CONSPIRACY WITH MALICIOUS INTENT
Volume 1

Jerry Raaf

Copyright © 2010 by Jerry Raaf

Conspiracy With Malicious Intent
Volume 1
by Jerry Raaf

Printed in the United States of America

ISBN 9781609573355

All rights reserved solely by the author. The author guarantees all contents are original and do not infringe upon the legal rights of any other person or work. No part of this book may be reproduced in any form without the permission of the author. The views expressed in this book are not necessarily those of the publisher.

www.xulonpress.com

An emotional story based on truth. A chronicle filled with pathos, fear, optimism and fleeting hope. This is a narrative for all ages; easy to read and hard to set aside. The author paints frightening images with colorful words, not easily forgotten.

L. Pillsbury, Toronto, ON

Many forces contributed to this historical event; Roman Legions, Centurions, an arrogant Governor and Praefectus, an egotistical King, naïve pilgrims and fearful citizens. The details of this documented event reflect human turmoil with soul wrenching results.

K. J. Rogers, Seattle, WA

This historical drama caused me to weigh the evidence and consider the outcome. Was this a murder or a sacrifice, and why have so many people been affected by this story?

Carl Redpath, Vancouver, BC

A GIFT TO

_____

FROM

_____

DATE

_____

RECENT PUBLICATION

FOREVER ELEVEN
ISBN: 9781425190033

Trafford Publishing, USA
www.trafford.com

Chapters Indigo, Canada
www.chapters.indigo.ca/home

AUTHOR WEBSITE
www.jerryraaf.com

COVER DESIGN
Brandon Schultz
The Graphic Garden Design Group
British Columbia, Canada

This book honors the memory of

~ **Sanford & Isobel Hanson** ~

Who provided me with
encouragement, love, genuine friendship
and trusted me with one of their own

I miss them greatly.

'Thank You' is truly an insufficient reward to those listed below for providing input and encouragement during the creation of this book. I am indebted to all of you.

Martin C. Abegg, Jr. PhD
Director, Master of Arts in Biblical Studies
Dead Sea Scrolls Institute
Chair, Religious Studies
Trinity Western University
Langley, BC, Canada
Website: www.twi.ca/biblical

Fra. Leo Barker O.S.B.
Westminster Abbey
Seminary of Christ the King
Mission, BC, Canada
Website: www.westminsterabbey.ca

Rene May
Lethbridge, AB, Canada

George Peck
Abbotsford, BC, Canada

Rainie I. Raaf
Abbotsford, BC, Canada

Virgil D. Raaf
Three Hills, AB, Canada

Beverly Thompson
Drayton Valley, AB, Canada

www.xulonpress.com

Chapter	Chapter Title	Page
	Book Dedication	xi
	Statement of Appreciation	xiii
	Table of Contents	xv
	Roman Numerals	xix
	Political / Social Overview	xxi
	Geography Location	xxv
	Roman Military Command Structure	xxvii
	Two Eldest Sons	xxix
I	The Decoy and the Fatal Error	33
II	The Zealot and the Stranger	43
III	The Miracle and the Cloth	49
IV	The Search for Athaliah	59
V	Seven Things Beno Said	67
VI	The Caravan Master's Critical Clue	79
VII	The Prophet, The Harlot, The Party	87

VIII	Bloodshed on the Tanner's Street	101
IX	The Ashes and the Memories	109
X	Amon's Escape	115
XI	The Long and Dusty Road	123
XII	A Soft But Firm Hand	131
XIII	The Sea, The Boats and the Fish	137
XIV	Varrus' Request	149
XV	Zebedee and The Messiah	157
XVI	Scythopolis / Beth Shan	165
XVII	The Battle and the Long Night	175
XVIII	The Officer and the Mirror	185
XIX	The Power to Interrogate	197
XX	The Gift of Negotiating	205
XXI	The Agreement	213
XXII	Varrus the Centurion	219
XXIII	The Blind Man and the Short Man	225
XXIV	The City of David	233
XXV	Pontius: Governor, Praefectus, Procurator	243
XXVI	The Promotion	249
XXVII	Chaos in the Temple	257
XXVIII	The Praetorian and the Executioner	263
XXIX	A Devastating Message	273
XXX	A Vile and Malicious Agreement	279
XXXI	The Passover Lamb and the Warning	289

XXXII	The Meal and the Betrayer	303
XXXIII	The Arrest and the Ear	315
XXXIV	The High Priest and the Betrayer	327
XXXV	The Governor and The King	337
XXXVI	Anger, Accusation, Distrust	351
XXXVII	The Trial, The Note, The Basin	365
XXXVIII	A Prisoner Now Free	379
XXXIX	The Betrayer and the Executioner	385
XL	The Place of the Skull	395
XLI	Darkness, The Earthquake, The Spear	405
XLII	The Request for the Body	413
XLIII	Guilt, Remorse and Exhaustion	425
XLIV	Securing the Tomb	431
XLV	The Angelic Beings at the Tomb	443
XLVI	The Gardener	453
XLVII	Broken Hearts and Good News	459
XLVIII	The Miracle and the Mandate	467
XLIX	Doubters, Deceivers and Believers	473
	Bibliography	477
	Pertinent Maps of the Region	481-482

ROMAN NUMBERIALS

I	One
V	Five
X	Ten
L	Fifty
C	One Hundred
D	Five Hundred
M	One Thousand

1. Read the LETTERS (numbers) from LEFT to RIGHT

2. No symbol is used more than three times in a row
    III = 3
    IIII is **NOT** acceptable except on a clock or wrist watch
    XX = 20
    XXX = 30
    XXXX is **NOT** acceptable

3. If a symbol of lesser value precedes a symbol of greater value, then subtract lesser
    IV = 4 (subtract one from five = 4)
    IX = 9 (subtract one to the ten = 9)
    XL = 40 (subtract ten from fifty = 40)
    XC = 90 (subtract ten from one hundred = 90)
    IC is **NOT** acceptable for 99

4. If a symbol of larger value is located before a smaller value symbol, then add their values
   VI = 6
   XI = 11
   XV = 15
   CII = 102

5. If a combination of symbols exist, begin on the LEFT, and apply these rules
   CIX = start with C (100) and add IX (9) = 109
   DC = 500 + 100 = 600
   XXXIV = 30 + 4 (IV) = 34
   CCXIX = 219
   CCCLIV = 354
   MMCDLIX = 2459
   CMXXXII = 932

POLITICAL / SOCIAL OVERVIEW

The Roman Empire consisted of many countries populated with tens of thousands of people, who spoke multiple languages, practiced diverse religions and lived by many ethnic and personal rules and laws. This Roman influence incorporated countries such as Britannica, France (Gaul), Iberia (Spain), Italy, Macedonia, Syria, Galicia, Mesopotamia, Palestine, Greece, Armenia, Egypt, Cyrenaica and most of the northern coast of Africa. This included inlands in the Mediterranean Sea and almost all lands surrounding the Black Sea and Caspian Sea. (See enclosed maps)

The Roman Legions oppressed the masses with an iron fist. Blood was the currency of that era; easily spilt for unbridled words, suspicious activities and outright confrontation spawned by religious convictions and political fervor. There was no identifiable difference between the guilty or the innocent. Much depended upon how resistant the citizens were to Rome's dominance and what kind of leadership the Legatus or Commander of the Legion exercised. Egotistical leaders led with absolute power and brute force, while only a handful led less aggressively. Bribery, arrogance, greed, theft, murder and other personal vices were evident throughout the privileged of society, who controlled the oppressed more by whim than reason.

A Legatus, Commander of a Legion, was required to provide countless reports to Caesar; highlighting his decisions and actions related to military matters, detailing confrontations with rebels, describing citizen reactions as well as itemizing imminent challenges that threatened Rome. It was an overwhelming task that required decision making skills, self-confidence and diplomatic proficiency to command six thousand men, manage the manufacturing and maintenance of weapons and equipment, supervise logistics related to acquiring and training of horses, secure food supplies, and ensure the housing and execution of political prisoners.

Capable men were seldom selected from the ranks to become qualified leaders. Often relatives and the sons of the wealthy and influential families received their positioning because of friendly favors. Caesar's expectations of the Legatus and his Assistants proved to be demanding, and those that were unable to manage their duties were transferred to other centers or demoted.

Some of the regions, such as the province of Judaea in Palestine, were further ruled by a Governor and Praefectus, who had authority to tell the Legatus what he wanted and how it should be done. The designated Governor and Praefectus collected taxes, sat as a judicial head on matters of civil and Roman law, and enacted laws to maintain peace and generate large amounts of revenue. It was not uncommon for disagreements to exist between the conflicting egos of these arrogant leaders, however the decisions made by the Governor and Praefectus, usually prevailed.

Twenty-eight Legions of legionnaires, cavalrymen and support personnel represented Caesar and the Roman Empire. Supporting these legionnaires were small armies of common people and slaves, who were conscripted and posted to isolated regions.

Each Legion included: Commanding Officers under the Legatus, Optio (Aides or Assistant to an officer), scribes, message couriers, infantrymen, cavalrymen, physicians, veterinarians, executioners, torturers, cooks, slaves, guards and men responsible to gather supplies, and men who made and repaired military equipment and maintained military strongholds and buildings. Though each Legion generally consisted of six thousand men, only five thousand, one hundred and twenty were active duty cavalrymen, infantrymen and soldiers; the rest provided logistical support.

Active duty legionnaires were divided into ten divisions known as a Cohort. The first Cohort was commanded by the most Senior Cohort Centurion, identified as Primus Pilus, whose responsibility was to take command of all active duty men if and when a major incident or insurrection occurred. During times of peace, he was responsible for only eight hundred men, who were commanded by five Centurions directly under his command. There was only one Primus Pilus in each Legion, and the Primus Pilus of Legion X (ten) was stationed in the city of Caesarea, a beautiful coastal city in Palestine, located on the most eastern coast of the Mediterranean Sea. The Legatus for Legion X also resided in Caesarea. (See enclosed maps)

The remaining nine Cohort divisions, each commanded by a Cohort Centurion with six Centurions under his authority, managed four hundred and eighty men. Rome's command structure sounded complicated but it was a simple system with clear strategies and rigid protocols. (See enclosed a list of ranks of Legionnaires)

Of the ten Cohort divisions, three were stationed in the city of Caeasarea; numbering one thousand, seven hundred and sixty active legionnaires. Three Cohort divisions were stationed in the city of Jerusalem and numbered one thousand, four hundred and forty men. Two Cohort divisions were stationed in the city of Scythopolis consisting of nine hundred and sixty men. The remaining Cohort was stationed in Jericho and consisted of four hundred and eighty men.

Isolated outposts existed throughout the region where a lone Centurion, his Optio and eighty cavalrymen patrolled the district to observe and control the activity of citizens in an attempt to maintain peace. Numbers in each Legion varied because of injuries and death. Recruitment was primitive. The most effective recruitment was public conscription with threats of violence and death.

****

GEOGRAPHICAL LOCATION

The country of Palestine was subject to Roman influence and harsh control. This rectangular shaped region was bordered on the west by the eastern coast of the Mediterranean Sea. The northern edge was an imaginary line that began north of the city of Caesarea on the eastern coast of the great sea, and ran north and eastward to Lake Semechonitis, a lake north of the Sea of Galilee. From there, the eastern border extended south toward the city of Capernaum and encompassed the Sea of Galilee, and continued southward along the Jordan River toward the Dead Sea.

A small territory west of the Jordan River belonged to Decapolis (Ten Cities), located east of the Jordan River. Legion X patrolled the area and managed all military confrontation. In that region were the cities of Scythopolis, Nain and other smaller towns. (See enclosed maps)

The southern border of Palestine vaguely existed from the Mediterranean Sea, eastward to a point twelve miles (18 kms.) north of the most southerly end of the Dead Sea. (See enclosed maps)

The area south of this imaginary line stretched toward Egypt and the Red Sea, and was a desolate desert known as Nabataea. Few people lived in this wasteland. Lack of water and great sand storms taunted the brave and foolhardy, who chose to risk these hazards because they were fugitives of Rome. Few were ever seen again. Caravans travelled throughout this region but life was extremely difficult.

Palestine was divided into four provinces. **Galilee**, the most northerly region, embraced the cities of Capernaum, Tiberias, Cana, Nazareth and Mount Tabor. **Samaria** encompassed the cities Caesarea, Joppa, Jericho as well as smaller towns. **Judaea** claimed cities such as Jerusalem, Bethlehem, Bethany, Kerioth, Beersheba and Hebron. The most southern province, **Idumaea**, consisted of countless sand dunes, the occasional oasis, and isolated nomadic tribes, who tended flocks of sheep, goats and camels. Water was the currency of that region. (See enclosed maps)

Caesarea, a beautiful city on the Mediterranean coast, was the command centre for Roman Legion X. Caesarea's shoreline and streets mesmerized merchants and seamen throughout the known world. Even King Herod chose to have one of his palaces built in that city. This palace could be seen from a great distance, and it became a major attraction to those that imported spices, gold, silver, horses, linens, silks, male and female slaves, unusual foods and exotic animals.

Here the Legatus of Legion X lived in considerable luxury and interacted with other high officials in that region. Occasionally, the Legatus from Antioch, who commanded Legion III in Asia Minor, would travel southward to Caesarea to meet the Legatus of Legion X so that they could mutually celebrate their status and plan strategies against mutual foes and religious Zealots.

Antioch was a major city, known for commerce, mixed culture and its large population. It was here that the Legatus of Legion III controlled the region northward toward Asia Minor, now known as Turkey. (See enclosed maps)

Pontius Pilate, Praefectus and Governor of Judaea, was proud of his primary residence in Caesarea but did, on occasion, reside with his family in Jerusalem to carry out his administrative duties for the province of Judaea. His tenure was filled with chaos, confrontation, violence and death.

Annually, additional cavalrymen from Caesarea and Scythopolis were temporarily assigned to be in Jerusalem during major religious festivals because people throughout the Roman Empire made annual pilgrimages to worship at a Temple the Jews considered to be sacred. It was during religious festival, known as the Pesach (Passover) that the population of Jerusalem increased six to eight fold, creating an uneasy calm and a potential trouble spot for Rome.

The population throughout the Roman Empire experienced continuous hardship, famine, oppression and uncertainty. Citizens did whatever was necessary to survive.

ROMAN MILITARY COMMAND STRUCTURE

Caesar	Emperor of the Roman Empire
Senators	Political Advisors, Law Makers
Magistrates	Judges of Military and Civil Law
Governor/Praefectus/Procurator	Appointed Bureaucrat
Legatus (Legate)	Legion Commander (4000-6000 thousand men)
Tribunus Laticlavius	Aide to the Legatus (Legate)
Tribuni Augusticlavii	Officer, Aide to Tribunus Laticlavius
Primus Pilus	Senior Centurion of a Legion
Cohort Centurion	Responsible for six Centurions
Centurion	Responsible for 80-100 men
Optio	Aide to an Officer or Centurion
Cavalrymen	Mounted Cavalry (horsemen)
Infantrymen	Foot soldiers
Legionnaire	Active Roman soldier
Standard Bearer	Carrier of the Aquifer and Roman banners
Aquifer	Metal Polished Eagle (symbol of Roman authority)
Captain of the Guard	Security Officer with specific responsibilities
	* Praetorian (prison), city gate, Officer's quarters
Keeper	Praetorian Slave/Keeper of prisoners in a cell block

* **Ranks with two titles** are similar to those in more modern military structures such as Sergeant Major, Lieutenant Colonel, Major General or Lieutenant General.

A Roman Legion consisted of:

One Legatus, several Commanding Officers, Assistant Officers, one Primus Pilus, Cohort Centurions, Centurions, Optio(s), cavalrymen, infantrymen, veterinarians, physicians, blacksmiths, cooks, stable hands, weapons makers, slaves, equipment repairmen, Captain of the Guard(s), logistics personnel responsible to gather food for men and horses, guards, executioners, floggers etc.

TWO ELDEST SONS

Amon Ben Gazahem, a Hebrew son of the Tribe of Naphtali, was born into a family of want, where only the essential needs for he and of his younger brother, Asa, were provided by the skilled hands and hard work of Beno, their father. He, like his forefathers, was a sandal maker in town of Nain for as long as anyone could remember.

Nain was a town known for its crooked and disorganized streets, countless shanties, sheep pens, two wells and fragile commerce, all surrounded by deteriorating city walls and two narrow city gates in need of repair. It was an unimportant town located in a remote and dry region of Palestine.

Beno modeled honesty, respect and reverence for the Laws of Moses. Both Amon and Asa were schooled in all Jewish traditions; the Ten Commandments, the Feasts and Festivals, including preparation for Shabbat, known as the Sabbath. Each son had been circumcised on the eighth day according to the Law of Moses, and each received religious education from religious elders, who taught the native sons about Abraham, Isaac and Jacob, the prophets as well as King David and King Solomon.

Beno and his sons were skilled at their trade, and clients in Nain as well as the surrounding region frequented their shop, located next to Joash the Tanner's Shop which was adjacent to a small market known as Sycamore Market, not far from a small synagogue. Though all major religious feasts and worship was centralized in Jerusalem, this community observed all essential Hebrew practices and observances including readings from the Tanakh made up from the three divisions of the Hebrew Bible: the Torah (Pentateuch or first five books of the scriptures), the Nevi'im (the Prophets) and the K'tuvim (Writings).

The citizens of Nain lived in isolation from the outside world except for two events: an annual visit from an Egyptian caravan which brought spices, linens as well as foods which could not be cultivated in this dry region, and the verbal reports from the devout who returned from religious pilgrimages to Jerusalem, the holy and sacred city.

Jerusalem, a city rich in tradition and history, was proud of its heritage and its mighty king named David and his wise and wealthy son named Solomon, who was credited with constructing buildings and gardens equivalent to the status of the Seven Wonders of the World. King Solomon's greatest achievements included the construction a lavish Temple, amassing great wealth and becoming known as the wisest man to have ever lived.

The citizens of Nain were surprised and outraged when Gentiles, identified as Romans, invaded their land and established a military presence with infantrymen and cavalrymen throughout their land. No reason was given why these uncircumcised heathens lived in their midst nor was an explanation provided for the oppression they experienced. The Hebrew citizens conducted all of their commerce, practiced all of their religious rites and feasts, and carried out their community activities under the guise of cooperation even though they secretly sought for and planned rebellion to regain their freedom and recapture their land they believed promised to them by YHVH (G_d).

Leah, mother of Amon and Asa, was of the Tribe of Asher. Both she and Beno were devout in their religious practices and spoke often of a Messiah to come. Though she was continually unhealthy, Leah was determined to raise both sons to respect and to obey the Laws of G_d given to them by Moses.

Neither Amon nor Asa was married, defying all attempts of matchmakers to find suitable wives. It was Asa's physical disabilities and Amon's reluctance to make a commitment that ensured their celibacy.

In a town the size of Nain, the Ben Gazahem family maintained a respectable reputation as valuable citizens. Despite their penury, they lived peaceful lives until the death of a young man, the only son of a neighborhood widow.

****

Varrus Marcius Cassius de Lonnea was born into a wealthy and influential family with enviable status because of his Roman lineage. His grandfather, Silicas Contantia Martoca de Lonnea, was a Roman citizen, who maintained his respected name with political influence and power as a Roman Senator and as a Legislative Assistant to Caesar. It was the family wealth and status that ensured that the family name of 'de Lonnea' would remain respected in Roman hierarchy.

Varrus' father was Legatus Cassius Silicas Metaro de Lonnea, Chief Commander of Legion XV, located in Macedonia. He was well known for his education and leadership in both battle and peacetime. Those under his authority and influence understood his four fold philosophy: 'Silence is strength, gestures convey vulnerability, words expose thoughts, and eyes display inner turmoil and tranquility.'

As a result of his demeanor, he was known as a silent and intimidating Legatus. His stoic stare and silence robbed many of confidence and challenged their convictions. He was not a mean spirited man but self-assured in all his ways. His presence commanded respect and caution.

Cassius' sons, modeled self-control and self-confidence just short of arrogance, and soon developed an ability to listen to more than words and to observe even the slightest cues from body language of those around them. They idolized their father and admired his power and influence. Though silent in private and in public, they were resolved to defend him, verbally and physically if necessary.

As the eldest of three sons, Varrus was required to learn the protocol of Roman dignitaries, to practice proper decorum, to develop decision making skills and to acquire the art of persuasion. From his father, he learned three key skills: to understand and outmaneuver human nature, to anticipate the potential for confrontation and to remain composed under pressure. Self-confidence became his core strength.

His mother, Hadassah, was a gracious and quiet woman, born of Greek and Hebrew descent of the Tribe of Benjamin. Her love for her sons was never in question, however it was easy to see that she favored Varrus, for she constantly monitored the servants and their interaction with him. In the privacy of their lavish residence, she taught Varrus about Abraham, Isaac and Jacob, and the history of the Jews. A Hebrew teacher became his private mentor and helped him understand the Feasts and Festivals and the Tanakh. His religious education included the Law of Moses, the Prophets and other writings such as the Psalms, yet he was not allowed to openly practice his mother's religion.

Varrus' privileged status meant that he was provided with a personal servant, carefully selected for his perceptiveness, kindness and mastery in the use of every weapon known to the Roman world. Pollus was his name. His lineage was unknown but it was rumored that he had a Babylonian father and an Egyptian mother, all of whom lived in Crete. Pollus became

Varrus' personal servant when Varrus was ten years old. He proved to be an invaluable mentor, a loyal friend and dedicated servant.

Varrus was respectful of his tutors and mentors, who taught him Latin, Greek, Aramaic, Egyptian as well as mathematics, geometry, astronomy, politics and navigation. He became particularly fond of hand weapons such as the gladius or short sword, and honed his skills as a rider. He also learned the use of larger weapons such as the catapult and battering ram but his greatest interest was in the study of military strategy and equestrian warfare. His riding skills were readily noticed by those around him.

When his father determined that he was ready for military training, he sent Varrus to serve under Legatus Flavion Amatanius Giovatalou, Chief Commander of the Legion XIX in Galatia. His father monitored Varrus' progress by requesting reports from Legatus Giovatalou. On one occasion, Varrus received one parchment in his father's handwriting, which he valued greatly.

His mother was greatly grieved, yet said little, but prayed daily for the safety of her son and that he would not forget all that he had been taught. She tried in vain to ease her pain by doing more for the other sons but the emptiness she experienced when Varrus left, was evident to all including her servants.

Varrus became an invaluable strategist, scribe and organizer of documents, and a skilled legionnaire. At the end of his fifth year, he was promoted by Legatus Giovatalou, to be an Optio or an Assistant to a Centurion in Legion III, under the leadership of Legatus Octavius Regallo. This meant that Varrus would be transferred to Antioch, a city near the northeastern shores of the Mediterranean Sea. There he would finalize his education and broaden his experience which would ultimately promote him to an authoritative position of Centurion or greater.

Upon completing his tenure, Varrus was reassigned to Legion X, in Caesarea where he served under Centurion Damarius. After one year of flawless performance, he was transferred to the city of Scythopolis, known to the Jews as Beth Shan.

Chapter I

THE DECOY AND THE FATAL ERROR

The Roman Legion's military might was frequently deployed against dissident groups, identified as Zealots, whose clandestine and subversive activities attempted to unify the Jews for a successful rebellion against Rome. Many of these groups were crushed in violent confrontations, and captured leaders were publicly flogged and then sadistically executed with the most brutal of all executions; crucifixion. But there were times when the rebels succeeded in killing or maiming their enemies. Such events were demoralizing to the Romans, who added additional patrols to flush out those resisting Roman authority and when such force was unsuccessful, gold coins were offered to the public to encourage betrayal. Collecting the reward, however proved to be difficult because rebels always seemed to find out and informants were seldom seen again.

The majority of citizens in Palestine chose to live their lives as though Rome were not present, nevertheless if given an opportunity they would kill rather than be ruled by 'uncircumcised pagans.' Rome may have had the upper hand but their brutality and presence did little to intimidate and solicit cooperation from the oppressed.

****

In the predawn muted light and glow of dozens of torches, Roman cavalrymen bridled and saddled fifty-two horses while stable slaves, thorough and experienced, carefully checked the lower limbs and hooves of nervous steeds that snorted and pawed the ground in anticipation of military maneuvers. Metal scabbards emitted dull clanging sounds as cavalrymen bumped into hitching posts and wooden stable doors.

Conversations of bravado stirred the emotions of the men, who readied themselves for an arduous day of patrol in an arid countryside soon to be bathed in sweltering heat. Occasionally, laughter and verbal taunts could be heard as the legionnaires prepared for their day.

Several geldings whinnied as girth straps and cinches were readjusted while the cavalryman responsible to carry the Aquifer, a shining eagle on a lance and symbol of Rome's presence, prepared to mount his horse.

Finally, those that were ready to ride stood next to their mount and awaited the arrival of their officer. When he arrived, he said little but motioned to his Optio, an Aide, who immediately moved closer for final instructions. When they had completed their conversation, Centurion Augusto Ramao called to the cavalrymen, "MOUNT UP," after which he raised his hand and motioned for the troop to follow him in military formation.

Centurion Ramao confidently led fifty cavalrymen and his Optio out of the city of Scythopolis, northwestward toward the town of Nain, located in an arid region of endless ravines and caves believed to be hideouts for religious Zealots and rebels.

Horses bobbed their heads and swished their tails as the Centurion and his men moved under the stone archway of the northern gateway of the city wall. Dust swirled around the eager hooves of the mounts as they began to canter over the hard dry soil.

It was to be a day of reconnaissance, not confrontation. The remaining fifty legionnaires, under Centurion Ramao's command, were reassigned duties to clean barracks and stables. They were not pleased with their assignment but by the end of the day, they would realize that they were the fortunate ones.

At first, the morning air chilled the riders but as the morning sun appeared over the eastern hills, it warmed their backs and made their morning ride more comfortable. When the sun was high overhead, they began a long steady climb toward a small mesa known for its many large boulders that surrounded a small resting area. In this seemingly peaceful setting, more than two hundred hooves carried the cavalrymen through a narrowing pass to the summit.

Overhead, birds flew in the warm air and off in the distance two jackals loped toward distant bushes and dead trees. Five hundred strides ahead of this troop lay the mesa and resting area. Here Centurion Ramao intended to give the horses a short rest before descending to a distant shanty next to three sheepfolds near an ancient well that would provide cool water for their mounts and a much needed rest for the legionnaires.

As Ramao slowed the pace of his mount, he could see three men with donkeys approaching the mesa from the other direction. When the men and donkeys were only fifty strides away from the troop, they moved off the roadway and waited near several dozen large rocks. One of the donkeys brayed and immediately several horses perked their ears. Centurion Ramao tightened the reins of his horse so that it would not shy from the donkey's raucous sound.

As the troop approached the men and donkeys, Ramao raised his hand and called, "HALT."

Immediately the troop reined their mounts and waited for further instruction from their officer.

"Where are you going?" asked Ramao as he turned his horse to confront the Bedouin travelers.

The eldest of them replied, "It is our custom to go to Jerusalem to worship."

"That's a long journey."

"That is why we travel while it is yet cool and there is yet plenty of time to travel before the sun gets too hot."

"What do you carry in those boxes on your donkeys?"

"Food. We need food for the donkeys and for our mouths. It is a long journey," was his reply.

"What else do you carry?"

"We have but a few coins and clothing for when we get to Jerusalem, and we have wineskins filled with water that we have filled at the well by the old sheepfold," he said as he pointed over his shoulder to where they had been.

Centurion Ramao turned to his Optio, "Have these men and their cargo searched. We have plenty of time, so let's see if they carry what they say they do. Search every box and every man."

"Yes Sir."

Immediately, ten cavalrymen were assigned to open the cargo boxes carried by the donkeys. As ropes were untied and boxes lowered to the ground, one of the legionnaires called to his officer.

"Sir, there are others approaching from the same direction as these men." The men inspecting the cargo raised their heads to see what he was talking about.

Turning to the mounted cavalrymen to his right, Centurion Ramao commanded, "Disperse, to escort those six men into this circle. We need to search them too."

Conspiracy With Malicious Intent

Within moments, fifteen cavalrymen moved in unison toward the six men who were approaching the rest area. As they did, one of the legionnaires searching the boxes of the first group of men looked up at Ramao.

"Sir, you need to see this."

Immediately, Ramao dismounted and stepped closer; a tactical error that would prove to be fatal. At that moment an arrow found its way into his throat and exited just below his hairline next to his spine. He immediately fell to the ground and his helmet rolled to the front feet of his horse. Unable to speak, he anxiously gasped for relief as his Optio turned to see what had happened. When his Optio reached down to Ramao, a second arrow entered Ramao's lower back and partially exited his abdomen, adjacent to his navel. Warm blood instantly splattered onto the ground and up to the rib cage of several horses.

Unaware of what had just happened to their Centurion, the remaining legionnaires watched as the six approaching travelers were brought toward them. Then without warning, dozens of men suddenly appeared from behind the large rocks on the both sides of the pathway. A flurry of arrows found their mark as did dozens of stones hurled with remarkable accuracy from countless Bedouin slingshots. Amid the sudden confrontation, the remaining legionnaires tried to turn their horses, only to find that they were surrounded by men carrying spears and swords. Five legionnaires died as they fell to the ground, each with a spear thrust through their back and chest. Four others felt the stinging ache of a sword slashing their thighs just as six horses stumbled and fell to the ground because they had been fatally wounded by spears into their abdomens as countless arrows pierced their necks and rumps.

It was impossible to guess how many nemeses rained death upon the vulnerable legionnaires. In the confusion, blood flowed from every cavalryman, even those that managed to break through the lines. Shouts and death surrounded the panicking cavalrymen. Within moments, all but five cavalrymen were knocked to the ground and slaughtered in hand to hand combat.

The five, who narrowly escaped the circle of death, realized that returning to the melee would result in certain suicide, so they rode blindly across an open field toward the city of Scythopolis.

Without looking back, the five frightened men rode as though the very flames of Hades were licking at the heels of their horses. Neither cast a glance at each other but focused solely upon their destination many miles away. One of the injured riders fell from his horse when it leapt over a large boulder and stumbled before continuing its breakneck speed over the arid ground and through knee high scruffy bushes.

When the five horses crested a knoll, shepherds in the distance suddenly stood to the their feet and tried to move a large flock of sheep out of danger, but soon the horses were among the flock and in the ensuing chaos, another horse stumbled and a second rider fell, never to rise again.

With the flock in total disarray, five horses continued on, two without riders and three carrying injured and terrorized cavalrymen. When a jackal suddenly appeared ahead of the horses, another exhausted rider slumped forward and almost fell to the barren soil, but regained his balance. None of the frightened horses lost stride but continued to run mile after mile as though unbridled.

A watchman on the city wall in Scythopolis shaded and narrowed his eyes as he peered at an unusual cloud of dust on the distant ridge. He moved into the shade so that his eyes would not have to deal with the glare of the sun. Moments later he called to another watchman and pointed to the clouds of approaching dust.

"HOW MANY RIDERS ARE THERE?" he shouted.

"I SEE . . . THERE SEEM TO BE TEN . . . NO WAIT . . . THERE ARE FIVE HORSES BUT WHY ARE THEY RUNNING SO HARD? ARE THEY ATTACKING?"

"WHY WOULD ANYONE ATTACK WITH FIVE OR TEN HORSES? MAYBE THEY ARE A DECOY TO GET OUR ATTENTION FROM SOME OTHER PART OF THE WALL OR ANOTHER GATE INTO THE CITY."

"WAIT. THERE ARE ONLY FIVE HORSES AND . . . AND ONLY THREE RIDERS."

Calling to the gatekeepers and legionnaires on the ground, he warned them that approaching horses would soon be arriving. Legionnaires moved to the city gate and prepared for confrontation while others were dispatched to inform Centurions of this unusual impending attack.

When the horses were within several hundred strides of the city walls and gate, a watchman called out, "THEY'RE ROMAN'S AND THERE ARE ONLY THREE OF THEM ON HORSEBACK!"

Moments later, one of the horses without a rider stumbled and fell, leaving a large plume of dust, and when the dust cleared the horse did not attempt to stand but appeared motionless.

Now three riders and one horse without a rider raced blindly up to the city gate and knocked over four legionnaires, who tried to slow or catch them. In the confusion of the moment, three injured and wounded legionnaires rode into the city and fell from their mounts. One of the horses dropped to its knees, unable to rise for its underbelly was bleeding uncontrollably. It moaned loudly as its body quivered while bloody foam frothed from its nostrils and mouth. Moments later it stretched and then all muscle tone suddenly ebbed away.

The horse that had no rider ran into the courtyard and as it reared up, it knocked over several legionnaires and a two-wheel cart along with a wooden canopy at the entrance of one of the guardhouses.

The second horse that had carried a cavalryman dropped to its knees and wheezed loudly and fell on its side. Dust from its nostrils swirled around its head but no one noticed because three exhausted legionnaires were carried to the shade of the city wall and cool water was poured over their sweating and hot bodies. They gulped cold water and gasped their fragmented message of horror to their officers and fellow legionnaires.

A Centurion ordered the men to pour cold water onto the remaining horses to cool them. "DO WHAT YOU CAN TO KEEP THEM ALIVE," he ordered as he knelt to listen to the gasps of the three exhausted and wounded men.

By the time one hundred and fifty cavalrymen were ready to ride to where the ambush had occurred, the four horses that had run all the way to Scythopolis were dead. Their bridles and saddles had been removed and a Centurion ordered that their bodies were to be dragged a thousand strides outside the city walls to be left to the jackals.

When the Centurion with the cavalrymen arrived at the killing field, he watched as six jackals moved among the dead bodies of legionnaires and horses. Centurion Caesan found that all that needed to be done was to gather the severed heads, limbs and bodies of the cavalrymen for burial. It was a massacre beyond imagination. Many horses had been killed and those that survived had their leg tendons cut, so Centurion Caesan ordered them to be destroyed. The bodies of the enemies of Rome were left where they fell, soon to become a nocturnal feast for countless jackals and scavenging birds, who soared high overhead.

Later in the day Centurion Caesan called to his Optio. "Take one third of the men and all the horses to the well on the backside of the mesa so they can be watered. The rest of us will remain here to bury the dead. And oh, I seem to recall that some people live in those buildings near the well. Find out if they know something about this massacre. When they see you with fifty men and all the horses, they may be willing to speak with you."

As the Optio and the men with all the horses approached the well, a small flash of sunlight, reflecting off a shining object halfway between the well and the sheepfold, caught his attention so he rode directly to where he had seen the flash of light. As they neared the spot, the Optio noticed five children running toward one of the shanties, so he spurred his horse into a gallop. When he was one hundred strides from the fleeing children he thought he saw the eldest child drop something behind a scruffy bush.

When the children were surrounded, the Optio rode to the bush where he thought the shining object had been thrown, and after dismounting, he picked up a Roman gladius which was lying on the ground.

Walking back to the children he knelt down with the gladius in his hand and asked, "Where did you find this?"

Immediately all of the children began to cry, so he motioned for them to walk ahead of him. As they approached the shanty and sheepfolds, two elderly men stepped from one of the sheepfolds and knelt down to hug the sobbing children.

When asked why the children were playing with a cavalryman's sword, the old men insisted that the children must have found it near the well where it must have been lost. They denied knowing anything about the massacre and recalled only a few men with donkeys passing by earlier that day. Off in the distance, the Optio could see two women tending sheep, and after walking into the sheepfold and looking around, the Optio called to his men to search all buildings including the lofts.

While the search in the sheepfolds and shanties was being carried out, a two wheeled cart arrived at the site of the massacre. It carried food that was immediately dispersed among the hungry cavalrymen. Spades that arrived in the cart made it easier for the cavalrymen to dig shallow graves. Damaged leather vestments, sandals and the helmets of the deceased, and the saddles and bridles from the dead horses were loaded into the cart. No weapons were found among the dead because all had been taken by the murderous rebels.

Late in the afternoon, the Optio and the men who had searched the shanties and sheepfolds returned to the killing site. While the men were tying up the horses that had been watered, the Optio rode directly to where Centurion Caesan was standing.

Stepping down from his horse, the Optio saluted and cleared his throat.

"You have been gone for a long time. What did you find?" demanded the Centurion as he squared his shoulders.

"Sir, we found eleven people at the shanties who claimed that they knew nothing about this battle but we did find some children playing with a gladius."

"Tell me about the eleven people," he demanded as his jaw tightened and his eyes narrowed.

"There were two old men, a blind and crippled woman, two young women and five children, and in the loft of one of the sheepfolds we found large amounts of food, spears, bows, arrows and twenty-two swords. Under three sacks of grain we found a broken Aquifer."

"You mean to tell me that they even had the Aquifer?"

"Yes Sir."

"Where are the weapons now?" asked Centurion Caesan.

"Because we had all the horses we were unable to bring the weapons so we hid them until we returned with the cart."

"What about the eleven . . . did your visit sharpen their memory?" asked Centurion Caesan, his eyes red with rage.

Shaking his head from side to side, the Optio responded, "Sir, their memory is now mixed with the ashes of the buildings and food we destroyed. All that remains are the scattered sheep in the distant fields, the well and the troughs. When we return for the weapons we can fill the well with rocks to prevent travelers from using it again, if you wish."

"No, leave it. We may need it someday. Oh and by the way, I am pleased that you have completed your duty so efficiently."

"Thank you Sir," responded the Optio as he saluted and rode to where the cart was standing. Sometime later, the cart, led by the Optio and fifty men returned to the ancient well to retrieve the weapons that had been discovered and then hidden.

As darkness surrounded them, the cavalrymen continued to toil by the light of several fires and torches. Others remained on guard to prevent rebels from returning. Hour after hour, the fires burned at the killing field, and when all the dead had been buried, and the Optio and his men had returned from the well, the caravan began its long trek for Scythopolis. After travelling all night, the legionnaires arrived at Scythopolis just as streaks of morning sunlight reached over the eastern hills.

One Centurion, his Optio and forty-five legionnaires perished in the ambush. Two of the five that had escaped the surprise attack, fell from their horses on their way to Scythopolis and were never found.

Of the three surviving legionnaires, who rode blindly through the countryside to Scythopolis, one died from his wounds before nightfall, another developed a massive infection and died several days later. Only one cavalryman survived the ambush and the frantic race to Scythopolis but was executed a week later for abandoning his troop in battle.

Chapter II

THE ZEALOT AND THE STRANGER

It was military disasters and massacres such as these that fueled the anger of the Legatus and the Tribunus Laticlavius, Commander of the city of Scythopolis. Rewards were offered and innocent people were executed, all in an attempt to intimidate citizens and force them to cooperate, however none of these actions proved to be successful.

The man the Romans diligently searched for, particularly in the two northern provinces of Galilee and Samaria, was a man named Athaliah. He was believed to have been responsible for the death of more than three hundred legionnaires and the maiming of Roman horses by cutting tendons in their hind legs. Eventually the Legion was forced to import two hundred horses as replacements.

Athaliah was elusive because fellow citizens harbored him and provided food and shelter for him and his gang. Rome increased the bounty on his head, but no one reported seeing him and no rumors existed as to his whereabouts. His last confrontation with the Roman cavalry was in a triangulated area between the cities of Nain, Nazareth, and Mount Tabor. It was here that twenty-eight cavalrymen and twelve horses were killed before Athaliah escaped into one of the many narrow ravines. It did not seem to matter how many rebels were killed, Athaliah was always able to recruit more replacements from surrounding towns.

Rome was clearly at a distinct disadvantage. First, they did not know what Athaliah looked like and secondly, they were unsure of how many men followed him because he recruited from every region he passed through. Thirdly, citizens did not want to speak to the Romans about Athaliah because they feared that he or his men would return to slay them and their families. Athaliah's existence and whereabouts was a mystery and every effort to capture ended in failure.

Nain, a small town in the dry hill country north and west of Jerusalem was known for its partially broken down walls and two narrow entrance gates. Rome's presence in Nain consisted of Optio Ataxia and fifty legionnaires; thirty cavalrymen and twenty infantrymen. Fifty men were unable to monitor all of the activities of its citizens, and since Rome did not consider Nain to be a critical point of confrontation or influence, these men served merely as a token reminder of Rome's presence in Palestine.

A reluctant informant, whom Rome financially supported, told them that Athaliah was in the hill region near the town of Nain. This rumor was embraced by Optio Ataxia because of a recent confrontation in that area and because the informant told him that Athaliah had family members living in Nain.

This information prompted the Legion to dispatch additional cavalrymen to search for Athaliah. One hundred men, including Varrus Marcius Cassius de Lonnea, under the leadership of Centurion Cassius Damarius, arrived in Nain with orders to search for, find and execute Athaliah.

When the cavalrymen from Scythopolis arrived at the small Roman barracks in Nain, Optio Ataxia and Centurion Damarius discussed what they knew of Athaliah and the possibility of him hiding with relatives in town. What made this search difficult was that Rome did not know who Athaliah's relatives were or what part of Nain they lived in.

During their discussion, Optio Ataxia told Centurion Damarius that a Jewish religious teacher named Jesus, from Nazareth, and twelve of his followers were on their way to Nain.

"I expect them to arrive on the morrow," said Ataxia. "I know nothing about them. They may be part of Athaliah's rebels for all I know."

Centurion Damarius dismissed Ataxia's concerns. "I don't think that this Jesus is part of Athaliah's murderous group for he has not broken any Roman laws that I am aware of and he has not provoked any Roman administrators to act against him. I think Rome's only concern is based solely upon Jesus' ability to gather hundreds of people to listen to his religious teachings, and all previous reports I have heard about him indicates that he has no political views. All he does is heal people of diseases and illnesses. Rumors of his activities include stories of mentally incompetent people being freed from vexatious spirits, spending time teaching Jews about some of their religious laws and playing with their children. The unbelieving religious leaders try to destroy his credibility, nevertheless crowds continue to increase in size wherever he goes." He reached for a cup of water and gulped loudly as he drank.

"All I have heard is that he is on his way to Nain," said Ataxia, "but I know nothing about him."

Centurion Damarius raised his hand, "On many occasions soldiers have been assigned to follow this Nazarene and his twelve men but all he seems to do is travel from the Sea of Galilee along the Jordan River to Jerusalem. When the crowds gather, he speaks of Jewish religious practices and interprets their religious scriptures. There's no report of any violence or vile words against Rome."

"So why is he coming here? There's nothing in this arid region except poor people," responded Ataxia as he stood and motioned for the others to follow him outside.

The timing of the arrival of Jesus during the search for Athaliah did not cause Centurion Damarius to alter his plans. He continued to focus on the search for and arrest of Athaliah. The next morning, he assigned eight cavalrymen to follow and observe Jesus the Nazarene, once he arrived. The remaining cavalrymen and infantrymen would search the city and surrounding area for clues as to where Athaliah might be, and to speak with citizens to determine who his relatives might be.

Since Varrus was an Optio, he was ordered to take seven cavalrymen to the city gate and wait for Jesus the Nazarene to arrive, but noisy mourners in the distance sufficiently distracted him so he turned down a side street to find out where the noise was coming from. Several moments later, Varrus saw a large crowd slowly moving along a narrow street. The crowd appeared to be distressed about something.

At an intersection where five streets converge, Varrus watched the restless crowd as it waited next to a small building. He motioned to four of his men to move to the other side of the street while he and the remaining cavalrymen watched from the shade of an abandoned building.

When the door of the small building opened, Varrus could see people carrying what appeared to be a dead body on a wooden pole stretcher. Immediately the crowd broke into wailing, shouting and swaying as they began to move along the street.

Varrus motioned for his men to remain where they were, allowing the mourners freedom to move wherever they pleased.

Slowly the funeral procession inched its way between the houses and shops that led toward a building that one of the legionnaires said was a synagogue. Varrus guessed that the procession was on its way to one of the city gates so the crowd could take the body to its burial site, so he was surprised when the funeral procession suddenly changed direction. He tightened the reins of his mount and motioned for his men to wait as the mourners turned down another street.

Moments later Varrus nudged his mount with his heels to move closer to the mourners. The long line of weeping and wailing mourners and those that bore the deceased on the stretcher suddenly stopped when a man, near the front of the procession, raised his hand. The wooden stretcher wobbled from side to side as those carrying it stopped.

The woman walking next to the stretcher ceased her wails and focused upon the man, who motioned for the stretcher bearers to lower the body so that it would be only waist high. The crowd pressed closer as the man placed his hand on the deceased and looked upward to the sky. Moments later, the deceased stirred as the shocked crowd stared in disbelief. It appeared as though the dead person was attempting to move off the stretcher.

Varrus nudged his mount again to move closer. He was unsure of what was happening, so he tipped his head to one side and shaded his eyes from the bright sunlight. To his amazement, he watched as the deceased frantically moved his arms and legs before stepping to the ground.

Hundreds of swarthy faces were frozen with amazement, their dark piercing eyes wide with awe, now looking at what appeared to be a young man, who stood unsteadily before them. Moments earlier this body, wrapped in rags, was dead and part of a Palestine funeral procession, accompanied by loud moans, piercing cries and agonizing wails. To the mourners' amazement, they watched the rag wrapped body and his mother desperately trying to unravel the tattered cloth from the body which had previously held him motionless on a fragile wooden stretcher.

Family members, that had been summoned to carry the deceased to his burial, stood in disbelief, their eyes not blinking as they stared at what appeared to be a youth, who was now desperately tugging at the burial cloth about its face. Gasping for a breath, the body moaned until its mouth was free of cloth rags. At that instant it began to frantically inhale dry desert air.

As tattered burial clothing fell from this once dead body, the mother turned with blurred eyes to look for the man, who had moments earlier stopped the funeral procession and touched her dead son to restore him back to life. Anxiously, she scanned the swaying crowd and when she was sure she had found him, she dropped to her knees and cried out, "YOU HAVE RESTORED MY SON TO ME. GOD HAS VISITED ME! WHO

ARE YOU SO I MAY THANK YOU? YOU MUST BE A PROPHET. OHHHH, THANK YOU! OHHHH, THANK YOU!"

The hand that had touched the dead body, now reached toward her and she, breaking with Jewish tradition, grasped the hand of the stranger, kissed it, squeezed it and tugged at it. Her tears of joy and reverence flowed from her flushed cheeks onto his hand and he, with patience, helped her to her feet.

Her son continued to stumble toward her and anxiously pulled at the remaining tattered pieces of cloth that were wrapped around his torso. Loud moans could be heard coming from the young man as he frantically inhaled more air.

A crescendo of whispers soon became voices of praise and thanksgiving, all directed toward this ordinary looking man, who had raised this lad to life. A rumor soon spread that this stranger had come from Nazareth, but many found it hard to believe, for everyone knew that nothing good ever came out of Nazareth.

To make things even more difficult to understand, this man was rumored to be a carpenter. Where had he learned to do such things? Who were his parents? Was he a prophet? Which one of the twelve tribes did his family belong to? Why had he come to Nain?

As strands of cloth fell from the lad's legs, the youth breathed deeply to fill his lungs. His tongue tried to form words but only garbled moans could be heard. He waved his arms and shoulders in desperation as his mother grasped at the remaining rags. Finally two men, who had been standing next to the stranger who had raised him, helped him by removing the last few strands of cloth on his body.

Varrus moved closer, unsure of what he had just witnessed. He sighed slowly as his left hand reached up to rub his chin.

Chapter III

THE MIRACLE AND THE CLOTH

Amon Ben Gazahem, a rotund, middle-aged sandal maker, stroked and tugged at his scruffy, grey beard with his right hand while squinting at the young man, who had just scrambled off the stretcher. After using his left hand to shade his eyes in the bright midday light, he began to move his head from side to side for a better view.

"Things like this have never happen in Nain," he whispered. Staring at the frantic young man, he tried to recall if anyone had ever spoken of unusual events like this. "Maybe my eyes, they, they have deceived me. How could this be? My eyes are not that old . . . but I did see a dead boy, but maybe he was not dead."

Confused by what he saw, he bit his upper lip and looked around. "Just because he was lying on that, that thing that carries dead people does not mean he was dead. But why would his mother make him lie on it if he was not dead? Maybe I did see what I thought I saw." Again he stroked his beard and then took a long slow breath.

As a youth, Amon recalled hearing of soothsayers and people, who seemed able to predict the future, and once his father Beno spoke about lepers being healed in a pool near the sacred city of Jerusalem, but this was something that he had never seen or heard of before.

He licked his bottom lip as he tried to catch a glimpse of the man, who had raised this lad back to life, but the swaying crowd and the dust from the street obstructed his view. He tilted his head to one side and then the other, but all he could see were the backs of heads. In frustration, he began to jump up and down and even stood on his tiptoes, but the crowd was too active for him to maintain his balance.

In the shade of several buildings, seven Roman cavalrymen and their officer stared at the young lad, but none spoke a word. The sway of the frantic crowd and their shouts made their steeds, noticeably uneasy.

One of the mounts pawed the ground and bobbed its head as the others perked their ears. Varrus' gelding snorted loudly so Varrus tightened his hold on the reins.

The people continued to move to and fro and it became evident that all of them were pushing for a better view of what they had just witnessed. Regardless of how loud the crowd had become, the voice of his mother could be heard as she expressed her joy over seeing her son alive.

Varrus glanced at his men, but they did not notice because they, like the crowd, were unable to look away from what they had just witnessed. One of the cavalrymen shaded his eyes to focus upon the woman and her son.

As Varrus looked back to the crowd, he asked, "Where is the man who caused this commotion? Could this be the man from Nazareth we were to meet at the city gate?"

"It must be one of those men next to that woman," replied a cavalryman as he pointed to the center of the emotional crowd.

Three legionnaires turned to Varrus but he remained motionless. Moments later, Varrus moved his head slowly from side to side, indicating 'No', to any of their questions or comments.

The crowd grew louder and pressed closer to see the young boy, and in the ensuing chaos several people fell to the cobblestone pathway. The mother's voice continued to be heard above the noise of the swaying and shouting crowd.

Again one of the steeds pawed the ground and bobbed its head. Several of the cavalrymen turned to Varrus, so he opened the palm of his right hand and held it above his horse's mane as a sign: 'Hold your position.'

Meanwhile Amon tried to stand on the tips of his toes and moved his head from side to side for a better view, but all he could see were more faces and the back of more heads. For a moment, he thought he had spotted the young lad, but amid the oscillating movement of the crowd it was impossible for him to be sure, so he pushed forward and felt goading elbows and heard angry insults.

Amon looked around to see if he could see a porch or a tree to climb, but the crowd was unforgiving as it began to move down the narrow street toward the synagogue. Amon forced his way into the crowd, but found that his footing was unstable, and when several people stepped on his foot, he became angry.

If it had not been for his crippled brother, Asa who was following some distance away, Amon might have fought his way through the crowd or climbed the small tree next to the butcher's shop. The tree would have given him an unobstructed view, however since the crowd was moving, this vantage point would have eventually become useless.

Asa called to his brother, "AAAMMMOOONN! AAAMMMOOONN!" as he continued to limp along, favoring his left leg.

Moving away from the mob to meet his brother, Amon raised his hands and asked, "Asa who is this man that did this, this thing? I have never seen such a thing, a dead person yet walking around and, and such crowds and never so much noise in Nain in my many years. I have never . . ."

Asa interrupted, "Yes and when we were back there," he said as he pointed to where the mob had been, "the dead boy hugged his mother in public. Who has ever heard of such a thing? Hugging a woman in public and, AND his mother yet?"

"Yes, yes, but how did he get alive again? That is what I want to know," ranted Amon. He looked at the crowd and then back at Asa. "Never worry about hugging in public, but what about becoming alive again, and in public? That is more important than hugging in public. Think about it Asa, dead and then suddenly alive! How can that be?" He waved his hands above his head as he spoke.

"Amon, we know that mother! She is Hannah and that is her boy. What is his name, Amon?"

"Yes, yes but who is the man that did this thing, Asa?" ranted Amon as he continued to move slowly toward the crowd. "I want to know the name of that man, who made him alive again. Think about it, Asa, alive then dead and now alive again. How can that be? I ask you Asa, how can that be?"

"Slow down Amon. I can't keep up with you," called Asa as he tried to follow Amon and the frantic crowd.

"ASA, I NEED TO FIND OUT IF HE'S A PROPHET OR SOMETHING," shouted Amon as he forced his way back into the crowd.

Within moments Amon was out of Asa's sight and though Asa tried to keep up, the crowd and Amon moved more rapidly than Asa could follow.

Amon's shouts were fading but his words could still be heard. "MAYBE HE'S THE PROPHET THAT WE HAVE HEARD ABOUT. SADAC SAID THAT A PROPHET FROM BY THE SEA OF GAGGALEE OR SOMEWHERE LIKE

THAT WOULD COME AND HE DOES MANY NEW THINGS? MAYBE IT'S HIM and he is the. . ." His words finally faded and became lost in the noise of the frenzied crowd.

"AMON, AMON," shouted Asa, who was too far behind the crowd for Amon to hear.

Varrus motioned for the cavalrymen to move along with the crowd.

"This world is hard to understand. What will happen next? No wonder, Sadac said that the rabbis and priests in Jerusalem are upset. People made alive again and sick people made good again. That would make anyone upset even the person, who was dead," mumbled Amon to himself as he tried to maintain his balance by leaning on a fellow citizen next to him.

No one seemed to notice that the Roman officer and his cavalrymen were following on the perimeter of the crowd. As the people moved along, Varrus stared intently toward the center of the mob and once he was able to identify the young boy and his mother, who were the object of all this excitement, he positioned his horse to walk parallel with them. The remaining cavalrymen followed without incident on the outer edge of the crowd.

Amon found himself momentarily isolated on the outer edge of the crowd, and as he tried to change course, one of the cavalrymen crossed in front of him. He immediately stood motionless as he felt his shoulder being nudged by the chest of a horse, so he cast his gaze to the ground to reduce the chance of confrontation.

Within those few moments of delay, Asa managed to come closer to the crowd and Amon.

"AMON, MAYBE," Asa shouted as he limped closer, "THE PROPHET IS GOING TO MAKE SOMEONE ELSE ALIVE." He gasped for breath when he suddenly caught up with Amon.

"How can the prophet make more people alive unless more people are dead? Asa, sometimes you make me think about things I don't want to think about. You make my brain hurt," Amon said as he raised his hands above his head and rolled his dark eyes. "You are a nice brother but sometimes, sometimes I think you don't think too good."

"Amon, someone stepped on my foot when we were back there," Asa said. "Maybe this prophet will heal it when we catch up with him."

"Never mind your foot. The prophet is getting away. Now I can't see him," Amon said disappointedly. "How can I keep my eye on the prophet and on you if you keep limping so slowly on that crooked foot?"

Another cavalryman's horse nudged Amon and he stepped back. He felt a warm surge of anger deep in his chest, but he knew that confrontation with a legionnaire could mean death, so he stopped and bowed his head in an act of apology.

"Soldier . . . Roman man," he muttered, before finishing his comment with a whisper once the cavalryman was gone. "Pagan, someday I will, I will, I don't know what I will do." Again he raised his hands above his head.

"But someday, I will do something to them. I don't know what, but I will do something. Right now I don't have time to decide what that will be, but someday," he said as he lowered is pointer finger and moved toward the perimeter of the crowd.

As the crowd came to a narrow part of the street, one of the cavalrymen on the other side of the street motioned to Varrus that he and the other men would go around several buildings to meet the crowd at a different intersection. Varrus nodded his approval and the cavalrymen disappeared behind several buildings as the crowd continued to move along the street.

Frustrated that he was at the back of the crowd, Amon verbalized his threats again. "I will have to kill people to get to the front of these, these people. They have lost their minds and are meshugga," he whispered.

At that moment a cavalryman's arm reached down and grabbed Amon's shoulder. "Who are you going to kill?" he asked in a gruff voice.

"Me! Nobody . . . I . . . I was just . . ." he stuttered as he shrugged his shoulders and cast his gaze to the ground.

The cavalryman turned his mount and left Amon standing alone and shaken. For a moment, Amon remained frozen with fear, and when he was sure that the legionnaire was no longer looking at him, he started running toward the mob and elbowed his way into the crowd. "All these people look alike but why are there so many strangers? Where did all of these strangers come from? Has all of Palestine come to Nain?" he muttered as he continued to force his way into the crowd.

Several people, including Amon, stumbled and fell to the cobblestone roadway and Amon found himself kneeling at the feet of a young boy, who was holding an old tattered piece of cloth which looked like a common rag. Amon watched when the lad dropped the rag that had been on his body. Surprised by what he had seen, Amon looked up at the boy and the sobbing woman, who was hugging and kissing her son.

She continued shouting, "MY SON, OH MY SON. THANKS BE TO THE GOD OF ABRAHAM, ISAAC AND JACOB!" She bent over and picked up the last piece of cloth and threw it to the ground and then spit at it.

Amon's eyes widened as he looked at the boy. Moments later, the boy and his mother were swept away from his sight by the pushing crowd.

Amon reached down and reverently picked up the grave cloth and stared at it. When he rose to his feet and shouted, "I SAW THE BOY BUT WHERE'S THAT PROPHET?" Clutching the cloth in his calloused fingers, he tried to look over the heads of his fellow citizens but he could not see anyone who looked like a prophet.

"Things like this don't happen in Nain," he whispered again as he moved along with the crowd. "How could an ordinary man do this? Only prophets do things like that . . . I think." He continued to elbow his way forward and suddenly found himself directly in front of the lad again.

"Are you alive?" he asked naïvely as he tilted his head to one side and narrowed his brows.

The boy did not answer but continued to jump up and down as he reached for the hand of his mother, who was shouting, "MY BOY, OHHH, MY BOY. HE WAS DEAD AND NOW IS ALIVE. GOD HAS GIVEN HIM BACK TO ME. THE GOD OF ABRAHAM, ISAAC AND JACOB HAS GIVEN HIM BACK TO ME!"

When Varrus heard the words, 'the God of Abraham, Isaac and Jacob,' he reined his horse to a sudden stop and turned his head to one side so that he might hear more. Momentarily, he remembered his mother and his Hebrew mentor using those names when he was a lad.

Family members crowded Amon out of the immediate circle and he found himself in the middle of the street, with the grave cloth still clutched in his hands. He stood there for several moments, when Asa grabbed and shook him until his white teeth chattered. For a moment, Amon thought that it was a legionnaire shaking him.

"AMON!" shouted Asa. "AMON, are you deaf? You look like you need to lie down. Did you see the prophet? What was his name? What is he like?" Asa's voice eventually became a whisper.

"Asa," Amon said, as he gasped for breath. "The boy was dead and here is a cloth that was on him," he whispered as he raised the cloth for Asa to see.

"Drop that cloth Amon or you can't go to the synagogue tomorrow. If you leave it here, I, I will pretend that I never heard what you said. Drop it on the ground, Amon. If anyone asks, I will say what cloth are you talking about?" Asa looked both ways for fear that someone had overheard what he had just said.

"Asa, this cloth," whispered Amon as he held it reverently in front of Asa's face, "this cloth, this here cloth is what the boy was wearing. I tell you that this, this here is the cloth, right here Asa." He clutched it as though it were sacred.

"Don't touch me with that cloth, Amon. Don't touch me! You know what the rabbi and priests will say if they know that you touched the cloth of that dead boy."

As Amon looked down at the cloth, his eyes noticed blood on Asa's foot so he knelt down. "Come Asa, I will take you home and I will bind up your foot. Let's go home, Asa. The prophet is gone by now. I will never find that prophet." His voice suddenly lost enthusiasm.

"Amon . . ." whispered Asa but was interrupted by Amon.

"These people, they are meshugga and have lost their minds, and the pagans, one of them grabbed me, but I escaped. It's not safe looking for a prophet these days. I thought these people were nice to be with, but no, I tell you Asa, a person could be killed."

"Amon!" said Asa as he eyes widened. "If you were killed, then the prophet could make you alive again and you could tell us how it was like!"

"That would be nice, but by now the prophet is out of town. Prophets move from town to town and don't look for men like me to make them alive again. They help only young people, like Hannah's boy, but not old men like me." His face saddened as he spoke.

"Did you see what the prophet's face looks like?"

"Nobody that I saw looked like a prophet, but I saw the dead boy, I mean, the alive boy. His father was Gazer, who died many Passovers ago."

"Let's go to the synagogue and ask a rabbi. He'll know. Rabbis know everything," said Asa as he slumped to one knee.

At that moment, twelve additional cavalrymen rode past Amon and Asa. Their horses were moving rapidly in the direction of the crowd, and as Amon looked up, his eyes met one of the riders, who looked disdainfully down at him.

As their horses moved past him, Amon bowed his head and with his right hand touched his forehead and respectfully moved it down to his chest. When the cavalrymen were gone, Amon kissed his bunched up fingertips as a sign of disdain. The soldiers did not see his motion nor did they see Amon tighten his lips and spit onto the ground.

"Pituuueee to you, you pagans. You uncircumcised Roman pagans," he repeated as he spit a second time onto the ground. Then he turned, "Asa," he said, "you are my only brother and it is sad to tell you that you are all that I have, but maybe, just maybe, I might tell my grandchildren about this day and what we saw."

Conspiracy With Malicious Intent

"Amon you don't even have a wife so how can you have grandchildren?"

"SHHHH, you talk too much," he responded as he put his pointer finger on his lips. "You need to think more and ask less questions. Come let's go home." Then placing his shoulder under Asa's arm, he helped him over the smooth stoned street near a grove of olive trees near one of community wells.

Soon all of the people were out of sight and the streets were empty and silent.

"Amon, do you think the prophet could heal my bad leg and foot?"

"Prophets can do anything they want. They can even fix your foot and whatever else you have that is not good. Think about it, if the prophet can make a person alive, fixing your foot is like nothing to him," Amon said as he snapped his fingers.

"Where do they live?"

"Jerusalem, I think but I don't know. Why do you ask me about things I don't know about? Ask me something I know about," Amon whispered in a gentle, yet disgruntled tone.

As they entered the narrow street that led to their sandal shop, they stopped to rest on the steps of an abandoned building.

"Amon, I heard someone say that the prophet comes from the Sea of Galilee. What is a Sea of Galilee?"

"Jerusalem, I know about, but this sea, this sea of Gagalee, I don't know about. Our father, Beno, told me about Jerusalem, but a sea called Gagalee, is not what I know about. I don't even know what a sea is." His voice ended in a higher tone than what he had been speaking in.

"Amon, you know so much, but why not this?"

"You should have been born with a broken voice and not a broken foot. You ask me too many things and then my brain hurts. Now come and limp in silence."

"Not so fast Amon. It hurts."

As the two brothers moved between the yellowing plastered houses, Amon whispered, "I am too old to know everything and about new things. If I did, then maybe I could be a rabbi, and if I knew more than everything, then maybe, yes me, I could be a prophet."

"Maybe you should be one," smiled Asa as he tightened his grip on Amon's shoulder.

"You need to be very smart to be a rabbi, but me . . . well I'm only a little smart. One day, I will go to Jerusalem to see for myself. Maybe, I will go with Sadac when he goes to Jerusalem next time. Until then, well, I must live with you and myself. Come, we're almost home. Then I can fix that bleeding foot of yours."

"Amon you are my favorite brother."

"Yes, yes I know Asa, but I am your only brother, so why do you say things that make me shake my head?"

A flock of sheep, making its way to the community well, crossed the brothers' shadows. Neither the flock nor the shepherds were aware of the miracle that had just taken place.

Meanwhile, Varrus and seven cavalrymen followed Hannah, her son and the crowd to the doors of the synagogue.

Chapter IV

THE SEARCH FOR ATHALIAH

Hannah, her son and her relatives entered the synagogue while the crowd anxiously waited for their return. As time passed, the people became less agitated and by late afternoon, the citizens began to disperse until only a handful of people remained.

Varrus however, was not interested in the woman or her son but continued to look for the man, who raised the lad back to life. He had been told to find and follow a Nazarene named Jesus so he rode his gelding around the circumference of the crowd until he saw what he believed to be the man who had performed the miracle. Leaning down from his horse, he touched a man on the shoulder and asked, "Is that the man who brought the boy to life?"

Somewhat defensive, the man withdrew, nodded and whispered, "I think so. But I am not sure."

"What is his name?" asked Varrus.

"Ask that man," he said as he pointed to a man with hairy arms. "He knows."

Varrus nudged his mount and moved toward the man with hairy arms and asked, "What is the name of the man who brought the lad back to life?"

"His name is Jesus," was his reply.

"How do you know that?" asked Varrus.

"I'm one of his followers."

"What is your name?"

"My name is John."

"Where are you from?"

Conspiracy With Malicious Intent

"I am from Capernaum by the Sea of Galilee and my father's name is Zebedee. Twelve of us follow Jesus. Do you wish to meet him?"

"There is no need," responded Varrus as he reined his horse to return where the other cavalrymen were waiting. There, he backed his horse into the shade of a building and said to three cavalrymen, "You remain here and wait for the woman and her son while I follow the man they call Jesus. I want to see where he goes."

Jesus, his followers and some of the crowd moved into a marketplace and at that point Varrus suddenly realized that Jesus was nowhere to be seen. Unsure of where he had gone, Varrus rode around the small group of people but could see that Jesus was not in the group. Despite his search for Jesus, he was unable to find him so he returned to the synagogue.

It was dark when Varrus and the seven cavalrymen returned to the barracks. When they arrived, Varrus entered the stone building and finding no one there, reasoned that the search for Athaliah may have produced some clues which were worthy of attention. He called for the horses to be groomed and tended to, and by midnight he and his men had eaten and were waiting for Centurion Damarius and Optio Ataxia to return. Meanwhile, he completed his report on what he and the cavalrymen had witnessed that afternoon.

When Centurion Damarius and his men returned to the barracks, Damarius sat at the table and ate by candlelight. "Tell me Varrus, what happened to you today?" he asked as he broke off a piece of the flat bread and then reached for a bottle of wine.

"Sir, we were on our way to the city gate to see if the man called Jesus and his followers had arrived, but were distracted by a noisy funeral procession not far from the synagogue. When we heard the noise from the mourners, we were surprised at what we saw. Suddenly a man stopped the procession of mourners and asked that the stretcher be lowered so that the stretcher and body would be only waist high. Then, the man did a strange thing." Varrus sighed before continuing. "He touched the body, looked up to the sky and said several words."

Damarius stopped chewing and with his mouth partially full of food he said, "A man touched the dead body? I thought these people's religion doesn't allow them to touch a dead body."

"That may be true, Sir, but it was the man we were waiting for. He must have entered Nain while we went to check on the noise."

Damarius sipped wine from a metal goblet and when he placed the goblet on the table, his eyes narrowed. "This man and his followers were already here, and he was the one that stopped the burial procession?" He wiped his mouth with the back of his hand.

"Sir, then a strange thing occurred. As I told you, this man raised one hand to the sky and spoke several words, and then," he paused as if he needed to build his courage to continue. "The dead body sat up on the stretcher."

Instantly Damarius stopped chewing and narrowed his brows. "The body did what?" He momentarily held his breath as he waited for Varrus to respond.

Varrus smiled before continuing. "The dead person stood to its feet in front of everyone and began to remove its grave clothes."

Damarius grinned in disbelief. "Varrus, ha-ha," he chuckled, "are you telling me that the dead person sat up?" He appeared shocked by what he had heard. "Varrus, you're the last person that I would expect to . . ."

"Sir, the live boy began to remove grave clothes from his face so he could breathe, and then there was chaos. People pushed and the entire crowd swayed back and forth. Some fell to the ground and the wailing changed into shouts to a god."

Damarius placed his food back into his plate and leaned back on the bench. "Varrus, you did say they shouted to a god?" His pointer finger and thumb tugged at his earlobe as he spoke.

Varrus nodded.

"How did you know it was a . . . a god, they were shouting to?"

"Everyone in this town saw the youth become alive again," said Varrus as he nodded his head up and down. "It's the truth, Sir. I saw it and so did the legionnaires with me."

"Varrus if it were not for your honesty," he smiled and continued chewing for a moment, "I'd . . . I'd think you were trying to make a fool out of me." The corners of his mouth rose slightly to create a doubtful smile.

"It's true Sir. The boy is alive. We followed him and his mother to the synagogue."

"Alive huh? Did the mourners have to hold him up as they moved down the street?" His eyes twinkled as they searched Varrus' face for clues that would indicate he was gently taunting his officer.

"Neither Sir, but the mother, her son and their relatives remained in the synagogue while we followed the man, who raised him back to life, but he disappeared into one of the buildings."

"Alive huh? This is not like you to make fun of your officer, or are you goading me to see how I will react?"

"Neither Sir. We rode through the streets looking for this man they say is a rabbi or a prophet, but we couldn't find him." He paused a moment before continuing, "What we did hear was that this man is named Jesus. Some said he was from Nazareth and some said he was from Capernaum near the Sea of Galilee."

"So where is this, this Nazarene now?" asked Centurion Damarius as he used a piece of bread to wipe his plate.

"He was in the crowd but because he looks similar to everyone else, we were unable to find him. He blends into the crowd and somehow he eluded us."

"Did this Nazarene or this Jesus Jew say anything when he awoke this dead boy?" Damarius continued to stare at Varrus as he reached for the goblet of wine.

"Not that we could hear, but the mother certainly was shouting. She thanked the God of Abraham, Isaac and Jacob for having mercy on her son."

"Varrus, you speak as if you know something about this, this Abraham and whomever. If I didn't know better, I'd say you know what this all means."

"Abraham, Isaac and Jacob are the three original descendants of all of these people." A moment later, Varrus asked, "And did you find anything that indicated that Athaliah is in Nain?"

Damarius chewed on some cheese and sipped wine from his goblet before responding, "Well, our day was not as exciting as yours, but it may have proven to be productive. We found or should I say, convinced several countrymen to speak with us and we found out that Athaliah has a brother in Nain. His brother is a tanner, and since I suspect that there are several tanners in this area it will take us some time to determine which one is related to Athaliah."

"Did they give you a name?"

"No, but if we can find this brother, we'll force him to talk."

"Who were these informers?" asked Varrus.

"Shepherds. I've always believed that if you can convince shepherds to talk. You can learn much about the area and who travels through the territory, day or night. Fortunately, the three we spoke to, realized that dying for someone else is not honorable, so they agreed to talk." He wiped his mouth with the back of his hand after finishing the wine in the goblet.

"Do you think Athaliah is in the area?" asked Varrus.

"He was last seen east of here, two days ago. The shepherds said that other shepherds provided food to him and his men. They think that he was coming to Nain, so he may be in Nain right now."

"My guess is that if he has a brother in Nain we have a chance of finding him Sir," said Varrus as he leaned back in his chair.

"All of these people are related to each other, besides they have a common enemy, Rome," continued Damarius as he pushed his empty plate to the centre of the table. After scratching the palms of his hands, he ran his thick fingers through his sun bleached hair. "A dead man back to life, huh? Are you sure Varrus?" Again he smiled as if he knew that Varrus was teasing him.

"Yes Sir. But about Athaliah, do you want us to go out tonight and look for these tanners?" asked Varrus.

Damarius stretched and yawned loudly, "No, we'll wait for Ataxia and listen to what he found out. I suspect that he's visiting the city gates and speaking to the guards. He should be back soon."

"We could go out tonight if you want, Sir."

"No, we'll look before dawn while most people are still sleeping. That way they'll be surprised to see us. The horses are tired and so are the men, but you should post a guard around the horses and the barracks. I don't want to find that some of our horses are missing or their tendons have been cut during a night raid. We'll start before dawn. Now be sure that you complete your report for me."

"I've already done so, Sir."

"Then set the night watch."

Varrus arranged for three night watches in the corral and then returned to his cot to read his report to be sure that it was complete.

Sometime later, Optio Ataxia arrived. He slumped into a chair and breathed a sigh of relief. "We found nothing. Not even a rumor of Athaliah," he said as he hung the scabbard that held his gladius, on the corner post of his bed and then removed his sandals.

Damarius rolled over to sit on the edge of his cot before rising to sit at the table across from Ataxia. He peered over the small candle on the table, "Well, we convinced several shepherds to talk, and they said that Athaliah was east of the city two days ago. He was moving in this direction and he's not alone, but has at least four to six men with him."

Optio Ataxia poured wine into a cup before looking at Damarius, "So he's in Nain, is he?"

Conspiracy With Malicious Intent

"Apparently, Athaliah has a brother, who lives in Nain. He's a tanner, but we have no name," said Damarius.

Placing the empty goblet on the table, Ataxia belched loudly before saying, "A brother in Nain and he's a tanner? Well, that's helpful."

Varrus turned to look at Optio Ataxia. "Any idea how many tanners live in Nain?"

After lowering his gaze, Ataxia scratched the side of his chin before speaking. "Well I know of two for sure, and one that works occasionally just outside the city gate. There must be more than three. I'm sure there are more if you think about the ones in the area outside the city." He paused, "Sir, do you wish to go out tonight?"

"No," replied Damarius. "Did you speak to the guards at the city gate?"

"Yes, just before I returned to barracks. Why?"

"Did the guards remember seeing any strangers entering the city within the last few days?"

"Yes. They told me about a caravan from Egypt. It comes through here once a year, and this afternoon a Jewish teacher and twelve of his followers arrived." He turned his head to the floor, "Now where did they say he came from?"

"We happen to know about that man and the twelve men that travel with him, but you mentioned a caravan from Egypt?"

"Yes, it comes here once a year."

"When did it arrive?"

"Yesterday."

"Any other strangers than those two groups?" asked Damarius.

"No. They did not remember anyone else. You have to remember that few people ever come to Nain. It's a rather out of the way place. If any others arrived or entered, the guards would have remembered." He rubbed his eyes and yawned.

"So why have guards at the gate if few people come here?" asked Damarius.

"Several citizens have been robbed during the night and four have been murdered, so I had guards placed there to question those that enter or leave. Some people believe that shepherds enter the city to steal food and then run off during the night."

"By the way, Varrus followed that religious man and his men today. Tell him Varrus, what you told me," said Damarius as he grinned and ran his fingers through his hair.

"We were on our way to meet this man called Jesus and the men that travel with him, but as it happened, he was already in the city. We saw him stop a funeral procession near the synagogue and that is when he raised a dead boy back to life." Varrus became silent and looked at Damarius, whose eyes twinkled as he continued to stare at Ataxia.

"WHAT? You saw what?" asked Ataxia as he looked at Damarius and then back at Varrus.

Centurion Damarius shrugged his shoulders. "Don't ask me about it. I wasn't there."

"A dead boy came back to life?" asked Ataxia. "You have to be..."

"I'll tell you about this later," Varrus said, "but were there any other people who entered the city?"

"I told you, NO," Ataxia said, sounding rather irritated.

"Is it possible that Athaliah could have entered Nain with the Egyptian caravan?" asked Varrus.

"I guess so," responded Ataxia as he leaned over to rub the lower part of his leg. "I guess that's possible." He scratched his head before turning to Varrus. "You may be right."

"That may be how Athaliah entered Nain undetected," said Damarius. He poured some wine into his goblet and emptied it with two gulps. After watching the glow of the candle slide over of the metal goblet, he said, "Dispatch someone to each gate and tell them that they must NOT allow anyone to leave Nain without my permission. If Athaliah is in the trap, I want to keep him here at least until daylight," insisted Damarius.

Optio Ataxia immediately put on his sandals and left the room to dispatch five additional men to each city gate. Before they left, he said to them, "Be sure that no one leaves Nain without Centurion Damarius' permission. That's an order."

When Ataxia re-entered the room, Varrus stood to his feet, "I did notice that the walls of Nain are not in good condition, so Athaliah could escape over one of the broken down sections."

"Yes, I know the exact sites you're talking about. Maybe we should send several men to each breach in the walls," responded Ataxia.

"That sounds good," responded Centurion Damarius as he blew out the candle next to his cot.

Ataxia strapped his gladius to his waist and before leaving the room, he turned to Varrus, "When I get back, I want you to tell me about this dead person, who you saw brought back to life. I've never heard of things like that before."

Before sunshine could warm the eastern walls of Nain, the legionnaires were preparing for the day. All horses were saddled and weapons prepared before they ate, and when Centurion Damarius spoke to them, they were reminded that finding Athaliah was the priority.

After Damarius mounted his horse, he motioned for Optio Ataxia to step near. When he did, Damarius said, "With the extra men at the two city gates, we'll be able to close the trap. If Athaliah came into the city with the Egyptian caravan, then we must keep him here."

Ataxia nodded in agreement. "I've been thinking Sir, about who the tanner might be that Athaliah is related to. Obed lives near the synagogue but he is old and quite ill. Joash, who lives next to a sandal maker not far from the market, is young and has publicly complained about Roman soldiers in Nain. Azera lives just outside the city wall and is a tent maker. Those are the only ones I can think of."

Damarius called to Varrus. "Find the caravan and see if Athaliah might have entered Nain with them. It will be difficult because they speak Egyptian only or at least they claim to speak only Egyptian, so I will leave that in your hands. Ataxia and I will look for the tanners."

Varrus moved his horse next to Ataxia. "Do we have a legionnaire who speaks Egyptian? If I am to question an Egyptian, then I will need someone who can speak their language."

"Yes, I have someone but he's guarding the east gate. His name is Phanal and when you see him, tell him to travel with you," responded Ataxia.

"So there are only three tanners that we need to see," responded Damarius.

"They're the only ones I know of Sir," responded Ataxia.

Damarius raised his hand, "All of you know what needs to be done today. Finding Athaliah is our priority." He turned his mount and everyone left the barracks yard.

As the last horse pranced out of the Roman courtyard, the sun crept over the eastern wall of the city, and somewhere a cock crowed.

Chapter V

SEVEN THINGS BENO SAID

Amon sat on the edge of his cot and rubbed his eyes. Light from a street torch flickered outside his window and cast strange moving shadows on the walls of his room, located at the rear of his sandal shop. It was the sound of horse hooves on the smooth stones of the street that had awakened him. He tried to guess how many Romans were approaching but decided not to look, lest they see him at the window.

After they had passed his shop, Amon lay back, stretched and yawned as his mind returned to the miracle that he and hundreds had witnessed the day before. "That man must be a prophet because nobody else could make sick people well, yet a dead boy is alive again," he whispered to himself. "How could he do that? Dead has always been for always, but this boy, he's alive." He shrugged his shoulders, "but I saw him walking around and he was hugging his mother. He looked alive, so he must be alive."

As he stared at the ceiling, he decided to speak with Sadac to see what he thought about the miracle, but remembered that Sadac was visiting his daughter near Jerusalem. Unable to think of any other person's opinion that he valued, he tossed the bed cover aside and made his way to the window where morning light sliced through the tattered curtains at the window. He reached into his pouch and removed the grave cloth that had fallen from Hannah's son and was about to look at it when he heard horses and foot soldiers approaching.

A chill ran through his body as he turned his ear to the window and held his breath. When the horses were very close to his shop, he listened for voices but all he heard were the snorting of the horses, the sound of sword scabbards and the squeaking sound of dry leather from the saddles.

Moments later, several dozen foot soldiers marched by in rapid pace. He closed his eyes before inhaling silently.

When the legionnaires were beyond his shop, he moved into the subtle light that was cast into his room by the torch outside. Moments later he looked down at the piece of grave cloth he had picked up the day before. So many questions and each one brought its own emotion. His fingers felt the cloth with reverence, knowing that he was now considered to be ceremonially unclean and unable to enter the synagogue. For a moment, he regretted picking up the cloth but reminded himself that the cloth came from a living person so he confidently put the cloth back into his waist pouch and made his way to a wooden stool near the entrance of the shop. It creaked loudly when he sat down and momentarily Asa stopped snoring. Amon waited in silence until he could hear Asa's raucous breathing begin again, and then leaned on the table, closed his eyes and took several large breaths.

"Who is this prophet? Maybe I will never be this close to a prophet again," he whispered to himself. "Now is the time to find him," he reassured himself as his mind wrestled with so many 'what ifs'.

Minutes passed before he returned to his cot even though he was skeptical of finding sleep. He adjusted the thin cloth that covered him, closed his eyes and eventually fell asleep.

It was the sound of the neighbor's cock crowing that awakened him. Morning light was now entering his room through the broken shutter that partially hid the torn curtains. Amon turned to face the wall as he covered his eyes with his forearm. "Someday, I will catch that cock and if he tastes as good as he crows, then he will not bother me when I sleep," he muttered to himself. "Loud cocks I don't like but cooked ones are very good." He smiled as he spoke to himself.

"Amon," whispered Asa. "Are you awake?"

Amon did not respond but lay in silence.

Again the cock crowed.

"Amon, are you asleep?" Asa's words were now louder than before.

"No. I'm still sleeping and only dreaming about silence and the sunrise, so don't try to wake me." He sounded irritated but Asa knew Amon's words were never intended to do harm. "Between you and that cock, I will never get much sleep," he mumbled.

"Amon, could we look for the prophet today? If he helped Hannah's boy, maybe he will help me and my crippled foot."

"We have sandals to make and food to buy, and . . . and I don't know where to look for prophets. One other thing, I don't know what he looks like, so how will I know when I found him," was Amon's skeptical reply.

"Would a rabbi or one of the priests know?"

"Alright, I will look," Amon said as he sat up suddenly. "You talked me into it. Today, I will talk to the rabbi at the synagogue to see what he thinks." He adjusted his weight on the edge of his cot and ran his fingers through his curly grey hair and then scratched his stomach.

"Rabbis know everything, Amon. Why did you not think of this before?"

Amon did not respond to Asa's question but rose from his cot and opened the shutters. Rays of sunlight streamed into their room and hundreds of floating dust particles danced in the warm sunlight. Amon pursed his lips and blew at them, causing the dust to swirl in concentric circles. He watched them for a moment, then returned to his cot and carefully stretched the ragged blanket over it.

After they were dressed, Amon and Asa sat down at an old table to eat figs, honey, goat cheese and flat bread. Amon reached for the last piece of cheese and then handed several dates to Asa. While Asa munched loudly on figs and flat bread, Amon stepped out of his shop and into the street.

"Good morning, Amon," someone said as he passed the shop.

"Yah, yah," was Amon's reply. "All mornings are good. This one I have not yet had a chance to find out about it, but maybe I need to wait and see." Again he scratched his stomach and yawned loudly. When he turned to enter his shop, a woman's voice called to him, "Amon, are my sandals ready yet?"

"This day is too early to fix sandals. I'm still thinking of sleep, but yes, yes you can come this afternoon. They will be ready by then."

As the woman walked away, Amon entered his shop. "Asa, today I want to have a good day," he said.

"Do you yet have that cloth from Hannah's boy?" whispered Asa, his eyes wide with enthusiasm.

"How did you know I still have that cloth?" asked Amon as he turned his eyes toward the window and then back to Asa.

"I know you," whispered Asa. "Remember you have been my brother for many years and I know you."

"SHHHHH about that cloth, Asa, someone may hear you."

"It's hanging from your pouch, Amon. Whatever you do, don't lose it. Maybe someday it will bring you and me good things."

"Asa, eat your figs. When you ask me questions, my brain hurts."

In the distance, they could hear sheep bleating and the sound of a monotonous bell ringing around the neck of an old ewe, and knew that a flock of sheep were rushed toward the water troughs next to the community well.

"Amon, can we ask a rabbi what he thinks about the prophet?"

Amon remained silent for some time before responding. "This time I will listen to your advice. Today, yes today, I will speak to the rabbi. He will know who this prophet is, and maybe, just maybe, he will know what makes a prophet."

"But Amon, you can't go."

"Why not?" asked Amon, his eyebrows gathered tightly and his mouth slightly open, "Why?"

"Because you have the cloth from a dead boy in your pouch and you're not supposed to touch anyone or anything from dead people and because . . ."

Amon interrupted him, "Asa, that cloth was on a boy that was alive, not dead, so that doesn't matter, and if the rabbi doesn't know about it or didn't see Hannah's boy being alive again, how can he know about the cloth?"

"Maybe, you should go and speak with Hannah and her boy. Maybe they can tell you who the prophet is," suggested Asa.

"I will speak to a rabbi after we fix these sandals, and then, maybe then, I will speak to Hannah," insisted Amon as he pulled his chair to the work counter and began to examine several pairs of sandals that had been carelessly tossed into a pile.

It was early afternoon when Amon and Asa stepped out of their shop and walked toward the synagogue. When they arrived, a rabbi opened a side door and began to walk in their direction.

"Rabbi, ah Rabbi," Amon called as he raised his hands and cast his eyes to the ground. "Rabbi, I know that you are a very busy a . . . a rabbi with much things and chores to do but," he said as he looked at Asa, " but as a son of Abraham, I too need to know what you think about what happened yesterday, especially about Hannah's dead son . . . who now lives."

"You are Amon, the one who makes sandals next to Joash the Tanner's Shop, are you not?"

"Yes, yes Rabbi, but can you tell me if this man, who stopped the crowd to make Hannah's boy alive is . . . is maybe is a prophet?" His voice became a whisper as he tilted his head so he could see the rabbi's facial reaction.

"Why is it important to you?" asked the rabbi as he moved his hand to scratch his chin.

"How often does a dead boy stand up and walk around, especially in Nain?" Amon asked as he raised his hands above his head.

"Very unusual, yes, very unusual indeed," said the rabbi as he stroked his long beard. "I too, have been wondering about that stranger some say is from Nazareth. Someone told me that he was a carpenter but how can that be? That I do not know. Why do you ask?"

"A carpenter and from Nazareth? We all know that nothing good comes from Nazareth, so how could he do that?" interrupted Amon as he nudged Asa with his elbow.

The rabbi raised his hand to interrupt Amon. "This stranger has been performing miracles from the Sea of Galilee to Jerusalem. I've heard he does some wonderful things for people but, I must say but," he raised his pointer finger before continuing. "I don't know by what power he does these things. We do not know the family he is from, and we don't know his parents. All of what he does appears to be good but, and I must say but, that doesn't mean everything is good."

Asa looked down at Amon's pouch to see if the grave cloth was visible.

The rabbi closed his eyes and shook his head from side to side. "Many people follow this man from town to town, and he does ask some very good questions and knows much about the Laws of Moses, and . . . he does things that are very unusual. Yes, very unusual, but from Nazareth, I just don't know. From some other town, maybe but Nazareth, I'm not sure." He closed his eyes and shook his head from side to side.

"But Rabbi is he . . . maybe a man from God?" asked Amon. Again he tilted his head to one side so he could watch the rabbi's reaction.

"All men are made by God, even you, Amon."

"Even me?" asked Asa.

"Yes, yes, a thousand times, yes," responded the rabbi as he stroked his beard and cast a momentary glance at Asa.

Asa moved closer. "My name is Asa."

"Oh yes I know of you. You're the one with the big foot," he said as he looked down at Asa's feet. "I knew your father, Beno. A good man, yes I knew him well and he made good sandals too."

With one easy hand movement, Amon pulled the grave cloth from his pouch. "Rabbi, this is a piece of the cloth that was on the dead boy that was on his way to be buried. Do you want to see it or hold it?"

"NO! NO!" the rabbi shouted as he stepped back. "Don't touch me with that cloth! It was touching a dead body."

"But Rabbi, the last thing it touched was a live boy so why is it not good to touch?"

Raising his hand, the rabbi interrupted, "I just do not know. I too saw the boy come back to life and I too saw this man," he said as he shook his head. "But these are things that I do not know about." There was an awkward moment, and then he looked both ways before whispering, "I must go." Immediately after saying that, the rabbi walked rapidly to the side of the synagogue and disappeared behind a heavy door used only by rabbis and priests.

Amon stood motionless for a moment and then put the grave cloth back into his pouch. Raising his hands up to the sky, he said, "Palestine is becoming a strange place. We are all the sons of Abraham. We speak to each other and try to survive, but now, now things are changing. Suddenly, Nain has crowds of people. Then a dead boy is made alive on his way to be buried and now, a rabbi, a rabbi I tell you Asa, says he doesn't know nothing. Why do I have to be with people who don't know nothing? Must I find out all these things for myself?" He turned his eyes toward heaven and reverently said, "I love rabbis but, but why did I have to meet one that doesn't know nothing?"

Asa waited in silence until Amon lowered his hands and then Asa whispered, "When you look up to the sky, do you think you will hear some answer?"

"Asa, you ask me too many questions. God made ears so can he not hear? So that is why I ask, besides, where does God live? Tell me, Asa, I want to hear you answer me, where does God live? I am waiting, Asa, tell me." His voice quivered as he ended his words.

"Amon, down the street, look" Asa said as he pointed, "there's a crowd and they are coming this way. What if it's the prophet?"

"Every street is crowded and what makes you think that a crowded street has a prophet?"

"Amon, what if the prophet is in that crowd?"

A moment later, Amon turned and started walking toward his sandal shop. With both of his hands waving frantically above his shoulders, he mumbled to himself as he walked along.

Suddenly, Amon realized that Roman cavalrymen were crossing in front of him, so he stopped and waited until they had passed by him. Turning,

Conspiracy With Malicious Intent

he saw infantrymen approaching so he moved to the opposite side of the street.

When they had gone, he realized that Asa was not following him so he looked around for him. Seeing Asa standing next to a donkey, he crossed the street. "Asa, another strange thing," he said as he raised his pointer finger into the air. "Asa, think about this. I am the oldest and as the oldest, I am supposed to do the thinking, and all you have to do is . . ." He suddenly stopped to listen to the sound of people approaching.

"Maybe the prophet is coming this way, Amon," repeated Asa as he looked back at Amon.

Staring at the crowd Amon responded, "But, Asa which one is the prophet? All of these people look alike."

The crowd stopped beside a row of sycamore trees and eventually moved to the steps of the building behind the trees.

"Asa," whispered Amon, "come with me and I will find this prophet, but you must stay close to me. Come," he whispered as he moved slowly toward the crowd.

Amon elbowed his way into the crowd and as he did, he exchanged verbal insults with several fellow citizens. When he successfully made his way to the centre, he stopped and looked at the strangers, who were in front of him. He furrowed his eyebrows as he moved his eyes from person to person trying to guess which one might be the prophet.

Laughing children crowded around the men, who hugged them and ruffled their hair. Amon was momentarily annoyed that the children were getting so much attention. "I think people like children because they are little, but what about us?" he muttered. "Some of us are little too, so does anyone care about that?"

After looking into the faces of all of the people whom he knew, he looked at the strangers. Amon said to himself, "The children aren't even looking for a prophet, and yet they get so close." He turned to look for Asa but did not see him. "Somebody must have stepped on his big foot again," he whispered to himself as he looked back at the children and the men playing with them.

All conversation stopped when cavalrymen rode past the crowd, and when they were out of sight, the crowd resumed their conversation with the strangers.

Amon studied their faces but was unable to determine which one might be the prophet because they looked so much alike. He moved his eyes from side to side, trying to convince himself that the prophet was somewhere in front of him. One man hugged several of the children and brushed their dark hair with his hands, and when the children giggled, he placed his hands on their backs and shoulders and called out their names.

"That must be the prophet," Amon whispered to himself as he tried to move closer. He did not take his eyes off that man. Then a man carrying a small girl placed her on the lap of a man Amon guessed to be the prophet. Amon focused on both of them.

When the strangers stood to their feet, the crowd followed them toward the synagogue and when they arrived, all of them pressed into the synagogue courtyard, and within minutes it was full. Some were forced to stand outside.

"Now we have no room in the synagogue. It is hardly ever full but now, now I want to go in, and it is too full," Amon grumbled as he stopped pushing and raised both his hands in frustration. "I hope that no rabbi gets run over in this place, at least not one that knows something."

Disappointed, he returned to where Asa was last seen, and when he found him, he put his arm around him. "Asa, what is happening? Is everyone losing their manners? Someday, I will meet that prophet and then I will . . ."

"What will you do Amon?"

"I suppose that I will tell him," he sighed, "that he should make people stop pushing. That's what I will tell him, Asa," he repeated what he had said and hung his head and closed his eyes.

On the outer edge of the throng, Amon noticed a rabbi and a priest standing on the steps of a moneychanger's building across the street, so Amon approached them.

"Ah, Rabbi", said Amon as he neared them. When they nodded to acknowledge him, he asked, "Has everyone in Nain been forgetting their manners? People are pushing and elbowing. My ribs are sore. Did you not see what is going on?"

In silence, the rabbi and priest began to move toward the side door of the synagogue. Neither spoke a word to Amon.

Shocked that they had walked away, Amon leaned over to a small scruffy donkey tied to a post, and turned the donkey's ear toward his mouth.

"Nobody is listening to Amon. Now," he said as he raised his gaze to the sky, "I must speak into a donkey's ear so that someone will listen to me." He leaned closer to the donkey's ear, "Do you know what is happening to Nain?" he asked in slow and deliberate words. "You are most lucky, Mr. Donkey because you don't have to know nothing, just keep flies from your

Conspiracy With Malicious Intent

nose and backend, and to stay away from heavy loads. I am thinking that being a donkey is better than a sandal maker. What do you think?"

The donkey turned his head away from Amon's hand and flapped his ears loudly as though scattering flies.

"Not even donkeys will listen to me, Asa." Frustrated, Amon started to walk toward his sandal shop. His eyes stared at every stone in his path. "Not even a donkey will listen to me. Maybe I am dead too."

"But Amon, I am listening to you," responded Asa as he tried to keep up with Amon. "I listen to you, Amon . . ."

"Yes, yes I know but," he did not finish his sentence.

As he passed the community well, Amon stopped to sit in the shade of a sycamore tree. "I must be too old to understand new things. Even my father, Beno, would have been confused by such things," he muttered to himself. After cupping his face in his hands, he sat in silence in the shade of the tree while his mind wrestled with all of the changing events around him.

Minutes passed and the voice of Obed brought Amon back to reality. "Amon, why are you not fixing my wife's sandals, like you said you would, and why are you yet sitting here?"

"Obed. Obed," Amon said as he lifted his face slowly to look at him.

"Amon what bothers you? You look so worried. Has the world squashed your face? I saw a donkey today that looked happier than you."

"Strange things are happening in Nain, and I'm afraid to think of what another sunrise will bring. Everything is changing. Roman soldiers come down my street many times every day, a dead boy now lives, a prophet is in this town and I can't find a rabbi, who knows something, people push and . . ."

Obed put his hand on Amon's shoulder. "Amon, Amon I too am not sure what will happen tomorrow. I have listened to this man some people say is a prophet, and he asks things that even rabbis cannot answer. He explains things from the Torah and the Law that makes rabbis to stroke their sacred beards."

"He does?" There was naïve tone to Amon's words.

"He raised Hannah's son from the dead, and I am too old to guess what will be next, but I cannot live with fear, Amon. These are times to watch and say nothing. Eyes work better when no words are used." He took a large breath as he patted Amon on the back. "The world never used to change but I have been thinking, even if it changes it will be here when I am dead, so why should I worry?"

Conspiracy With Malicious Intent

"Sit with me, Obed. I need to talk to someone who will listen. I tried to talk to a donkey today but even he didn't listen to me."

"Why are you yet so troubled?"

"I was there, Obed, when the prophet made Hannah's boy alive again and I have one of the cloths that fell from the dead, I mean the alive boy. Do you want to see or touch it?" he asked as he reached into his pouch and showed him the grave cloth.

"NO, NO, Amon, you should never have taken that cloth. It is from a dead person."

"No, no" insisted Amon as he shrugged his shoulders. "It was from a live boy when I found it."

"What would the rabbi say?"

"He doesn't know," responded Amon in a disgusting tone. "None of them knows nothing, so how can they know about this?"

"Here, let me see that cloth but you hold it. I do not want to touch it," said Obed as he stepped back to stare at the cloth in Amon's hand. "Why do you yet carry it?"

"So I can remember what happened. Maybe it could bring me good things if I keep it."

"Well, maybe," whispered Obed as he continued to scratch his beard and look at the cloth in Amon's hand. He tilted his head from one side to the other. "I know that you said it came from the boy that was alive but . . ."

"You know that things used to be simple," responded Amon. "Your parents told you what to do when you were young and then the rabbi told you what you should learn. Now our parents are dead and we have rabbis that don't know nothing." He shrugged his shoulders as he spoke.

"Amon, Amon, Amon, I am older than you, and I have decided long ago to stay away from new things because, well because I don't know about them. If it is not in our tradition I stay away from it, and from crowds I stay away because there are too many people in crowds, and sometimes I think . . ."

Amon interrupted, "My father told me that there are only seven things you need to stay away from."

"Your father Beno said to stay away from seven things? I didn't know that your father knew seven things."

"He did," responded Amon as he nodded his head up and down.

"What did he tell you to stay away from?" asked Obed as he sat down.

Conspiracy With Malicious Intent

Amon raised his right hand and spread his fingers as he spoke, numbering each one with his left pointer finger. Number one, you need to stay away from tax collectors because they give you a disease called poverty. Number two, you need to stay away from lawyers because they make you pay while they talk. They do nothing but talk and you must pay. Next, you need to stay away from Pharisees because they listen to lawyers, and then make more laws that we cannot keep. Then, you should stay away from Sadducees because all they do is argue with Pharisees. And next, you need to stay away from Roman soldiers because they will kill you just to keep the peace."

Obed narrowed his eyes as he stared at Amon.

"Next, you need to stay away from Gentiles because God's judgment is upon them and the last thing, stay away from a bossy woman, for when she marries you, she binds you with children like sheep in a pen and then she tells her mother to come and live with you to guard you."

There was a long period of silence as Obed stared at the ground, and then he wrinkled his eyebrows and moved his fingers through his beard as though in deep thought. "Your father, Beno, said all those things? I have known Beno many years . . . but, I don't remember him saying or even knowing that many things. What else did he say?"

"Yes. He said other things too, but they did not mean so much as these."

"Is that why you never married, Amon?"

"I don't want to talk about it," responded Amon as he stood, scratched his chin and started for his sandal shop. He paused several feet away and turned to look back at Obed, then raised both his arms to his waist and shrugged his shoulders. "I wish people would stay away from Nain. This was such a nice town and now . . . now everyone comes here to get in my way. If the prophet wanted to speak to people from Nain, then the others shall wait until he comes to their town."

Shaking his head from side to side, Obed adjusted his hat. "Amon, Amon, Amon . . . you are troubled by many things, but I need to know only one thing. Are my wife's sandals ready yet?"

"A man should not be rushed when he works. If you rush me, Obed, I might charge you double the price."

"The price you charge me is already too high so how can you double it?" responded Obed who chuckled and shook his head.

Amon put his arm around Obed's shoulder, "Come with me Obed and I will see if your wife's sandals are fixed."

Both men walked disquietedly from the shade of the sycamore tree, through the town's silent inactive market, and on toward Amon's Sandal Shop.

Asa followed without saying a word.

Chapter VI

THE CARAVAN MASTER'S CRITICAL CLUE

The organized search for Athaliah resulted in rumors only. Both city gates were secured with strict orders not to allow anyone to leave without Centurion Damarius' permission. Additional guards were dispatched to three locations where the city walls were partially broken down, and every street was searched for Rome's elusive nemesis.

Optio Ataxia's plan was to speak to every tanner that he knew so his first call was to a man named Amiel, who had been a tanner just inside the east gate, but because of his deteriorating health, he had given his shop and tools to his eldest son. When Amiel and his son were interrogated, they admitted that they knew of Athaliah because he had lived in Nain many years before, but insisted that they believed he was in Capernaum. Their comments seemed reasonable because Optio Ataxia knew that Athaliah began his violent campaign against Rome on the western shores of the Sea of Galilee. In their tanning shop, only two cups and a small amount of food was found, so Ataxia decided to continue their search elsewhere.

Joash the Tanner, whose shop was next to Amon's Sandal Shop, claimed he knew nothing of who Athaliah was or where he lived. He insisted that he and his family moved to Nain many years ago and had never heard of Athaliah. When soldiers walked through his shop and residence, they found five beds, one each for Joash, his wife and three children. No weapons were found and there was barely enough food for the entire family. They found no unusual clothing or sandals that did not fit members of the family.

Tanasha was the only other tanner Ataxia knew of, and he lived outside the city wall, next to several dead trees within several strides of a shallow well. He lived alone and willingly complied with a search of his deteriorating shack but no indications of visitors could be found. All that was found was one cup, one plate and very little food. Poverty was evident everywhere.

Centurion Damarius divided his men into three groups. He reminded them of their purpose when he said, "If Athaliah is in Nain, I want him found and captured. If you must kill him, then so be it. I remind you that citizens who hinder your search must suffer for their interference. Now find him and that's an order."

Varrus looked for and found the Egyptian caravan in the largest market in town. He spoke with the Caravan Master through an interpreter and insisted that he speak with every Egyptian.

Eventually eleven swarthy men and one boy stood next to the Caravan Master and when the interpreter asked questions he found them to be evasive, cautious and apprehensive. Often they would shrug their shoulders and smile.

Before leaving, Varrus insisted that the interpreter inform the Caravan Master that he and his servants would not be allowed to leave Nain without permission from the Centurion. They nodded giving Varrus the impression that they would comply, however Varrus knew that if given an opportunity to leave, they would not hesitate to flee.

Ataxia and his men searched every street and spoke to many citizens, yet no information indicated that Athaliah was in Nain. They continued to search near the walls of the city and the area occupied by the very poor.

Damarius and his men searched the area outside of Nain. This included a distance of two thousand strides from the city walls. Every gully, ravine and grove of trees was searched, but there were no signs of anyone or any objects that indicated anyone had been there.

When Damarius, Ataxia and Varrus met later that afternoon, they discussed what they had learned and reviewed their strategy.

"I don't believe that Athaliah is in Nain," said Ataxia. "I know that the people are fearful of us, and this causes many to remain silent, yet someone would have accidentally said something that would have made me suspicious. We've covered the entire town, but something bothers me. What about the man who stopped the funeral procession? Maybe he's the one we are looking for and he is . . ."

Shaking his head from side to side, Varrus interrupted, "No. He's not the man we want. He's not a violent man. Athaliah is different because he would not raise the dead boy back to life. That's something that Athaliah wouldn't do or could do. Remember that Athaliah is a ruthless murderer and a thief. The man, who raised the boy back to life, speaks of peace and is not known for any violence."

"So how did Athaliah get into Nain if he is here?" snapped Optio Ataxia as he loosened his sandal straps.

"We had reports that the Nazarene and the twelve men who travel with him, were on their way to Nain. They did not hide their travel plans but openly walked into Nain with the approval of the guards but the only other people the guards remember entering Nain were with the caravan. No other people entered Nain for the last, what . . . six days? No shepherds entered nor did anyone else, so if Athaliah is here he must have come into Nain with the caravan."

"If we are convinced that only Egyptians entered with the caravan and that Athaliah did not enter with the Nazarene, then there is no need for us to do any more searching," said Damarius as he refilled his goblet with wine. After drinking the wine, he sighed and said, "I've heard this Jesus travels mainly from Jerusalem to Galilee and from Jericho to the Jordan River. So why is he up here in this dry, forsaken, out of the way place?"

Varrus adjusted his weight on the stool and cleared his throat. "Jesus does not teach killing and resistance to Rome, but teaches that people must serve god. The only other thing he does is heal the sick. That does not sound like a murderer to me. He's much different than Athaliah and I can't see him as part of those murderous rebels. Why would he kill people and then bring others back to life?"

"Where is this Jesus now?" asked Damarius.

"I don't know, maybe at the home of the widow. She's the one whose son was brought back to life," said Varrus. "Maybe he's staying there."

"Varrus, tell me about the dead boy coming back to life," insisted Ataxia. He remained silent and stared at Varrus as he began to tell his story. When Varrus had finished telling about the lad being raised back to life, Ataxia lowered his gaze and said, "When I was in Egypt, I watched soothsayers and magicians perform some strange things. One of them handled a cobra and it appeared to have bitten him, but he did not die. A woman seer played with asps and did not die when she was bitten, so strange things do happen and when I was in North Africa, I saw an old woman point at some dry wood and a flame started. I never forgot that."

"Ataxia, this is different. This boy was dead. They were taking him out to bury him but he became alive when this Nazarene touched him. This man has power to raise a dead person back to life. What you saw may have shown that some people have power to overcome the threat of death but what about those who are dead, like this boy?"

"You may be right Varrus but it does seem rather strange that some people have such powers."

"Back to Athaliah. He must have entered Nain with the caravan. That's the only way he could have entered the city or maybe he isn't here and we just think he is," interjected Damarius.

"Let's speak to the Caravan Master again," said Varrus. "They're like shepherds that travel throughout the countryside and always know more than they are willing to admit to."

"Very well," said Damarius as he started for the door of the barracks. "I'm going with Varrus. Ataxia, you resume your search while there is still light."

Hoping to speak with the shop owners and retrace his steps, Ataxia entered the street adjacent to the tanner's shop. Meanwhile Damarius and Varrus arrived where the caravan members were selling their wares. Centurion Damarius dismounted and walked over to the man that Varrus pointed out as the Caravan Master. The language barrier was evident, and so one of the guards, who had been with Varrus on his original visit became the interpreter.

The interaction between the three men was obviously strained for the Caravan Master provided few words and constantly shook his head and raised his hands to everything the interpreter asked. Damarius was becoming impatient and eventually drew his gladius and placed it to the throat of the Caravan Master.

"Tell him," said Damarius in a strong nonsensical tone, "that I am taking all of his men to the barracks."

When the interpreter finished speaking, the Caravan Master was bound with cords and all of his men and a young boy were forced to walk to the Roman barracks. Two legionnaires remained behind to protect the Egyptian wares from thieves.

At the barracks, the Caravan Master was taken into a room at the rear of the building while his men were tied to corral posts not far from the open window of the room the Caravan Master was in. None of them could hear the conversation with their master but they were well aware of the seriousness of the situation and how quickly things could change.

When Varrus entered the room with the interpreter, he called for the cords to be removed from the Egyptian's wrists and then offered the Caravan Master some wine, which he refused to drink. Varrus drank some of the wine from the goblet and motioned to the Caravan Master, who smiled and shook his head from side to side, indicating, no.

The interpreter said to him, "The wine is not poison for this man has swallowed much of it. You need not be afraid."

Eventually, the Caravan Master reached for the cup and drank.

Damarius moved a chair to within a cubit of the Caravan Master's right shoulder and stared at the side of his head. Moments later, he began to speak. "There is no need for someone like you to receive trouble for what you were paid to do. We suspect that you allowed a stranger or strangers to enter Nain with your caravan. We take no pride in killing you and your servants, and selling your camels and wares. Remember that dead Egyptians will not be missed or found in this countryside."

The Egyptian said nothing as his eyes continued to stare at the wall directly in front of him.

Damarius continued, "I have not killed an Egyptian in a long while. I have no fear of killing one or a thousand, but I am willing to listen to you. All I want is for you to tell us if a man or several men entered Nain with your caravan."

The interpreter spoke to the Caravan Master, who glanced at the open window, and wondered if his men were able to hear the conversation.

Varrus sipped on wine before stepping near. "We will allow you to return to your camels and wares, if you will identify the man, who entered Nain with you. What does he look like? Does he have scars, a limp or anything that would make it easy for us to identify him?"

The Egyptian remained silent as the interpreter spoke.

"I suspect that you are afraid to speak because this group of rebels will attack you when you return to Egypt. I also suspect that these rebels know that you are in our barracks this very moment, so the only way to prevent a murderous attack against you after you leave Nain is for you to turn him over to us so we can deal with him. If we find and arrest him, then you will be safe. But if you leave while he is free, you will not likely make it back to Egypt. You know that . . . and so do we."

The Caravan Master remained stoic.

When Damarius stood to his feet, Varrus moved the chair to face the Caravan Master and sit directly in front of him. Varrus remembered his father's tactical interrogation so he remained silent and slowly moved his head from side to side as he continued to stare into the Caravan Master's eyes.

The Caravan Master was visibly uncomfortable but remained silent.

Conspiracy With Malicious Intent

Varrus leaned back and waited for a response and when none materialized, he turned to a desk and began to write notes on a parchment. Eventually, he set the quill on the desk and turned to face the Caravan Master. "Death is death regardless of whose sword is laid against your chest or throat. Do you agree?"

After the interpreter had finished speaking, the Caravan Master nodded in agreement.

Varrus placed his elbow on the table and cupped his chin with the thumb and pointer finger of his left hand and sighed loudly as he continued to stare at the Egyptian. After some time, Varrus told the interpreter to walk the Egyptian to the window to select a man that he was willing to sacrifice.

Nervously the Caravan Master looked out the window at his servants, who were secured to corral rails. After the interpreter repeated his instructions, the Egyptian turned away from the window and refused to select a slave, so the interpreter allowed him to return to his chair.

"He refuses to choose anyone," said the interpreter.

"Then I will choose," said Varrus as he stood to his feet and went to the window. "I will select the young boy. Bring him to me. He will be the sacrifice for the indecision of this Egyptian."

The Caravan Master turned to look at Varrus, who summoned one of the legionnaires to bring the lad into the room, and when the lad arrived, Varrus placed the lad in a chair next to the Egyptian.

Turning to the interpreter, Varrus said, "Ask him . . . if he would rather be slain or should we slay the boy."

Damarius, the interpreter and Varrus watched as the Caravan Master put his hand, momentarily on the lad's back.

The long silence must have unraveled the Caravan Master's confidence because he began to speak and when he had finished, the interpreter said, "He does not want any of his servants or camels killed and wants you to assure him that all his wares will not be stolen."

The room became silent.

Varrus nodded and eventually picked up a quill and stroked the feather before speaking. "Egyptians need not die for any Hebrews. We will return you to your wares and grant you permission to leave, after we have arrested the man we seek. Now where is he, and what does he look like?" Again Varrus' question turned the room into icy silence.

Damarius remained silent as he watched Varrus.

Conspiracy With Malicious Intent

The Caravan Master nodded in agreement. The interpreter waited as the Caravan Master began to speak, and when he had finished, the interpreter turned to Damarius and Varrus. "He said 'The man you seek is in Nain.'"

"How many are with him?"

The interpreter said, "Six."

"How will we recognize him?" continued Varrus.

The interpreter listened to the Egyptian's response and then turned to Varrus, "Him say, 'He has a wound on his inner arm that causes him to sway it by his side. He does not move it when he walks. He has two teeth missing and an old cut under his nose.'"

"Which arm is injured?" asked Varrus in an icy tone.

The interpreter turned to the Caravan Master, who looked at the lad and then down at his arms. In silence, he raised his left arm and pointed to the inner part just below the elbow.

Varrus continued to stare at the Caravan Master and then dabbed the quill into the ink and wrote something on a parchment, folded it and placed the quill onto the table. The silence made the interpreter, Damarius and the Caravan Master uncomfortable.

The silence continued and eventually the Egyptian began to speak again and the interpreter responded, "Him say, 'We were stopped in the valley of the fig trees. Sixteen men suddenly appeared with their weapons. The leader paid me and told me that he needed to go to Nain, but if anyone found out who he was, all of us would be killed when we returned to the open road.'"

Varrus remained silent.

The interpreter asked the Caravan Master a question and when he responded, the interpreter looked at Varrus. "Him say 'The man is still in Nain for he saw him this morning with a man, who was pushing a cart loaded with animal skins.'"

Varrus moved his chair closer to the Egyptian. "Tell him that the information he gave me is important to him, his men and the young lad. Secondly, it is important to us. One other question, how many men entered Nain with him?"

The interpreter responded, "He already say, 'Only six but the rest disappeared into a small valley.'"

Varrus smiled at the young boy.

The Egyptian nodded for he knew he had made a wise choice.

"Tell him that we owe him no favors nor do we plan to pay bribes. We have allowed him and his men to live. That is reward enough. Tell him that he will be remembered but that does not allow him to break the law or expect us to turn our eyes away from any of his activities now or in the future."

The Caravan Master sighed after the interpreter finished speaking.

"So he is in Nain," whispered Damarius.

Varrus walked over to the young lad and helped him to his feet. "Take this young man and his father, and all of those tied to the corral rails back to the market, and remind them that they must not leave until I give permission. We must go through Nain one more time. After we have found Athaliah, then they will be allowed to leave."

The Egyptians were escorted to their tents, animals and wares by three cavalrymen while Varrus and Centurion Damarius remained at the barracks.

"How did you know that the young man was the Caravan Master's son?" asked Damarius.

"Sacrificing an old person is no loss for they will likely die anyway but sacrificing a young man is different. Did you see what the Caravan Master did to the young man?"

"No."

"He put his hand momentarily on his back. Egyptians do not touch slaves or anyone except their children. He is not about to sacrifice his son for people he does not know or care about."

Chapter VII

THE PROPHET, THE HARLOT, THE PARTY

It was late in the afternoon when Asa returned to the sandal shop. He appeared to be physically exhausted as he slumped onto his crooked stool and sighed loudly.

"Only donkeys that carry heavy loads should sigh that loudly," said Amon as he tossed a repaired sandal into a box near the front door. A moment later he said, "What makes you so tired? You have not worked today." Tapping on a different sandal with his mallet, he looked up at Asa and smiled. "Well where were you?"

"Today, the prophet looked at me and smiled. My heart felt warm and I wanted him to touch me and make me well, but I couldn't get close to him. I think he is more than a prophet, Amon. I think he's . . . he's maybe the Messiah that our mother told us about."

Amon stopped tapping on the sandal and shrugged his shoulders. "He does not need my permission."

"Amon, you must come to listen to him. He said that the greatest man to live was someone called John the Baptist. Amon, what is a Baptist? Is that like a tentmaker or a butcher?"

"Do I, a simple sandal maker, know what a . . . a Bastisma is?"

"No, no Amon, a Baptist."

"Asa, who am I to know such new words?" He shrugged his shoulders as he continued to tap on the sole of the sandal. "I am a sandal maker and you, you were born with a big foot, a crippled hand and now the hot sun has hurt your head. Clean the floor or do something. Just be quiet. I need to think."

"Amon, I tried to ask one of the rabbis but . . ."

"Yes, yes I know but the rabbi doesn't know who the man is," interrupted Amon as he turned to the sandal over in his hand and held it up to the light. After looking at it, he tossed the repaired sandal into the box with the other repaired sandals, and began to search for the matching one.

"How did you know, Amon?"

"That is the way things are Asa," Amon said as he looked at a matching pair of sandals. Moments later he asked, "Did you say that the prophet looked at you? Where did he look at you?"

"Into my eyes."

Amon closed his eyes and shook his head. "Asa, I mean where were you when the prophet looked at you?"

"I was by the city gate where the road goes out of town, and many people were listening to him talk. He sounded so nice to listen to. I didn't understand all what he said, but I felt good when he talked and I listened."

"You saw him and . . . and you did not call me?" asked Amon as he wiped perspiration from his forehead.

"Sorry Amon but I was talking to Ammash and then we saw the crowd, and I did not have time to come to get you."

Amon placed the mallet on the table and shifted his weight on the creaking stool. "So now you go to find the prophet without me and, and when I wanted to see the prophet, it was you, yes you, who made me spend all my time looking for you and, and that big foot."

"Amon, I think the prophet will be here for another day. Maybe he will raise another dead person or maybe do some other good things."

"Strange things are everywhere, Asa. A prophet comes to this town and nobody wants to work, only listen to him, and I, yes I am the one who must work alone while you are somewhere listening and looking at . . . a Messiah."

Asa opened a small cupboard, "I'm hungry Amon. Is there any food to eat?"

Following their meager meal, Asa sat at his usual place, in the doorway of the sandal shop and watched children playing. Amon was restless and when he could no longer contain his emotions, he decided to go for a walk. He walked down the street, leading to the synagogue and when he arrived, he stopped next to the side door of the synagogue, hoping to speak with a rabbi. The door suddenly opened and a rabbi stepped out of the building.

"Oh, Rabbi," Amon said with his eyes cast to the ground.

"Yes, what is it?"

Conspiracy With Malicious Intent

"Do you know what the word Baptisma means or something like that is?"

"Baptisma? That word I do not know. Baptisma, hmmm, I know of no such word. Are you sure that the word is Baptisma? The only word that is close to your word, is Baptist?"

"Yes, yes that's the word," replied Amon as he stepped closer.

"Baptist is a very strange word indeed. My, my, my . . . why do you ask and why do you want to know?"

"Today the prophet, I mean the stranger to Nain that raised Hannah's boy to life, said that no man was better than some man named John the Baptisma." His eyes narrowed and his brows wrinkled as he studied the rabbi's response.

"Who told you that?" asked the rabbi.

"My brother Asa. He heard the prophet say that before he came home and told me."

"Strange you should ask. I heard the stranger to Nain say that too. The only man I know with the name, John the Baptist is a man who dips people in the Jordan River after they confess their sins to God." The rabbi shook his head slowly from side to side as he stared at the ground. A moment later, he stroked his beard and continued, "I don't know why that should be done. Those, who have witnessed this, say John the Baptist constantly tells people to turn from their evil ways because the Messiah will soon be here. I know we have been waiting for the Messiah to come but . . ." he said as he shrugged his shoulders, "but the prophets have told us that the Messiah will be born in the city of David in Judah, and Isaiah tells us, that God will call his son out of Egypt. How is that possible, I do not know." He pursed his lips and shook his head. "I don't know how he can be born in a city in Judaea and yet come from another country. Maybe we're backwards or upside down about all of this. I just don't know."

"What is a Jordan River?"

"The Jordan River, ah the Jordan River I have seen it. It is water flowing from the Sea of Galilee to the Dead Sea." He paused, "This John you are talking about immerses people in the Jordan River after they confess their sins."

"I have not heard of water except from one of our wells," said Amon in an apologetic tone. "When he puts people in water, does he wash them?"

"I just don't know," the rabbi said in a soft tone as he stroked his whiskers. "I have not seen what he does with those who confess their sins but

I have heard about it from those that have seen it while they were on their way to Jerusalem."

"You already said I don't know. What do you know?" asked Amon, feeling frustrated"

"Amon, your tongue is too fast for your ears. God in His wisdom, gave you one mouth, so don't wear it out. Ears don't wear out because they work without moving and because they don't make a sound." He sighed loudly before continuing, "God gave you two ears and one mouth. Listen to twice as much as you talk, Amon. That's my advice for you."

"Thank you Rabbi, but I want to find out if what Asa said, is true." He studied the face of the rabbi before continuing, "Asa thinks that this stranger is not just a prophet but maybe the, the M-e-s-s-i-a-h?" He deliberately slowed the word Messiah to emphasis it. Then he intensified his stare on the rabbi's face.

"Amon, God does not need my permission to do and or send who He wants. In the past he sent many prophets, but a Messiah? That I don't know." He folded his arms across his chest as he stared at the cobblestones. "This stranger does miracles like a prophet, speaks about the Law and discusses difficult things. Maybe he is a prophet and maybe a . . . the Messiah, but I don't know."

"When will you know?" asked Amon in a naïve tone.

The rabbi shrugged his shoulders. "I wish I could tell you because I would like to know about these things myself, but and I say but . . . some things are hard to understand."

"Where is the Messiah now?" asked Amon in a whispered tone.

"Quiet, Amon," he said as he raised his finger to his mouth. "Do not call him the Messiah yet. What I do know is that he was invited to Simon's house tonight and I will listen carefully when I am there. I'm on my way there as soon as Rabbi Malachi comes out of the synagogue."

"You and Rabbi Malachi are going to Simon's house to listen to the Messiah?" Amon's eyes widened as he spoke.

Putting his pointer finger to his lips, he said, "SHHHH, when you talk about a Messiah. No one is sure of that yet. The priests and rabbis will decide about this, not sandal makers and tentmakers like you."

Several people walked by and when they were beyond hearing distance, Amon leaned forward, "My mother said that we have been waiting for a Messiah for a long time and I have been thinking that maybe this is he. Have you yet thought about that?"

"Yes but . . ."

"Rabbi," whispered Amon, "look what I have. I have one of the cloths that fell from Hannah's dead son. Do you want to hold it?"

"NO!" shouted the rabbi as he stepped back. "It was from a dead man! You must not touch it."

"But Rabbi, it was from a live person when I found it. Does that not make it just a piece of cloth?"

"NOT just an ordinary piece of cloth," he quickly responded as he stepped back several paces. "I . . . I . . . well maybe, but I don't think so."

Amon raised his eyes and hands to the sky, closed his eyes and shook his head. "Rabbis are supposed to know but you . . ." his sentence was interrupted as Rabbi Malachi stepped out of the side door of the synagogue.

After Rabbi Malachi acknowledged Amon with a nod he walked past Amon, and he and Rabbi Jehocim walked away in silence.

Amon decided to follow at a distance and as he did he carefully put the cloth back into his pouch. At that moment seven cavalrymen and five infantrymen approached Amon, so he folded his arms and backed against a wall and held his breath.

Once the cavalrymen and the infantrymen had passed him, Amon started to run until he was only steps behind Rabbis Malachi and Rabbi Jehocim. When they arrived at Simon's house Amon could hear loud music coming from within the courtyard next to a large house.

Amon remembered who Simon was when they arrived at his house. He was a very wealthy man with much influence in Nain and in the synagogue. His servants had been to Amon's sandal shop many times to buy new sandals and though Amon had never spoken to Simon, he remembered what he looked like.

Amon followed Rabbi Jehocim and Rabbi Malachi past a manservant at the gate and into the courtyard. Once inside, Amon stepped into a doorway and peered around the large room. There was a great crowd of men, some whom Amon recognized and others he had never seen before. He folded his hands as if he was about to pray and tried to walk beyond the doorway, but a servant stopped him. Amon slowly backed out of the room into the courtyard when the servant pointed at him.

From the courtyard, Amon could hear the greetings offered to Rabbi Malachi and Rabbi Jehocim. He heard Simon introduce both of them to all of the guests, and wished he could go inside. After looking around, he moved quietly toward a large open window for a better view. The music was rather loud so the conversations were difficult to understand, so Amon decided to move to another doorway and as he did, he bumped into

Conspiracy With Malicious Intent

one of the many trees in Simon's yard. He was about to climb the tree for a better view when two men grabbed him and wrestled him the ground. Something struck him on the head, causing him to moan and almost lose consciousness.

Amid his momentary confusion, Amon was forced to stand on unsteady legs and when his head began to clear, he realized that he had been struck by one of the two house guards, who had him pinned against the wall. The noise in the garden brought several of the servants to the doorway and they in turn summoned Simon.

"We found this man in your garden and knew that you would not be happy to have a criminal in your courtyard," said the tallest of the guards as he placed a dagger against Amon's throat. "If you desire, I will slay him."

Simon put his hand on the guards arm and looked at Amon's face, "No, no, no wait. First let me find out who he is."

"Please, Simon. I am Amon the sandal maker and am not a thief. Please, Simon, I only came to hear what the prophet has to say."

Simon folded his arms across his chest and frowned. "Sandal maker? I trust that you were bringing back sandals that my servants brought to you several weeks ago."

"No . . . I followed Rabbi Malachi and Rabbi Jehocim to your place so that I could listen to the prophet."

"What prophet do you speak of?" asked Simon with an angry and disparaging tone. He instantly looked over his shoulder for he did not want any of his guests to overhear this verbal confrontation.

Amon moaned as he rubbed his head.

A moment later Simon spoke, "This man you call a prophet is a guest of mine." Looking over his shoulder again to see if anyone was eavesdropping, Simon turned to one of the servants and whispered, "Take care of him but do him no harm."

The guards walked Amon out of the courtyard and garden, leaving him standing in the street. As Amon rubbed his head, a servant of Simon's arrived from the market, and as he was about to enter the doorway, Amon reached out, "Shaka," he whispered. "I'm Amon the sandal maker. Do you remember me? I have come to listen to the prophet that is inside with the rabbis and scribes. Please let me in so that I can listen to what he says."

Unaware of what had just happened, Shaka replied, "Yes, Amon I remember you."

"Please let me follow you into the garden. I will be very quiet. I just want to hear the prophet."

"Well, I'm not sure that . . ."

"Thank you Shaka," Amon said as he grabbed the food that Shaka was carrying and pushed Shaka through the doorway. Once inside the garden, Amon gave the food back to Shaka and moved cautiously toward the house.

Just as Amon found a quiet spot next to a curtain by a doorway, Simon stepped into the courtyard to speak with a servant but his eyes noticed Amon and he walked over to him. Knowing that other guests were watching him, Simon was careful not to be unkind, so he whispered, "So you are still here?"

"Simon, I mean no harm. I just want to listen to . . ."

"What makes you think that this guest of mine is a prophet or is even interested in a sandal maker such as you?" His voice was low so that others were unlikely to hear his confrontational words.

"Well," replied Amon still rubbing the back of his head, "I have a piece of the cloth from Hannah's son who was raised back to life by this man, and I just wanted to see what this man looks like. Asa, my brother told me that this prophet talks about interesting things and I wanted to hear him." He grinned as he spoke and his white teeth seemed to glisten.

There was a moment of silence, and then Simon looked over his shoulder and turning to Amon, pointed to the stairs. "Sit on these steps and be silent. If you make any noise, I will call the servants back and this time they will flog you. Do you understand me?" Simon's eyes glared with anger, but he tried to appear congenial because some of his guests had come to the windows to see what the commotion was about.

Amon nodded as a sign of his agreement to the conditions of this informal invitation. He watched as Simon walked into the house. When everyone had turned away, Amon positioned himself on the stairs so that he could see Simon moving among the reclining guests.

Simon squatted next to the man Amon remembered seeing with the children, and convinced himself that this man was the prophet. Knowing that Simon was a man of his word, Amon remained silent as the guests continued to speak with each other. Soon the servants served roast lamb, dates, cheese, lentils, fruit and wine. Amon positioned himself so he could watch both the prophet and Simon.

The evening meal at Simon's house smelled so good but all Amon could do was smell the aroma of roasted lamb coming from the kitchen and from the room where the guests dined. He would have watched in silence, but his growling stomach drew the attention of a servant, who quietly handed him several figs to eat.

As darkness enveloped Nain one of the guests, named Jehoshada, started the post supper debate. He turned to the prophet and in a probing way began to speak. "Earlier today someone asked you about this current generation. In fact, the question as I recall was, 'Is this generation different than previous generations?'"

The prophet continued to eat in silence, looking only at the basket of fruit in front of him. After swallowing what he had been chewing, he looked up and into the faces of every guest.

"Does each generation," continued Jehoshada, "become better or worse than the previous one?"

The prophet dabbed his mouth with a white linen cloth and appeared to be considering his response when Nathan, Simon's eldest son leaned forward, "Is God more pleased with our generation than with the generations before us, like my father's generation or my, my papa's generation?"

All eyes were on the special guest.

"Why do you ask? Do you think that people become better as they age or are they better because of the generation they belong to?" asked the prophet. The silence in the room was deafening. Reaching for more grapes, the special guest began to speak. "Each generation is known for its actions, attitudes and what they value. Each generation tries to improve what they have learned and been taught, but does that make them better simply because of their efforts or desires?"

Simon and his guests looked at each other and after a marked moment of silence, this question stimulated a series of mini conversations, each varying in different levels of intensity and loudness. Some of the guests were concerned about the younger generation and their lack of commitment, and some were disappointed by the serious need for discipline and accountability. Others agreed that keeping tradition was as important as keeping the Law. The debates lasted for quite a long time before Simon raised his hands and interrupted.

"Well," smiled Simon who lowered his hand for the guests to become silent. "We seem to have varying opinions about this question. Our generation is much different from my fathers, and our children's generation is much different than what we expected." He paused as he reached for more wine. "What about our generation? Our forefathers taught us to observe the Laws of Moses and we have kept all the Feasts and we . . ."

Conspiracy With Malicious Intent

"Let him answer, Simon," someone interrupted and all of the guests chuckled.

Simon turned his head and smiled. "We follow all of the conditions and requirements set down by the Torah so I think that each generation is getting better. We understand the Tanakh, the Torah and the Laws of Moses better. And, we have been teaching all of it to the younger generation, so what about this new generation?" He opened his hand toward his son and several of his young friends as he spoke. "They may have new ideas about God but are they better than the ideas we had or what our fathers acted upon? What about our tradition? We have followed all of it. We keep the Ten Commandments and the Shabbat and all the Festivals and Feasts, and the Passover. Is that not important?" The guests immediately resumed their independent discussions.

When silence was restored, the honored guest from Nazareth reached for several more figs. Then he leaned back and asked, "Why do you think that your generation is better than the previous ones?"

Again there was discussion among the guests.

After silence was restored Jehoshada responded, "Well . . . we have not killed any prophets sent to us by God. We have not built groves to false gods, and we read the Torah every day. We carefully give our tithe to the synagogue and pray in public to be examples to all people, including our younger generation. All of us live our lives according to the Law and tradition. What more can we do?"

Some of the guests began to speak while others just nodded their heads in agreement.

Rabbi Malachi raised his hand. "Many of us have gone to Jerusalem to worship as required and have returned better people. Is that what makes us better than those who do not go up to Jerusalem?"

Another teacher of the Law asked, "All of us keep the Law and avoid idols. We do what has been taught to us and we in turn teach our children who are ultimately responsible to do what is right in the sight of God, or are we responsible for what the next generation does because we were the ones that taught them?"

Amon watched the prophet as he reclined on a soft cushion and swallowed what he was chewing.

"That was a good question," said the prophet. "I guess what you are really asking is, what are people like? They are like, like children playing in the marketplace and calling to each other. Each calls for different reasons and each perceives that they are correct."

"Are you saying that each generation calls out its opinions to the following generation? I guess another question is, are they listening to what is said?" asked the eldest guest, who was sitting next to Simon.

"One generation plays a sorrowful tune and then requires the next generation to follow by being sad as a sign of godliness, while another generation calls for happier traditions. Each believes that they know best, but do they? What you do is less important than what your purpose is for doing it. If you do deeds for the poor and care not that others see it, then you have done well and have acted in obedience to God, but if you do deeds so others will see what you have done, you have already received your reward. Each generation . . ."

Just then, Amon noticed a curtain slowly opening behind and to the prophet's left, and there stood Peninnah, a harlot from the other side of the market. At any distance, she was riveting. Amon could tell that her eyes were focused solely upon the prophet. Her beauty had lured many a shopkeeper, soldier, merchant and occasionally a rabbi to her door. Paupers envied her clients, and whispered their desire for her, but only to their closest friends. She was alluring, sensuous and her charms were bewitching.

She was a foreigner, yet no one dared ask where she was from, particularly when they were within arm's length of her charms or intense gaze. Often her perfumes made its way from her window to the men, who passed by her window. When she walked through the market it was easy to hear the sound of her wrist and ankle bracelets, which appeared to be made of pure gold, all adding to her charm and sensuality.

She remained hidden from the guests and for a moment, Amon had the feeling that only he knew that she was there. Her royal blue veil with golden tassels framed her long, tar-pitched, curly hair, which shone even in candlelight. Her dark eyes appeared to be focused upon the prophet, like an animal thinking only of its prey. Amon felt a need to warn everyone, but his throat was too dry to speak. The conversations in the room were now unimportant to Amon.

Silently, Peninnah moved from one pillar to another as she narrowed the distance between herself and her prey. Her sandals appeared to be made of gold, her nails were red with color and her dark unblinking eyes mesmerized Amon. He held his breath as she moved effortlessly with the skill of a stalking predator.

Amon stood to his feet for a better view, even though his knees were weak from the earlier confrontation with Simon's servants. Unable to hold his weight, he leaned against the archway as his eyes remained riveted on the harlot. He tried to swallow but his throat seemed unable to move.

Again, the harlot moved closer to the prophet, and Amon noticed something shiny in her hand. Was it a dagger? Was she about to strike down the prophet? If he was a prophet, why did he not notice her standing there, or know he was in danger?

Her long fingers were covered in rings, and her wrists and forearms were looped in pure gold chains. She moved without sound. Even her wrist bracelets were silent as she inched ever nearer. No one seemed to notice her, their eyes were solely upon the prophet.

Then the prophet turned his head slowly toward the pillar to his left, and she with tears in her eyes, suddenly knelt beside him. Her tears began to fall upon the prophet's feet. Silence was so loud that it could be heard from outside. No one breathed. Everyone's eyes focused upon the prophet and the harlot. Then the prophet looked down at her and for a few moments no one was aware of the deafening silence as all watched in disbelief.

Peninnah sobbed loudly, and when she saw that her tears had wet the prophet's feet, she tried to wipe them with her long, coal-colored hair. Only her intermittent sobs could be heard.

Amon unknowingly moved closer for a better view. He had hoped that he would see another healing but this . . . this was far from what he expected to experience in Simon's house.

When Peninnah finished wiping the tears from the prophet's feet, she kissed the right foot and then his left foot. Then, she opened a gold container and poured the entire amount of rare perfume upon the prophet's feet. The perfume was so strong that it permeated the entire house and its compelling odor seemed to mesmerize every guest, even the servants in the kitchen because they left the kitchen and entered the room to find out what that alluring odor was.

The prophet did not seem surprised but sat up and gently placed his hand on Peninnah's head as she remained motionless before him.

Simon, the owner of the house, seemed to view this as an indication that the guest of honor was NOT a prophet or else he would have chastised her and sent her immediately from his presence.

The prophet nodded as she looked up at him. Her sobs now became less audible. "Simon," said the honored guest without looking at Simon, "I have to tell you something."

"Y-e-s," responded Simon in a rather slow sarcastic and questioning way. His dark eyes scanned his guests, seeking support for these rather intimidating words. Finding none, he responded, "What does my guest wish to say?"

"Two men owed money to the moneylenders. One man owed five-hundred denarii, and the other man only owed fifty denarii. Both of them were unable to save or make the payment. The moneylender knew that both of them had tried to repay it, and so in an act of mercy, the moneylender cancelled both of their debts."

"Very unusual," whispered Rabbi Malachi. Other guests nodded in silent agreement.

The prophet continued, "Which person do you suppose appreciated and loved the moneylender the most?"

Simon, clearing his throat in an effort to delay his response, folded his arms across his chest and narrowed his eyes at a basket of fruit in front of him. "Why I . . . I guess the one who had the larger debt." He looked at his guest, confident of his answer.

"You have judged correctly Simon," was the prophet's reply as he looked at Simon and then back to Peninnah. "Do you see this woman? I came into your house this evening, and you did not follow our tradition by giving me water to wash my feet, but she wet my feet with her tears and then wiped them with her hair, a sign of true humility."

Simon, in silence anxiously looked at his other guests and then to the food in front of him.

Amon suddenly realized that he was standing next to some of the guests, so he backed slowly toward the doorway.

Then the prophet continued, "Our tradition is that you give me a welcome kiss when I entered your house but you did not give me a kiss. This woman, from the time she approached me, has not stopped kissing my feet. Everyone here knows that you should have put oil on my head but you did not, and yet she has poured valuable perfume on my feet."

Again Amon leaned closer to hear every word. Simon, as well as his guests, was notably uncomfortable with the words from the prophet.

"I tell you, Simon, that her many sins have been forgiven because she has loved so much. But he, who has been forgiven little, loves little."

Again the silence was deafening and every guest became increasingly uncomfortable.

Simon sighed, held his breath for a few moments and then slowly and silently exhaled.

Then the prophet turned to the woman and said, "Peninnah, your sins are forgiven."

Immediately the guests began to whisper to each other, "How did he know her name? Who is this that can forgive sins? Only God can forgive sins," muttered the oldest guest seated to Simon's far left.

"Peninnah," continued the prophet, "go in peace, for your faith has saved you. Sin no more." Then he smiled at her.

She stood slowly to her feet and backed out of the room, with her hands over her face. Her bangles and ankle bracelets chimed her departure.

Amon stopped one of the servants and whispered "Do you know what the prophet's name is?"

"I think, his name is Jesus," was the reply.

"Where is he from?"

"Someone said he was from Nazareth."

"Is he the one that raised Hannah's son from the dead?"

"I think so."

"How can this be? Things like this don't happen in Nain."

"I don't know," responded the servant as he walked into the kitchen.

The room was very quiet for a long time. Eventually whispers could be heard and soon the guests turned to each other and began to discuss what they had just witnessed.

Simon remained stoic and withdrawn by what had just happened.

Chapter VIII

BLOODSHED ON THE TANNER'S STREET

It was dark when Ataxia and his men arrived at the barracks and while the horses were drinking, he entered the building to speak with Varrus and Damarius.

"How was your search?" asked Varrus.

Ataxia cleared his throat as he sat down. "We believe that we have located the tanner's shop owned by Athaliah's relative. The tanner's shop is the one owned by Joash and is next to the sandal maker's shop. Did you learn anything from the Caravan Master?"

"He admitted that six men entered Nain with him, and earlier today the Caravan Master saw them with someone pushing a cart with animal hides in it," responded Varrus.

"Has any of you seen a cart loaded with hides?" asked Damarius.

"Now that you ask, several infantrymen remembered seeing a cart with hides outside Joash's shop this morning and there were several men moving it toward the synagogue."

"The Caravan Master described the man that entered Nain as having several teeth missing, a scar on his upper lip and unable to use his left arm. Apparently he lets it hang by his side as he walks," continued Varrus.

"I recall seeing that man . . . and he was between the synagogue and Joash's place. That proves that Athaliah is here and that Joash is his relative," said Ataxia as he stood to his feet. "But we have already searched Joash's shop and found nothing, so where is Athaliah?"

"He is likely to be hiding in the synagogue," responded Varrus.

"This is an excellent opportunity to catch him," said Damarius as he leaned back in his chair and grinned.

"I have left men to watch Joash's place and I have several men watching the synagogue," responded Ataxia. "So if Athaliah is in this city, he must be in the synagogue."

Varrus stood to his feet as he began to speak. "We know what Athaliah looks like so if we have any doubt, approach whoever fits that description."

"What if he's in the synagogue? Should we enter it?" asked Ataxia.

"If we force our way into the synagogue, then the Jews will complain to the Legatus and the Governor and maybe to Caesar. We'll enter only if we are absolutely sure," responded Damarius. "Gather the men and go to this tanner's shop. Ataxia, distribute your men between the synagogue and the tanner's shop. Sit and wait because he'll come out some time. In the meantime, Varrus, have some of your men check the carts in other parts of the city to draw attention away from the street between Joash's place and the synagogue."

As they were preparing to leave the barracks a rider arrived, and jumping from his horse, he rushed into the building. "Sir," he said without saluting, "we watched Joash the Tanner enter the synagogue and sometime later he left through a rear door, crossed the street and entered a garment shop. Shortly after that, he crossed the street near the sheepfold and entered the house of a silversmith. Eventually he and another man came out of the silversmith's house and followed a herd of sheep that were passing by, and then they entered Joash's shop."

"Anything else?" asked Damarius as he adjusted his scabbard. "What did these men look like?"

"One of the men walked as though his arm was painful to move, Sir. It hung by his side as he walked."

"MOUNT UP," ordered Damarius. "Varrus, you enter the street from the synagogue and I will go to the rear of the shop as Ataxia moves to the front. We have him trapped. Remember he's dangerous and desperate. Squash all resistance. Spare no one, not even women or children. If he's here, I want him now."

When Varrus arrived on the tanner's street, he was informed that Ataxia and his men were already in position, and that Damarius was at the rear of Joash the Tanner's Shop.

With their swords drawn, Varrus and his men moved cautiously along the street, and when they were within fifty strides of Joash the Tanner's Shop, Varrus observed a door slowly opening and then three men emerged. In an instant, Ataxia and the legionnaires were engaged in a battle, but the legionnaires were too distracted to notice adjacent doors opening, allowing additional armed men enter the battle. Hearing the foray at the front of the building, Damarius and his men forced their way into Joash's shop and finding no one there, rushed to the front door where they became involved in a fierce hand to hand battle.

Varrus and the men immediately drew their swords and rode into the fray. Soon the street was awash with shouts, cries of pain, metal on metal and gasps from the dying. The citizens initially gained the upper hand but when Varrus and his men arrived, the battle suddenly turned in favor of Rome.

Varrus could see several civilian archers at the top of a building across the street. Their position and skill struck down several legionnaires in the blink of an eye. The street was very narrow and that made it very difficult to maneuver their horses to defend or attack. Varrus rode his horse to the stairs that led to the roof of the building where the archers were raining death upon the men on the street below.

When Varrus and six men reached the top of the stairs, the archers were taken by surprise and immediately leapt to the roof of the adjacent building, which provided an escape route. Varrus pointed at the escaping rebels and four of his men followed while he and the two remaining legionnaires rushed down the stairs and ran to where he believed the archers would appear, but when he arrived there was no sign of them, so he and his men returned to where the major battle was raging.

Centurion Damarius was unsure of who or how many enemies they faced. When Optio Ataxia accidentally met Damarius at the front of a garment shop, Damarius shouted in both fear and rage, "KILL AS MANY AS YOU CAN. WE DON'T KNOW HOW MANY ARE HERE!"

Moments later, Optio Ataxia dropped to his knees for he was mortally wounded. He fell upon the body of a dead child and did not move. In the melee, Damarius continued to shout orders and suddenly fell when he was struck by a spear. When the cavalrymen and infantrymen thought their ranks had been depleted, they gathered the torches that were on the walls of the buildings and set fire to many of the houses. The battle seemed endless. Amid the cries of the innocent, the bewildered, the anxious and the fearful, the foes battled as flames continued to devour the homes of the innocent.

The frenzy of the battle raged on the edge of panic and insanity. Innocent children and their mothers were cut down with the sword. Panic stricken horses without riders ran through the streets knocking over citizens and stepping on frightened children. Torches on the sides of homes flickered

Conspiracy With Malicious Intent

above the swirl of activity and the cries of the wounded chilled the hearts of even the seasoned legionnaires.

A dog barked but soon yelped in retreat. Eventually the sound of metal on metal abated and all that could be heard were cries of despair and the moans of the dying. Nearby a fire began to engulf three additional buildings and soon smoke hid the wounded and dying.

****

When Amon left Simon's house his mind was filled with emotions which he had never experienced before. "If the stranger was a prophet and could raise the dead, why did he allow Peninnah to touch him and why did he touch her?" he whispered as he walked along. "And forgiving sins, only God can do that and he doesn't look like a prophet or a messiah"

In silence his mind tried to reason through additional things that added confusion to his thinking. Yes, the prophet did have a way of asking and answering questions that seemed to puzzle the religious leaders and his voice was gentle, especially to Peninnah, but why did he let her touch him? Did he not know what she was? The prophet did raise Hannah's son back to life but why break so much tradition?

Then Amon recalled how Simon had cleared all of the servants from the room to protect his reputation. When all the doors and windows were closed, Amon found himself standing in the dark street.

There with downcast eyes, he started for home. His steps were small and he was so deep in thought that he was unaware of noise in the distance because his mind was revisiting all of the events of the evening.

"But the man looks so ordinary," is what Amon kept mumbling to himself as he walked through the darkened streets. When he passed the synagogue, he noticed a light in the window, but resisted the urge to knock on the door because he knew that it would not be opened to people, who were out this time of night. Only soldiers and troublemakers would be passing through the streets, so he moved as silently as possible toward his home.

"How can this be the Messiah that our mother told us about? Maybe he was only a prophet," he said to himself as he turned the corner near a grove of stunted trees. Amon convinced himself that he would look for the prophet at first light.

The smell of smoke touched his nostrils and caused him to stop for a moment and that is when he became aware of the loud noises and people shouting and women screaming. It seemed to be coming from his street so he started to run but felt his chest desperately needing more air so he slowed to a jog. Moving steadily toward the strange glow of lights and confusing sounds, he was unprepared for what he would find around the next corner.

Near the community well, he forced himself to stop and leaned against a sycamore tree to catch his breath. He breathed deeply and tried to slow his heart rate. "What was this town of Nain becoming? A dead boy is alive, a prophet touches a harlot and forgives her sins, and now, there are loud cries from this neighborhood in the middle of the night."

Again, he started to run but this time faster because the momentary rest had renewed his strength. Fifty paces later, he rounded the corner of the butcher shop and what he saw caused him to stop in horror. His eyes dilated, his mouth opened in shock as his hands began to shake.

Soldiers seemed to be everywhere. Many of his neighbors were frantically running to escape violent assaults. Their faces were partially hidden by the smoke from the burning houses and the glow of torches was not sufficient for him to recognize them as they ran by him. The terrified screams of women deafened him, and a chill ran along his spine and out to the hairs on his arms. When he moved forward, he tripped over a child that lay at his feet.

Acting as though he was in a dream or trance, he tried to make sense of the lights, the screams, the fire and smoke. He looked toward his home, and realized that the chaos was next to his shop. Without regarding his life, he ran directly toward the door of his shop and home.

Suddenly, someone grabbed him and pulled him into the shadows. With dilated pupils, he tried to identify the one, who had a hand over his mouth. It was Achim. He whispered, "SHHHHH Amon, I'm Achim. Be silent."

Amon stopped struggling momentarily and looked over his left shoulder to see Achim's face next to his ear.

"Don't go there!" he whispered in a quivering voice. "They have already killed many people and they will kill you too!"

"But why?" Amon managed to utter in a muffled tone.

"SHHHHH, they have found Athaliah, the rebel, hiding in his brother's house next to your shop."

"Athaliah?" whispered Amon. "You mean the one the Romans are looking for?"

"Yes, he's the man, who has killed so many Roman soldiers."

"Here in Nain?" asked Amon in a muffled sound.

Conspiracy With Malicious Intent

"Yes! His brother is Joash the Tanner, the one who lives next to you. The soldiers are going from house to house, and they have been in your house and mine. They have killed many people and I think they have killed Asa, too."

"ASA! But . . ?"

"SHHHHH! Our lives depend on your silence. SHHHHH!"

A cold chill ravished Amon's body and all his senses became numb.

"SHHHHH!"

Amon tried to free himself from Achim, but Achim was a younger and much stronger man. Both men stood silently in the shadows of the money-lenders building. Their hearts were pounding and the veins in their necks were pulsating. In the distance, women could be heard pleading for the lives of their children.

"SHHHHH, I know they're very close," Achim whispered. "I know they are near. I can feel it."

They dared not move so Amon and Achim held their breaths. Neither man was aware that a legionnaire was approaching from behind.

A metal spear suddenly penetrated Achim's back and exited the left side of his chest, narrowly missing Amon, who was standing in front of him. A deep gurgling sound escaped from Achim's throat, then a deep moan as he fell to the ground. Out of the corner of his eye, Amon remembered seeing light from the fire shining off of the soldier's helmet and shiny leather vest, so he ran blindly through the market. The glow of many fires bathed the streets as Amon ran for his life. As he ran, he wiped Achim's blood off his cheek and smeared it onto his clothing.

Amon's energy seemed endless as his legs ran as never before. Passing the synagogue, he momentarily recognized Rabbi Malachi and Rabbi Jehocim, returning from Simon's house. Blindly, he ran past Simon's house, and stopped one hundred strides from the eastern city gate, where he crawled under a two wheeled cart to catch his breath.

He tried to slow his breathing, but found that he could not. His hands gripped the soil he lay on and suddenly he began to shake. Remembering that soldiers guarded the city gate during the night, he cautiously and quietly got to his feet and tiptoed over to where he knew a basket weaver lived. There, he found a very large basket, lifted the lid, stepped into the basket and lowered the lid over himself. It took a long time for him to gain control of his breathing and heart rate because every time he closed his eyes he thought of Achim and remembered the gurgling sound in his dying throat.

The basket was very confining, and breathing was difficult but as time passed it became more comfortable. All of the events of the evening had overwhelmed Amon. He remembered seeing Rabbi Malachi, Rabbi Jehocim, Simon, Peninnah and Achim. He wondered about Asa. Was he alive or dead? His conscience gripped him, knowing that he had abandoned Asa in the midst of all that terror. Tears washed his hot cheeks and his clothing was wet from perspiration from his run for freedom.

Emptiness gripped him and he regretted running without trying to help his neighbors. He closed his eyes and tried to gather his thoughts.

Chapter IX

THE ASHES AND THE MEMORIES

Soldiers, searching through the debris and ruins, found a man they believed to be Joash and placing a sword to his throat, heard him whisper, "Athaliah has escaped. You'll never find him." Moments later, he breathed his last as the soldier opened his abdomen with one slash of his sword.

Centurion Damarius, though seriously injured, called for Varrus. "SELECT A RIDER TO GO TO SCYTHOPOLIS AND BRING ADDITIONAL MEN, AND VARRUS," his voice suddenly became barely audible, "I want you to be sure to crucify Joash . . . and his sons outside the city . . . so that . . . those that go to bury their dead will see what Rome is prepared to do to those who resist."

"But Sir, Joash is dead and so is his family."

"Well hang their dead bodies on a cross anyway," he wheezed. "I want everyone to see . . . Joash and his sons on crosses . . . and that's an order."

"We are now removing our dead and caring for the injured. I'll do it at first light."

"Care only for . . . the legionnaires but as for Joash and his sons, hang them on crosses, as soon as possible."

"Yes Sir."

"Have we found Athaliah?"

"There are many dead and until we see all of them, we will not know."

"Is the battle over?" asked Damarius as he turned his head to allow blood to flow from his mouth.

"All will be silent soon, Sir. The battle is ours."

After Varrus was sure that the area was secure and all weapons collected, he divided the legionnaires into three groups. One group was assigned to take Centurion Damarius and the wounded to the barracks, the second group were to wrap the dead legionnaires in canvas cloth and bury them three hundred strides outside the city, and the final group were to drag the bodies of Joash and his sons through the dark street and hang their bodies on crosses fifty strides outside the main gate.

So the bodies of Ataxia and thirty-two legionnaires were buried, and the bodies of Joash and his sons were hung on makeshift crosses; all by the eerie light of several torches and the streaks of dawn peering over the eastern hills.

It had been a long and arduous night for Varrus and the legionnaires, and by midmorning everyone was extremely tired and could not wait to return to the barracks for a rest.

****

Hours passed before Amon fell asleep but before doing so, he made up his mind that he would take Asa, if he was alive or dead, to look for the Messiah. His dreams were of flickering torches, screaming people and legionnaires.

Rays from the morning sun found Amon's face in the basket. He stirred and opened his eyes and stretched. He almost tipped over the basket he was hiding in. Lifting the lid, he glanced around to see if anyone was near. He was hungry and the pressure on his bladder made him realize that he had to relieve himself. He listened for sounds, and off in the distance he could hear sheep bleating and a bell ringing on the neck of an older ewe.

Peering through the slits of the basket, Amon could see several sheep lying next to the city wall, so he lifted the lid again and looked around. Seeing no one, he stepped from the basket and was about to replace the lid, when someone called to him, "Why are you hiding in my basket?"

"I . . . I . . . I was not hiding. I mean, I needed a safe place to sleep," Amon replied as he brushed dust from his clothing.

"I've seen you in the synagogue several times. Why are you on this side of Nain?" It was the basket maker.

"Last night, the soldiers came into our homes and killed some people because the soldiers found Athaliah, the rebel, in the house next to mine. I must return to see if I can find my . . ." he stopped when he was interrupted.

"Athaliah! He's the one who has been killing Roman soldiers. Some say he has killed several hundred Romans."

Conspiracy With Malicious Intent

"That's the one," whispered Amon as he nodded his head up and down. "We never knew he was there. Joash the Tanner is his brother and he lived next to my sandal shop."

"Is it safe for you to go back there?" asked the basket maker.

"I must find my brother. Someone said he was killed but that I do not know." He turned and started walking toward his house, not knowing what he would find.

Eventually, he neared Simon's house but saw no one, not even servants. He continued walking until he neared the synagogue and then slowed his pace, fearing what he may find. Nearing his street, he hesitated even more as he listened for unusual sounds. He stopped when he heard sobbing and loud wails. Peering around the corner of the butcher's building, he saw grieving women and some children, but no men and no soldiers. The women were sobbing loudly as they knelt to hug their dead: charred, mutilated, disfigured and strewn across the cobblestone street as worthless cargo.

Carefully walking beside the buildings, Amon approached the group of women as he stared in horror at the carnage. Dried bloodstains were on the roadway and on the walls of several buildings. The bodies had been carelessly placed in a row and it was easy to see that the majority of the dead were men.

Amon moved cautiously toward the legs of the dead as he looked for Asa but found Achim. Amon leaned over to look at him and became nauseated by what he saw. Near the end of the line, he began to breathe easier because he had not found Asa but as he was about to leave, he spotted Asa lying at the entry to their shop. His yellowing hands and purple fingernail beds were holding his wounded side, yet his face did not show fear. He appeared rather peaceful.

"ASA, ASA!" Amon sobbed as he dropped to his knees. "Why have they done this to you? You were such a soft and gentle brother. ASA, OHHHHH ASA."

He placed his face on Asa's bloodied chest and sobbed uncontrollably for a long time. Raising his head, he looked at Asa and in a whisper said "Asa, I will take you to see the prophet. He will bring you back to life, Asa. The prophet will raise you like he did to Hannah's child. OHHHHH, Asa my brother. OHHHHHH Asa." The sound of his words faded into whispers and then changed into loud audible moans.

Conspiracy With Malicious Intent

When Amon tried to lift Asa, he found Asa's hands and arms were rigid as were his legs, so he placed him back onto the ground. It was evident that he had died hours earlier, from the brutality of a sword.

Amon reached into his pouch and pulled out the cloth that had fallen from Hannah's son and placed it upon Asa's face. "Here, Asa. Maybe this will help you be alive again." Minutes passed but Asa did not move.

"Asa, Asa," he whispered as he readjusted the cloth over his forehead and face, but Asa did not move. "Asa, get up! I will take care of you. Oh, Asa my brother," he sobbed uncontrollably. "If I knew where the prophet was I would take you to him. He would bring you back to life." Amon's body began to convulse with painful sobs that eventually ebbed into silence.

Amon used the grave cloth to wipe his tears and then looked toward the sky. "I will kill any soldier that gets in my way. Even if they find me and put me to death, I will kill more than what it takes to find me," he vowed as he placed the grave cloth back onto Asa's face. "I do not want God to see your dead face." Tears ran down his cheeks and into his beard.

A gentle voice behind him interrupted him. "We will see to it that Asa as well as the others will all be buried today, but you must leave now." It was Rabbi Malachi.

"Why? What have I have done?" asked Amon with tears continued to flow down his cheeks. There was a subtle angry tone in his voice.

"You were living next to Joash the Tanner, so they are looking for you too." Rabbi Malachi nodded his head up and down as he reached down to help Amon to his feet. "Amon, there are thirty-three men, twelve women and nine children dead. Come, you must leave now. Come with me," insisted Rabbi Malachi as he tried to calm Amon's rage.

"That means that I must kill thirty soldiers and some for the children," said Amon. "That means one soldier for every man." His eyes radiated both hate and anger.

"I know you are filled with anger but the sixth commandment tells us not to murder."

"But why can uncircumcised pagans kill without," he stopped suddenly when he became aware of an unusual sound approaching him, and turning, he realized that several men had arrived with two-wheeled carts to load the dead.

"I will stay and help with the burial. They will not drive me away," Amon insisted even though Rabbi Malachi tried to convince him to leave.

Many women and people from the other side of town brought old cloth strips and tattered rags to wrap the dead. For hours, they prepared the bodies for burial, and eventually two men carried Asa to the death cart. When they placed him on the cart, Amon sobbed loudly as he clutched Asa's rigid deformed leg.

"Asa . . . how could I have been a better brother? It is now that I know you were here for me, oh Asa."

Amon became a man with a purpose. He worked harder than anyone and cared not about his safety or if the Roman soldiers would return. His face hardened and tears did not flow as he handled the dead with dignity. Occasionally, he stretched his back before eagerly resuming his work.

When the two death carts were filled, the citizens moved them toward the city gate but were refused passage to a burial site. As they patiently waited, a legionnaire rode to the barracks and informed Centurion Damarius that citizens requested permission to leave the city to bury their dead.

"Varrus," Damarius growled, "take ten men and follow them out of town to bury their dead, but be sure that all of them return. If twenty leave, twenty must return. And Varrus, I want you to check every dead body to see if one of them has an injured left forearm, teeth missing and a scar under its nose. If Athaliah is one of the dead, I want to know about it, and if you do NOT find him among the dead, let me know immediately," demanded Damarius.

"Yes Sir."

When Varrus and the legionnaires arrived at the city gate, they followed the grieving citizens and the two carts into a small ravine where the dead were buried. Off in the distance, three crosses could be seen and everyone knew that it was Joash and his young sons.

"They crucified them this morning," whispered one of the women as she walked beside Amon.

One of the soldiers on the wall called out, "THAT'S JOASH THE TANNER AND HIS SONS. YOU COULD BE NEXT!" Other guards laughed and jeered as the mourners continued their slow march toward the burial site.

"Where is the prophet when I need him? He should be here for all of these men. Especially, Asa," mumbled Amon as they plodded along.

It was a long and perilous experience for the families of the dead because Varrus supervised his men, who inspected every body before it was buried. They checked every man's inner left arm to see if an old injury existed and the two men that had severe injuries to their inner left arm had their mouths forced open with spears to see if teeth were missing. Not one body matched the description of Athaliah.

After the dead were buried, the mourners returned to the city gate, and Amon pulled his head covering over his face as sign of mourning. When inside the city walls, he stopped by the synagogue, unsure of where he would spend the rest of his days. Eventually he walked to the community well and watched a flock of sheep drinking water. Later that evening, he walked to where he had spent the night in the basket but returned to the synagogue, where he chose to sleep next to a sycamore tree.

For the first few hours, he could not lie still enough to fall asleep. A combination of his anger and grief held his spirit in indescribable emptiness and pain. Despite his attempt to sleep, he could not find a position of comfort and often doubled over into a fetal position as he moaned loudly. Fortunately, no soldiers passed near him or heard him. His agony engulfed him when he least expected it. The night was too long for anyone to bear.

Shortly before sunrise, Amon fell into a restless sleep.

Chapter X

AMON'S ESCAPE

A flock of sheep awakened Amon when they arrived to drink from the water troughs at the community well. He listened to the monotonous sound of the bell around the neck of the old ewe, and silently wished that it would suddenly fall over and die. "At least it would be quiet," he muttered to himself as he rubbed his eyes and rolled over. "Sheep should be roasted and eaten, not listened to."

He rose from his uncomfortable place of sleep and started to walk toward his sandal shop and home. He was aware that returning could be dangerous, but he cared less at that moment and walked confidently into the doorway of his partially destroyed building. He touched the blackened walls, marred by the flame, and closed his eyes as he tightened his jaw and ground his teeth.

"This is the worst dream I have ever had. I would like to wake up and see Asa but I don't think . . ." He could not finish his sentence. He shook his head and ground his teeth as tears ran down his leathery skin to drip onto his vest cloth. The pendulum of emotion moved radically from hate and violence to nostalgic memories of Asa. Again he vowed that if given opportunity, he would kill every Roman soldier that he came in contact with.

"If I can kill one, then we will be even for what you, you pagan Gentiles did to Asa." He clinched his fists as he spoke. "If I can kill more, then I will sleep better," he assured himself. "And if I kill a thousand, then I will sleep so good that I will not even snore."

He moved damaged stools and the table to one side and then sobbed loudly as he dropped to his knees. Everything was destroyed. The only things that he found were a small wooden mallet, a leather awl, his father's

Conspiracy With Malicious Intent

old walking staff and a small sharp knife, which he had used to cut and trim leather. Picking them up, he held them in his hands and vowed again to use them or anything else available to return the painful favor to the cold-hearted pagans in leather vests.

"This is the place of my birth and my father, Beno, was born here and who knows who else was born here. Now all that is here is death and memories. My mother, Leah, died here and now . . . now Asa died here. God do not watch while I break the sixth commandment. You said in the commandment not to kill but this will not be killing, it will be . . . paying back for what they did to Asa, my brother."

Glancing furtively around to see if anyone was looking, he stepped into the back room where he and Asa slept, and removed a stone from the wall. Inside the small hole in the wall was a tiny pouch with coins that he had managed to save over the years. He emptied the contents into his hand, replaced the stone in its place and then placed the coins into his waist pouch.

He tried to sweep the floor after tossing out the broken stools, the table and cots, but when he found blood on the dirt floor, he raised his hands toward heaven and said, "God, could you just this once not watch me when I break the sixth commandment. Killing Gentiles should not even count against any of us, because they have been killing us for years. Please don't watch me when I kill Roman soldiers because they are pagans." He wiped his eyes and continued, "If you don't watch, then I will not be guilty of breaking that commandment."

Tears ran down his cheeks again, and he found it difficult to clean out the ashes of his previous life. It was late in the afternoon when he realized that his cleaning was a useless effort, so he placed the old broom next to the door and started for the synagogue. He did not look back to the street of his birth.

On the way hunger pangs drove him to the marketplace. He walked among the merchants and when he had selected several things to eat, he leaned over to the merchant and said, "I have lost all and have nothing to eat. I, Amon," he said as he tapped his chest with his fist. "I have lost everything including my brother, and now I am a common beggar. What must I do for this food? Tell me."

"Amon, I know what has happened to you and your shop, yet I must have something for this food. I have six children to feed. Do you yet have anything that you can give to me for this food?"

Conspiracy With Malicious Intent

"Nothing. I tell you, nothing." His voice ended on a higher note than before.

"You have a walking staff in your hand. I will take it for the food," replied the shopkeeper. "I need something. What do you think . . . the food for your walking staff?"

"But this was my father's walking staff." responded Amon.

"Is he yet alive?"

"No."

"Does he need it?"

"No."

"Well, if he doesn't need it anymore and you need the food then," he paused to look into Amon's face, "then we can trade for the food," continued the shopkeeper, now feeling confident that he had gained the upper hand. When Amon hesitated, the shopkeeper continued, "Your crooked stick for my food. I'm sure that I'm losing on this trade but," he raised his hands, "but I am willing to do this for you because I know you and I knew your father Beno."

Amon reluctantly exchanged his father's walking stick for an armful of food, which he carried to the steps of the synagogue. After sitting down, he ate until all the food was gone. With nowhere else to go, he started for the Basket Weaver's Shop, where he had spent the previous night but found many infantrymen standing near the city gate, so he decided to return to the market.

As he approached the market, he noticed more infantrymen so he decided to join several grey-bearded men sitting under a tree. Their conversation was of no interest to Amon, so he immediately left once the soldiers were out of sight. He wandered the streets of Nain until it was dark and never considered that he would be arrested if they knew he had been living next to Joash the Tanner.

The night was becoming cold and lonely, and sleeping on the ground next to one of the community wells was dangerous but he hoped that a leather-vested soldier would try to awaken him. He assured himself that he would be ready to plunge either the awl or the knife into his stomach.

Amon positioned himself on his side and tried to sleep with the awl in his right hand and the knife in his left hand. At first, his anger kept him from sleep, but eventually his eyes became heavy and he drifted off to sleep.

He was awakened before sunrise, by a flock of sheep drinking at the troughs next to the well. When Amon sat up, he found himself surrounded

Conspiracy With Malicious Intent

by dozens of lambs and ewes pressing toward the water troughs. In the melee and confusion, he realized that his awl and leather mallet were missing. Looking for the objects was impossible because of the sheer number of sheep pushing and shoving their way to the troughs. The only thing he had was the sharp leather knife, which he carefully guarded for future confrontation.

Standing to his feet, he moved to the side of a building to sit and watch as the sheep drank from the leaking troughs. After they had gone, he searched for the awl and the mallet, but did not find them. "Maybe the shepherds found them," he reasoned to himself.

Eventually, he moved to the steps of the synagogue where he spent some time recalling what he had seen and what had happened over the last few days. When someone touched him on the shoulder, he jumped to his feet, fearful that it was a soldier, but it was Rabbi Malachi.

"Why do you yet stay here? If the pagans find you, they will kill you. I have heard them asking for you because you lived in the same building as Joash the Tanner, and remember, yes remember that they crucified him even though he and his sons were already dead. They kill even the dead. Did you hear me? So what will they do to you?"

"I have nowhere to go. I have nothing, not even a brother," Amon said as he lowered his head.

"SHHHH, not so loud," whispered Rabbi Malachi as he looked in several directions and then put his arm around Amon's shoulder. "Come with me and I will hide you, but then you must leave Nain."

"Where will I go, and how will I get past the pagans at the gate?" asked Amon.

Rabbi Malachi took Amon into a side door of the synagogue where he remained until early morning. During the night, Amon dreamt of Asa and what his damaged body looked like in the doorway of the shop. His was a restless sleep.

Rabbi Malachi awakened Amon. "Come with me. Now is the time," he said. Moments later he ushered Amon into a room where some food had been prepared. "I have arranged a safe departure from Nain. Eat now and I will be back shortly."

Amon was eating when Rabbi Malachi returned. "You will be executed if they find you, so you need to leave Nain this morning."

"But where do I go? I have never been very far outside of Nain. My father, Beno, went to Jerusalem many times but I . . . I have never been there." He sounded fearful and confused.

"Well, Jerusalem is a place you could live and then there is Caesarea or Joppa, or maybe you should go to the Sea of Galilee, but you must NOT stay here." His voice had the sound of urgency and fear.

"I don't know anyone so . . ."

"You don't need to know anyone, but at least you'll be alive. Come."

"I don't know what a Sea of Gagalea is and . . ."

"I have arranged for you to leave the city. It will take you several days to travel northeast to the Sea of Galilee. Remember that our father Abraham, Isaac and Jacob traveled many miles and lived in tents for our benefit. Moses led our forefathers out of Egypt, and they traveled many, many years to find this place, so a two or three day trip for you to another Hebrew town will be easy. I just do not want you to be killed by these pagans."

After handing Amon a cloth package with food in it, Rabbi Malachi motioned for Amon to follow. "Now, is the time and be silent. Ask no questions. Do you understand? Just follow me."

Amon agreed and began to follow Rabbi Malachi down the hallway. He resigned himself to go to a new land and different city but when Rabbi Malachi closed the door of the synagogue, Amon became very uncomfortable. He followed Rabbi Malachi along several streets in the early morning twilight. They walked in silence until they came upon the caravan of camels, several hundred strides from the east gate. The caravan appeared ready to leave town because the camels were already loaded and restlessly grunting and moving their heads from side to side.

"This is your way out of Nain," whispered the Rabbi. "Say nothing, but do what they tell you. They are Egyptians passing through this country on their way back to Egypt. If you go with them, they will take you safely out of Nain."

"Egyptians? But why?"

"They come through here only once a year with spices and food. Come with me, and do not speak, but do as they tell you."

Rabbi Malachi walked over to a swarthy skinned man, who was removing the hobble from the front legs of a camel. Amon could not understand what Rabbi Malachi was saying, but he did see Rabbi Malachi hand a small pouch to the Egyptian. The man looked at Amon and stepped closer for a better view.

Rabbi Malachi turned and walked away before Amon could thank or speak with him. When Rabbi Malachi was out of sight, Amon looked at the Egyptian, who motioned for him to follow. After Amon stepped closer, the Egyptian handed him a rope that was tied to the halter of a camel. Within

Conspiracy With Malicious Intent

moments, the caravan started for the city gate, and Amon was now leading a camel, an animal he knew nothing about.

"Why do you smell so bad, Mr. Camel? Not only do you stink, but you look like no one cares about you. How could God make something that looks like you?" asked Amon as they neared the gate. The camel continued to chew its cud and plod along with a strong and rhythmic gait.

When the caravan arrived at the eastern city gate, five guards stepped out from behind a wall and stopped the caravan. As the members of the caravan waited, the guards walked past every animal and every person. They stared at each man for several moments and then moved on. When the guard stared at Amon, Amon moved his hand slowly toward his pouch where he held his small knife. Amon's heart pounded in his chest and the palms of his hands became cold and damp.

"You don't look Egyptian. Where are you from?" asked the guard as he grabbed Amon's chin. Turning Amon's head to the side, he sneered, "You do not look like an Egyptian. You look like someone I have seen before."

Amon's hand held the knife tightly, as he looked over at the Caravan Master, who stood motionless except for his right pointer finger which was pointing at the ground. Amon could feel his stomach become hot but remembered what Rabbi Malachi said to him, 'Say nothing but do only what they say,' so Amon only smiled, shrugged his shoulders and lowered his gaze.

The guard began to pull on the ropes that held the load in place on the camel's back. Several camels moaned and one burped loudly, but the Caravan Master did not move.

A man next to Amon moved slowly to the other side of a camel as the guard spoke. "We have orders from the Centurion that no one will leave without his permission, so you will have to wait until he arrives."

The delay caused the animals and the Egyptians to become restless. The wait seemed to be endless but finally Centurion Damarius arrived and rode around the entire caravan. He appeared to be ill and rather unstable but he continued to allow his horse to walk among the camels. He stopped next to the Caravan Master and spoke to him through the interpreter. "You have made a wise decision," he said.

The interpreter responded to the Caravan Master and then turned to Centurion Damarius. "He say, 'We have done what you have asked and now we trust you to let us go.'"

After waving at the guards at the gate, Damarius shouted, "Let them leave." Immediately, the guards opened the gates and the Caravan Master raised his hand, shouted something Amon did not understand, and the caravan moved slowly out of Nain, just as the morning sun was rising over the eastern hills.

One by one, the men and the camels exited the city gates toward the barren hills and valleys. This was a new adventure for Amon for he had never been outside of Nain, except to bury his brother.

He was not happy with his traveling partner, the stinky cud chewing camel on the end of his rope, but he reminded himself that he had little choice in the matter. His heart was fearful, angry and confused. He was fearful of his future, angry about his loss and confused about the prophet. Convinced that he would never return to Nain, he did not even look back for one last look.

The caravan did not stop to rest until the morning sun was high overhead. Amon's feet began to hurt but the caravan continued moving. The camel that Amon led continued to sway and grunt, and eventually it began to pass Amon so he forced himself to walk faster.

Eventually the caravan stopped near a grove of dead fig trees, just beyond a junction in the road. Moments later, the Caravan Master walked back to where Amon was standing, reached down and took the halter rope from his hand.

Amon stood motionless, unsure of what he had done wrong.

The Egyptian placed his pointer finger on Amon's chest and then pointed to a road that travelled northward. In the distance, Amon could see nothing but hills with narrow valleys. Then the Egyptian placed his finger onto his chest and then pointed to the other road that traveled southward.

Amon smiled and nodded. "Gentile," he whispered out of the side of his mouth as he stepped back.

"Hebrew," responded the Egyptian as he handed Amon a small cloth bag with objects in it. At that moment another man, who was standing nearby, was handed the rope that Amon previously held. Amon looked intently at the man, and noticed that his left arm hug motionless at his side and when the man grinned, Amon noticed a scar under his nose and several teeth missing. As the man turned to walk away, Amon noticed blood splatters on the man's clothing, sandals and feet. When Amon looked at the man's back as he walked away, he noticed several drops of blood falling to the ground.

The Caravan Master shouted several words that Amon did not understand and the caravan began to move southward, leaving Amon on the side of a road he had never seen before.

Amon watched the caravan for a long time and when it disappeared around a distant hill, he sat down and began to rub his aching feet. Several moments later, he remembered the bag that the Caravan Master had given him. In it, he found figs, dates, goat cheese and flat bread. After eating several items, he placed the remaining items in the bag and was about to start walking when he noticed cavalrymen approaching in the distance. He remained seated as they rode past him toward Nain.

Once they were out of sight, Amon began to follow the narrow path that moved northward and when he rounded a corner, he could see two travelers approaching in the distance. When they met, Amon asked, "Where does this road go to?"

"Where are you going?" asked one of them.

"To a sea . . . a sea of gagalee."

"This road will take you to Nazareth and there you can turn east toward the Sea of Galilee or south toward the Jordan River," the eldest man said.

Amon did not ask what a Nazareth or a Jordon River was because he did not want to appear ignorant, so he nodded, smiled and started to walk away when one of the travelers called to him, "Come eat with us. It is yet early," said one of the men, so Amon joined them. They shared figs and goat cheese with him before continuing their journey.

As they walked away, Amon stood and watched until the travelers disappeared around a distant hill.

Chapter XI

THE LONG AND DUSTY ROAD

One hundred cavalrymen from Scythopolis arrived in Nain and were immediately dispatched to patrol the streets and resume their intense search for Athaliah, but there was no sign of him. Rewards were posted but no rumors surfaced as to his whereabouts. Varrus was sure that Athaliah had escaped but there seemed to be little he could do about it, so he divided the cavalrymen into three groups and told them to ride through the countryside and check every ravine and cave, and to speak with every shepherd within a day's ride.

The Egyptian caravan was now gone and all contact with the Caravan Master had ended. Now it was time to re-establish order in Nain.

****

In the meantime, Amon continued north toward Nazareth. Occasionally, he stopped to rub his aching feet. "I have never walked so far in my life. If I knew my feet would hurt so much I would have made different sandals."

He had never been to Nazareth before, but had heard many disparaging stories about the people, who lived there. He was unsure of what he would find when he arrived. He did not know that Nazareth was only seven miles, as the crow flies, but a walking man in this region is not always able to take the shortest route to where his is going, especially if he is not familiar with the area. Following the road meant that the path was easier, but additional distance was added to his journey.

Along the way, Amon stopped several travelers to ask if they had seen the prophet. Eagerly, they told him of what the prophet had done in Nazareth, and Amon told them about Hannah's son being raised to life. They visited

Conspiracy With Malicious Intent

for some time, and Amon was now sure that he was on the right road. This newly acquired information encouraged Amon, so he tried to walk faster but his aching feet soon made him slow down and eventually stop.

"Why would a prophet come to such a place like this? There are no wells and it's hot," he mumbled to himself.

It was a dusty and a lonely walk, and often Amon cried in memory of his brother, Asa. With his food nearly gone, he thought about asking for something to eat when he passed a group of travelers, but his pride prevented him from doing so. As he neared the city of Nazareth, he decided that he would keep the few coins that he had saved, and if he had to ask for food, that would be acceptable. Somehow he justified that asking for food was better than begging.

After laboring up several long hills, he was pleased to see a gentle valley with trees and many houses on a hillside. It was a valley several thousand strides wide from east to west but significantly shorter from north to south. A large hill was located to the northwest, and to the east he could see many ravines.

Amon approached Nazareth with some reservation. It appeared to be the same size as Nain. The first thing he discovered was that the citizens were similar to those in Nain. For some reason, he pictured them as being different. He stood on the outer edge of the town for a long time and watched the sheep, donkeys and people. He could hear children playing in the distance, and began to feel less apprehensive.

"Maybe Nazareth is not such a bad place," he mused to himself as he neared the small and narrow city gate. He did not notice two soldiers silently approaching him from the rear because he had been too busy looking at all of the people and buildings. One of guards carried a gladius and the other a spear.

"Where are you going?" asked one of them.

Amon turned his head to look at them. "This is . . . this is my first time to this city. What is its name?"

"I ask the questions," said the guard with the gladius. He placed the tip of the blade onto Amon's chest as he widened his stance and then narrowed his eyes. The bright sun flashed its reflection off the legionnaire's helmet and Amon turned his head to momentarily close his eyes.

"If they kill you for asking the name of this place, then I will not need to know," Amon said as he opened one eye as his hand touched his small dagger under his vest.

"Where are you from?"

"From a place far away," Amon replied. "After coming this far over the hot and dry road with sore feet and an empty stomach, I wish I was back in Nain." Momentarily, Amon regretted telling what place he had come from.

A mounted legionnaire arrived at that moment. "Who is this beggar and where is he from?"

The legionnaire returned his gladius into the scabbard as he spoke, "He won't answer."

The cavalryman moved his horse within a hand's width of Amon's chest. "Where are you from?" he demanded in a strong voice.

"I told him," Amon said as he lifted his left hand above his head while the other hand gripped his dagger, "I told him that I wish I was in Nain. That's where I am from; Nain." Again Amon regretted saying Nain because he remembered that the Romans may be looking for him.

"What is your business here?" asked the cavalryman.

"It may sound foolish to you, but I am looking for the prophet that heals people and, and raises dead people back to life. Many people have told me that he used to live here. I'm looking for him. Have you seen him?"

"A prophet?"

"Yes, I have come to find him," said Amon as he turned to face the foot soldier. "Look at me. I am too old to make trouble," he said. "I'm but a simple man just looking for a prophet."

The mounted soldier said something in a language that Amon did not understand, and then motioned to Amon, allowing him to walk through the gate.

When Amon realized that he was free to enter, he looked up at partially collapsed walls before moving ahead. "It seems like such a nice place, so why did so many people say that nothing good ever comes out of Nazareth?" he asked himself.

Amon's stomach growled loudly and he poked at it with his pointer finger. "Am I to blame that you have no food? Never have you ever thanked me for all the food that I have given you over these years, but now, now you only know how to growl and complain," he muttered disgustingly.

Tired from his long walk, he chose a shady place just inside the city gate, where he could rest. Sometime later, he walked several hundred strides and was surprised to find a group of beggars sitting on the steps of a synagogue. Cautiously approaching them, he stopped some distance from them and sat down.

Seventeen gaunt and disfigured faces appeared to be annoyed and skeptical of him because he did not appear to be like them. He appeared well fed, his clothes were not tattered or shabby and his face and hands were not disfigured from leprosy.

As they stared at him, one of them asked in a raspy voice, "What do you want with us?"

"I've just come from Nain and all I have has been destroyed by Roman soldiers. They have killed my only brother, so I have come here to find the prophet; the one called the Messiah." He wondered why he had added the word Messiah.

Hollow eyes continued to stare at him and he became uncomfortable with their silence. When the tallest of them approached him, he planned an escape route. The man's lips were deeply scarred, his hands were deformed and one ear was missing. His unsteady gait and swollen feet with missing toes emitted a muffled scraping sound as he walked. The filthy faced man adjusted his shabby rags. "Wish I had something soldiers could take from me or a family they could kill. Me, I've been a beggar since a child and now look," he said as he lifted his rags to expose his white arms and chest. "Leprosy," he whispered with disfigured lips, and with that, he shuffled off in disgust.

Amon was now reduced to the depths of associating with lepers and beggars. With no home and no family, he felt empty. Tears trickled down his cheeks and into his dusty beard. Alone, hungry, forsaken and without hope, he lay over and tried to sleep. His night was restless, to say the least. Amid the snoring of sixteen disheveled lepers, there was the occasional sound of horse hooves passing by, and Amon knew that Roman cavalrymen were nearby. Every time they drew near, Amon renewed his vow to kill a soldier or two. The much coveted killing did not occur because the soldiers only cast despising glances at him and the sleeping beggars.

In the early morning light, a flock of sheep drew near just as they did in Nain. Seeing a young shepherd boy, Amon approached him but two large fierce looking men quickly approached with staffs in their hands.

"I only want to know if you have seen the prophet, who heals people," Amon said as he carefully planned an escape.

"Yes, we have," was the response of the eldest shepherd. "He was here several days ago and I think he's gone to Gennesaret, by the Sea of Tiberius."

"Where is that?" Amon asked.

"The Sea of Tiberius is the same as the Sea of Galilee," replied the younger shepherd. "It's not too far from here."

"Does the prophet live there?"

"I don't know where he lives."

"I saw him raise a dead boy in the town of Nain several days ago," said Amon, with renewed enthusiasm. "The dead boy was the only son of a widow named Hannah. I had a piece of the grave cloth that fell from him but when my brother was murdered by Roman soldiers, I left it on his face so I could look for the prophet."

"A dead boy was raised back to life?" The shepherd stepped closer, unsure of what he had just heard.

"Yes, the boy was dead but now lives. The prophet stopped the people as they were going to bury him, and that is when the prophet made the dead boy alive," responded Amon. "I saw it and so did others."

"We saw him heal sick people, but never making dead people alive. You saw this in Nain?"

"Yes."

At that moment, Amon's stomach growled loudly. He rubbed his abdomen, hoping to silence it with some external massaging. "I haven't eaten since yesterday," he apologized.

"While the sheep drink water, we eat and when they are finished, we go back into the hills. Come join us. My name is Arrah."

"My name is Amon," he said as he followed Arrah to the shade of several trees. Soon the beggars followed, hoping for some charity from the shepherds and two young boys.

Bleating loudly, the sheep continued to jostle for an opportunity to drink from the broken troughs that were being filled by one of the young boys.

In the shade of the trees, the shepherds ate cheese, figs and drank goat's milk. Amon tried to be gracious, but hunger made him covet whatever everyone else was eating. The four beggars that joined them were given some cheese but no milk.

"What is the name of this here town?" asked Amon.

"This is Nazareth. It's a small place but we still have too many Roman soldiers. They are . . ."

"Someday I plan to kill some of them," said Amon, hoping to gain some respect with that comment.

"Why?"

As he told his story, another flock of sheep arrived and both flocks began to mingle with the sheep that were already drinking, causing Amon wonder how they would ever separate all of them. Sometime later, a third flock arrived, and by now the plaza was filled with sheep. The shepherds exchanged stories and laughed loudly as they visited and drank milk.

Arrah walked into the midst of the massive number of sheep and started to sing and make calling noises. Soon several sheep and their lambs began to follow him as he walked out of the centre of the large number of sheep. He continued singing and calling as he walked, and soon forty-three sheep followed him through the city gate, out to the warm and sunny plain.

Amon followed them for several hundred strides before stopping. He was amazed that the sheep knew whom to follow. He could hear the sound of a bell that was tied around the neck of a ewe. Eventually the men, the boys and the sheep faded into the horizon.

"How can this have happened to me? Only a few days ago, I had a home, a brother and a business, sat in one of the most powerful Pharisee's home, saw the prophet and now . . . now I am in a strange place, sleeping with beggars and begging for food?"

Amon hung his head, closed his eyes and sighed loudly. "This pain is here in this chest of mine and is more than I can stand. If I breathe, I hurt. If I walk, I hurt. If I sleep, then and only then, I have rest from this hurt. When will I ever feel better as I did when Asa was alive? What do I do now?" He cupped his hand over his face and sat on the ground for a long time.

Eventually, he returned to the steps of the synagogue as it was the only familiar place that he knew. Moments later, he saw several priests approaching the steps of the synagogue and when one of them accidentally bumped into Amon's leg, he smiled but they withdrew in disgust.

"Why do you yet lie here and do nothing?" asked the youngest priest. "Lepers and beggars are NOT welcome on the steps of this place."

Amon smiled and raised one hand. "Rabbi, I am not a common beggar and I do not have leprosy. I have come from Nain and I need to know how to find the prophet, the one who heals people. I even saw him raise a dead boy in the town of Nain. It was Hannah's boy. Do you know where this prophet is?"

"This man you speak of may heal people but he is not a prophet," said the eldest priest. "If you want to follow after that troublemaker, take the east road to Capernaum." With that said, they entered the synagogue and slammed the door.

Disappointed with the priest's response, Amon asked several people where the market was and when he found the place, he purchased food. As he walked and ate, he came across a shopkeeper that sold sandals so he stopped to talk with him. During their conversation, Amon learned that

Conspiracy With Malicious Intent

the shopkeeper was in failing health and needed someone to help him, so Amon asked if he could work for lodging and food.

It was a unique relationship. The shopkeeper was pleased that someone with experience was willing to work, and for Amon it was an opportunity to go back to an occupation he knew.

Chapter XII

A SOFT BUT FIRM HAND

Several days following the bloody confrontation on the streets of Nain where Joash the Tanner and Amon's Sandal Shop were located, Varrus assigned citizens and legionnaires to remove all of the debris. Burned out buildings were torn down in an attempt to remove all memory of the past. When not enough men were found to complete the task, Varrus and his men rode through the streets conscripting others to help.

Varrus considered removing the decaying bodies of Joash and his sons from the crosses, but decided to leave them as a reminder to Nain citizens of what would happen to those who chose to rebel against Rome.

Centurion Damarius remained in command of the city even though it took some time for him to regain his strength and heal from his wounds. Before returning to Scythopolis, he provided Varrus with additional legionnaires and a promise to return in the near future.

His final words to Varrus were, "This is your town. It's your chance to prove yourself worthy of command. Ave." After they exchanged salutes, Centurion Damarius and fifty cavalrymen returned to Scythopolis.

Varrus immediately assigned legionnaires to supervise the workers, who were rebuilding the damaged walls, the shops and houses. He insisted that the guards at the city gates were to notify everyone entering or leaving Nain and they had to register with the Captain of the Gate. He required every person to provide their names and what they planned to do in Nain. The registry was submitted to his office on a daily basis.

Varrus requested younger horses and when new ones arrived, he immediately dispatched the old ones to Scythopolis. He scheduled cavalry maneuvers as an everyday activity and introduced hand to hand battle exercises to hone the skills of the men under his command. All legionnaires were required to appear for inspection every morning, and that meant that they be in full uniform with polished weapons and leather vestments. He insisted on decorum and respect, continuously insisting that every opportunity to reduce confrontation between citizen and soldier was a priority. At first citizens were suspicious of this young leader, but soon witnessed positive changes to the Roman presence in Nain.

One day Varrus stopped at the synagogue, tied his horse to a tree and entered the outer court. Immediately several servants and a priest appeared and insisted that he leave, but he told them he would leave under one condition, that rabbis and priests agree to meet with him once a week at the public well next to the moneychanger's building. At first, they were reluctant but cautiously agreed.

At their first meeting, Varrus met with resistance but soon tensions were eased when he asked the religious leaders if they were pleased that the broken down walls and the destroyed buildings had been repaired. He explained that the guards at the city gate kept a registry so that citizens would not have thieves entering to steal their goods. He told them that he would continue to provide legionnaires to help citizens to clean the town of filth and debris. They soon realized that Varrus was not an arrogant person desiring power but an organizer, demonstrating quality leadership skills.

They were shocked to find that Varrus asked stimulating questions about the Laws of Moses, Festivals and Feasts. He asked about King David and King Solomon, and requested an explanation of life after death, prompting Pharisees to immediately give their opinion. He asked about Abraham, Isaac and Jacob to see if what they told him matched what his mother and mentor had taught him when he was a lad.

On one occasion, Rabbi Malachi and Rabbi Jehocim were listening to Varrus' questions, when they spoke Aramaic to each other. One said, "It is sad that Gentiles will never understand these things, so why do we need to explain?"

Varrus immediately responded in Aramaic, "Wise men guard their words lest they be understood or misunderstood." From that day on, both rabbis and priests were more cautious about what they said when they were near Varrus. Eventually, they began to trust him.

Shortly after Varrus' promotion, he sent a parchment to Macedonia requesting that his personal servant, Pollus, be sent to Nain so he could attend to Varrus' personal needs. One month later, seven cavalrymen escorted an elderly man into Nain. He had little in the way of personal possessions but what he brought was more than fabric, gold or food. When Varrus and he met, Pollus knelt before Varrus and kissed his hand as a sign of renewed devotion.

Often Varrus sought Pollus' wisdom and opinion on events in Nain. He trusted Pollus' perception and used it to fortify his decisions. Pollus was pleased to attend to Varrus again and remained strong physically and emotionally.

The time that Varrus remained in Nain provided him with many opportunities to hone his leadership skills and political interaction, especially with indifferent citizens. He earned great respect from infantrymen, cavalrymen and the rabbinical leaders.

****

When six weeks had passed, Amon decided that he needed to resume his search for the Messiah. He stood at the entrance to Naaham's leather shop to say, "Shalom my friend but I must find the Messiah. You have saved my life and been a good brother to me." They hugged before Amon departed. When he arrived at the city gate, he left Nazareth by the east road, just as Naaham had directed to him to do.

Shortly after leaving Nazareth, he met several travelers and asked, "Is this the way to a place called Caper . . . Capermum?"

"Yes, Capernaum is some distance along this road. You'll be there before nightfall, if you walk without much stopping," said one of them. They remained at distance and appeared fearful of Amon.

"Don't be afraid of me," Amon said. "I'm from Nain, and have nothing but hunger and thirst as my companions. All I am looking for is a prophet that heals people. Do you know where he is or where I might find him?"

They said nothing but looked at each other and shrugged their shoulders.

"I'm a Hebrew and not a Roman. Why do you fear me?" asked Amon as he held both of his hand open, to show that he had no weapons and meant no harm.

"In these regions, robbers will approach in a friendly manner but will slit your throat for a bite of food," said the eldest, who stood behind the young man, who held a large staff in both hands.

"Are they Hebrews that will kill you?" Amon asked with childlike innocence.

"Yes Hebrews, Samaritans and Romans. Anyone will kill and rob you for food and valuables," was the youngest one's response.

"How can a Hebrew kill another Hebrew? Is that not breaking the sixth commandment?"

"You are new to this region and have much to learn," he heard one of them say. "Many who travel this road are robbed." After a moment of silence, one of men spoke, "You asked about a prophet?"

"Yes, do you know where I might find him?"

"His name is Jesus and he comes from Nazareth."

"Nazareth! I was just in that town," responded Amon.

"He's now at the Sea of Galilee at the house of a fisherman named Zebedee."

"What is a Sea of Galilee and who is a Zebanee?"

"Have you never seen the sea before?"

"No," Amon replied apologetically. "Is it something that I must fear?"

"No, no," one of them laughed. "It's a place with much water where people sail boats and catch fish."

"Fish? Boats? What are they?" Amon asked.

"Oh yes, you're from Nain. The only water you have in that region comes from wells."

"Yes and what's wrong with that? Is not all water in a well?" asked Amon as his stomach growled loudly. He gripped it in an attempt to silence it, and then smiled.

They offered Amon dates and a piece of flatbread and told him of things he did not understand. They spoke of boats fish, nets and the prophet. He munched loudly and did not take his eyes off of them. As they spoke, he tried to understand but was unable to picture any of the things that they spoke about. All of this was so different than his former life in Nain. What interested Amon most were the stories that they told about Jesus. They told of his miracles, his interaction with people and his teachings.

"Is he the Messiah?" asked Amon in a childlike way. "My mother told my brother Asa and I that a Messiah would come and free us from many things, including," he paused to look around and then leaned forward to whisper, "even the Romans."

"Some believe that he is the Messiah but some do not. The Pharisees, Sadducees and priests think he is a blasphemer and troublemaker."

Amon told them of Hannah's son and how everyone could not believe that a dead boy could be raised from the dead. He spoke of his losses and the death of his brother, Asa. They listened intently to his stories.

"We must be on our way," one of them said as he stood to his feet. The others responded, "Shalom," before they walked away.

"Shalom," Amon replied, disappointed that they were leaving.

By late afternoon, Amon was near the town of Dalmanutha, a small community on the western shore of the Sea of Galilee. Amon was now hungry, thirsty, weary and physically and mentally drained. He was sure that he could not go any farther. His steps were unsteady and his arms hung loosely at his side.

Dalmanutha was within eyesight when Amon stumbled and fell to the ground, too weary to go on. The heat and lack of water to drink affected his ability to continue. Breathing heavily, he tried to rise but could not generate the strength, so he crawled to the side of the road, hoping to regain his strength some time later.

A hand touched his shoulder as he lay face down on edge of the dusty path. All Amon could do was moan but even that took effort. He opened his eyes as he felt water on his hot face and in his mouth, so he tried to roll over and grasp the liquid. Through his blurred vision, he saw, what appeared to be several people looking down at him.

"You will die here," said a gentle voice. "Drink slowly no, no . . . not so fast. Slowly, slowly, ah that's better."

Amon had no idea where he was nor how long he had been there. Somewhere in his confusion, the strangers helped him to sit in the shade of a tree next to a crumbling rock wall. They provided him with water, food and stayed with him until he gained his senses.

At early dawn, loud shouting awakened him. When he opened his eyes, he was somewhat confused and unsure of where he was, but when he came to his senses he saw what appeared to be soldiers wrestling and fighting with several men, who were next to several wooden carts. Roman weapons struck down two men as the remaining three defended themselves against the aggressive legionnaires.

Shaking his head for a moment to clear his mind, Amon watched the confrontation and tried to make sense of it when the odor of food entered his hungry nostrils. There, several strides to his left were platters of uneaten food and a pot of stew, still on the fire. Amon realized that the soldiers must have been in the middle of their morning meal when the men with the carts interrupted them. This confrontation was more than pushing and shoving. Another man screamed and fell to the ground, and Amon heard swords clashing. The shouting continued, and again someone cried out in pain.

Amon stood to his feet, reached for a plate of food and started to gulp as much food as he could. The battle between the guards and one man continued for some time because the man had backed himself into a corner and demonstrated that he was able to defend himself.

Amon kept eating and when he could eat no more, he grabbed some of the food next to the fire and ran toward a side road and disappeared behind a row of trees.

Sometime later, Amon became violently ill. His stomach refused to keep its stolen treasure. Now nauseated, he lay next to an empty sheep pen to rest. Several hours passed before Amon was able to stand and as he did, the morning sun appeared over the eastern ridge of hills.

Chapter XIII

THE SEA, THE BOATS AND THE FISH

Amon rested next to a large rock and looked off into the distance. What he saw confused him. There appeared to be an extremely large, shiny object in the distance that was as bright as the sun, yet it was below the sun and seemed to be surrounded by hills. It seemed as large as the entire valley. He stood unsteadily on his feet and gazed at it for a long time. His stare was so intense that he did not notice the vineyards and groves of trees nearby. Unsure of what this very bright object was, he started to walk toward it.

After several hundred strides, he realized that the area of this shiny piece of land was even larger than he had initially estimated. It seemed to be moving back and forth and for a moment, it occurred to him that the soft breeze made the shiny object move from side to side. He was surprised to see several birds soaring effortlessly above it but what baffled him most was how these birds would suddenly rise and disappear into the white and grey wool looking objects above the shining object. He had never seen anything like it before and had no idea what it was so he motioned to a man, who was walking by with a donkey that was laden with wood.

"What is that piece of . . . that . . . that thing that shines like the sun?" Amon asked with a naïve tone. "And how can birds disappear into those, those wooly looking things in the sky?"

The man withdrew momentarily and looked at Amon as if he were meshugga or crazy. "Do you mock me with questions that are that foolish?" the man responded in anger.

"I have never seen such bright land. What is it?" asked Amon without looking at the man. "And that, that wool in the air, how do they keep it up there and why?"

"That's a sea, the Sea of Galilee. Have you never seen this place before?"

In childlike wonder, Amon tipped his head from side to side. "What is a sea? Why does it shine and what are those boxes out there doing?" He raised his arm and pointed toward ships in the distance.

The man stepped closer before responding, "You're new here, aren't you? Where are you from?""

"Yes," whispered Amon, unaware of his response. "I . . . I'm from Nain and we do not have anything shiny like that," he said as he shook his head from side to side. "What is it made of?"

"It's water. Do you not know what water is?" the man responded as he continued to stare at Amon.

"Water, yes, but . . . but how did you find so much water that you could set it on the ground and it just stays there? The water where I come from is in wells and when we pour it on the ground it disappears. So why does this water yet stay there and where is the well that it came from? It must be a big well."

The man smiled, "I suppose that, that the Creator put it here. We couldn't live without it. Much of our food comes from this sea."

Amon stared in awe. "What are those boxes doing out there? They seem to be moving."

"Those boxes are ships and boats. Men sail in them and use them for fishing."

Several minutes passed before Amon responded. "That much water and nobody cares about it. It doesn't sink into the ground like the water in Nain. I don't understand." He slumped to his knees and looked intently at the shimmering surface. His words were soft and drawn out. "I have never seen . . . something like this before."

The man was about to leave when Amon raised his hand, "And how do people get wool to be above the water and it does not fall down?"

"Those are clouds and they bring rain and give shade. They move around and disappear only to be back tomorrow."

"Clouds . . . rain? I have never seen or heard of them before. Did the Creator make those too?"

"I must go," said the man as he tugged on the donkey's halter.

Amon did not watch the man walk away but continued to look at the bright surface of the water. "The Creator must have forgotten to bring these to Nain."

A second man, who was carrying a wooden crate with birds in it, walked near Amon and when he was about to pass by, Amon called to him. "Wait!"

Conspiracy With Malicious Intent

"Why?"

"Someone told me that bright land is water, but how . . . how does it stay there . . . and not disappear into the ground?"

"It's the Sea of Galilee."

"I'm from Nain and we do not have such things. We have water, yes but not like this," he said as he shrugged his shoulders and raised both hands. "Our water is in the well or sometimes in a trough that sheep drink from, but this . . . will I be able to go close to see if it is water?"

Moments passed and finally the man said, "Come with me and I'll show you." He reached out and touched Amon on the arm and both of men walked down the hillside toward the shore and the piers.

Amon was reluctant to step onto the wooden pier, but when he saw that other men were walking on it without falling through, he cautiously stepped forward. He raised his hands as he spoke, "How do those boxes move? They have no wheels or donkeys to pull them, yet they move like large carts and, and they are so silent. They don't squeak like the wheels on a cart. Did the Creator make those too?"

"The ships move because of the wind. It blows on the sails and that is how they move," the man said as he turned and walked away, leaving Amon standing on the pier.

"Our carts have wheels but no cloth on tall wooden sticks like these boxes," he said to himself. He remained on the dock for a long time and watched the boats moving effortlessly through the clear blue water. "I have never seen so much water. It must have taken many wells to fill this place," he reasoned to himself.

Overhead, he heard many birds calling to each other and when he looked up he stared at the clouds. They appeared as wool, and he marveled that they moved and continued to change shape. "I wonder what they do up there," he whispered to himself.

To Amon's right were fish market patrons, actively negotiating, debating and arguing over changing prices and varying qualities of fish. Amon walked over to see what they were buying. He was reluctant to touch one of the fish, especially when a fisherman held one out to him. "Do you want to buy one? It's fresh today and you will never find one so good," he said.

"What do people do with them?" asked Amon as he stepped closer for a better view.

"People cook them and eat them."

"But they have no legs or ears or udders. Do they make a noise like a sheep or a goat?"

Confused by what Amon said, the fisherman tried to explain. "N-O, but they are good to eat. Here touch one," he said as he held one out to Amon.

Amon withdrew his hand at first but cautiously reached out to touch it. The silver body did not move. "Where are their legs?"

"Fish don't have legs. If you want to buy legs then buy a lamb," replied the fisherman, who shrugged his shoulders.

"Do they make any sound?"

"No . . . I don't think so. If they do, I've never heard it."

"So how do you know when they are close to you or where they live?" asked Amon as he tilted his head to one side. "Sheep don't smell good and these, these things don't smell so good either." A moment later, he looked at the confused fisherman. "Where do you raise them?"

"No one owns them and nobody raises them. They're in the sea," he said as he pointed over his shoulder toward the water.

"Who feeds them?"

"They eat other fish and food from the bottom of the sea."

"Are you a fish herder?"

"No, I'm not a fish herder," the man chuckled, "but I'm a fisherman. I catch them and people buy them to eat them."

"If so many people buy these fish and you don't own them, then you must have many coins."

The fisherman shrugged his shoulders. "I make a living, not so good but I feed my wife and six children."

"These things you call fish are silver like some coins," said Amon as he lowered his head to have a closer look at the largest one. "I'm a sandal maker. Everyone needs sandals but it is difficult to make money, but you, you must make much money since these, these fish are not yours and you don't need to feed them, yet you sell them. Whose are they?"

The fisherman turned away to make a sale to several women standing nearby.

Amon ignored their conversation to enjoy every moment of this new world. All of this unusual activity excited him. Here were new people, wooden boxes on much water and fish that people said they ate.

"Did the rabbi say that these things can be eaten?" he asked. "Lamb, I know about, but this, this fish . . . I don't know about."

"Yes we can eat them."

Amon walked along a narrow pathway on the shore and stopped next to a house to purchase some dates and flat bread with one of his coins. After eating, he felt better and then spent the remaining part of the day sitting on a flat rock and stared at the waves that moved over the smooth rocks of the shore. He could not take his eyes off the water and by late evening he moved away from the shore to sleep next to several trees.

In the morning, Amon was awakened by the voices of men, who were walking on the wooden pier. He rolled over and tried to sleep, but they kept shouting to each other as they cast ropes from the pier into a boat. Eventually, they raised the sails and lifted anchor to sail away.

Amon walked along the shore to watch the ships. He was unsure of how the wind moved the giant boxes but when a gust of wind moved over the shore and touched his face, he realized that the cloth on the large sticks was how the wind moved the wooden boxes. Intrigued by this, he sat down and marveled at their size and the speed at which they could travel.

Sometime later, a conversation between several fishermen on the pier stirred his curiosity, so he walked over to see what they were doing. As he approached, they acknowledged him by nodding and smiling.

"What are you doing," asked Amon.

"We're mending our nets," responded one of them. "If we don't fix the nets, the fish will swim out and we won't catch anything."

All of the men chuckled at Amon's question.

"So that is where the silvery fish come from. You catch them in those crisscross ropes," Amon said as he scratched his head and then reached down to touch it.

"We call them nets."

"But how can you fix these, these nets because they already have holes in them. What if some fish swims through and . . ?"

"Through these holes?" asked one of them as he held up the net. "Yes."

The men laughed loudly and one of them responded, "The little ones swim through but we'll catch them some other day, when they are bigger."

"I have never seen so much water and . . . and fish, I know nothing about them. And your wooden boxes that you move in," he said as he pointed at the ships. "I have never seen them before. They have no wheels."

Again the men chuckled as they continued to repair the nets.

"Who are you and where are you from?" asked the eldest of the group.

"My name is Amon and I come from Nain in the hill country," he said as he turned to look back at the sea. "I have come this way to find the prophet, the one some call the Messiah. Have any of you seen him . . . or know where I might find him?"

"Several days ago, a prophet and his men bought fish from us and I heard them say that they were going to Capernaum."

"What is that?"

"Capernaum is a city farther up the shoreline," the man said as he pointed to his right. "It'll take you some time to walk there, but it's a beautiful road. Just follow the shore."

"How did you know about the prophet?" asked the eldest man.

"He was in Nain and stopped a burial and then raised Hannah's boy to life again. It was something that I have never seen before. Then, he left Nain before I could speak with him." Amon paused, "Are you sure he is a prophet? Maybe he's a Messiah. Have you thought about that?"

The men looked at each other before one responded, "He healed many people in the town square. Many people follow him. His words are sometimes hard to understand because he speaks in stories."

Just before noon, the men carried their nets to their ships and Amon started walking along the path toward Capernaum. He passed through the heart of the small community and purchased food before leaving town. The journey northward was beautiful as far as Amon was concerned. After living his entire lifetime in the arid hills of Nain, this place seemed to have an endless bounty of trees, boats and buildings. The air was certainly easier to breath than the dry air in Nain.

Gennesaret was the first small town that he passed through, and when he saw a market he bought figs and flat bread. After he had eaten, he stopped by a sandal maker's shop and looked at sandals, pouches, belts and straps. When he noticed several leather objects that seemed unfamiliar to him, he asked, "What is that?"

"Those are saddles and they are used on the backs of donkeys and horses. It is easier to tie a load onto a donkey or horse when you have one of these strapped on its back. We got the idea from the Romans," said the old man as he held one up for Amon to look at.

"I too am a sandal maker and I come from Nain. My shop was destroyed by the Romans, who also killed my brother, Asa," he said as he turned the donkey saddle over in his hands. "I have made many, many sandals over many years but some of these things are different." He placed the donkey saddle on the table and picked up an unusual sandal. "These look like sandals that the Roman soldiers wear."

"Roman soldiers come to me and I make their sandals. They are very different because they are made of heavy leather and cover the entire foot and toes. Some cover the front of their leg up to the knee."

"The leather is very thick," said Amon as he examined it carefully.

"The nails in the soles make them last longer. It is difficult work but they pay me well."

"I need work to live. I will do a good job for you if you let me work for you. I'm hungry and on my way to Capernaum, but a few days of work would be good."

"Are you in a rush to get to Capernaum?" asked the old man.

"I have come this way to find the Messiah, but now I need food before I go farther. Can I work with you? You can teach me about these here saddles."

"My name is Nabal. Come in, and I'll give you work to do. I have thirty sandals to make for soldiers and many others that need repair. I will show you how to make Roman sandals and saddles."

Amon entered the dimly lit shop and when the odor of leather, dye and glue entered his nostrils, he felt as if he had come home.

"You can work here. If you do well, you can sleep over in that corner," said Nabal.

"What about food?" asked Amon.

"First you work, then we bring food to eat."

"Hungry workers do not see too good and their hands are not steady without food," said Amon as he tipped his head to one side.

After they had eaten, Nabal showed Amon how to make Roman sandals.

****

Just when Varrus was becoming comfortable with the progress that he made with the religious leaders in Nain, he received a parchment from Scythopolis informing him that he had been promoted to the rank of Centurion and was to move immediately to Capernaum, a city at the north end of the Sea of Galilee. He was not provided with a reason for his new assignment and so he asked Pollus, his servant, to pack his personal items for the trip. Pollus was told that he would be escorted to Capernaum several days later.

When Centurion Varrus arrived in Capernaum, he immediately asked Optio Demetrios to assemble the men for an inspection, and while Demetrios was gone, Varrus immediately read through the documents that were left on the desk by the previous Centurion. Following inspection, he and Demetrios rode through the city so that he had a better understanding of the streets and where the synagogue, the markets and wells were.

Conspiracy With Malicious Intent

After they returned to the barracks, Varrus spent the evening with Demetrios to establish what their priorities were, their duties and his personal expectations.

"You are responsible for all documentation, maintaining accurate records, planning logistics and preparing schedules related to patrols and preparing reports regarding any confrontation between citizens or between citizens and Rome. I want the patrols to report on migrants passing through our region and any violent acts against citizens. I will handle discipline, training and all aspects related to dealing with the religious leaders and those who have influence in the city."

"Yes, Sir," responded Optio Demetrios.

"Also, I want you to notify me if a man named Jesus and his followers are in our region. Some people refer to him as a prophet and some call him a Messiah. He and his men are not violent and are not a threat to anyone, including us, but I wish to know if they are in the region."

"We are aware of this prophet and have followed him from place to place many times," responded Demetrios.

Varrus secretly hoped to meet and speak with the prophet. He never did forget the young man that was raised to life in Nain. He thought often about it and wanted to see more of what this Jesus could do.

Two days later Varrus was told that Jesus was in the area so he and ten cavalrymen rode to where Jesus was last seen. When they found him, Varrus listened to Jesus speaking to the crowd but did not understand everything that Jesus spoke about. He heard Jesus referred to God as his Father. Varrus was pleased to see children healed of various diseases and injuries, and marveled at the size of the crowds that followed the prophet.

One day Varrus was told that the prophet was speaking to several thousand people, so he took Demetrios and ten men with him to the hillside just outside of Capernaum. He watched as Jesus' followers organized people to sit in small groups. After the crowd was seated, Jesus' disciples gave him some food and he held it up to the sky. Immediately after, he gave the food he had been holding, back to his disciples, who began to distribute it among the people. Varrus marveled when he realized how much food was distributed to the large crowd.

"Sir, where did he get all the food to feed these people?" whispered Demetrios.

"I don't know but there must be at least five thousand people on this hillside," responded Varrus as he moved his hand over his eyes to shade the bright sunshine from his eyes. "There are one, two," he pause a moment before continuing," at least one hundred groups of people and each group must contain fifty people. This is amazing."

"Sir, there are no carts or anything that could have brought all of this food, so where did it come from?"

Varrus said nothing, but watched in silence.

"I have counted about fifty people in each group and there are about five thousand or more people, Sir. That is a lot of food."

"I can see that Demetrios. Thank you."

When most of the food had been distributed, Varrus said, "Demetrios go down and join the people, so that you can receive some of that food, and Demetrios, bring it to me. Do not eat one crumb of it, but bring me what is given to you."

"Yes Sir."

The crowd continued to receive food from the prophet's twelve men, and when Demetrios arrived in their midst, he received some food which he immediately brought to Varrus.

"Sir, they have given me all of this barley bread, and look at all of the fish. There is enough here for . . ."

Varrus interrupted, "Give some to every cavalryman here. I want them to see what is happening." He turned the fish and bread over in his hand before eating it and marveled at how so many people had been fed.

After the five thousand and the soldiers had been fed, the prophet spoke about the Kingdom of God. He spoke in parables and when the day was well spent, the prophet called for children to come to him. He placed his hand on their heads and hugged each child.

"Remain here," commanded Varrus as he dismounted and walked down the hillside toward the prophet.

"But Sir," Demetrios pleaded.

Varrus did not turn his head but motioned for his men to remain where they were. When he arrived in the middle of the crowd, he noticed that the twelve followers were gathering up the remaining food that the people could not carry home. He marveled at the amount of food left over and watched as the prophet's followers were placing it into twelve large baskets.

One of the prophet's followers stood erect as Varrus approached him.

Varrus nodded. "There were several thousand people here. Where did you find enough food for all of them?" he asked as he squared his shoulders.

"A small boy had five barley loaves and two fishes, and he gave it to us. We gave it to Jesus and when he gave thanks to God for it, we began to hand it out to the people."

"That's all the food that you started out with? Five barley loaves and two fish?"

"Yes Sir."

"What is your name?" asked Varrus.

"My name is Levi and many call me Matthew."

"Matthew, what did you do before you were a follower of this prophet?"

Before I became a follower, I was a tax collector for Rome, but now I remain with him." He pointed toward Jesus.

Varrus' silence made Matthew uncomfortable. He felt a need to speak. "Is there anything else, Sir? Do you want to meet my Master?"

"What is his name?" asked Varrus.

"His name is Jesus."

"Is he a prophet?"

"More than that Sir. He's the Messiah sent to Israel from God."

"Messiah? Is he the one that is spoken of in the book of Isaiah?"

Matthew seemed momentarily speechless. "How do you . . . a Roman know of these things?"

Varrus did not answer the question but smiled. Before returning to the men on the hillside, he asked, "Were you with your Master when he was in Nain some time ago? A woman had a son that was dead and was being taken out to be buried. I remember seeing Jesus raise that young boy back to life. Were you there?"

Somewhat surprised, Matthew stepped back. "How do you know about that?"

"It is I that asks the questions. I have asked you two questions that you have chosen to ignore."

Matthew swallowed and tried to hide his momentary fear as Varrus stepped closer.

"Well?" insisted Varrus as he waited for a response.

"Kind Sir. We were in Nain and the event you speak of is true."

"I know that you and your Messiah cause no harm, but I now wait for your final answer."

"Yes, the book of Isaiah, and the Psalms that was written by King David, spoke of a Messiah to come."

"From my understanding, the Messiah, who is to be sent by God will save his people from their sins," said Varrus to a speechless and surprised Matthew. "Is he THAT Messiah?"

"I . . . I believe that he is the one that has been sent by God."

"Where was he born?"

Conspiracy With Malicious Intent

"In Bethlehem, the city of David in Judaea."

"I thought he came from Nazareth."

"Yes, he and his family lived in Nazareth. His father was a carpenter."

"Tell me, what caused you to follow his teaching?"

"I told you that I was a tax collector for Rome. When Jesus spoke to me, I believed what he said, and gave up my public status to become his disciple."

"That is honorable but are you sure that you have made the correct decision?"

"Oh, yes, kind Sir, I am able to listen to him, be with him and see miracles like this one every day. It's a decision that I have not regretted. But kind Sir, may I ask you a question?"

"You may," responded Varrus as he narrowed his brows and tightened his lips.

"How do you know of these things . . . about the book of Isaiah, and why do you care of what the Messiah does?"

"That is two questions. Which one do you wish me to answer?"

"I have overstepped my boundaries," Matthew said as he lowered his gaze, "but I am surprised that you, a Roman would know about Isaiah and the Messiah."

"It is not necessary to be a Hebrew to know of those things. Not all of us are ignorant and have no interest in those things. Make no assumptions as to who I am, for though I am a Roman Centurion, I know about Feasts and Festivals, and have knowledge of the Tanakh. I am familiar with the Law of Moses, the Prophets and other writings such as the Psalms.

Matthew seemed unable to speak.

"Why do you find this a strange concept, when you a Hebrew were a servant to Rome? Why then are you surprised that I'm interested in Hebrew history and prophesy?"

"I have not judged you correctly and require your pardon, Sir," responded Matthew as he bowed low.

"I harbor no offense. You have been gracious to me." Varrus turned away from Matthew to look at Jesus, who was speaking to a group of small children. Before walking away, he said, "Continue with your duties and when you have finished, be sure to tell your Master . . . or should I say Messiah, that I have listened to his words and have observed him often. Someday I will speak personally with him."

"I will do as you have requested kind Sir."

When Varrus walked toward the cavalrymen, Demetrios immediately nudged his mount and led Varrus' horse down the hillside to meet him. After mounting his horse, the cavalrymen followed Varrus back to the city.

Chapter XIV

VARRUS' REQUEST

Several days later, five cavalrymen arrived in Capernaum. They brought with them a cart with Varrus' servant, Pollus, and all of Varrus' personal belongings. When they stopped at the front of the building where Varrus' office was, the most senior legionnaire dismounted, dusted off his vestment, removed his helmet and entered the building.

"Good day Sir," he said as he saluted Varrus, who was seated at a table with several maps in front of him. As Varrus looked up, the legionnaire said, "I am Cavalryman Nartanos, who has just arrived from Nain. It is I, who has escorted your servant Pollus and your belongings, Sir."

Immediately, Varrus stood to his feet and returned the salute.

"If I may, Sir, there is one thing I need to talk to you about. Pollus is quite ill. It has taken us two days of travel to get here and . . . and we were fearful that he would die during the journey, Sir."

"What's the matter?" Varrus asked, as he narrowed his brows.

"Just as we were about to leave Nain, he complained about a severe headache, stiffness in his joints, blurred vision and great pain throughout his entire body."

When Varrus stepped from the building, he found Pollus lying in the shade of the porch at the front of the building. Varrus immediately knelt next to him. "My dear Pollus, what seems to be your illness?"

"It seems as if my head and body are not connected. What I wish to do and what I can do is not the same. Even now I see you with only one eye and my left arm does not move as I wish."

Turning to Demetrios, Varrus responded, "Find a physician, NOW."

As Demetrios left the porch, Varrus turned to Nartanos, "Has it been the hot sun or . . ?"

"Sir I think it's the palsy. I have seen this twice while I was stationed in Egypt."

Pollus motioned with his hand and Varrus placed the back of his hand on Pollus' forehead. "I am old and much of my years have already passed. Worry yourself not about me and . . ."

"Get him inside. He has a fever. Bring wet cloths to rid him of this fever," Varrus commanded. Once inside, Varrus tried unsuccessfully to make Pollus comfortable and soon Varrus realized that Pollus' life was ebbing away before his eyes.

Every physician was consulted but little could relieve Pollus' symptoms. It seemed that every day Pollus suffered additional difficulties. At one point, he was unable to eat and if he did, nausea immediately overwhelmed him. Soon he was unable to lift his head from his bed. His breathing became labored and his complexion waned.

"In my opinion," said one physician, after he had summoned Varrus to an adjoining room, "he has the palsy. There is little that I or anyone can do for him. I fear that . . ."

"You mean that he will die?" interrupted Varrus.

"I wish that I could help," the physician said before leaving the room.

Varrus immediately returned to Pollus' side and slumped in a chair and closed his eyes.

"Master Varrus," whispered Pollus, "do not cause yourself any pain for I am ready to go the way of my fathers."

"You will not die for I have decided to look for the prophet that heals people. I have seen him raise a young man back to life and I believe that if I speak with him, he will help."

"You have told me of him, but does he not heal Jews only? Remember that I am a Gentile but you . . ."

"I'll find him, Pollus. He will help us." Turning to his Optio, Varrus said, "Demetrious, dispatch several groups of men to find the prophet. I need to speak with him as soon as possible."

When the cavalrymen could not find Jesus, Varrus called for his horse and rode to the synagogue to speak with the religious leaders to see if they knew where Jesus was."

The religious leaders did not know where the prophet was but said that they would ask if anyone had seen him. A day later, one of the patrols saw Jesus on the shore of the Sea of Galilee. Immediately, Optio Demetrios dispatched a rider to summon Varrus.

Conspiracy With Malicious Intent

When the rider stepped into the doorway of Varrus' office, he saluted. "Sir," he said as he held his position.

"Yes what is it Kaddel?"

"Sir, Optio Demetrios has sent me to tell you that we have located the man you call a prophet. He is on the shore of the Sea of Galilee. Optio Demetrios said that he will remain there until you arrive and if the prophet plans to leave he will ask him to wait."

"Call for my horse. We will go to meet him."

When Varrus and cavalryman Kaddel arrived, Jesus was standing next to Optio Demetrios and the crowd was anxiously wondering why a Roman patrol was detaining Jesus.

Varrus dismounted and walked through the crowd. As he stepped near he said, "Thank you, Demetrios." Then looking at Jesus, Varrus removed his helmet and tipped his head slightly forward as a sign of respect.

Jesus returned the nod, smiled but said nothing.

"I know this is highly unusual, but I have observed you when I was in the city of Nain and you raised a young man back to life. I have witnessed you feeding several thousand people and I have observed many of your miracles while on my patrols."

"What do you want me to do for you?" asked Jesus.

"I know that you heal and help those of the house of Abraham, Isaac and Jacob but I have come to ask you to heal my servant, who is very sick with the palsy. Even now he is near death."

"It is true that I have come for those of the house of Israel but I am willing to come to your house."

"There is no need to come into my house, but if you say the word, you can heal Pollus my servant. For I too am a man of authority for I say to one go and he goes and to another come and he comes. I know that you have authority over illness and death. Say the word and Pollus, my servant will be healed and will live."

Turning to face the crowd around him, Jesus said, "I have not seen such faith in the house of Israel." Then turning to Varrus, Jesus said, "It shall be as you have asked. Go, for your servant Pollus is now healed."

Varrus lowered his gaze. "Thank you for your willingness to help me. I am grateful." Turning to Demetrios, he motioned for his men to step back and allow Jesus and the crowd to leave.

"Demetrios, continue your patrol. You have pleased me by finding this prophet." Moments later, Varrus returned to his home to speak with Pollus.

When he arrived, he rushed into the building and found Pollus walking toward the front door.

"POLLUS! You are well just as the prophet said you would be. When did this happen?"

"A short time ago, I suddenly felt strength in my arms and legs, and my head was suddenly clear, so I stood to my feet and was on my way to tell you about it"

"Pollus, the prophet that I told you about granted my request to restore you back to health. I owe him a great debt."

"I too owe a great debt to this prophet but I also owe a great debt to you for going to speak to him on my behalf."

****

Amon's stay in Gennesaret was longer than he had planned. During those six weeks, he learned how to make Roman sandals, cargo saddles, belts and scabbards for the Romans. When the Roman soldiers came into the shop, Amon would smile and ignore the warm anger in his chest, but once they were gone, he reminded himself of what they had done to Asa and his shop. Their appearance always left a bitter taste in his mouth for the remainder of the day.

He tasted fish, but complained about the odor and the small bones in the meat. His cot became comfortable and he managed to become friends with Nabal, who in turn learned several sewing techniques from Amon. The business flourished because of their unique friendship and honesty with clients and with each other.

Every evening, Amon went down to the shore to watch the boats. He marveled at the concept that the water did not disappear into the ground like it did in Nain. Often he would remove his sandals and wade into the water to cool his feet, but when he remembered that fish were in the water he quickly retreated to the shore.

He watched as women washed their clothing and bathed their children. Some of the larger children would swim in the sea and he learned that just because a child disappeared below the surface of the water, it did not mean that it was dead or being swallowed by fish. He marveled at the sea and the different sizes of boats, but turned down every invitation to be onboard.

One evening a small gust of wind swirled about Amon and he marveled at the clouds that swirled overhead and when rain began to fall, he ran for cover but when he arrived, he laughed at himself for allowing his clothes to become drenched with water from the sky. He wiped his face with a cloth and laughed loudly as he shook his head to dry his hair and beard.

Nabal was significantly older than Amon, yet they respected each other's artisan skills. On several occasions, they went to the synagogue together and often spoke about the prophet. Nabal's grandchildren played with Amon and he enjoyed playing games with them. Nabal's health began to deteriorate, so Amon continued to work at Nabal's shop to help the family.

"Maybe, I should have had children," he said as he and Nabal were taking a much needed break. He swallowed the date he was chewing on and continued, "But then I would need a wife."

"So what is wrong with that?" asked Nabal as he raised his hands. "My wife is a very nice person. I did as the Torah tells me. I married her after my brother died and they both did not have children, so here I am with a wife and children."

"Children yes, a wife well maybe, but her mother, NO," Amon said as he closed his eyes, shook his head and chuckled.

"But why Amon?"

"They cost you food and always tell you what they want you to do."

"We know a matchmaker in town, who would be happy to help you find a good wife, one with children or one without children. What kind of wife do you want?"

"If I wanted a wife maybe she should have teeth and . . . and some money but I have nothing that she needs so I . . ." He did not finish his sentence but shrugged his shoulders and smiled.

"What else should your wife have Amon?"

"She should have no mother that runs the house or . . . or makes me run too."

Again they laughed loudly until Nabal's wife appeared in the doorway.

"Much laughter means no work is being done," she said as she placed her hands on her hips.

Amon stood to his feet and raised both hands above his head. "See, what I tell you, Nabal. They may be nice, but now you know what I mean."

Later that day someone entered the shop to drop off a pair of sandals that needed replacing rather than repair when Amon responded, "These sandals look older than you," teased Amon.

The man responded, "They must be fixed. My wife cannot afford new ones." He smiled and grinned.

Conspiracy With Malicious Intent

One day while in the market, Amon approached several rabbis. They were visiting with several merchants, so he waited for an opportunity to speak with them. When they were about to walk away Amon motioned to them.

"Rabbi, my name is Amon and I have come from the hill country and the town of Nain. I have a question to ask."

As he spoke, the rabbi walked to the stairs of a nearby building, sat down and folded his arms across his chest.

"Yes. What is it? Questions are good. Yes questions are good."

"Rabbi, I have come to find someone. Some people call him a prophet and there are those who think he might be . . . a Messiah. Have you seen him?"

The rabbi's face tightened and his eyebrows narrowed into one. "There is a Messiah in this here town? Where is he?" He sounded rather surprised and asked, "Why do you ask me such a question?"

"Have you seen him?" responded Amon.

There was a long pause before the rabbi placed his hand to his beard and then shook his head. "Why do you bother me with such a question? Ask me something that has answers, but this . . . this question, I know not about."

Amon told him of Hannah's son and how the young boy was brought back to life and how some people believed him to be a prophet.

The rabbi closed his eyes and moved his head up and down. "I have heard of such things and God has sent prophets to us in the past to do unusual things, but," he paused, "I say but, as to your question if I think he is a Messiah, No!" The rabbi brushed his beard for some time before continuing. "A prophet tells us many things and is a messenger from God. People do not always listen to him," he shrugged his shoulders as he spoke. "They listen not like they should, but this man you speak of, does say some interesting things and people listen to him. Why do you yet ask me if I think this man is . . ?"

"Well is he a prophet or a . . . Messiah?" interrupted Amon.

"First be quiet and let me finish," said the rabbi, somewhat irritated at Amon's interruption. "Now as for the man you want to know about, he certainly knows the Laws of Moses and the Pentateuch, and I hear that in Jerusalem many priests and lawyers have asked him many question, and he answers all of them. This man asks questions of the Pharisees, Sadducees, lawyers and the rabbis, but few are able to answer back. Very unusual, yes very unusual," he continued to say as he stroked his beard.

"Prophet, maybe, yes maybe, but a Messiah . . . no!" His head moved from side to side for a few moments.

"What is a Messiah?" asked Amon. "My mother said the Messiah would come from the line of King David. Is this man from the line of David?" Amon did not take his eyes off the rabbi.

"That I do not know. Some people said he comes from Nazareth and has been a carpenter there for many years. The scriptures do not mention that the Messiah would be a carpenter. The book of Isaiah tells us that the Messiah will come from a city of David and that God will call his son out of Egypt, so does that mean he will be Hebrew in exile in Egypt or an Egyptian? If he is an Egyptian, then definitely no . . . but, if he is of the House of Israel . . . well maybe but I do not know."

"I met some Egyptians when I escaped from Nain."

Ignoring Amon's comments, the Rabbi continued, "This prophet does not seem to fit what Isaiah tells us, so I do not think he's the Messiah." He stood to his feet, waved to another rabbi that was passing by and started to walk away. Amon jumped up to follow.

"Have you seen him or talked to him?" continued Amon.

"I have seen him from a distance, but have not yet talked to him."

"Well, how do you know where he was born and if he was in Egypt unless you ask him?"

"You ask too many questions," the rabbi said and forced his way through a crowd, making it difficult for Amon to keep up.

Greatly disappointed, Amon returned to Nabal's Sandal Shop.

Unable to sleep that night, Amon walked down the shoreline and sat on a rock and recalled the raising of Hannah's son. "If only the Messiah had been there for Asa," he thought to himself as he wiped several tears from his face. "It's hard to find a good Messiah when you need one but I cannot even find this one," he mused. I cannot even find a rabbi that knows something."

As the moon shone down on the quiet community of Gennesaret, Amon listened to the waves lapping along the shore. "If only Asa could be here," he whispered. "We could go to Capernaum together. If the Messiah can raise dead and heal others, he could have healed his foot and, and raised him from the dead too, but I could not find him. I did my best, yet I could not find him."

In the yellowing light of the moon, two Roman soldiers approached.

"Who are you?" asked one of them.

"I am Amon."

Conspiracy With Malicious Intent

"You're a sandal maker at Nabal's shop."

"Yes. It's true that I am yet a sandal maker at Nabal's shop, but tomorrow I will go to Capernaum to find a prophet, who heals people," responded Amon as he tossed a small stone into the lake.

There was a moment of silence before one of the legionnaires stepped near. "When this man that you speak of was passing through here, he stood on the shore by those boats," the legionnaire said as he pointed to several boats swaying on the water. "He spoke to many people and we listened to him too."

"He was here?" asked Amon as he turned to face them.

"Yes and a crippled man could walk, after he was touched. Others brought their children, who were sick and they were all made well. I saw these things with my own eyes, but I do not understand it."

"Here in this town? Right here."

"He made children well, but in the city I have come from, they sacrifice children," said the other legionnaire. "The man you are looking for has gone to Capernaum."

"I do not understand," said Amon as he stepped back. "Romans talking to me, a Jew?" he said as he tapped his chest. "Why are you yet talking to me? An uncircumcised Gentile wants to talk to me, and all about a Messiah." As he spoke, his hand reached for the dagger under his belt. "Just remember," Amon said, "this prophet is OUR Messiah. If you Romans want a Messiah, then go find your own. How can a Messiah be a Messiah for us and the Gentiles at the same time?"

They turned and walked away, leaving Amon standing all alone.

Chapter XV

ZEBEDEE AND THE MESSIAH

The mutual joy that Varrus and Pollus shared was beyond the regular protocol of Roman decorum. Large amounts of food were prepared and six groups of two legionnaires were immediately dispatched to find the prophet and his disciples so that they could be invited to celebrate what the prophet had done for them.

The message to be delivered to Jesus was clear. "Tell Jesus," said Varrus, "you and your disciples are invited to come and dine with us. Food will be served outside so that you do not have to come to my house for I know that it is not acceptable for a Jew to enter my house."

Varrus was greatly disappointed that the legionnaires were not able to find Jesus and soon rumors suggested that Jesus was on his way to Jerusalem, so the legionnaires were granted permission to enjoy a day of celebration with Varrus and Pollus. They ate and willingly listened to the story Varrus told them about what Jesus had done for Pollus and for other people. Varrus also told them of what Jesus did for a widow in Nain and how he had fed five thousand people. Varrus was humbled that Jesus was willing to heal his servant.

The following day there was a knock on the door of Varrus' office. When he looked up, he saw a Centurion and motioned for him to enter.

"Ave," said Varrus as he stood to his feet. "What is your purpose for your visit to Capernaum?"

"I am Centurion Averia from Caesarea. I have been sent to replace you, and you are to return to Scythopolis immediately. Here is the parchment telling you of the transfer."

"Scythopolis? I have not been here very long time and . . ."

Averia interrupted, "Apparently, you are to return for a short time to Scythopolis and rumors are that you will eventually be assigned to Jerusalem. This is only rumor, but the person I heard it from said it twice, so it is likely to be true."

"Well, I'm not pleased that I have to return, but I have had the most wonderful thing happen to me in Capernaum. Let me tell you about it," said Varrus as he offered Averia some wine."

****

Amon eventually broke the news to Nabal that he was leaving to resume his search for the Messiah. Nabal understood and was visibly disappointed and hugged Amon several times. They parted as friends.

Amon started for Capernaum with food and coins in his pouch. It was a long walk but when he arrived in Capernaum, he asked the first person that he met, if they knew where the prophet might be. Excitement gripped his heart when the man told him that the Messiah had been in the city four days earlier.

In the market, Amon saw a rabbi and hurried to speak with him. "Oh, Rabbi," called Amon as he slowed his pace to speak with him.

"Yes," responded the rabbi as he turned to face Amon.

"I have a question," Amon said as he stopped to catch his breath.

"You are new in this area, are you not?" interrupted the rabbi. "I can tell from your speech that you are from not here but from . . . from maybe the hill country."

"Yes, it's true that I am from Nain and have come a long way but I need to find the prophet that raised a boy to life in my town. Do you know where I might find him?"

"A dead boy now lives? Where and when has this happened?"

"In the town of Nain. Let me tell you that I saw the dead boy and his mother, Hannah. The boy was dead, dead I tell you but the Messiah made him alive."

The rabbi narrowed his eyes as he tried to understand what Amon had just said.

"But I'm sad," continued Amon, "because I couldn't get my brother, Asa, to be brought back to life. He was killed by Roman soldiers."

"A Messiah, a dead boy and you have a brother named Asa who was killed?" said the rabbi as he studied Amon's face.

"Yes," responded Amon, "but what about the prophet?" Eager to hear what the rabbi would say, he leaned closer. "Where is the Messiah now?"

"There was a prophet and a Messiah in Nain? When was this?" The rabbi seemed eager to hear more of what Amon was talking about.

"I followed him here and I'm sure that the prophet and the Messiah are the same man."

The rabbi stepped back to look at Amon. "Why do you speak in riddles? Why do you think there is yet a prophet and who do you think is the Messiah? We have been waiting for a Messiah and have seen many prophets in the past, but what makes you think that, that there is a Messiah somewhere that we do not know about?"

"The man named Jesus is the one that heals people and I saw him raise the boy back to life in Nain. That is why I think he is a prophet or maybe the Messiah."

"Yes, I too have seen very difficult things to understand and explain, and yes there is a man . . . a Galilean or is he a Nazarene . . . I don't know, but he does miracles and seems to speak about the Torah and he knows about the Tanakh, yet I'm not sure whether he is a prophet." He stroked his beard before continuing. "I know the Torah and the Tanakh too, but I am not a Messiah. Why do you yet think there is a Messiah some where in this here town?"

"You are like the rabbis in Nain. They say they don't know. Everywhere I go, every rabbi I meet says to me, 'I don't know.' I need a rabbi, who knows something. Where can I find one?"

"You are impatient and must learn that all questions do not have easy answers, especially when you ask them all at once. Questions are easy but the answers, oy," he paused, "sometime they can be hard. We ask questions so we can discuss them and learn from them," said the rabbi as he folded his arms across his chest, "but you, you ask questions and talk at the same time. It causes me to think too many things at once."

"Where should I be looking for this here Messiah?" asked Amon.

"That I don't know," replied the rabbi as he walked away.

Amon raised his hands above his head and expressed his frustration. "Who am I that I should complain against rabbis, but why do they not know anything. How can he be a rabbi and not know something. In that case, I could be a rabbi, too."

Three days passed and Amon seemed no closer to the prophet. As he walked along the shore, he stopped by a moored fishing boat next to a pier to inquire about the prophet. The older gentleman smiled and with a Galilean accent, began to tell him about the day the Messiah asked his sons to join him.

"Yes. I know him," was the Galilean's reply. "He has stayed in my house many times and has used my boats. He and the men that follow him were in my house last night but left for Jerusalem this morning. He's not here now, but he'll be back again."

"HE STAYED AT YOUR HOUSE . . . last night? Who are you?"

"My name is Zebedee."

Amon listened carefully to every word that Zebedee was saying.

"My sons are with him now. At first, I was unhappy that they left me so suddenly. They left everything to follow him because he speaks about God. But if I didn't have these boats and workers, maybe I too would have gone with him too."

"Am I too old to go with him?" asked Amon.

"That I don't know. When you see him, ask him."

"How can you say I don't know when you know so much? Are you a rabbi?"

"No, no," the man chuckled as he raised his hand. "No, my name is Zebedee and I am not a rabbi, but a fisherman."

"All the rabbis I meet don't know nothing, and say 'I don't know.' Why don't they know something?" complained Amon.

"Come with me," motioned Zebedee as he walked over into the shade of the small boathouse and pointed for Amon to sit next to him.

Amon's eyes narrowed as Zebedee began to tell his story.

"We had listened to Jesus many days and found his words to be peaceful. He was kind with everyone, played with all of the children that live in this area, and taught from the Torah. His words touched our hearts." Zebedee paused as he waved at two men, who were mending nets some distance away. "Judah and Palti are good workers and have been with me for many years. They too, listened to Jesus," continued Zebedee, "and wanted to follow him, but I needed workers, especially since my sons decided to travel with Jesus."

"They have seen Jesus too?"

"Yes. One morning, about three hundred strides from shore, right over there, I suddenly heard shouting. When I looked up, I could see that one of my boats was in trouble and about to sink. Soon, other boats were sailing toward it to help it. I was on shore, and when I shaded my eyes, I recognized that it was one of my larger boats. The other boats circled my boat, and there seemed to be much activity. At first, I watched in silence and then ran to my rowboat and started to row out to where all the trouble seemed to be. When I arrived, I could see the net between my two boats was so full of fish and that the net was starting to break."

"What happened?" asked Amon as he leaned over to listen more intently.

"The net bulged with moving fish, and it seemed for a moment that all of them would escape because the net was tearing. It looked as if a thousand fish were in the net."

Amon's eyes were wide with imagination.

Zebedee continued. "My sons and the hired hands tugged on the net and finally all of the fish were safely on board. I was afraid that my boat would sink but eventually it made its way to shore."

"Then what happened?"

"When they arrived at that pier, I looked up and saw Jesus standing on the pier. Then I remember hearing Simon Peter say to him, 'Don't come near me, for I am a sinful man.'"

"Was he a sinful man?" asked Amon with childlike innocence.

"You don't know Simon, do you? Nice man, but you never know what he'll do or say next."

"Then what happened?"

"When they unloaded the boat, we counted one hundred and fifty five fish."

"Is that many?"

"That is more than what we catch in several days, and Jesus stood nearby as my sons and the workers counted them. That is when Peter ran over and knelt before Jesus and they spoke in private for a long time."

"What did he say?" asked Amon.

Zebedee cleared his throat and smiled. "My sons and my employees had fished all night and caught nothing, and that morning Jesus called to them from the shore and told them to cast their nets on the other side of the boat. That's how they caught . . . what must have been a record catch of fish."

"Where is the Messiah now?" asked Amon as he stood to his feet and shuffled his weight from one foot to the other. "You said he was at your house last night."

"I'm not finished my story," said Zebedee as motioned for Amon to sit. "Sit and I will tell you. Jesus is a carpenter and he is the one who told my sons how and where to fish. Have fishermen ever told carpenters how to build? NO! But this carpenter told fishermen how and where to catch fish, and look what happened."

"Is there yet more?" asked Amon.

"Jesus told my sons to follow him and that he would make them fishers of men. I could not say no, so I gave them my blessing. If Jesus is the Messiah, then who am I to say NO to him or my sons?"

"Where is he now?"

"He and my sons, along with several other men, are on their way to Jerusalem."

"Will they be back soon?" Amon asked.

"Yes, they will be back, but I don't know when."

"Well," said Amon, "I want to find them as soon as I can. Can I go now?"

"No, no, no," said Zebedee. "Stay with us for the night and in the morning you can start out for Jerusalem. Now tell me, why you have become interested in Jesus, the Messiah.

On their way to Zebedee's house, Amon began his story which started with Hannah's son being raised from the dead. They sat on the porch until Zebedee's wife, Salome, called them for supper.

Zebedee's home was small and needed repair, but it was a peaceful place and Amon felt welcome. Supper was a new experience for Amon. Salome prepared the fish and her husband immediately took a large portion and placed it in front of Amon, who looked at it for some time.

"Is this what I am to eat?" Amon asked, somewhat unsure of what to do.

"Have you never tasted fish before?" she asked.

"I've seen them and tasted them, but," he poked at it, "but they do not smell so good," said Amon in an apologetic tone.

"Well be careful of the bones," Zebedee said. "They are very different than the bones a lamb has. The bones are small and very sharp."

Salome interrupted as she sat down, "I have tried to take all of the bones out before and after it was cooked."

"Fish is good if you are not hungry. Do you know what I like about lamb? The bones are big and easy to find. Not like fish. Fish bones are . . . they're too small and hard to find. It takes too long to take them out. When I'm hungry, I like lamb." He smiled apologetically.

After supper, they spoke about Jesus and all the things that Zebedee and his sons had seen and heard.

"I heard someone say that the Messiah must be born in a King David town. Is that true?" asked Amon.

"His lineage is from King David and he was born in Bethlehem, which is the city of David. Jesus claims to be the Son of God; the God of our Fathers Abraham, Isaac and Jacob."

"But one rabbi said that the Tanakh tell us that God would call his son out of Egypt. I met some people from Egypt and they do not seem to be special people." He paused and then continued, "Is the Messiah Egyptian?"

"No," replied Zebedee. "Shortly after Jesus was born, King Herod made a decree that all Hebrew boys under the age of two should be put to death and that is when Joseph and Jesus' mother, Mary, escaped to Egypt until Kind Herod died. When they returned from Egypt . . . I guess in a way, he came out of Egypt."

"Who was his mother?"

Zebedee smiled, "His mother is of the line of David. Her name is Miryam (Mary)."

Their conversation continued until midnight and shortly after, Amon fell asleep with his head leaning against the kitchen wall. He snored loudly, so Zebedee and his wife went to bed and left him where he was.

It was the sound of a cock crowing in the neighbor's yard that awakened Amon. He moaned and opened one eye. After several attempts to sleep between the obnoxious crowing, he shouted, "Hey, Mr. Rooster, if God would have allowed us to eat the neighbor's birds like you, we could have kept you quiet a long time ago." He yawned loudly before mumbling, "At least we could get some sleep."

A few minutes later, he scratched his stomach and opened his eyes. "Hey, Zebedee who is the person that wakes those cocks so they can crow so early in the morning? I would like to know who does that job. I would like to speak with that person and tell him to wait a little longer in the morning."

Zebedee opened the door of his sleeping chamber. "What is it Amon?"

"Hey, Zebedee, if we would have had that cock for supper last night instead of that fish, maybe we could have slept longer." Amon rose from his nocturnal nest as Zebedee pulled back the tattered curtains to let the morning light enter the room.

Amon stretched and scratched his head again. "Today, I must find that Messiah. He may not come here until I am an old man."

After they had eaten, they went down to the pier and on their way, Amon turned to Zebedee, "I need to find the Messiah but I do not know where this Jerusalem is. My father, Beno, talked about it, but I do not know how to find it."

"If you wait a few days I'm sure my sons and Jesus will return from Jerusalem."

"What road do I take to get there?"

"No, Amon. Walking will take too long. I will sail you to the south end of the Sea of Galilee, but we can't leave today because a storm is coming.

The sky was very red before dawn and there is an east wind. All birds are gathering near the shore, so we may have to wait for a day or two for it to settle," said Zebedee.

"The sky and wind tell you that much?"

"When you have lived here as long as we have, you look at the sky, feel where the wind is blowing from and watch the birds. They will always face into the wind if there is a strong breeze."

The men spent the day quietly visiting and repairing nets in a small building attached to the pier. Amon had many questions about boats, fish and the trip to Jerusalem. He seemed eager to learn about everything around him, and after supper the two men remained in Zebedee's house because of the strong wind that was blowing across the sea.

Chapter XVI

SCYTHOPOLIS / BETH SHAN

Scythopolis, known to the Jews as Beth Shan, was a city that Varrus knew well because he had served there under Centurion Damarius prior to his days in Nain. Diversity was the most obvious aspect of this city. The population consisted of Jews, Romans, Samarians and people from the eastern side of the Jordan River. There were ten cities in the region and as a result that area was identified as Decapolis. Some emigrated from the Far East and regions north of Babylon while others came from the city of Ur, between the Euphrates and the Tigris Rivers. There were those, who came from the Elburz Mountains, south of the Caspian Sea and from Susa, on the western slope of the Zagros Mountains.

Violence east of the Jordan was the norm. Patrols sent from Scythopolis encountered many ambushes and eventually, the Legatus refused to send troops into that region beyond a half days ride. What the rebels in that area desired most were the horses that Rome had to carry out their raids.

When Varrus entered the barracks, he was greeted by Damarius his former officer, who had been promoted to Cohort Centurion. They spent the day discussing scheduled patrols north and west of Scythopolis. It was a region of many confrontations where numerous legionnaires were ambushed and killed.

For the first few days, Varrus drilled his cavalrymen until he was confident in their abilities to ride and use their weapons in battle. The Optio assigned to him was named Kofea, who had extensive experience in North Africa.

Shortly after Varrus' arrival, he summoned Pollus to join him.

****

Conspiracy With Malicious Intent

In the early morning light, Zebedee and Amon walked down to the pier to see if the boats were safely moored and if any damage had occurred during the night storm. Amon watched as the boats swayed amid the noisy and splashing waves. Sails rattled and overhead sea birds floated in the steadily increasing gusts of wind. Foam was forming around the algae covered rocks along the shoreline and occasionally, waves crashed loudly against the mossy wooden floats that were moored to the pier.

"There's a very strong wind today and on days such as this, fish are difficult to catch and sailing can be dangerous," said Zebedee. The wind has sunk many a boat out here so there is no reason to risk sailing when you don't have to."

"How do fish know that there is a wind when they live down there where there is no wind?"

"Well, I suppose, they . . ." he paused and looked inquisitively at Amon, "I don't know, but they seem to know because they are very hard to catch."

"Maybe the wind scatters them like it does the sheep."

"Maybe you're right. I never thought about it," responded Zebedee as he opened the knot of the rope that was used to hold the door of the shed closed.

As they spoke a large wave crashed against the side of one of Zebedee's boats causing it to bang noisily into the pier.

Palti shouted, "The storm is not over, so let's wait until noon."

"I agree," called Zebedee as he turned his face into the wind. "No one else is out on the water, so let's go into the shed and check our nets."

The storm on the Sea of Galilee became more intense and lasted four days. No one dared leave the shore for the waves were higher than many people remembered. Moored ships and small boats had to be tied with additional ropes to keep them from smashing against the pier. Some of the nets that had been left on the pier for repairs had been washed into the sea and there was considerable damage to several piers farther down the shoreline. Many of the boats needed to be emptied of water from the waves which often swept over the sides of the boats and threatened to sink them.

During the storm, Zebedee and his employees as well as other fishermen sat and visited with each other until the storm ended and then they repaired the pier, emptied water from their boats and reset the ropes and sails. Amon eagerly worked at every chore that was assigned to him. He was pleased to help Zebedee and the other men.

Conspiracy With Malicious Intent

The day following the cleanup was the Shabbat or the Sabbath, so no one sailed, fished or repaired nets. The following morning, the waters appeared calmer and soon ships began to appear on the sea.

Palti called to Zebedee, "We're almost ready to sail."

Zebedee waved to them as he and Amon neared the pier. Zebedee turned to Amon and said, "Have you ever been to Jerusalem?"

"I've heard about that place from my father Beno when he was alive. He went there several times to pray and told me that one day he would take me and Asa, but my father died from what we don't know."

"Well today we'll sail you to the south end of the sea and you can leave for Jerusalem from there. It will be quicker than if you walked from here, and besides you are less likely to be robbed when we sail than when you walk."

"I have never been in one of those wooden boxes. What if it sinks down to the place where fish are?"

"I have sailed since I was a child and have not drowned, so you'll be safe if you sail with me," insisted Zebedee.

Amon looked down at the boat and then at Zebedee. "What will happen if we suddenly stop moving, and maybe fall into the water? Will we be able to walk on the bottom?"

"Ha, ha, ha," laughed Zebedee. "You won't drown. It's safe to sail in a boat. Since you have been with me, how many times have you ever seen a boat sink into this water?"

"Does wood always stay on the upside of the water? Maybe I'm too heavy for it."

Zebedee continued to laugh, "Ha ha ha, my fathers and I have sailed on this sea for many years, and we have not died once. If all of us and all the fish cannot sink the ship, then you will be safe with me. Now trust me, grab the rope and step aboard."

"I have seen donkeys jump to make people fall off when they do not want to carry them, but . . . but if this box can jump when the wind pushes it, I'll fall and then disappear and, and I don't know how to walk under that water."

"Hurry," Zebedee urged as Amon raised his leg to step into the boat.

Palti and Judah, Zebedee's hired servants, were already on board, and they smiled as Amon grabbed one of the ropes and lifted his leg to enter the boat. After some hesitation, Amon said, "My foot is . . . he is willing but this hand of mine, he . . . he tells me that they do not want to die." Amon wobbled back and forth as the ship moved up and down with the waves.

"LET GO OF THE PIER AMON! IT'S SAFE," shouted Palti.

"ALL THESE YEARS MY HANDS HAVE OBEYED ME BUT NOW, THEY WILL NOT LISTEN TO ME AND LET GO OF THIS HERE ROPE."

"Don't be afraid Amon," coaxed Zebedee as he reached for Amon.

Once Amon was onboard, Palti and Judah adjusted the sail and Zebedee turned the boat out to the middle of the sea as Amon finally slumped onto a large roll of nets. A few moments later, he sat up to see where they were going. His eyes darted from the shore to other boats and back to the shore as the ship swayed from side to side as it responded to the waves and the breeze.

Overhead, seabirds floated in the wind and occasionally swooped to the surface as though they had seen something to eat. Ropes and rigging snapped loudly when the breeze tugged at the sails.

"Are you sure that we can get back to your house from where we're going?" asked Amon.

"Yes," replied Zebedee as he waved to some lifetime friends in another boat that was passing some distance away.

Occasionally gusts of wind caused the ship to sway and roll so it was no surprise that Amon was beginning to feel ill. He made his way to the edge of the deck and was about to lean over, when Palti taped him on the shoulder.

"If you are going to be sick, then go to the other side. The wind in your face will make you very unhappy."

"I . . . I . . . I'm trying to like this here ride, but my stomach tells me, NO." He leaned over for several breaths and then looked at Palti. "Can you help me to the other side and . . . and be quick?"

Amon hung his head over the side of the ship for a long time and when he looked up, Zebedee called to him. "Amon, you look like the inside of a pomegranate. Your eyes are red and the rest of your face is yellow."

"This is worse than riding on a angry donkey."

Palti and Judah looked at each other and laughed.

"I don't feel so good. I feel worse than I remember. Will I ever be well again?" asked Amon as he rubbed his stomach, closed his eyes and moaned loudly.

After several hours, the surface became calm, and their ride became more enjoyable.

Amon looked over the edge and saw his reflection on the surface of the water and tried to smile. His beard was wet, his hair was messy, and with childlike innocence, he waved at himself.

"Zebedee, I think dying in the water is easier than living on it. My eyes don't see too good, and my stomach . . . he will never eat again, unless it is roasted goat or lamb."

"You'll be fine. Just let the breeze blow in your face and breathe the fresh air. Oh, by the way, keep your eyes on the shore."

Some time later, Palti asked, "Do you feel better now?"

"I think so, but I'm still not sure. At first I thought this was as bad as riding a donkey that was meshugga, but now I feel that this is much easier when the wind stops. It is better than riding on a camel, too. Besides, this smells much better and there are no flies out here."

In the late afternoon a breeze blew the spray from the bow over the starboard side and splashed Amon's face. He smiled and rubbed his wet beard and licked his lips. "Zebedee," he called as he motioned for Zebedee to join him, "has the Messiah been on this here boat?"

"Yes."

"This very boat? The Messiah has been here?" Amon pointed to the deck as he spoke.

"Yes."

"Where did he stand and where did he sit?"

"Everywhere, I guess. He even helped pull the nets and helped unload fish from the boat."

"If he is the Messiah from God, how come he does work?"

"I don't know. When you see him, ask him."

Zebedee's boat continued southward toward the end of the Sea of Galilee, where the Jordan River begins to flow southward toward the Dead Sea. The sun sat on the peaks of the western hills and the sky glowed as the valley began to darken. A warm breeze danced among the trees along the shoreline and small waves lapped at the side of Zebedee's boat. Overhead, the moon flooded the landscape with subtle yellow light. In the distance, the glow of evening lamps in houses could be seen along the shoreline.

"We'll sleep on the boat tonight and in the morning we'll drop you off at that pier by the trees," said Zebedee. "Palti and Judah will let down the anchor, so let's go down and cook some food."

"I cannot eat because my stomach is not ready for food. It still wants to be sick so can I stay up here and smell the fresh air?"

Later that evening, the men visited by the candlelight and retold stories of their past. Amon was particularly interested in what the Messiah had said and done.

Conspiracy With Malicious Intent

"Zebedee, tell me more about the Messiah."

"Well when my sons stopped at our house just before I met you, they told of a very interesting thing that happened at Capernaum. A Roman Centurion came and asked Jesus if he would heal his servant, so when Jesus said that he would come to the Centurion's house, the Centurion told Jesus to just say the word and the servant would be healed. Jesus said he was amazed at the faith this Centurion had, so he healed him without going to his house."

"The Messiah heals Gentiles. I thought he was our Messiah."

"I guess Jesus did it because he likes people." Zebedee yawned, stood to his feet and said, "Well I don't know about you three, but I'm going to sleep." He walked over to the corner where there was a coil of rope and lay on it, and soon the others found comfortable places to sleep.

In the morning, Zebedee called to Amon. "SAILOR. Did you have a great sleep?"

"Yaaaaaaaaawwwwwwwnn . . . yes," moaned Amon as he stretched until he shivered. "Is it morning already?" When Amon sat up he could see that Palti and Judah had prepared food, so all of them ate before going to the main deck.

"Where do I go, Zebedee?" Amon asked as he leaned over the railing of the ship to look at the distant pier.

"Just follow the Jordan River, and when the sun is almost overhead, you will pass Mount Tabor on your right. Follow the river until you meet a main road from the other side of the river. Many travelers use it to go over the western hills to the coast of the Mediterranean Sea."

"It will not take me to this here place called Egypt, will it? I was with some of those Gentiles in Nain, and one of them made me carry the rope of a stinky camel."

"What's wrong with Gentiles?" asked Zebedee.

"They hate us Jews and they are not to be trusted," said Amon, confidently.

"Palti is a Gentile. Do you trust him?" asked Judah.

"Palti . . . he is . . . one of those Gentiles?" Amon's eyes widened. "How did he become a Gentile? He seems like such a nice man, that I thought he must be a . . .!"

"He's a Samaritan, who saved my life. If he can be nice to a man like me," said Zebedee, "then I can be nice to him."

Amon put his hand over his mouth, as he looked a Palti.

Palti came over to Amon. "Zebedee has been very kind to me and my family. His kindness has fed my family for many years, and he has never told the people in Capernaum that I am a Samaritan."

"How did someone nice like you become a Samaritan?"

"My father came from Thebes and I think my mother was from the Tribe of Reuben. When they died, I was alone and so to survive I traveled around the Sea of Galilee and that is when I met Zebedee."

When the boat neared the pier, Zebedee motioned to Amon. "If you go on that road," he said as he pointed to the shore, "it will take you to a beautiful city called Beth Shan. The Romans call it Scythopolis. It is some distance away. When you near it, cross the Jezreel River and begin the gentle climb to a valley. In that valley, you will find the city."

"It sounds easy."

"Just remember to stay to your right and follow the main road into Scythopolis. If you miss the main highway, you will end up in the rough terrain of the Seddan Valley and the climb is rather difficult and very dangerous because of thieves in the area."

"Zebedee, if I get lost, can I come back and find you?" asked Amon with a twinkle in his eyes.

"You won't get lost. Once you're in Scythopolis, you can take the high road to Shechem and then on to Jerusalem. Both roads are known to have many thieves, so I think that you will be safer to take the road to Shechem."

"Robbers? But I have nothing to rob. What will they want?" asked Amon as he shrugged his shoulders and raised his hands above his waist.

"To be safe, travel in the daytime and rest for the night at an inn."

The ship touched the pier and Palti jumped out of the ship and secured the boat to the pier. After Zebedee and Amon were on the pier, Zebedee nervously shifted his weight from one foot to the other. "Stay away from thieves."

"What kinds of Hebrews are out here?" asked Amon. "Don't they know the commandment about not stealing?"

"Those who disobey the commandments and the Law care less whether they break the sixth or the eighth commandment," responded Zebedee.

"Robbers don't kill you or they would be called murderers. Robbers rob you, so be careful," Palti said as he smiled at Amon.

"When you find Jesus, be sure to tell my sons that you stayed at my house. They will be pleased."

"Here is some money to help you and may God go with you, my friend. I hope that you have a chance to meet Jesus. He's a marvelous person, who has been sent by God. As I told you, he teaches from the scriptures, heals and feeds the people. He has done great things for my sons and their friends." With sadness in his voice he said, "Shalom, my friend."

Zebedee returned to his boat as Palti and Judah pushed the boat from the pier. Within minutes, the sails were opened and Zebedee's boat began to sail northward toward home.

"SHALOM," shouted Amon and Zebedee waved.

Amon watched the ship until it faded into the distance and then he sat on the pier and became melancholy for he found this separation difficult to accept. He remained seated until noon. Several times, he looked for Zebedee's boat but it was out of sight. Reluctantly, he started walking toward several buildings in the distance and eventually found a market, so he walked around the market to see what the vendors were selling. When he was about to leave the market, he happened to see a rabbi.

He moved among the people and animals to intercept him near a row of trees. He approached the rabbi, who was about to sit under at tree. The rabbi was busy discussing something with an elderly man, so Amon waited for an opportune moment to interrupt their conversation.

Every time Amon raised his pointer finger to speak, the rabbi would raise one hand, indicating that Amon should stay out of the conversation, so Amon sat down and leaned against the tree next to them but fell asleep.

Unaware of how long he had been sleeping, he was startled when the rabbi touched his coat, so he sat up and tried to adjust his blurred vision to see who had awakening him.

"You are new here, are you not?" asked the rabbi. "Did you want to speak with me?"

"Yes! Yes, I am Amon," he managed to say as he shook his head to clear his mind.

"That is nice but what is your question? There's no rush. I can wait," responded the rabbi. "Rushing will make you old, so what is it that you want?"

"Oh, yes. I remember," Amon said as he blinked his eyes. "Have you seen the Messiah that travels here?"

"A Messiah is here? What makes you think a Messiah is somewhere in this here place?"

"He's the prophet that feeds the people and heals others. I saw him raise Hannah's boy back to life, when he was in Nain."

"So, who said he's a Messiah?" asked the rabbi as he narrowed his brows. "Did he ever say he was a Messiah?" he demanded.

"In Nain and in Capernaum, people say that he's a Messiah," replied Amon in an apologetic tone."

"You're from Nain? That is not far from here, but why do you ask me such a question?"

"Have you seen him?" asked Amon. "I'm looking for him."

"We are all waiting for the Messiah, but what is he to you and why do you think he's a Messiah?"

Amon spent an extended amount of time telling his story about Hannah and how he had come to the Capernaum and to the south end of the Sea of Galilee. The rabbi sat quietly, nodded and grunted occasionally.

When Amon ended his story, the rabbi looked at Amon. "I'm just glad that you didn't come from some place farther than Nain. It would have been dark by the time you would have finished your story. Are you yet finished?"

In a long and breathy sound, Amon answered, "Y-e-s."

The rabbi rubbed his chin as he spoke, "So what is your question?"

Amon raised his hand as he looked at the rabbi, "I guess now that I'm here, I'm afraid to go to Jerusalem."

"Fear robs men of their dignity and potential. Do you have dignity?"

"I think so," Amon whispered in an apologetic tone.

"What about potential?"

"I don't know!" responded Amon. "What is that?"

"SEE! I told you. It will rob you in some way." The rabbi paused, "So you want to go to Jerusalem, do you? It is yet far from here. Jerusalem you can find, but a Messiah, I don't know about. Go to Jerusalem and may God go with you." With that, the rabbi stood to his feet and walked away, leaving Amon sitting alone under the sycamore tree.

Chapter XVII

THE BATTLE AND THE LONG NIGHT

It was Amon's fear that prevented him from leaving the village and by the time he decided that waiting would not be helpful, it was too late to leave for the open countryside, especially since he had never been on that road before. He walked to the south end of the village and looked for a comfortable and safe place to stay for the night. When he saw a man milking a goat, he cautiously approached him.

"My name is Amon and I have come from Nain."

"That is not far from here."

"My distance has been long. I have come from Capernaum and towns along the way. I need a safe place for the night. Can I stay by your back door? It will be safer than leaving for Jerusalem tonight."

They spoke for some time before the man agreed, and so Amon spent the evening alone on a porch facing a small pen with animals. When darkness fell, he lay over to sleep and some time during the night, the owner of the house, asked him to move to the trees near the pen because of his loud snoring.

He was awakened by the sound of a cock crowing and thought about throwing something at it, but realized that the man, who had let him stay for the night may not be too pleased, so he rolled over and covered his ears with his hands.

Later that morning, he ate some of the food that Zebedee had given him and then walked down to the banks of the Jordan River. There, he listened to the birds and enjoyed watching the animals drinking. He remained there for a long time before beginning his journey along the Jordan River.

At first he walked at a rapid pace, but soon slowed his walk and by late afternoon his feet were becoming very sore. He realized that he had left too late and since he was unsure of the remaining distance, he looked up at the sun to determine how many hours of sunshine were left in the day. The journey may have been only twelve miles but by now Amon was exhausted. When darkness was about to overtake him, he moved to a grove of trees that would provide cover for the night.

When he awakened, he was stiff and sore from sleeping on the ground, but was pleased that he had saved some of the money that Zebedee had given him. It never crossed his mind that his loud snoring could have been his demise for it would be easy for robbers to know where he was.

After he had eaten, he began the journey with full intentions of arriving in a city by noon. When the sun was at its zenith, he passed a large hill on his right. "That must be the mountain that Zebedee told me about," he muttered to himself.

When three merchants, leading four donkeys, approached him he asked, "What is the name of that mountain."

One of them replied, "Mount Tabor."

"There is a city somewhere with a name . . . Scythe something. Can you tell me where it is?"

"Scythopolis? It's straight ahead," the older man said. "We Jews call it Beth Shan." Then they turned and walked away.

Amon continued along the road while looking for landmarks that Zebedee had told him about. Ahead of him, he spotted a large group of men walking toward him and fear caused him to leave the path prematurely. He turned to his right and walked along a small path leading toward a tiny valley that ultimately led him up a long incline toward the top of a hill.

He had forgotten that he was to walk southward, until he crossed the Harod River in the Jezreel Valley. Just beyond that river, he would have intersected with a large cross-country road that came from the eastern side of the Jordan River. There, he was to turn to his right or westward, and follow the road to Scythopolis, a major Roman military centre.

Amon's error in calculation led him onto a narrowing path and into a ravine. After several thousand strides, he realized that the valley was becoming increasingly steeper and narrower, so he decided to climb to the top of the ridge to see where he was. When he got to the top of the ridge, he noticed a large hill in the distance. Unknowingly, he was looking at Mount Gilboa not far from Scythopolis.

Amon was about to choose a pathway down the southern slope when he heard something in the distance, so he turned to look into the valley. In the distance, there appeared to be a large group of men on foot, fighting with mounted soldiers. He shaded his eyes with his left hand and squinted for a better view. It was difficult to count the number of men because of the heat waves, but Amon was certain that there were more men on foot than mounted soldiers. He crouched to the ground to hide his presence, as he watched the battle. It appeared to him that some of cavalrymen were being dragged from their mounts. The battle raged on for a long time. Amon watched as spears, swords, arrows and slings found their mark. The activity riveted Amon's attention and he became unaware of time.

"What does this have to do with me?" Amon mumbled to himself as he turned his back to walk away. Leaving was difficult for him, so he squatted down and continued to watch the battle. Eventually, every cavalryman was on the ground and in a fierce hand-to-hand battle for their very lives. Even though they seemed outnumbered, the soldiers seemed to be gaining control of the battle.

Amon sat motionless, unsure of what to do next. After some time had passed, he noticed that some of the horses were trotting away because several men were chasing them. The battle seemed over and Amon watched as men began to strip the injured and dead of their clothing and weapons. Several men used swords to slash wounded soldiers, who were lying motionless on the ground. Only a few soldiers remained standing as the enemies abandoned the fight.

Amon lay on his belly to hide his presence. Another hour passed and by now the battle had abated into an eerie silence. Time seemed insignificant as he observed little or no movement by those lying on the ground.

In the quietness that followed, Amon rose to one knee and looked in every direction to be sure that no one had seen him. Eventually, he stood to his feet but when he was about to leave, his conscience gripped him as he mumbled to himself. "They need the Messiah, but I have not found him yet."

He stared at the killing field as he spoke to himself again. "Maybe the Messiah would heal them, or maybe raise the dead ones back to life." A moment later he asked himself, "What has this got to do with me? I don't like Roman Gentiles. Look what they did to Asa."

He turned his back to walk away, but stopped again to have one last look. "I know what the Messiah would do. He would make them all alive again," he whispered and cautiously started down the hill toward the downed warriors. As he approached, he became suddenly aware of the massive injures that had been inflicted during this battle. His heart pounded and his mouth was dry at the thought of being in the midst of this battle zone.

Dead men and horses seemed to be everywhere. At first glance, he counted thirteen Roman soldiers on the ground and at least double that number of ordinary men, whom he realized were fellow Jews.

He knelt beside the first soldier, who had been struck with an arrow through the throat. "Gentiles," he mumbled as he recoiled. "I knew it. God doesn't mind if they die so why should I?"

Moving from body to body, he found many dead. One had his arm severed, who must have bled to death. The next two lay on their side with spears thrust through abdomens. Two rebels had been killed with a blunt object and the sixth had been stabbed through the abdomen with a large crude sword. Other warriors had been slashed with swords and two them had their bowels spilt onto the ground. There was an odor of death and violence amid the eerie silence.

Amon stopped next to four horses that had fallen, the result of spears being thrust through their rib cages. Another horse staggered several strides away from where Amon stood, and then it moaned as it fell to the ground with a loud thud. Its last gasp heralded death spasms and convulsions.

To his left, Amon came upon two cavalrymen, moaning in pain, their life ebbing away before him. Without realizing it, he had been to the side of every downed cavalryman and every rebel that had been part of the battle. Amon tried to bind their wounds by using strips of cloth from his outer cloak and his blue sash that had been around his waist. He tore clothing from dead bodies and used them to control the bleeding of those that were writhing in pain.

Tirelessly, he worked under the late afternoon sun until he was near exhaustion. After Amon had bound the wounded, he returned to where he had started his triage. On his second round of assessment, he realized that only five cavalrymen and nine renegades were alive. Again, he went from man to man, not favoring anyone.

On his final assessment, five soldiers and one renegade remained alive. All others had succumbed to their injuries. He sat down on the ground and looked at his blooded hands as tears marked his dusty cheeks.

"What am I to do? I have had bad dreams, but this, this one does not yet end." He closed his eyes and hung his head in silence until he heard a voice.

The only surviving renegade called as he motioned for Amon to come near. When Amon knelt beside him, the injured man whispered, "If you're smart," he wheezed and air bubbles mixed with blood oozed from his chest, "you'll kill the . . . the Romans and . . . and . . ." This time he coughed loudly and placed his hand on his wound. "Wait until they come back for me . . . and I'll tell them what you did." He paused to catch his breath. "Kill the Romans. Do you hear me? Kill them!" His words became difficult to understand and ignore. Again, he coughed and blood oozed from his chest as he raised his hand to Amon. "If you are the son of Abraham, you'll kill the Romans. Kill them while you can. They will kill you when they arrive." He coughed and moaned loudly before continuing. "If they return," he paused to take a shallow painful breath, "they will think you are one of us, so kill them . . . now!" His voice ebbed into a whisper and silence.

"You have been so busy killing that you forgot about yourself," said Amon.

After taking another breath, the wounded rebel whispered, "If the Romans return . . . and find you here . . . they will cut you up like strips of fish." He coughed and winced in pain as blood ran freely from his mouth and nostrils. "They'll think that you're with us. So kill them and live."

Amon nervously licked his lips, and his eyes did not blink. This was his chance to kill Gentile soldiers for what they had done to Asa. He stared at a spear lying on the ground near him and memories of Asa flashed into his mind. He felt the heat of anger in his stomach.

"It will be easy," whispered the injured rebel as he gasped for a shallow breath. He did not take his eyes off of Amon.

Amon bent down to grasp the spear and started to walk toward the legionnaire nearest him. As he raised the spear, he heard the soldier whisper, "If you . . . if you will take us back to Scythopolis . . . I will personally see that you . . ." he coughed and lay still. His shiny leather vest did not move but blood ran down his cheek and dripped onto his partially severed hand.

A second legionnaire propped himself up on his elbow and said, "If you get help for us and my officer, we'll see to it that you'll be rewarded." He fell back onto the ground and moaned.

Amon looked off into the valley and saw several horses in the distance. Some of them appeared to be injured and one of them crouched to the ground and fell slowly to its side.

Amon dropped the spear and looked at the injured mounts in the distance and suddenly felt sorry for them. "I don't know anything about horses, except that they are noisy and snort at both ends when they walk but they did nothing to deserve this."

He walked slowly to the bottom of the hill to where the horses stood. When he was within several strides of them, he realized that he had never touched one before, so he cautiously reached for the reins.

"Mister Gentile horse, I have led a camel and several donkeys but you look different. So Mister Gentile horse, here is your chance to be gentle. I hope that you are easier to lead than stubborn donkeys or that stinky Egyptian camel I had to lead out of Nain." He swallowed as he grasped the reigns. Instead of shying away, the mare stood still and breathing heavily. Blood dripped from a large wound in her rib cage, and when Amon led her to where an injured legionnaire lay, it limped on a severely injured right front foot.

Three other horses followed and only one of them started to walk away to join eight others farther down the ravine. They seemed so exhausted from the heat and the battle. Six of them had serious wounds to their sides, three had arrows impaled into their necks and one had a spear handle protruding from its stomach. Foam clung to their flanks and bubbles of air mixed with blood ran down to its underbelly.

It was late afternoon when Amon realized that he would have to spend the night with the injured men. He walked up the hill to retrieve his personal items and food. When he returned, he opened the pouch and walked to each man to offer some food. Later he offered each man a drink of water from several water canisters he found tied to the horse's saddles. Only one of the legionnaire refused to eat or drink.

The only surviving rebel remained silent as he watched Amon and when Amon approached him with water, he grabbed Amon's arm, "Do it now," he whispered, "or I will personally kill you."

Amon pulled his arm away from the rebel's grip. "Your hatred is greater than mine. If it were I lying on this sand, you would not help me, a fellow Jew. Maybe you deserve this, this death. I am a son of Abraham yet I control my hatred to help you."

Amon was aware that the sun was now touching upper rim of the western hills, and that transportation was out of the question. He rested for several minutes and then walked among the dead to be sure that he had not missed any that were alive. He gathered all of the weapons into one pile and placing them at a safe distance from both legionnaires and the rebel. He watched as one injured horse lowered its head to the ground and continued its labored breathing. It was the first time that Amon felt sympathy toward an animal. He stood near the injured animal and felt uneasy as it swayed restlessly, from side to side in an attempt to relieve its pain.

"You were forced to come into this valley to die. I will be sad that you will not live through the night," he said as he watched the blood dripping from the nose of injured animal. "Let me take that heavy saddle off your back so you can breathe and die without a load." He approached the horse and opened the buckle of the cinch and watched as the saddle slid to the ground, allowing the horse to breathe with less effort. Amon realized that the horse had a wound in its ribs, so he ran to bring a dressing for its injury.

By the time he returned, the gelding was on the ground and grunting loudly. Blood was now flowing from his mouth and nose, and its breathing became eerily irregular. Amon knelt beside the horse as it moved its head toward him and he felt the urge to reach out and touch it, when suddenly it shivered, stretched his legs and eventually stopped breathing. Amon remained next to the dead horse for some time before standing and wiping his blooded hand on his clothing.

Amon decided to place the legionnaires in one group, so he tried to carry the youngest legionnaire to the side of his fallen officer. The soldier moaned loudly and held his abdomen as Amon dragged him across the dry rocky soil. When they could go no farther, both he and the injured young man slumped to the ground.

"You know that as a Jew, I should not even be touching you. Come lay here for it will soon be night," said Amon.

The injured cavalryman gasped for breath and whispered what Amon thought was 'thank you.'

When Amon had regained his strength, he rose to his feet and dragged another young man to the side of a large irregular shaped rock. "Here, lie down beside this other Gentile," he whispered as he laid the young man on the ground. "Both of you can talk to each other while I, a Jew, keep you from dying."

As he walked away, another legionnaire cried out in pain.

When Amon passed the injured rebel, he raised his bloodied hand and said, "It is almost night time and soon my friends will be back." He coughed and Amon heard a gurgling sound in his throat. The rebel continued, "They are probably watching you right now . . . and planning what they will do to you."

"Save your breath," growled Amon as he moved away from the renegade. "If they are busy watching, why are they not coming and helping?

Have you thought of that? Are they afraid they may have to help? Not only are they murders but they are lazy. Let them watch all they want. Maybe they will learn something." His voice was angry and he sounded impatient.

Amon tried to help the third soldier to his feet but his body suddenly went limp and he slumped forward onto his face. He struck the ground so heavily that his helmet fell off and it rolled several feet away. Amon picked up the helmet and tried to place it back onto his head, but it fell off again, so he left the legionnaire where he had fallen.

"Why should I . . ." Amon gasped, "a Hebrew, help you Gentiles? If I had been out here alone today maybe you, yes you, and your fancy swords would have killed me like you did my brother, Asa."

The officer closed his eyes and rolled onto his back. "How many of my men are alive," he whispered as he held his abdomen.

"How many of you Gentiles were there?"

"Sixteen and . . . and I."

"Well, all I found alive are here with you. Count them, there are three of you Gentiles," he said as he slumped to the ground, exhausted from his last errand of mercy.

"HOW MANY OF US ARE ALIVE," shouted the injured rebel.

"Only you, but I should not help you because you are a murderous fool too. If I had been out here alone today, maybe you and your murderous friends would have slit my throat for the food in my sack. It is you I should kill, and not these Gentiles. A murderous Jew, who is willing to kill another Jew for food should not live. Do you not know the sixth commandment?" He sighed before continuing, "Why should you remember the sixth commandment when you forgot the eighth commandment about not stealing?"

Amon eventually divided the flat bread, figs and dried fish that he had in his pack and returned to the injured. "Here, eat to keep your Gentile hides alive," he said as he handed them some of his food. Two of them ate, but the officer refused.

As they ate, Amon mumbled, "God, I have come to find your Messiah and not to help these evil, hopeless Gentiles and this, this murderous Hebrew. All I wanted to do is find the Messiah. Why did you decide to bless me with these, who do not keep your commandments?"

"Give the food to my men," the officer insisted. "They're the ones that need it, besides, I may not live through the night, and I do not want to waste any . . ." His words became a whisper.

Amon offered the last piece of flat bread to the rebel, who grabbed it ungratefully from his hands and sneered at Amon as he said, "If you want to live, you will kill the Romans and keep me alive until my friends come back."

"If they're coming back," replied Amon, "they'd better hurry before I decide to break the sixth commandment and KILL YOU MYSELF," he shouted. "NOW EAT AND BE QUIET! I saved your miserable life and you are ungrateful. You're worse than those pagans," he said as he pointed to the cavalrymen on the ground. Then he stood to his feet, spit on the ground and mumbled as he walked away, "The Romans are grateful for what I have done, but you . . . you do nothing but bleed and complain, so bleed, but do it in silence."

Chapter XVIII

THE OFFICER AND THE MIRROR

Soon after the sun had set, the five unfortunate men, including Amon began to feel the cool night air. Amon considered starting a fire but he feared that unwanted guests would arrive, so he made one final effort to be sure that each of the men were in a comfortable position. Then he went from dead man to dead man looking for clothing which he distributed among the wounded.

"This will keep you warm during the night. The dead won't feel the cold," he said as he handed extra clothing to the injured. He made sure that all weapons had been gathered and placed next to where he lay.

The Roman officer called to him, "You've done well, but I would suggest that you," he paused to cough before continuing, "gather wood to burn because the night air will be cold and the fire will keep the jackals away from the dead."

"What is a jackals? Is that another Roman thing I need to know about?" asked Amon as he tried to make himself comfortable on the ground.

"They're animals that will feed on dead carcasses. They will be here soon and a fire may keep them away." Again he coughed to remove the phlegm and blood from his throat. "If you listen, you can hear them calling to each other."

"Yes, start a fire," said the rebel. "My companions will see it and come back to save me."

"What do jackals look like?"

"They're wild dogs that travel in packs," responded the other injured cavalryman.

Amon ignored their comments and just before total darkness enveloped them, Amon wrapped himself in a torn cloth he had taken from a dead rebel. Before he fell asleep, he considered what he should do when the morning light would appear. Just as he was about to fall asleep, the officer heard Amon mumble, "If the Messiah was here, he could raise some of these people but then they would fight again so what would be the use?"

Fortunately the ground was warm from the sunshine it received during the day but it was very uncomfortable because of the small rocks and thorns. The cool night air caused Amon to shiver, but it did not seem to interrupt his snoring. Several times, the moaning of the injured men awakened him, but he managed to fall asleep again.

In the distance, jackals called to each other, and their calls came ever closer, knowing that the darkness would provide cover to a feast that they and their pups were looking forward to.

One nocturnal howl was particularly close and it awakened Amon. "I have heard cocks crowing in the morning, but now some other animal calls in the night to wake me. What kind of place is this?" He mumbled as he rolled over and pulled a piece of cloth over his shoulders.

He was suddenly awakened as a cold chill ran up his spine, and the hairs on his arms reacted to create dimpled skin. The rate of his breathing increased and he suddenly felt threatened. In the early morning twilight, he could see forms like thin dogs creeping among the corpses.

A legionnaire suddenly screamed, and Amon jumped to his feet. He tilted his head so that his eyes might adjust to the dim light. There before him were several animals that resemble dogs. One of them growled at Amon.

He kicked sand at it and shouted, "YAH!"

Again the legionnaire screamed and Amon, now lacking fear, ran to where he heard the scream and knelt down beside injured young man.

"My arm," gasped the legionnaire, "one of the jackals bit me." Moaning loudly from the new injury, the legionnaire pointed into the darkness. "There, over there, that's where it went."

"I told you to light a fire to keep the jackals from coming near us," said the Roman officer. "If they're willing to attack the living, you can count on them eating the dead."

"They look like dogs," said Amon as he scanned the immedate area. "You probably scared them off," said the officer.

"What do I do now?"

"They'll be back, so you may have to sit up to keep them away," the officer replied.

Conspiracy With Malicious Intent

In the subtle morning light, Amon heard something and suddenly sat upright. He looked at the cavalrymen lying next to him and then stood to his feet to look for the rebel, who was nowhere to be found. Amon scanned the horizon for him but saw no one. He tried to count the horses but realized that he never did know how many were alive before darkness fell.

The Roman officer tried to lift his head but slumped back to the ground. The youngest of the three soldiers did not move and when Amon knelt beside him, he discovered that he had died during the night.

"Your friend here is dead. Did any of you talk to him during the night?" Amon asked. He looked around and noticed that another horse was lying on its side, and guessed that it had also died during the night.

"I heard something this morning, but it was too dark to see anything. Maybe that's when the rebel ran away," said the second legionnaire as he coughed to clear his throat and gain control of his breathing.

"Rebels, I think they are worse than Gentiles," Amon mumbled to himself. He shared the last of piece food with the officer and last surviving legionnaire.

By now morning light was painting the eastern sky with bright orange and yellow light. Amon felt less fearful of jackals as he stood next to the Roman officer.

"I cannot carry you and you cannot carry me, so what do we do now? Should I use a horse to carry you?"

"We're too injured to be carried by horses but if you can find my grey horse, the one with the red beads on the bridle, you will find a mirror in my saddlebag," said the officer. "Bring it to me."

"Grey horse? What will I find?" asked Amon.

"A mirror. It's a shiny piece of glass that shows your face."

"What is my face doing in a Roman soldier's saddle?" Fear suddenly gripped Amon's heart for he was afraid that the officer knew of his escape from Nain.

"The saddlebag is a leather pouch on my horse."

"I know what they are because I made them in Nabal's shop but how did my face .. ?"

"Just go and bring my horse," interrupted the officer as he cleared his mouth of blood and mucous. "If my horse is dead, then open the saddlebag and bring the mirror to me. It may save all of our miserable lives," he said as he tried to control his painful breathing.

Amon ran down the hillside and when he found a grey horse with the red beaded bridle, he walked over to it. It lay dead with a javelin deeply thrust into its rib cage. Amon approached cautiously as if he expected it to suddenly stand to its feet. He reached into the saddlebag and pulled out several parchments, a knife, some dressings for wounds, several pieces of dried meat and an oval shaped shiny piece of glass. Amon turned it over in his hands and to his shock, there before him, was his face.

"Gentiles! How did these pagans get my face and put it into this, this thing?" He tilted it downward and noticed that his face disappeared. "Where did I go? This must be what that pagan wants. How will he be able to save our lives with this?" Moments later he ran to where the officer lay. "Is this what you want?" he called as he waved the mirror in his hand.

"Yes," he whispered.

"But my face? How did you . . ?"

The officer reached for the mirror, his voice much weaker now than before. "Now listen to me. You," he cleared his throat again, "you must do exactly what I tell you or we will die. If the rebels come back to pick up the swords and spears, they will kill both of us and I know that they do not need you anymore."

"What have I done to make them angry? I have fed them and tried to keep them alive so for that they will kill me? If they do, they are worse than pagans. I will do what you say but I . . ." he paused.

The officer raised his hand. "See that hill over there, that tallest one?" When Amon turned, the officer repeated his question, "Do you see it?" before he lay back on the ground and closed his eyes.

Amon nodded.

Again the officer took several shallow breaths before opening his eyes. "If you climb to the top of that hill, and tilt this mirror toward the sun, it will cast light toward Scythopolis. Someone will see the light and will come to our rescue." The officer held the mirror up to the light and when he tilted it away, Amon saw the strong reflection of the sun on the ground. When the officer moved it again, Amon's eyes followed the blinding reflection on the dry ground.

"Do you see how the sun hits the mirror and then . . . then it sends the light to the ground?"

Amon nodded and cautiously responded, "Y-e-s," in a slow and drawn out manner.

"That bright light is what you must send to Scythopolis. When you get to the top of the hill, face the sun." The officer paused and breathed slowly. "Tip the mirror upward toward the sun and then move it down toward the ground until you see the reflection on the ground." Again he paused to take a painful breath before he contining, "Tilt the mirror slowly to your right about two long strides and raise it up to the horizon and point it toward the city in the dark valley. Do you understand?"

"How will I know where the . . ?"

"Look for the lights of Scythopolis. It's a city and it's in the dark valley this time of the morning. Do you understand?"

"Yes. I think so, but I have never done this before and why is my face in that thing?"

"Your face is not in the mirror."

"But I saw it in there and . . ."

"Once the reflection is on the city, move it side to side for some time and then do it again and again. Do it for as long time as the light will shines to the city."

"I will do my best," responded Amon as he slowly reached for the mirror.

"Only three of us are alive. You must go as fast as you can. The light is at the top of those hills . . . but it is still dark in the valley where Scythopolis is. So when you send the light into the dark valley, the watchmen will see it. Go hurry!"

Amon started for the distant hill as the officer lay back onto the ground. Many thoughts raced through Amon's mind as he ran. "What if I meet the rebels? What if the rebel, who escaped finds me? What if the sun doesn't shine to this here Scythos city?" he mumbled as he climbed the steep hill.

He was often too tired to continue the steep climb, but a combination of fear and excitement motivated him. His ankles hurt and the muscles in his calves burned. He stopped once to look back to where the soldiers were and to the site of the battle, but found it difficult to see them because twilight was still in the ravine where they were. Momentarily he waved at them and then rushed up the slope, and when he reached the top of the hill, Amon was unsure of where to stand, let alone where to point the mirror's reflection.

"Well, first I must," he paused, "the sun is over there and that Scythos place is, whatever the name of that place is, must be over down there somewhere. If I was walking up that hill," he said to himself pointing with the pointer finger, "that city must be in that dark valley over there." He blinked his eyes, "I think I see some lights."

Nervously he fumbled with the mirror and discovered to his amazement that the reflection of the sun was very bright on the ground in front of him. For practice, he shone it on various rocks until he began to understand what to do. Facing the sun, he raised the mirror and then tilted it downward until the reflection was at his feet. Turning toward Scythopolis, he tried to aim the beam of light into the dark valley. He moved the mirror back and forth hoping to see something.

"I forgot to ask that pagan how long I should shine this thing toward that place. Maybe I'll have to stay up here until dark," he said to himself. "Well, let me see. I should do this again to be sure."

Amon found it difficult to aim the sun's rays toward Scythopolis because the city was now receiving some sunlight. "God made the sun to move across the sky so maybe there is too much light there already to see anything," he said to himself as he lowered the mirror. Then he turned it over in his hand. His image fascinated him and he tried to smile. So this is what Amon looks like. I remember seeing my face in a pail of water but this thing doesn't shake like water. Amon," he said as he smiled, "you're an old man but still look like a good man. Maybe, your beard is too grey and your eyebrows are too bushy, but you, yes you are still looking good." He waved at himself in the mirror before he started down the hillside toward the killing field.

When he arrived, he looked at the two soldiers and handed the mirror to the officer, but the officer insisted that he keep it.

"This, this thing," Amon said as he spoke reverently, "this here thing is nice and makes me look tall and maybe a little old, but, and I say but, I'm yet a nice man. What do you think?"

The officer closed his eyes and smiled.

Amon continued to look into the mirror. "Yes, you know it makes me look smart too. Well, maybe it just makes me look old and maybe a little smart but I don't know. What do you think?"

"Yes, you look very smart," responded the other cavalryman.

"Is that the truth? If you do not tell the truth then you are breaking one of the Ten Commandments."

"Yes, I know," responded the officer. "It's the ninth commandment; the one about bearing false witness."

"You . . . you a Roman also kill and that is breaking . . ."

The officer interrupted him. "That's the sixth commandment."

"How do you know all of those things about our commandments?" asked Amon. They're our commandments. Don't you have commandments of your own?"

"I may be a Roman in your eyes, but I am aware of many Hebrew things, including the Ten Commandments."

"What else do you know?" asked Amon.

The officer raised himself on one elbow and looked at Amon. "I have listened to you and have tried to decide where I have heard your words before, and now I know." He coughed up more blood. "You speak as if you lived in the hill country and near the town of Nain. Do you come from that town?" he asked as he repositioned himself on the ground.

Amon's eyes widened. "Yes! How did you know that?"

"People from Galilee have an accent, hill people have a different accent and those near Jerusalem speak differently."

"How do you know about Nain?" asked Amon.

"I was in Nain some time ago because of the rebels in this region."

Amon stomach tightened and his eyes started to glare at the officer. "Was it you who killed my brother, Asa?" asked Amon as straightened his spine and narrowed his brows.

"The only people that I killed in Nain were those that battled with me. Why do you ask?"

"My brother, Asa, was killed the night they found that Athaliah man in the house of Joash the Tanner. My brother and Achim and others were murdered by Roman pagans like you." Amon's hands dropped the mirror and it broke into many pieces. "You were there . . . and so was my brother, Asa. Maybe it was you, who killed him."

"I remember that evening," said the officer. "The only people that fell to my sword were those . . . those that battled with me when we surrounded the tanner's shop." Instantly he began to cough uncontrollably.

"So you were there when Asa was killed?"

The officer raised his hand to interrupt Amon. "I was initially assigned to speak to the Caravan Master to find out if the rebel, Athaliah was in town."

"But you . . ."

"I was in Nain for many days after the battle with Athaliah. I remember other things that happened in Nain. I also saw the prophet raise a dead boy back to life as they were taking him to be buried. Did you see that?"

"Y-e-s, I saw the prophet raise a young boy back to life," said Amon as his eyes widened. "I was there and saw it and I was at Simon's house later that evening, but my brother was murdered because he was living on the TANNER'S STREET!" He finished his sentence loudly and the sound of his voice echoed in the distance.

After a long pause, Amon shouted, "MY SANDAL SHOP WAS NEXT TO JOASH THE TANNER." In his anger, Amon turned away and when he did, he noticed what appeared to be clouds of dust in the distance.

Conspiracy With Malicious Intent

For a moment he was unsure what that meant but slowly he begain to realize that riders were approaching.

He shaded his eyes with his right hand. "I think soldiers are coming. Yes, some men are coming and, and," he paused, "they look like soldiers because only pagans ride horses in a long line. Jews do not ride horses so it must be Romans." He watched as they approached.

"I want you to know that I did not kill your brother. I was on the tanner's street that night and the only ones that I," the officer's voice changed to a whisper and stopped. "It was a terrible battle, and many people were killed including Roman soldiers."

"What is your name?" asked Amon as he leaned forward to look into the eyes of the officer.

"My name is Varrus, Centurion Varrus Marcius Cassius de Lonnea."

"So you were there when my Asa, my brother was killed. Do you know who killed him?"

"No, but what I do know is that it was not me, unless your brother was one of the rebels who attacked us with swords and spears."

Amon knelt down so he could look into the officer's eyes. "Asa, my brother . . . he was too sick and weak to kill anyone. The only knife he could use was the one we use to cut leather in our sandal shop." Amon sounded angry and momentarily overwhelmed by what he had just heard. At that moment, he felt his small knife in his pouch; the one he had used for cutting leather in his shop.

"I'm sorry about your brother. In the middle of the battle, it is hard to know who our foe was and . . ." He did not finish his statement but waited to regain his strength. "You know my name but you have not told me your name."

"It doesn't matter."

"Yes it does. I want you to know that I did not kill your brother." He waited a moment before saying, "Now tell me your name."

Rising from his kneeling position, Amon responded, "My name is Amon; Amon Ben Gazahem." His last word was barely audible.

"Amon, Thank You for saving our lives."

"I did not plan to save Gentile pagans and now that I know who . . ." he closed his eyes and shook with grief, "who you are and that you were in Nain, I wish I could . . ." he did not complete his sentence.

"Amon, your grief and hatred is understandable, but I did not kill anyone unless they had a sword or spear in their hand."

Conspiracy With Malicious Intent

Moments passed as both men felt uneasy about their conversation. After an extended period of silence, the officer continued, "By the way, we never did find Athaliah, who was Joash's relative."

"So all that killing was . . . not worth it?" asked Amon.

"We knew what he looked like but no one fit that description." He paused momentarily before continuing. "He had several teeth missing and a scar under his nose and had an injury to the inside of his arm, so when he walked it hung by his side as if he could not use it."

Amon turned his head slightly, "I think I saw a man like that and he had a scar under his nose or somewhere on his face."

"Where did you see that man?" asked the officer.

"He was with me when I . . . I saw him with the caravan from Egypt. He was leading a camel when they left Nain."

"So he's alive," responded the officer.

The other injured cavalryman asked, "Sir, do you think the men will be here soon?"

Amon walked away to regain control of his anger and when he returned, he pointed at the officer. "What is that on your arm?"

"This tattoo shows others that I am a Centurion."

"What is that?" asked Amon.

"A Centurion?"

"So what is that?"

"I am responsible for legionnaires," Varrus said as he held his chest while he coughed. "Can you tell me how far way the soldiers are from us? Can you wave at them or run out to meet them?"

"They're coming," said Amon. "They should be here soon."

Turning to Varrus, Amon knelt down and said, "So now you know I am a Jew, who lived next to Joash the Tanner. All I know is that I saved your pagan skin and now you might take me to your city and . . . what will you do to me when we get there and who are you?"

"I was born in Italy, and my father is a Legatus, who is Chief Commander of a Roman Legion in Macedonia." He held his rib cage as he coughed. "My mother, she spoke often of Palestine, so I saw this as an opportunity to see the many places she taught me about." He paused again to draw a painful breath. "I came to see where Abraham, Isaac and Jacob lived and what Jerusalem is like."

"You . . . you know about our father Abraham? How did you know that unless you . . . Are you a Jew?"

Varrus narrowed his brows and readjusted his position. "Are you Hebrew?" repeated Amon.

"No."

"But then you must be a . . . a Samaritan?" whispered Amon.

"My mother is Jewish of the house of Benjamin."

"How can that be?" asked Amon. "Samaritans are people, who are . . . they are . . ."

"Yes I know," responded Varrus. "You Jews despise people, who are half Jew and half Gentile. I cannot help that." Again he coughed for several moments. "My mother paid for me to have a mentor to teach me about Abraham, Isaac and Jacob." He turned to spit blood from his mouth. "I know of the Torah and the Tanakh, and about all the Feasts and Festivals, the requirements of the sacrifices."

"Romans I don't trust, but Samaritans I have been taught to hate."

"I HEAR HORSES," said the wounded legionnaire as he tried to raise his head off the ground. "They're coming! I can hear them coming!"

Amon walked toward them to wave at the approaching cavalrymen, and as he did, he muttered to himself, "I had a chance to kill Roman soldiers for my brother and all I could do is let them live and . . . he is yet a Samaritan." Raising his hands above his head, he continued talking to himself. "Asa, I'm sorry that I did not avenge your death." Grieved at his failure, Amon slumped to the ground, closed his eyes and clenched his fist with dirt. Just before the troop arrived, he threw the dirt into the air and shouted, "ASA, I AM SORRY," as tears ran down his cheeks.

When the cavalrymen were within a hundred strides, he returned to where Varrus and the other legionnaire were lying.

"All I wanted to do is find the Messiah and what did I find . . . but you Roman soldiers and many dead people. How could this happen to me that I should save the life of a Roman that was with Asa when he was killed? All I want now is to talk the Messiah."

"I think the Messiah that you are looking for is in Jerusalem," whispered Varrus. "When we get to Scythopolis, I'll ask . . . some people if anyone knows where he might be."

As dust from four hundred hooves swirled about the dead and wounded, Varrus whispered, "I'll see to it that you will be rewarded for your help. It may not mean anything to you, but I . . . I believe in that man who is a prophet, the one you call the Messiah. I have listened to him many times and seen his miracles."

Conspiracy With Malicious Intent

Within minutes the legionnaires surrounded the dead and the living, and faced their horses outwardly to watch for any possible approaching foe. Five cavalrymen dismounted and immediately walked among the dead, while a mounted officer moved his horse to where Varrus was lying.

"Varrus?" He sounded surprised. "You left two days ago."

"It's good to see you, Theodoius." Varrus' words were weak and faint.

"What happened?"

"We entered this valley because we thought we saw a fire and when we approached, we saw a small amount of smoke . . . rising from some ashes." He paused again to take a breath, "And instantly, we were ambushed."

A soldier knelt down and offered Varrus a drink and then moved to the other injured legionnaire.

After drinking, Varrus looked up at Theodoius, "We drove off most of them but they ravished our numbers. As the battle raged . . . I estimated that we may have killed thirty to forty, but the rest escaped into the hills." He lay back totally exhausted.

"Are any of the enemy alive? By the way, who is this Jew?" as he pointed at Amon. "Is he one of them?" asked the Centurion Theodoius.

"No. He saved my life and Romas' life." After moaning and holding his abdomen, Varrus raised his hand before speaking. "He tried to save the others and stayed with us during the night. Do not harm him."

A soldier approached Theodoius, "Forty-two enemy dead and fifteen legionnaires dead, Sir. Are these men the only ones who survived the battle?"

"More than forty-two against seventeen? The odds were in favor of the rebels," said Theodoius, "but you have done well."

Varrus lay motionless for some time before responding. "Some of the rebels escaped. The only surviving one fled during the night . . . but he is severely wounded and will not likely travel very far."

"Ride to the supply cart and direct it here," commanded Theodoius as he turned to a legionnaire next to him. "We have much work to do. Move, NOW!"

As the cavalryman turned his mount, Amon heard him reply, "Sir" and he rode off in the direction that the soldiers had come from.

Theodoius looked down at Varrus, "Varrus, I will never thank a Jew for saving a Roman soldier's life, so be sure that YOU tell him, because I won't." Then he climbed into his saddle and rode into the killing field to count the number of dead.

"Amon, I am to thank you for saving our lives. How can I repay you?"

"By leaving Palestine," responded Amon with a subtle smile.

"Amon, ask me for something I have the power to do."

The dead bodies of the rebels were stripped of clothing and their bodies left for the jackals, but the dead cavalrymen were buried after the supply cart arrived.

It was almost dark when the cart began its long and bumpy journey back to Scythopolis. Amon had a choice to make. He either remained behind to travel alone or he could walk behind the Roman troop or he could ride in the cart. He chose to ride.

Chapter XIX

THE POWER TO INTERROGATE

Amon's trip to Scythopolis, in a Roman military cart, was slow, bumpy, dusty and extremely uncomfortable. The cool night air chilled him so he tried to nestle next to some of the clothing that had been gathered at the battle site. The two-wheeled cart carried Amon, Romas, Varrus and weapons: swords, spears, slingshots, bows, arrows and some primitive weapons made by the rebels. Also, there were saddles, bridles, helmets and sandals, all tightly packed into the cart. The six surviving horses, tethered to the cart, appeared equally uncomfortable with the journey. In the middle of the journey, one of the horses dropped to its front knees and was unable to rise again. After several attempts to make it stand, it was untied and the troop and the cart moved on, leaving the horse behind.

Theodoius and one hundred cavalrymen escorted the cart through the dark, barren countryside toward Scythopolis. The rhythmic sound of hundreds of hooves, the creaking leather from saddles and uniforms, along with the squeak of the cart wheels made the journey almost unbearable for Amon. Sleep was impossible.

Varrus watched Amon, even though it was almost impossible to see his face in the darkness. "Thank you, Amon, for saving my life," he whispered. "I know that you see me as a foreigner and a pagan but . . . ."

Amon interrupted without looking at Varrus, "And don't forget a Samaritan and a soldier that was where my brother was killed too."

"Yes Amon, but I remember my mother speaking of a Messiah that would come." The cart suddenly struck a hole in the road and Romas, as well as Varrus, moaned loudly as they sought a position of comfort.

When Varrus was in control of the pain and his breathing, he uttered, "I have seen the prophet and have listened to his words. If there is such a thing as a god, then he must be one. Maybe he is the Messiah."

Amon nodded his head as if he understood.

The ride was a painful experience for the wounded because every pothole produced a deep moan and a painful grunt. When the cart eventually stopped, the three passengers breathed a sigh of relief. As the driver stepped down from the cart, Amon stood to his feet to stretch his legs and arms.

"How come that man leading us has a red bushy thing on his shiny helmet?"

"The red horsehair at the top of the helmet indicates the rank of the Centurion," responded Varrus.

After the driver relieved himself and spoke to some of the cavalrymen near him, he climbed into the cart, snapped the reins and the cart moved forward, instantly responding to a rock on the roadway.

Amon repositioned himself but another bump in the road caused him to grimace and seek another position of comfort.

"If you remember my words, I told you that . . . I would speak with my Superior officer, Marcus, and tell him of your bravery," said Varrus just as the cart struck another pothole. Again Varrus moaned loudly.

After a long silence, Amon looked at Varrus and asked, "Hey, are you yet alive."

"Yes."

"Varrus, did you say that you would speak to someone about me? What will you say?"

"I will tell Marcus that you tried to save some of the soldiers. He needs to know that you tried to save the horses too."

Amon smiled and nodded just as the cart struck a large rock in the road. Varrus was not sure if Amon had intended to nod or the bump in road caused the nod.

"We spent many hours together," said Varrus just before the cartwheel jarred the cart and its passengers one more time. After moaning and gripping his side, Varrus continued, "What did you do for an occupation?"

"I was a sandal maker," responded Amon, "until I saw the Messiah bring Hannah's boy back to life. My mother and father told us about a Messiah that was coming, and then my brother was murdered by you Romans." He paused as the pain re-established itself deep in his soul. He looked off into the distance for several moments and then narrowed his brows before speaking. "Here I am, just a Jew looking for the Messiah, and all I find is murderous pagans and, and a Samaritan who I worked to keep alive. Why. I cannot answer especially since I swore that I would kill as many of you as I could."

The driver coughed from the dust and said something to a mounted cavalryman who was riding beside the cart. Again the cart struck another large pothole and the wheel next to Amon creaked loudly.

Amon looked at the mounted cavalrymen that surrounded the cart and then turned to Varrus. "You know, Varrus, if I had not met you, any one of those men would have slit my throat because . . . why . . . because I was walking in the wrong place. I'm angry that I didn't let all of you die. The sixth commandment tells me not to kill or murder, but it does not say anything that I must keep all of you alive."

The cart wheel dipped into a pothole and all contents including the passenger were jolted again. Amon looked at the driver, "Did they teach you how to hit every hole in the road or are you just careless?"

The driver ignored Amon's comments, brushed the dust from his uniform with his left hand and snapped the reins of the team of horses pulling the cart.

If it were not for the moon, darkness would have totally enveloped the entourage. The cavalrymen and the cart moved slowly and steadily over the yellowing moonlit countryside. In the distance, the lights of Scythopolis brought hope to Amon. He had never been to Scythopolis, yet in a strange way it seemed to be a haven.

"You know," said Amon after he had remained silent for some time, "I was on my way to this city but never planned on riding with pagans in such a terrible cart, especially surrounded by, by people who hate me. This shows me that what happens is not always what I plan."

"Amon, you know that not all Romans are your enemies, and now that I know you, I'm pleased that you had mercy on me and helped us," responded Varrus.

The cart driver slowed the cart to accommodate a narrow curve in the road and when the cart and cavalrymen were several hundred strides from the city gate, a dozen riders rode out to escort them into the city. Several horses snorted and tossed their heads for they sensed that they were now on familiar ground.

When the entourage stopped inside the Roman stronghold, the cavalrymen dismounted while Amon stepped down from the cart. He complained about the ride to the driver as Varrus and Romas were lifted from the cart.

When both men were carried into the barracks, Amon tried to walk away but a cavalryman placed his hand on his shoulder. "Come with me," he said.

"Why?" asked Amon. "What have I done?"

"Centurion Varrus has asked that you remain here," and with that, he rudely pushed Amon toward a building. Amon looked around as the large wooden gate that was being closed. Amon was amazed at the many burning torches on the rock walls.

"Here, sit here," the legionnaire said as he pointed to a wooden block next to a fire pit. Amon watched the sparks rising from dying embers, and wondered where they went when they didn't glow anymore.

Any thoughts of leaving quickly vanished when two guards came and stood next to Amon. He waited for a long time before he was ushered into a large room and told to sit on an old bench. A guard stood next to each of the four doors of the room, making Amon feel very uncomfortable. He mumbled to himself, "Gentiles, no wonder God chose us instead of them. They don't know enough to say thank you. Just because they carry long knives and sticks with sharp things on the end, they think they own the world. Well, maybe they do, but they don't own Judaea or Jerusalem. It's ours, not theirs and if they want a Messiah, they should get their own Messiah and leave ours alone."

The events of the previous day, the long night and the dusty ride to Scythopolis made Amon very sleepy. He stretched, yawned and tried to keep his eyes open when suddenly one of the heavy wooden doors opened and a middle-aged, bald man entered the room. Immediately the four guards snapped to attention, their arms moving in unison, as they saluted an officer. They held their arms across their chests until the bald man sat in a large padded chair behind a desk.

The man sniffed loudly as he cleared his nasal passages and focused his dark eyes upon Amon. The lights from the candles and torches on the walls made it difficult to see his face, so Amon moved his head from side to side for a better view.

"Few Jews have ever entered this room," he said as he leaned back and folded his hairy arms across his chest. "We do NOT owe any of you Jews anything, but in this case . . . I suppose we'll consider making an exception."

Amon felt uncomfortable but he knew there was little that he could do about his situation, so he remained silent. He focused upon the warmth of the fire behind him.

The officer paused and again cleared his nasal passages. When he snapped his fingers, a young servant poured wine for him and when the young man had filled the goblet, the bald man picked up the wine goblet, lifted it to salute Amon and drank all of it. Amon was unsure of what that meant, but decided that he should remain silent and listen to what the man had to say.

"I'm Marcus, a Cohort Centurion, and I want to hear about your journey into the Seddan Valley."

Amon nodded his head but did not say a word.

"What is your name and why were you in that valley?"

"My name is Amon and I lived in Nain all my life. I was," he stopped and rubbed his chin as he looked up at Marcus, "by the way, how will you know if I am telling you the truth when I answer your questions?" There was a certain sound of innocence in his voice.

Marcus stopped in the midst of his drink to cast a sideway glance at Amon. After emptying the wine in his goblet, he set it on the table, leaned forward as his eyes narrowed without blinking. "You know, the only thing worse than a Jew is an arrogant Jew."

His lips were so tight that Amon thought they lost their color.

"I never ask a question twice but in this case I will make an exception. WHY WERE YOU IN THE SEDDEN VALLEY?" he shouted as his fist struck the top of the table. The goblet he drank from almost toppled over from the jolt of his fist striking the desk.

"I was coming to this here Scythos place because I'm on my way to Jerusalem to look for a Messiah. You do know what a Messiah is, don't you?" Marcus remained motionless and did not blink his eyes.

"When I was in Nain," Amon continued, "I saw this man, sent by God to," he wrinkled his brow, "you do know what a god is, don't you?"

Marcus did not move but continued to stare in silence. His rigid face appeared as immobile as a portrait painted on a canvas.

"God made all things, including you Romans, and he told us that he would send a Messiah. He told us about this long ago in the Tanakh. As a Gentile you may not know what the Tanakh or Torah are but . . ."

"Do I look like a person, who wishes to become a rabbi or Jew? NOW ANSWER MY QUESTION." A vein on his forehead pulsated as he shouted.

Amon was beginning to feel uncomfortable with Marcus' stare.

"WHY WERE YOU IN THAT VALLEY?" Marcus asked as he smashed his fist on the top of the desk again. This time his voice was louder than before.

"I think that the Messiah was in Nain some time ago when he raised Hannah's dead boy from the dead. I was there and saw it, and now I'm looking for him. Zebedee, who lives at the Sea of Galilee, told me that the Messiah was in Jerusalem so," he shrugged his shoulders as he spoke, "I decided to walk there. I found wounded pagans and the others and then I stopped to help. That's all I did. I stopped to help and now you . . . you are angry at me. Is there a law or rule that someone should not help?"

The silence in the room seemed to have an echo.

Amon looked down at his hands before speaking. "We Jews have laws given to us by Moses that tell us not to touch dead bodies, Gentiles or go into their buildings, so," he shrugged his shoulders "the only law I'm breaking now is being in this," he looked around, "this here Gentile building."

"Why should I believe you?" asked Marcus in a more subdued tone. He snapped his fingers and his servant poured more wine.

"If you don't believe me, ask Varrus your Centurer. He will tell you that I helped keep him alive. He was in Nain when Hannah's boy was raised and he saw that too."

Marcus rose from his padded chair and walked directly over to Amon, placed his left hand on Amon's shoulder and drew a dagger with his right hand from within his left sleeve. Amon tried to withdraw but Marcus was desperately strong. "YOU STILL HAVE NOT TOLD ME WHY YOU WERE IN THAT VALLEY," he yelled at the top of his voice and as he spoke his face reddened and veins protruded from his neck. Droplets of saliva touched Amon's face, so he closed his eyes.

Unsure if he should speak, Amon kept his eyes closed as he tried to withdraw from Marcus' grip.

"I asked you a question. Now what is your answer?"

"I was on my way to Jerusalem and, and stopped for a rest and saw the fighting. When it was over, I couldn't leave," said Amon as he shrugged his shoulders and raised his hands, "so I went down to help whoever did not want to die."

Marcus loosened his grip slightly.

Amon continued. "Have you asked Varrus or this Romas man? I tried to save others but during the night some died and, and I guess I only saved two of them."

Marcus returned his dagger to his left sleeve and walked around his desk to sit in his chair.

"If I was an enemy, I would have let everyone die or even killed them myself," said Amon in a low tone, "but I," he raised his pointer finger, "I am a gentle man, who knows the Ten Commandments and could not even kill pagans." His voice was now soft and more convincing.

Marcus shouted at a soldier next to the door which Amon had entered. "BRING ME VARRUS AND ROMAS, NOW!"

The large wooden door creaked loudly on its rusty hinges as the guard opened the door.

"What about me? Can I go to Jerusalem?"

"No! Sit and be quiet. If you talk, I will have your tongue cut out. Do you understand me?"

Amon nodded and remained silent.

Marcus' servant poured more wine. Marcus coughed loudly and then drank the dark liquid, before placing his elbows on the table. "I do not like it when Roman soldiers and horses are killed. It is my responsibility to find out who these rebels are. Do you happen to know who they are and where they might be?" His voice was strong and commanding.

Amon shrugged his shoulders and wagged his head, indicating 'no.'

Several minutes passed before the dispatched soldier returned. "Sir, Varrus is in the infirmary and unable to come. He's alive but did say that a man named, Amon, saved his life, Sir."

Marcus folded his fingers together as though he were praying and placed them under his chin. Rubbing his thumbs together, he scowled at Amon but remained silent. Moments later there was a knock on the door. The door opened and Centurion Theodoius, who had ridden the rescue mission to the killing field, entered the room and saluted.

Marcus narrowed his eyes.

"Permission to speak, Sir."

Marcus nodded his approval.

"This man," Theodoius said as he pointed to Amon, "saved Varrus and Romas' life. Apparently, he attempted to save other cavalrymen on the battlefield. His actions made a difference and he was the one that sent the signal to Scythopolis, using Varrus' saddle mirror."

Marcus said nothing and the silence became uncomfortable for everyone.

Amon stood to his feet, "If this is my reward for helping you then I've been a fool. Jews will say thank you and Shalom, but here I am greeted with trouble."

His words were interrupted when Marcus stood to his feet and shouted. "SIT DOWN."

Amon looked at Theodoius, who did not move.

"Take this man," said Marcus, "and let him sleep in the inner court near the rear wall and be sure that he does not leave the compound. That's an order. Inform the walled guards that he must not leave because I want to see him later tomorrow. Is that clear?"

Theodoius responded with, "Sir," and Marcus rose and left the room.

"Come with me," Theodoius said as he exposed the palm of his left hand to point the way. When he and Amon were outside, they walked over to a corner where the horses were being fed. There, Theodoius pointed to the ground. "Here, you stay here. Marcus plans to listen to you again, but you must not leave. If you leave and are caught, Marcus will have you flogged. Do you understand?"

"So this is a Hebrew's reward for helping Gentiles. No wonder so many people want to kill you," he said as he shuffled his feet in the hay to form a bed. "I will be here when you need me, but I shared my food with Varrus and Romas, so am I to eat this straw?" Amon continued to make a bed for himself and mumble, "So this is my reward for doing good?"

Amon tried to sleep but the noise in the barracks constantly disturbed him.

Chapter XX

THE GIFT OF NEGOTIATING

Shortly after a cock crowed, a guard kicked Amon's leg and he shouted, in a gruff and unfriendly tone, "Get up you dog and come with me."

Amon stood unsteadily to his feet and rubbed his eyes so they could adjust to the morning sunlight. "Where are we going?" he asked, but the legionnaire said nothing but pushed him toward a door in a large stone building.

Once inside the building, Amon was led down a long hallway and up several flights of stairs to the top floor where two guards opened the door so they could enter. Seven padded chairs were positioned in a semicircle all facing a larger, padded chair. Near the back of the room were several ordinary chairs, a small wooden table and two stools. On the walls were Roman flags, maps, written parchments and banners, as well as a large oil painting of Caesar. Several brass utensils and unlit candles were on one of the smaller tables.

"Sit here," said the legionnaire that had awakened him. Then he pointed to one of the stools and when Amon sat down, the legionnaire moved to stand behind him.

Some time passed before the door opened and two guards assisted Varrus into the room. Varrus smiled and raised his hand to wave at Amon, but when Amon tried to stand, the guard, behind him, put his hand on his shoulder and forced him to remain seated.

Varrus and Amon sat in silence, one at one side of the room and one on the other. When Marcus entered the room all of the guards snapped to attention. Marcus paused next to Varrus, who tried to salute with his injured arm but it was too difficult to move.

"So this . . . this Jew saved your life?" asked Marcus in a sarcastic tone as he moved to sit in one of the padded chairs.

"Yes Sir!"

"You were in Sedden Valley when you were ambushed. Are you not trained to recognize the potential of an ambush?" asked Marcus.

"We were on patrol near the entrance to Sedden Valley when we thought we saw smoke from a fire, so we cautiously approached. Suddenly, we were hopelessly outnumbered with bows, slingshots, arrows and spears," responded Varrus. "The rebels must have been lying on the sand behind the bushes. We did not see them when we approached. When the battle started, I realized that all of them wore clothing the color of the soil, Sir."

Marcus shifted his weight in the chair before dragging his chair over to where Varrus was sitting. Their knees almost touched when Marcus began to speak. "I do not understand why you use the word, we. Are you not the commanding officer of this troop?"

Varrus nodded as he responded, "Yes Sir."

"Then why do you use the word, we? Should it not be I?"

"Yes Sir."

"Now, who was in charge and who led these men into a trap?" asked Marcus.

"I did Sir."

"Now we can move on?"

"Yes Sir."

"This man," Marcus said as he pointed casually over his shoulder toward Amon, "tells me that he was just passing by and happened to witness the battle. Was he part of the battle?"

"No Sir. He arrived just as the last of the rebels were leaving."

"How can you be sure that he was not a member of the rebels? He could have been their lookout. Maybe, just maybe, he knows who these murderers are or where they may be."

Varrus turned to look at Amon. "He actually separated the wounded of each side, gathered the weapons, bound up the wounded, gave us some of his food and stayed with us the entire night. He could have killed any one of us at any time or just abandoned us, Sir."

Amon stood to his feet and was about to speak when the guard's hand pressed on his shoulder again so he sat down and remained silent.

"If he were one of them," continued Varrus, "he would not have tried to keep us alive, Sir."

"Did he keep any of the rebels alive?" asked Marcus.

"Yes only one, Sir."

"So he kept one of the rebels alive? Where is that rebel now?"

"The patrol that came to our rescue found him a thousand strides from the killing field. He was dead. He must have tried to sneak away during the night and died from his wounds."

Marcus turned to Amon and when their eyes met, Amon tried to smile. Turning back to Varrus, Marcus continued. "What is this about a Messiah and a dead boy brought back to life? Do you know anything about that?" Before Varrus could respond, Marcus raised his hand. "This man," he pointed at Amon, "said that you saw what happened in Nain, when you were stationed there."

"Yes Sir!"

"Hmmm. Do you think that this . . . this Messiah is part of the rebel group?"

"Oh no Sir."

"So tell me about the dead boy in Nain."

"I did see a young boy brought back to life while he was being escorted out of the city for burial. That is true, Sir."

"How long have you been in Palestine?"

"I have served in the Legion for eight years and have been in Palestine for four years."

"Have you ever seen dead people brought back to life anywhere else?"

"No, Sir." Varrus shook his head as he spoke.

There was a long period of silence before Marcus stood to his feet and walked over to his desk to sit on the front edge of it. As he crossed his legs, he stared at the shiny marble floor. "Where is this Messiah now?" he asked. "If he can make people alive, where is he when I have all of these dead legionnaires?"

No one responded to his question.

"Maybe he could have brought the rebels back to life so that we could crucify all of them," Marcus continued in a mocking tone. Then he adjusted his position on the edge of the desk and rubbed his eyes with his pointer finger and thumb of his right hand. After taking a large breath, he walked over to Amon and leaned forward so that his warm breath was on Amon's face.

"I know that the Legatus would want me to give you something as a token of appreciation for your heroic acts. What do you think of that?" asked Marcus as Amon withdrew slightly from his warm breath that reeked of garlic and wine. "What do you want? I am willing to listen to your request."

Conspiracy With Malicious Intent

Amon cleared his throat and looked at Varrus and then back at Marcus. "I will think about this today, and return tomorrow with my answer. I would like some time to eat, sleep and think about this generous offer."

Marcus walked to the door and before he exited, he pointed at Amon. "Be here before midday tomorrow. If you are late, I will consider that you are not interested and have no request." He nodded and the door was opened for him, and he stepped out of the room.

Amon turned his eyes to Varrus. "What will happen to you?"

"I have time to heal and then will be sent for more battle training. Rumor has it that I'll be transferred to Jerusalem. I have been a cavalryman and legionnaire for many years and know the risks of war."

"Healing I can understand, but why do you have to learn how to fight and kill? You lived through that battle, so you don't need to learn more about killing."

Two guards helped Varrus to his feet.

"You said something about knowing where the Messiah was," said Amon as he stood to his feet. "If you meant that, then where is he now?"

"You mean to tell me that you actually heard some of the things that I was saying to you while we rode in that cart?" responded Varrus.

Amon shrugged his shoulders, "Yes, I listen best when I am not talking and, and that night I wasn't talking."

"The Messiah was here in the synagogue in Scythopolis a few days ago, but now I don't know," Varrus said as two men assisted him to the door.

Amon shifted his weight from one foot to the other.

"The synagogue," Varrus continued, "is down the broad street near the well and the moneylenders building. You can't miss it. But tomorrow, be sure to be here before midday." He turned and left the room with the aid of the two legionnaires.

Amon raised his hands as though he wanted Varrus to wait but the door was closed before he could continue.

Some time later Amon was escorted to the barracks gate. Walking along the widest street he could find, he spotted a building with many people entering a courtyard. "Is this the synagogue?" he asked an elderly man.

"Yes," he said as he turned to Amon. "If you must ask, then you must be new in this here city." The man speaking to him had a white beard and carried a long wooden staff. "We are getting ready for the Sabbath," the man said as he started to walk away and after several steps, he turned, "Why are you yet not ready for the Sabbath? You act as if you did not know when the Sabbath is. Are you not a son of Abraham?"

"I must speak to a rabbi. Do you know where I can find one?" asked Amon.

A rabbi? You need not a rabbi to prepare for the Sabbath."

"No but I wish to speak to a rabbi," insisted Amon.

"Well in that case I am a rabbi. What is it that you need?"

"As a son of Abraham, I have some questions."

"Why not? Everyone has questions but remember it is getting late, so I can listen fast if you can talk fast." Then he motioned for Amon to follow him to the steps of a building where garments were being sold. There, Amon told the rabbi the entire story, starting with the Hannah's son being raised from the dead, his trip to Capernaum and the battle in the Sedden Valley.

Rabbi Beraiah responded with, "O my, I'm glad that we were sitting for this story. Did you know that it would take so long to tell?"

Amon shrugged his shoulders and grinned sheepishly. "I need some advice."

"You need more than advice. You need help," said Rabbi Beraiah. "So what do you want me to tell you?"

"I have two questions. First, I want to know where the Messiah is."

Rabbi Beraiah folded his hands and yawned loudly. "That happens with old age. You sometimes yawn without getting ready. Sometimes a yawn will catch you when you are not looking." He adjusted his hat and brushed his whiskers with his wrinkled hands. "First, what makes you think that there is yet a Messiah in this here place? Messiahs just don't exist like everyday loaves of bread. They must be sent by God, and if God does send a Messiah, so be it." He stared at the ground as he continued, "And if he does not send a Messiah, then what he sends us we call prophets. Messiahs are not easily found. If there is one, that is how many we get. One and no more: just one. God is good but I don't think he will send more than one Messiah. What makes you think there is yet a Messiah nearby?"

"A Roman soldier that I helped in that Sedden Valley said he saw the Messiah blessing children several days ago."

"Just because a man blesses children, he's suddenly a Messiah?" he said as he raised his hands above his head. "Oh my, my, now a Roman soldier, a pagan tells you that there is a Messiah. Maybe the soldier thinks he's the Messiah, besides when a Messiah comes, we will know him."

"But this Messiah heals children and makes them well again."

"Physicians also make people and children well but that does not mean they are Messiahs."

"But this man plays with children."

"That man, I might know, but a Messiah, I don't know about." "Well where is he now?"

"Now if you are talking about a man, who heals and blesses children that are not his, well I might just know of him. He left for Jerusalem this morning."

Amon's frustration surfaced as he stood and clenched his fists. "How will I ever find him when he always goes to different places?"

"You said that you had two questions. One I have just answered but the other question I have not yet heard."

Amon paused to gather his thoughts. "But Rabbi while I was walking from the Sea of Galilee to this here place, I came across a fight between Romans and rebels. Many of them died and I did what a good Jew should do. I saved some of their lives."

"So what is wrong with that? That is not even a question."

"Well I stayed with the dead people and injured soldiers all night long, and kept some Romans alive." He withdrew slightly, fearing what the rabbi would say.

"So what? Just as long as you didn't touch any of the dead bodies or any of those Gentiles, you will be alright."

"But Rabbi, I had to talk with the Romans in . . . in their building."

"Oh my," responded the old man as he scratched his head.

"Well the Centurrers and the man of the Roman building are going to give me something for being a good citizen to the injured soldiers. What should I ask for?"

"You speak in ways that my mind cannot keep straight, but if I understand what you are trying to tell me, the Romans want to give you a reward for saving some of their uncircumcised lives."

"Yes," responded Amon, pleased that the rabbi understood his question.

"Well, now let me think what I would ask for." He rubbed his beard for some time and then raised his pointer finger. "You should ask him to give me a written parchment that you can carry with you wherever you go. The parchment should say that you helped Roman soldiers and saved their lives. This may be very valuable someday to you, but, I must say but, I must ask you, why would you help Roman soldiers? That I do not understand."

Amon narrowed his eyes as he thought about the rabbi's' question and suggestion. "Thank you, Rabbi Beraiah. Finally, I have met a rabbi that knows something. In Nain, rabbis know nothing because they always say, 'I don't know.'"

Rabbi Beraiah rose from where he was sitting and started to walk away and as he did, he raised his finger and said "Just remember tomorrow is the Sabbath and it is not a time for you to make any deals. Before sundown today maybe, but not tomorrow for you must not desecrate the Sabbath, and when you travel, it must not be more than a Sabbath day's journey. Do NOT forget."

"SHOULD I ASK FOR ANYTHING ELSE?" shouted Amon.

Rabbi Beraiah did not look back but again raised his pointer finger and said, "Greed has a way of taking away what you have, so be careful."

Amon stopped at the market to purchase some fruit and flat bread with several of his coins, and then he returned to the barracks walls. There he lay under a sycamore tree, ate and prepared for the night. His tired body ached from all of the walking and from the stress of the former evenings. He closed his eyes and quickly drifted off to sleep.

Chapter XXI

THE AGREEMENT

It was a difficult night for Amon. Sleeping next to the city gate and a military base is noisy, and an empty stomach is not easy to ignore. When he slept, his dreams were of Asa. He whimpered when his dream reminded him of when they were boys and played next to the city wall and surrounding ravines of Nain. In this dream, he saw his father and mother dying again from an unknown disease. When he saw Asa's body after a spear had been thrust through him, he moaned so loudly from the emotional pain, that a guard nearby shouted at him. He stirred and went back to sleep, as tears wet his sleeve that was supporting his head.

Soon the morning sun warmed his back so he rolled over, and when it shone on his face, he squinted and covered his eyes. Eventually, he sat up, smacked his lips and scratched his empty stomach. Several minutes passed before he rose to see what was around him and then he wandered over to the front gate of the barracks.

"I'm supposed to see a bald man called Marcus," Amon annouced to the guard, who looked at him and mumbled something he did not understand. When the guard returned from the guardhouse, he pushed Amon away from the door without saying a word, so Amon walked over to where he had spent the night, sat down and waited until different guards replaced the existing ones.

When he saw other guards arriving to relieve the night watch, he approached the entrance. The aroma of food from the barracks tempted him to walk through the gate without waiting for permission. As he stood there, a side door opened and two guards appeared.

"I was told to meet a man named Marcus. He said that I must be here this morning," Amon said.

Conspiracy With Malicious Intent

"Come with me," said one of the guards. "I saw you here yesterday."

Amon found himself back in the barracks. He followed the guard up the stairs where he had been the day before, but this time six men guarded the office door. After a long wait, Amon became very restless but he reminded himself that if he were not here before midday, Marcus would believe that he wanted nothing for his life saving efforts.

Amon's wait was longer than he had imagined but he eventually heard footsteps and a door suddenly opening. Marcus entered the room accompanied by two soldiers. This time Marcus did not sit on his padded seat but walked over to where Amon was standing.

After placing his hands on his hips, he said in a sarcastic tone, "So you have returned. You must be eager because you're early."

"As a Jew I am not allowed to make any deals today or travel very far because today is the Sabbath, so I want to ask you if I can come back tomorrow."

"I care not what today is to you Jews. I have no intention of meeting you again, today or tomorrow. So what do you want for your efforts to keep Roman soldiers alive?"

"I guess my request is that you let me come back tomorrow when it is not the Sabbath."

"You are wasting my time. Now do you want something or not?"

"I was hoping that you would . . . maybe give me some food to eat, like I did when I gave MY food to the injured soldiers."

"Food . . . huh? So that is what you want?" Marcus said as he grinned.

"No, no," insisted Amon as he moved his head from side to side. "No, no."

"So if it isn't food that you want. What have you decided would be the exchange for your heroic actions?"

"Well," said Amon confidently, "there are three things that I want but I want to come back tomorrow because I am not to do any business deals on the Sabbath."

"THREE things? I expected you to be greedy and you did not disappoint me. Oh by the way, I will not meet you tomorrow. You must tell me what you want today or you will receive nothing."

"Hunger makes people want food," responded Amon.

"Your hunger is not my concern but I must admit that I did hear that you gave your food to the legionnaires. What else do you want?"

"I am very hungry and I would like some food to eat."

"So it's food that you want?"

Amon raised his finger, "Well food is only part of it."

"Food," said Marcus as he tilted his head to the side. "Food, yes I can allow that."

"Next, I would like a parchment from the man, who has the most power in this city. The parchment should tell others that I, Amon Ben Gazahem saved the lives of injured Roman soldiers. It must say that I am a good person and good man." He tilted his chin up as he spoke, a sign of confidence.

"What soldiers? Only two survived. Two out of . . . how many, sixteen or seventeen? You saved two. HAHAHAH. What else do you want? This is interesting."

"And, I would like several denarii for my trip to Jerusalem. Coins are sometimes as important as food."

Hearing this, Marcus raised his arms and said sarcastically, "How about an armed escort to Jerusalem? Why did you not ask for that?"

Amon lowered his head and thought for a moment. "That would be nice, but I don't want to be greedy."

Marcus walked over to a window and stood in silence as he looked over the parade square. "Three things huh? You want three things."

"Yes," responded Amon. "It sounds like much but . . ."

"How about two things for the two soldiers that you saved?" asked Marcus as he turned from the window to look at Amon.

"Well, then I will take the parchment and some coins."

"Really?"

"With denarius, I can buy food and . . ."

"Have a seat," Marcus said as he pointed to a stool in the corner. As Amon moved to the stool, Marcus walked over to his padded stool, dragged it noisily over to Amon's side, and sat down in front of him. He closed his eyes, brushed his sparse wiry hair with both hands and clicked his tongue several times. After taking several large breaths, he began to shake his head. "Greed is what I expected and for that, you will receive only one thing. What will it be?"

Amon swallowed noisily as he stared at the door. "You said two things so how did it become only one thing?"

"One," was the cold reply. "Your greed deserves only one thing, and one it will be, so what do you want?"

"Then, I will take the parchment," Amon responded. "A parchment that I can take with me that will tell others that I helped save and fed injured Roman soldiers."

Crossing his left arm across his abdomen and placing his right elbow on it, he raised his right hand to his chin, "We do not have a Legatus in Scythopolis and I am not in the mood of giving you such a parchment, especially to a Jew," Marcus said in a cold tone.

"I did help by keeping some of your Gentiles alive. I could have killed them or walked off in the night, and you would have never known. I was the one that sent the light to the city with the Varrus' shiny glass. I did more than two things. I did many other things."

Marcus walked to his desk and sat in his chair. "I have considered your requests. I will grant you two things: some food and a parchment."

"For this I will be grateful," said Amon as he lowered his gaze.

Amon was ushered into a dining area and he sat where they indicated. Soon a large metal plate, filled with food was presented to him, so he began to eat. He did not ask what it was or how it had been prepared, but pretended that the food was ceremonial acceptable and that Hebrew silversmiths made the plates, so that he did not violate any Leviticus Laws. He was sure that the meat was lamb but did not ask. The lentils and fruit were very tasty, so he ate until the plate was empty.

After he had eaten, a soldier ushered him back to Marcus' office. Once inside the room, he sat where they indicated and waited for Marcus to arrive. While he waited, Amon scanned the maps on the wall and looked at the posters that were written in a language that he could not read. The room had an odor of old books and papers. Amon suspected that few Hebrews had ever been in this place.

When Marcus entered the room, all soldiers snapped to attention. He walked directly over to Amon and stared into Amon's eyes as the muscles in his cheeks tightened several times. Amon tried not to look at him, but when he turned away, he felt a chill pass through the back of his neck.

"I hear that you have eaten," said Marcus.

Amon felt his warm breath on his cheek. He raised his eyes momentarily and then looked down again. "Yes," he whispered.

Marcus sighed before speaking, "I have had time to think about your request for a parchment and began to wonder why you would want one and," he scratched his chin and paused before saying, "and what should be written on it."

Amon listened intently.

"Varrus, the Centurion you assisted, has offered to give you several coins." He tossed a small bag of coins to Amon, who immediately opened it to count the contents. When he put the pouch of coins under his belt, he mouthed the words, "Thank you."

"I want to know why you have requested a parchment."

Amon moistened his lips. "Someday Roman soldiers may want to take me where I do not want to go, and then I will be able to show them what you have written about me," his voiced cracked slightly.

"This parchment will explain that I am not a rebel or a Zealot but a good citizen."

Marcus reached into the drawer of the desk and removed a silver coin and placed it on the desk. "Do you know whose inscription is on this coin?"

"No, I have never had a silver coin like that before."

"That is Caesar. He is more powerful than I and he would be pleased with your contribution to our presence in Palestine."

Amon looked at the coin. "Is that coin mine?"

"Not yet," Marcus responded. "I do, however want to know why you want a parchment? Are you planning to break the law?"

"No. I could be on my way to Jerusalem and soldiers stop me and ask me questions, and then I could show them what you said. It may save my life." Somehow the thought of a parchment seemed to be a poor request at that moment, and just before Amon was about to cancel this request, Marcus interrupted.

"I can give you a parchment but it will NOT allow you to commit a crime or be in any restricted areas. All it will do is state that you have been recognized for helping Roman soldiers during an uprising. If any officer, including the Legatus wishes to override this note because he feels that you are a danger to citizens or Rome or its contents, they have the power to ignore what has been written. Is that clear?"

"Thank you," said Amon.

Marcus reached for a quill, dipped it into ink and scribbled words on a parchment. When he had finished, he said to his Optio, "Wax it and place my seal on it."

"Yes Sir!"

After several moments of activity, the parchment was handed back to Marcus, who rose to his feet and handed it to Amon.

"Here you are," he said.

Amon glanced at the silver coin that lay on the desk top. Marcus smiled as he turned to pick it up, "And here is the coin that we spoke about."

"Now that I have received these generous gifts, I may try to save more Gentiles and maybe Romans too," said Amon as he smiled.

Conspiracy With Malicious Intent

The room became silent.

Under his breath Amon whispered, "Gentiles, maybe, just maybe God made them for us and we didn't know about it."

Before leaving the room, Marcus said, "Oh, it is still unclear to me as to why you were in that valley on that day."

"I was on my way to Jerusalem to find a Messiah. Did you hear about him?"

"I know the man you speak of. We have observed him many times. There are times when I think he is a rebel and a troublemaker, and at times he seems to be a peacemaker. My compliance with your request is because of Varrus and no one else."

"Thank you," said Amon in an apologetic tone.

Marcus stepped into the hallway, turned and pointed at Amon, "You have your parchment, a silver coin, money from Varrus and you have been fed. Am I correct?"

Amon nodded.

Marcus steps could be heard as he walked away and the room became silent.

"Well, you were given all that you have asked for, so now we will have you escorted back to the front gate," said the eldest guard.

The guards escorted Amon to the front gate and after standing outside for several moments, Amon started toward the synagogue. He did not go to Jerusalem that afternoon because it was too late and it was certainly more than a Sabbath's day journey, so he decided to wait until the morrow.

Chapter XXII

VARRUS THE CENTURION

Two days later, Amon went to the open market to buy some food for his trip to Jerusalem, and while he was there, he noticed several Roman soldiers walking among the people. They appeared to be searching for someone but he never suspected that they were looking for him. After he purchased dates, cheese and figs, he was surprised when two soldiers moved closer to him.

He stopped at a sandal shop to speak with the owner, and while he was there, he heard someone ask, "Are you Amon?"

Turning slowly, he saw a soldier standing in front of him. "Yes. Why, what have I done?" he asked as he tried to control his surprise.

"Centurion Varrus wishes to speak with you, but he is not well enough to be here, so we are to bring you to the barracks gates. Follow me," he said as he turned and motioned with his hand for Amon to follow. Before committing to the invitation, Amon looked at the second soldier, who nodded and pointed for him to start walking.

They moved through the crowd and entered the military gate where they proceeded to walk along a narrow hallway to a set of stairs. When the door at the end of the hallway was opened, Amon was surprised to see Varrus sitting in a chair. He motioned for Amon to enter.

"Thank you for coming," Varrus said. "I was fearful that you had already left for Jerusalem. I have some news about the Messiah. I have asked my servant Pollus to speak to several of the parents of the children who were healed by the Messiah."

Amon stepped closer, eager to hear more.

"Pollus, my servant, will be glad to take you to their homes. They will be pleased to tell about how the Messiah healed their children and other things that he has done."

"Who is Pollus?" asked Amon.

"Pollus is my personal servant. He was purchased by my father to be my personal servant when I was a very young boy. I trust Pollus with my life. I asked my father to send Pollus to me, when I lived for a short time in Capernaum. Pollus became very ill with the palsy and was about to die and I feared that I would lose him. When I remembered seeing the Messiah raise the sick, I decided to find him and have him come to my house to heal Pollus."

Amon turned his head slightly so he could hear every word.

"I told the legionnaires to look for the Messiah. As Pollus neared death, several soldiers reported to me that the Messiah was not in the region so I prayed to the God of the Abraham, Isaac and Jacob that he would send the Messiah to heal Pollus."

"What happened?" asked Amon, somewhat surprised by Varrus' words.

"I was desperate, so I asked the elders of the synagogue if they would ask Jesus to come and heal him. The elders seemed to be rather surprised that I would ask, and Hagri, a respected elder, along with several others spoke kind words about me to Jesus."

"Did the Messiah come?" asked Amon as his eyes widened.

"Word came to me that the Messiah was just outside the city so I immediately rode out to meet him. When I saw him, I dismounted and walked toward him to speak with him."

"Then what happened?"

"I told him that I have seen him raise a lad back to life in Nain and that I had seen him heal children and other people. I told him that my servant, Pollus, was near death and asked if he could come and heal him."

"Then what?" asked Amon.

"The Messiah said that he was willing to come to my house but . . . I said that he need not trouble himself by coming under my roof for it is not acceptable for a Jew to come into a Gentile building."

"Did he come?" whispered Amon.

"I said, I am a man of authority and say to one go and he goes, and to another I say stay and he waits, but you have power and authority over illness and death. Just say the word and my servant will be healed."

Amon moved closer.

"If the Messiah has that much power, all he needs to do is say the word, and illness would leave Pollus and he would be healed."

"Was he healed?"

"The Messiah did not come to my house, but the very hour that I spoke with the Messiah, Pollus was healed."

"You must have been very happy," said Amon as he grinned.

Varrus lowered his gaze. "I have sent many messages to the Messiah, to thank him for healing Pollus. In fact, my orders have always been to my men, if you see him, please tell him that I think often about the miracle he had done for me. I will never be able to repay the debt I owe."

"The Messiah helps Samaritans?" asked Amon. "This is something I do not understand. Don't Gentiles and Samaritans have their own Messiah?"

"Gentiles don't have Messiahs and," Varrus sighed, "and you Jews don't understand that those of us who have a Jewish ancestor are . . . well we think that you Jews should share your Messiah."

"S-h-a-r-e" Amon said slowly as he wrinkled his brows. "Share our Messiah?" Maybe the Messiah does not want to be shared. Have you thought about that?"

Varrus nodded his head up and down.

"I have been taught that having one parent that is Gentile makes you worse than a Gentile and you, you still want to see the Messiah? How can that be?" asked Amon as he scratched his forehead.

Varrus shrugged his shoulders. "I know of Abraham, Isaac and Jacob. My mother taught me many things about the Law and the Prophets. Amon, you may be in a rush to go to Jerusalem, but before you go, I need to say, thank you for listening to me and my story."

Amon turned to see a swarthy skinned elderly man standing next a table that had grapes, figs and wine on it. The man bowed to acknowledge Amon.

"That is . . ?" Amon said as he pointed at Pollus.

"Yes . . . that is Pollus."

Amon looked at every part of him, from head to toe. After some silence, Amon asked, "Is he also a . . . Samaritan?"

"No, he is a Gentile and the Messiah healed him."

"How can that be? He is our Messiah and now uncircumcised people claim him?"

"I cannot answer that. All I know is that he healed Pollus and I am indebted to him."

Amon needed some time to think about that and while he was deep in thought, Varrus said, "Since you have not been here before, and you know of the stories of King David and Saul, I thought I would tell you that this city is an important part of Hebrew history."

Amon appeared shocked.

Varrus smiled. "Yes I know about King David because my mother told me about Moses, Daniel and arranged for a rabbi to teach me from the Tanakh. I am able to speak Aramaic as well as many other languages."

Amon was momentarily speechless. When he gathered his thoughts, he responded. "You know about the Tanakh?"

"Yes Amon. The Tanakh is a word made up of the first parts of the word, Torah, Nevi'im and the K'tuvim."

Amon remained silent.

"Come to the window," insisted Varrus as he motioned for Amon to join him. "That mountain," said Varrus, "in the middle of this city is where King Saul and his sons were killed in battle."

"That mountain over there?" whispered Amon as he opened his mouth in awe.

For the remainder of the afternoon, Varrus continued to tell Amon about the history of this area and what Jesus was teaching to the common people. He told Amon about the disciples that followed him and who the leaders of the synagogue were and how confrontational they were with Jesus. Their time together seemed to pass so quickly.

When it was late, Varrus gave Amon instructions about traveling to Jerusalem. He told him that he would have to go through the City of Jericho, one of the oldest cities in the world. He also told Amon what areas to stay away from and when to travel. He recommended an inn for the night because of the thieves in that area.

"The worst part of the journey is between Jericho and Jerusalem. It is a steep climb and there are more thieves and robbers in that area than you can imagine. Many people have been murdered for small amounts of food," Varrus said. "It seems that priests seem to be the only ones, who are not attacked and beaten."

"How am I to get there?" asked Amon as he stepped back.

"Travel when a Roman cavalry is passing through that area or follow a priest. Be very careful when you pass through that area because it is very dangerous."

"How do you know about that area?" asked Amon.

"I've been there before, and it is an area that I don't like. We have found many murdered people in that area."

"Are you be going there sometime soon?"

"My orders are to take three hundred men to Jerusalem, but I will not be able to take you with me. First, I must allow my injuries to heal before I am able to travel."

"Can I follow?"

"We'll be on horseback. This is a mounted cavalry, remember."

"I can travel very fast if it means that I'm not to be killed," insisted Amon. "When will you be going?"

"In a week, but I need to get stronger before I leave."

"Why are you going?" asked Amon.

"I'll still be a Centurion, but I'll be given different duties when I arrive in Jerusalem."

"Is that good?"

"Yes, I suppose, if it were in a peaceful city, but Jerusalem is not as peaceful as Scythopolis. War is a constant threat to everyone that lives there, especially during the Passover Feast because of the many pilgrims."

"I don't like war and things like that. All I want to do is find the Messiah," insisted Amon.

"I'll find out if my rank will change when I arrive in Jerusalem. A promotion could make me a Cohort Centurion, but I don't know what will happen. Amon, since I have listened to the Messiah and he healed my servant, I find war to be very hollow. Peace is what I wish, but my military responsibilities and promotions keep me where I am. I will have Pollus take you to the families that Jesus has helped. Shalom Amon, and I hope that you find the Messiah."

Amon nervously shifted his weight from one foot to the other before whispering, "Shalom. I never thought that I would say that to a Samaritan."

"And if you speak to the Messiah, tell him that you know me and that I am very grateful for what he has done for me and my servant Pollus. He will remember."

Pollus walked with Amon several hundred strides from the Roman barracks and introduced him to a garment maker and a family which Varrus had spoken about. They welcomed Amon when Pollus explained why they had come to their house.

After Pollus left, Amon spoke to the father and knelt beside the young child that had been healed by Jesus.

Conspiracy With Malicious Intent

"Tell me the story again of what the Messiah did," said Amon as he turned to Abbiahk, the garment maker. "I want to hear it one more time so I am sure to understand."

"When," explained Abbiahk, "a neighbor told us about the Messiah who healed a man, who could see again and about a woman who was able to walk, we decided to find out where this Messiah was. When they told us that he was at the Jordan River, we knew it was too far for us. Several days later our neighbor's wife, Tziddel, told us that Jesus was going to be in Scythopolis, so we waited. Then one day when I was leaving the synagogue, I saw many people standing next to the three wells, and when I went near I saw the Messiah healing a blind man. I rushed home and brought Dunya, my daughter, and the Messiah touched her ears and whispered into them. All I remember is that she cried out and made sounds that we had never heard before."

"What did she say?" asked Amon, his eyes wide with surprise.

"She could not say words because she had never heard words before, but she pointed at both ears and covered them with her hands."

"Why?"

"Well, she had never heard sound before and it was strange for her until she got used to it. Now she is learning to hear and speak."

Amon watched the young girl as she played with two other girls. He was pleased that he had the privilege of hearing about this miracle and seeing who it was that had been healed.

Amon stayed at their home for ten days and asked many questions. He was introduced to other parents of children that had been healed, and eagerly watched every child.

Chapter XXIII

THE BLIND MAN AND THE SHORT MAN

During the twilight hours of the eleventh morning, Amon was awakened by the sound of many horses. He sat up in the moonlit darkness, rushed to the window to see what was happening. He could see small slivers of light reflecting off dozens of cavalrymen's helmets, silver shoulder straps and spears at the barracks gate. The moonlight flashed boldly off the large metal eagle or Aquifer, which was held high above the legionnaires as they moved near the barracks gate.

Amon dressed as rapidly as he could and ran to the main road just as four horses nervously pranced through the barracks entrance. He hurried to the shadows of the sycamore tree and watched in silence.

A cold shiver ran across Amon's neck and down his arms, when he heard a voice calling orders from within the barracks gate. Suddenly, the sound of a thousand hooves took Amon's breath away. He watched as the cavalrymen began to pour out of the military fortress like a swarm of bees. Leather creaked and metal scabbards rattled as the faceless beings rode by him in an organized frenzy. It was difficult for Amon to comprehend how many cavalrymen and horses flowed out of that narrow wooden gate.

Seven horses led the swarm in a nervous dance toward the tree where Amon stood hidden from view. Again chills ran up his arms as the moonlight created a silent and cold halo of authority over the souls of the men, who rode past him. An imposing aura hovered over the shiny eagle, located on a long, thick, wooden staff. Amon could not take his eyes off the Aquifer, a symbol of Rome's authority. The Standard Barer, who carried the Aquifer, found it difficult to master his anxious steed when they rode within strides of where Amon stood. At that moment, he felt the urge to hide behind the tree but his legs seemed unwilling to move.

All of this happened so fast that Amon had little time to notice if Varrus had been leading the swarm of potential killers on their midnight maneuver. Almost as quickly as this event started, it was over. All that Amon could remember hearing was the sound of nervous hooves moving over the cobblestones. The soul stirring sound eventually faded into an eerie silence.

The chill that he felt when this armored hoard and spirited horses pranced by him, remained in his body for several minutes and he had to literally shake himself for it to ebb. He knew that soon it would be sunrise, so he rushed into the house where he had been staying and began to pack his personal things. As he quietly closed the door of his room, he assured himself that today was the day that he had to leave for Jericho. Disappointed that Varrus had left and that he was unable to follow, Amon reminded himself of his purpose to find the Messiah.

As he was about to leave, Abbiahk called to him. "Amon, are you alright?"

"Yes, but I must leave for Jerusalem today."

"Can you not stay for some food? It is a long journey and there is yet plenty of time."

Amon ate, bade Abbiahk farewell and started his journey southward along the Jordan River. It was an easy road for it descended toward the Dead Sea. The first part of journey was uneventful but he did have several opportunities to speak with travelers who he met along the way.

He was sure that the Roman Cavalry had traveled this road only hours earlier because of the manure that marked their passing. To avoid stepping in it, he walked on the rocky edge of the road, and soon his feet became tired. Fortunately, the road did not have any steep inclines.

Later in the day, he approached a group of homes with two sheep pens and stopped to see if they would allow him the safety of their location for the night. After the man agreed, he offered Amon food and listened to his endless stories. When it was dark, he walked over to one of the sheep pens and slept under three small trees.

In the morning, he drank water from their well and started for the city of Jericho. Only once did he worry about a group of men approaching him. They seemed to be excessively loud but when they ignored him, he was relieved. He walked very rapidly after he had passed them because he was hoping to put significant distance between himself and the group.

It was late afternoon when he found himself approaching the city of Jericho. When he saw a large crowd off to the side of the pathway, he decided to see what the commotion was about. Off in the distance, he could hear someone calling at the top of his voice, so he stopped at the edge of

Conspiracy With Malicious Intent

the crowd to listen. Amon peered between the heads of men, women and their animals to see who it might be. Some people were sitting on donkeys while others stood on large rocks by the side of the road. All seemed to be looking in one direction.

The shouting became louder and louder and it was hard to understand what was being said, so Amon elbowed his way into the crowd to see who was making the noise.

Suddenly Amon became aware of what was being said. A man, off to the side of the road, was shouting at the top of his voice, "JESUS, SON OF DAVID, HAVE MERCY UPON ME. JESUS, SON OF DAVID, HAVE MERCY UPON ME." The man repeated the phrase over and over again as the crowd slowly moved toward Jericho.

Suddenly the crowd stopped and a man, whom Amon recognized as the prophet and Messiah from Simon's house in Nain, called for the shouting man to be brought to him. Two men assisted the man across the dusty roadway to where Jesus was standing.

The man's clothing was tattered and filthy, and his hands and hair appeared unwashed. The man moved his head from side to side, as though listening for someone speaking to him. Then he said, "I am Bartimaeus, the son of Timaeus. Please do not harm me. Do not harm me." He held his arms in front of him as he shuffled his swollen and bruised feet toward the Messiah.

Amon heard the whispers of the people near him. "He's blind. Maybe the Messiah will heal him."

The man became silent as the Messiah placed his hand on the blind man's arm. "What do you want me to do for you?" asked the Messiah.

As Bartimaeus' head continued to sway from side to side, he pleaded, "LORD, that I may receive my sight!" At that moment, he slumped to his knees.

The crowd remained silent as Jesus said, "Receive your sight, Bartimaeus. Your faith has made you well."

A moment passed and the blind man began shouting. "I CAN SEE. I CAN SEE. THERE IS A TREE AND PEOPLE," he voice suddenly calmed. "Jesus, OHHHHH, thank you. Thank you Son of David." As he spoke tears flowed from his now seeing eyes.

The crowd shouted and praised God. Some jumped off their donkeys to push closer to look at the once blind man.

Amon asked the man beside him, "Who is that man?"

"That is Bartimaeus. He lost his sight a long time ago and now begs."

"Not that man! The man who made him see?"

"That is Jesus, the prophet."

"Is he the Messiah?" asked Amon as he began to force his way to the front of the crowd. Suddenly a hand touched him on the shoulder. "Please don't push," the gentle voice said.

Turning to the voice, Amon asked, "Who are you?"

"My name is Andrew and I'm one of Jesus' followers."

"Is he . . . is he the Messiah?" whispered Amon with childlike innocence as he pointed at Jesus.

"He's the Son of God, and he has told us that he has been sent by God to the lost of the House of Israel. Even John the Baptist told everyone he was coming. We believe that he is the Messiah."

"What is a John the Bapatisma?"

"He's the one who came to make the way for Jesus to begin his ministry. He's the one who . . ."

Amon interrupted. "My friend Zebedee told me about this John the Bapatisma."

"You know Zebedee? How do you know him?" asked Andrew as he narrowed his brows.

"He's my friend in Capernaum. I know him and Judah and Palti. They're nice people. Do you know them too?"

"My brother Simon, the one who is leading the crowd and I listened to Jesus, who told us to follow him and he would make us into fishers of men. So we chose to follow him."

Amon continued to walk beside Andrew. "Yes. Yes. But do you know Zebedee too?"

"Those two men walking over there," he said as pointed at two men, "are James and John, Zebedee's sons. Yes, we know Zebedee, Judah and Palti, too."

"Is John the Bapatisma here too?"

"No. John has been beheaded by King Herod."

"You mean?" Amon said as he moved his hand horizontally across his throat, "He's . . ?"

Andrew closed his eyes, nodded his head up and down. "Yes I'm afraid so. King Herod had him put to death."

Some people remained behind to be with Bartimaeus, while others continued to follow Jesus as he walked toward Jericho. Amon was not aware of how many were following, but he felt as if his journey had finally come to an end. He had so many questions, so he walked along with Andrew and the crowd toward Jericho.

Andrew patiently told Amon of the feeding of the five thousand and the feeding of the four thousand, the calming of the stormy sea, the healings and about the people who had been delivered from evil spirits. Their conversation continued until they and the crowd entered the city of Jericho.

The crowd seemed to increase in size when Jesus arrived in Jericho and by now, it was difficult to remain with Andrew for the crowd was trying to be closer to Jesus.

Amon noticed a dozen cavalrymen watching from between two large buildings. The crowd was too busy to notice them but they continued to follow Jesus. Amon would have become lost had it not been for Andrew, who continued to speak with him as they walked along.

The crowd suddenly stopped under a sycamore tree when someone pointed and shouted, "LOOK UP IN THE TREE. IT'S ZACCHAEUS THE TAX COLLECTOR. What is he doing up there?"

"He's found a new place to tax people."

The crowd laughed while others in the crowd continued to taunt him. Someone shouted, "ZACCHAEUS. WE KNOW YOU'RE SHORT. DO YOU NEED A TREE TO SEE JESUS?"

Another shouted, "ARE YOU GOING TO TAX JESUS AS YOU DO US?" Someone shouted, "DO YOU PLAN TO TAX THE OWNER OF THAT TREE?"

"ZACCHAEUS, IS THAT THE ONLY WAY YOU CAN SEE WHAT'S GOING ON?" taunted another.

As the crowd laughed, Jesus walked under the tree and waved at him. "So you are Zacchaeus are you?" the Messiah asked.

"Yes," responded the man rather sheepishly.

"Hurry, come down Zacchaeus. I would like to meet with you. In fact, I'm willing to come to your house for supper."

"You would?" Zacchaeus' eyes widened as he began to look for a way to come down.

"Yes, come down," motioned Jesus. "I am glad to meet you. Tax collectors are interesting people."

The short man slid to the ground and nervously approached Jesus. Then he grinned before saying, "I would be pleased if you would come to stay with me. Why did you pick me?"

Jesus replied, "I don't often meet people in trees."

Again the crowd laughed.

"Watch out Jesus, or he will find a way to tax you," someone said.

Jesus smiled and motioned for Zacchaeus to come near.

"You're willing to come to my house?" asked Zacchaeus again as he looked around at the people who were still laughing at him.

"Yes. Your house is very nice place."

"Well come, it's not far from here," motioned Zacchaeus as he turned to show the way.

As the crowd moved along the street toward Zacchaeus' house, Amon heard some of the people complaining that Zacchaeus was a Jew, who was known to be a dishonest tax collector for the Romans. Many questioned were asked as to why Jesus would even talk to someone like him, let alone go to his house.

Jesus continued to speak with Zacchaeus as they walked along the street, when suddenly they stopped. Zacchaeus turned and raised his hand. "IF I HAVE CHEATED ANY OF YOU," he announced publicly, "I WILL REPAY YOU FOUR FOLD, AND HALF OF MY GOODS I WILL GIVE TO THE POOR."

The crowd was shocked at what they had just heard.

"What did he say?" whispered a man beside Amon.

"He's going to give some of his money away," Andrew said.

The man beside him whispered, "What has happened to him? Is he meshugga? Only a man out of his mind would do that. Why would he do that?"

Jesus turned to the crowd and said as he pointed to a luxurious house, "Today salvation has come to this house. All of this has happened because he is a Son of Abraham. The Son of Man has come to seek and save that which was lost."

The crowd watched as Jesus and his disciples walked through a gateway into the courtyard of a lavish house. Amon and the crowd remained outside. After waiting there for a long time, the crowd began to disperse for it was late in the day. Eventually only eight people remained.

Amon turned to the man beside him. "How far is Jerusalem?"

"Not far, but don't leave tonight. The road is very bad with thieves and murderers. They will beat you, take your valuables and think nothing of killing you. It is the worst place to travel in all of Palestine." Then the man offered Amon a place to stay for the night, and this provided him a full evening and opportunity to learn more of what Jesus had done for those in that area.

Amon ate with the man's family but lay awake for hours as he tried to understand all of the stories that he had been told. It was fortunate for the homeowner that Amon did not sleep, for his snoring would have kept everyone awake.

Chapter XXIV

THE CITY OF DAVID

Amon's eagerness to find the Messiah led him back to Zacchaeus' house the following morning. It was early when he arrived, and he considered knocking on the garden gate but when he saw how large the house was, he was initially intimidated so he moved to other side the street. From there he could see several fountains and two large gardens among the trees. Some time later, he returned to the Iron Gate to see if he could see anyone in the courtyard.

As he stood there, a servant approached the Iron Gate. He was not rude or aggressive, but appeared to be prepared for confrontation, rather than small talk. Amon knew another servant was standing behind one of the trees, so he waved at him but received no response. In an upper window, two other servants stood motionless next to lace curtains.

Amon called to the servant behind the tree. "Yesterday a Messiah came to your house. Is he still here?"

There was no response, so Amon called louder, "I know that you're behind that tree. All I want to know is where the Messiah is. Is he yet here?"

A moment later, the servant replied, "No. He left early this morning with the men who follow him."

"Where have they gone?"

"I do not know."

"Is your Master here? He would know."

"No."

After that, the servant refused to respond to Amon's questions, and when Amon was about to leave, a well-dressed man approached, so Amon turned to him, "What is the name of the man, who lives in this nice house?"

"He's a tax collector for the Romans. He's a betrayer of our people and we cannot trust him because of his allegiance to Rome." The man spit on the ground before continuing. "He's worse than a pagan." Again he spit onto the ground.

"I don't care what he does, all I want to know is his name," insisted Amon as he raised his hands above his head.

"He's a betrayer. Anyone that is a tax collector for the Romans should be put to death for betraying his people. Look at the house and that will tell you what he does to us."

"All I want to know is his name," interrupted Amon as he turned back to look at the house.

The man, now twenty paces from Amon turned and replied. "Zacchaeus is his name and he's at his tax booth between old Jericho and the Roman Jericho. He's made all of this off our backs because he takes our money. Look at his house and that will tell you what he has done to us and what he's like."

"I remember seeing him yesterday. He's a very short man," said Amon.

"Yes and all of his riches have come off our backs." Again the man spit on the ground, turned and walked away.

As Amon neared a small building at the end of the street, a herd of sheep and goats crossed in front of him, so he slowed down until they had passed. He watched the herd and herdsman walk toward the Jordan River and wondered if the Messiah might be there.

Amon roamed aimlessly through the streets of Jericho, looking for any sign of the Messiah, or anyone who knew where the Messiah might be. He stopped in the market and was about to buy some food when three cavalrymen rode past him.

He called to them and ran after them. One of them looked back at him and turned his mount to face Amon. The sight of the horse bobbing its head made Amon nervous so he stood still.

The cavalryman nudged his horse to move closer to Amon, and as it did, the cavalryman placed his hand on his sword.

"All I want to know," said Amon as he raised his hands and backed up, "is if you have seen the prophet. He heals people and speaks to them. Do you know where he is?"

"If you are looking for the man that walks around Jericho with many people following him, he's . . ." He turned to the other cavalryman who had been riding with him. "Where did we see that man that has many people following him?" asked the first legionnaire.

"Find him yourself. We're not your servants," was his reply.

"I mean no harm. All I am asking is where that man is?"

Ignoring Amon, they turned their horses and moved down the street.

While Amon was standing there, an elderly man with a scraggly beard approached. "Don't talk to those Gentiles. They will kill you if you bother them." He adjusted his weight with the crooked staff he was carrying and moved to a boulder next to a white washed house. When he was comfortably seated, he waved at Amon. "Say nothing to those pagans. They know not our ways and are heathens. Why God has allowed them to desecrate our land, I know not, yet they are here." He shrugged his shoulders as he spoke.

"Why not ask them questions?" asked Amon.

"You must be new in Jericho. Those Gentiles will arrest you if you bother to talk to them."

"Yes, I'm new here, but yesterday I saw the Messiah speaking to a short man, who climbed a sycamore tree. He's a tax collector and his name is Zaccass."

"Yes, yes. I heard that the prophet stayed at Zacchaeus' house for the night. I used to think he was a prophet until I heard that he decided to eat with Zacchaeus and stay in his house. Now I'm not sure."

"Is he the Messiah?"

"If he's the Messiah then the Messiah should live by the laws and keep our traditions, not be with tax collectors and sinners. I used to wonder if he might be our Messiah but he now stays and eats with sinners. Maybe I am upside down about this man, but if he's a Messiah, why does he do things that are not like a Messiah?"

"Why does it make any difference where he eats or sleeps? A Messiah is a Messiah. He's not a Messiah just because he eats with sinners and tax collectors."

The man stood to his feet and entered a shop because he was unwilling to continue speaking with Amon.

Amon stopped a man and his boy, who were walking by. "Do you know where the Messiah is?"

The man did not seem to know or care about Amon's question but continued walking without saying a word.

Amon spent the remaining part of the afternoon walking through the city, and realizing it was too late to walk to Jerusalem, he looked for a place to stay for the night. Some distance away, he saw an inn and stepped into the doorway.

The innkeeper, after letting the room to Amon, spent most of the evening telling Amon of many of the miracles that had happened in the area. He told Amon about John the Baptist, how he dressed, what he looked like and what he spoke about. He told Amon of what happened to John the Baptist, and spoke about the religious leaders and lawyers, who seemed determined to trip up Jesus with their many questions about the Mosaic Law.

Amon's many questions kept the innkeeper up for most of the night. The stories interested Amon but he was not pleased to hear that the Messiah and his disciples had gone to Jerusalem.

The next morning, Amon purchased a dagger from the shopkeeper for his trip to Jerusalem. His purchase was prompted by the rumors of thieves in the area. He left by the south road, which eventually turned westward, and when people approached Amon while on the road, he would reach into his sleeve and nervously hold onto the newly purchased dagger.

The distance to Jerusalem is one hundred furlongs or twelve miles (20+ kms) as the crow flies, but the crooked road and switchbacks made the journey closer to one hundred and sixty furlongs. It was a desperate climb that tires many a traveler and animal. Since Jericho is 820 feet below sea level, the climb to Jerusalem, 2500 feet above sea level, results in a grueling climb of 3400 feet.

It was late in the day when Amon neared Jerusalem. There he came to a fork in the road; one road turned to a southeasterly direction and other continued westward. Amon stood by the diverging roads, hoping that someone would be able to tell him which one to choose, but no one was in sight. He looked up at the angle of the sun and decided that he could not wait any longer, so he chose the road that traveled westward. The continuous climb exhausted Amon so he had to stop several times.

Eventually, he met two priests who were walking toward him. When they drew near, he waved his hand to stop them, but they nervously stood at a safe distance.

"WHICH ROAD LEADS ME TO JERUSALEM?" he called to them.

They approached cautiously and when they felt safe, one of them responded, "That road leads to Bethany," as he pointed to the southeast, "and this one will take you to Jerusalem."

"I'm looking for the Messiah. Have you seen him?" asked Amon.

"A Messiah does not live in this area," the priest said. "If you are looking for the troublemaker, who challenges all what is taught by the Laws of Moses and the priests, then you are looking for trouble too."

Amon told them of Hannah's son, Zebedee and the healing of a blind man in Jericho, but the priests just looked at him as though he had a disease. They remained aloof, regardless of how hard he defended the Messiah. Eventually, they walked around him and left him standing in the middle of the road.

"Rabbis and priests know nothing," he muttered to himself as he raised his hands above his head, "or maybe they pretend to know nothing." Disappointed, he watched them walking away.

In the distance he could see the walls of Jerusalem and the sight of that place momentarily took his breath away. "So this is where my father Beno came to worship and this is where King David lived and, and . . ." He did not finish his words because he became too emotional to speak. He wiped the tears from his eyes and moved slowly toward the city gate.

As he neared the city, he became more aware of Rome's presence. Mounted cavalrymen seemed to be everywhere. On the wall of the city were dozens of soldiers and at the gates, he could see many travelers waiting to enter the city.

When he was within several hundred strides of the walls of Jerusalem, he became emotional again because of what his father, Beno, had told him about the City of David. He remembered the stories of Solomon's Temple and the altars, and where sacrifices were offered. He remembered his father's excitement as he told his sons of this Holy City.

When Amon was within several strides of the gate, he stopped and wiped the tears from his eyes. Momentarily, he was unable to enter, so he stood there overwhelmed by the stone walls, the gates and the spiritual aura of the city.

He was nudged from behind as a strong voice said, "Move out of the way. Others want to get in, so get out of the way."

He turned and found several legionnaires forcing him aside so others could pass through the gate.

"Gentiles!" Amon mumbled. "You are not worthy to be in this special city. Why did God let you pagans be in this city?"

Once inside, he could not believe how many people were walking with camels, donkeys and carts. It was the busiest place that Amon had ever seen. He wandered as a child in a store, unable to take in the sights and sounds of the moment. Often he stopped to stare at the walls and buildings, wondering what his father, Beno, had seen when he had been here so many years ago. He enjoyed the sounds of donkeys braying, sheep bleating and music in the market place. Children were running and playing among the buyers and sellers, and oh, the smell of the food was so enticing. The breads and the meats that were being cooked made his stomach growl.

He stopped to look at the jewelry, clothing and food displays. It was the first time that he saw a black man, and found it hard to take his eyes off of him. Occasionally, a chariot passed by so he watched as it moved through the crowd. He watched as a merchant was selling slaves and marveled at the wild animals that were in cages. At one intersection, he watched as women, who dressed and looked like Peninnah, stood near a doorway of a small building. Two men arguing drew his attention away from the women so he wandered through the marketplace. There were many things that Amon had never seen before.

Amon stopped at several shops to ask about the Messiah, but he was forced out of the way by vendors, who were interested in sales only. They seemed disinterested in Amon and his questions. When he purchased some dates and a pomegranate, he asked the proprietor "Is this place always so busy?"

"You must be new to Jerusalem," said the man as he smiled at Amon. "I have lived here most of my life and it is always like this, especially before the Passover Feast."

"I've come from Nain." As he told his story and explained his reason for coming to Jerusalem, the man seemed willing, if not eager to hear Amon's stories.

"Everyone has a story to tell," the proprietor said as he raised his hands. "If you sit down, I will tell you about Gilam, who lives down the street from me. He was in Bethany some time ago and saw the Messiah raise a man from the dead. That's right. Dead for some days and just like that," he snapped his fingers as he spoke, "he was alive. Have you ever seen something like that?"

Amon interjected, "I just told you I TOO HAVE SEEN THAT. A boy was dead and just like that he was alive too."

The proprietor cocked his head to the side, "So it is possible, is it? I mean to be dead and then, then alive?" Again he snapped his fingers as he spoke.

"Yes," insisted Amon, "but tell me the story about the man from that Bethany place."

"This man was yet in the tomb for four days, yes, four days, and the man they call the Messiah called his name and then the dead man came out of the grave. He was still wearing grave clothes when he crawled out. Think of it. Dead and then alive." Again he snapped his fingers. "How can that be? The rabbi said that after three days the spirit leaves the body and you are for sure dead."

"I once had a grave cloth from Hannah's dead son. The cloth was no good because it did not help my dead brother but Hannah's son was alive, like I told you. Do you know where the Messiah is now?" Amon asked eagerly anticipating an answer but when the man did not answer, Amon said, "And I saw the Messiah make a man to see a few days ago and I heard he fed many people. Do Messiah's always do many things like that?"

"That, I cannot tell you but I do know that the priests, Sadducees and Pharisees would love to kill him because he is able to explain the scriptures better than they can, and," he raised his hand as he spoke. "I heard that he answered all of their questions, from lawyers too. Can you yet image that?"

"What are Sadaseas and Pharikese?"

"Pharisees?" corrected the shopkeeper, "are men that think they know more than any other people. They argue about everything and do not agree on anything, but when the Messiah comes near, they become jealous. I have seen with my own two eyes, what is in their eyes." He raised both hands and pinched his thumbs against the pointer fingers as he spoke. "They, they are jealous I tell you. Why? I will tell you why. Because the Messiah can do things that they cannot do. They call him a sinner and a blasphemer but can sinners and blasphemers heal people and raise people back to being alive? Sinners cannot do that. Blasphemers can't do that either I tell you." He closed his eyes and shook his head from side to side. "No, no, no they cannot do that."

"How can a man be jealous of a Messiah? The Messiah must know about their jealousy and maybe, just maybe, God knows that too. That's not good," said Amon as he shook his head from side to side.

"I've been talking to you all this time and do not yet know your name. Who are you and who are your family?" asked the shopkeeper.

"My name is Amon and my father was from the Tribe of Naphtali and my mother, she was from Jacob's son, Asher. What is your name?"

"I am Adakal. I've lived in Jerusalem almost all of my life. It is a city like no other. Come and tell me about this place you call Nain and, and then tell me about your brother. What was his name?"

Amon told of his life in Nain, his brother and the fateful night when he lost everything. At times, he stopped to wipe tears from his cheeks, but he continued until there was little left to say.

Adakal told Amon of the many miracles that the Messiah had done, even on the Sabbath. He spoke of the words and some of the debates between the Messiah and lawyers. Amon could scarcely take it all in.

In Adakal's house, Amon spent the entire night looking out of the window of his bedroom. He reminded himself of his purpose to find the Messiah and to speak with him. "I've been so close and heard him talk to others except me. I, Amon from Nain, want to talk to the Messiah. Yes, me, that is what I want," he said as he gently tapped his fist on his chest. "That's what I want."

In the morning, Adakal reminded Amon that Passover was coming, and since Amon had nowhere else to stay, Adakal invited him to remain with his family. During the day, Adakal showed Amon around the city and took him to the Temple.

In the courtyard, dozens of people bought doves and lambs from the moneychangers, who handled and exchanged coins from pilgrims, who had traveled from many different nations. Again Amon was surprised to see several black men, especially ones that were allowed into the courtyard. He watched them and stood near them to see if they had five fingers on each hand. One of them asked Amon a question, but Amon did not understand his language or accent, so he shrugged his shoulders and walked away.

"Where do those, those dark people come from? Why are they yet here in Jerusalem?" he whispered to Adakal. "Jews only should be in this here place."

"They come from Egypt and other parts south of there. They claim to be of the line of Abraham, Isaac and Jacob through King Solomon but, and I say but, no one knows for sure and . . . no one stops them, so who am I to ask or know that answer?"

"Tell me more about this King Solomon. My father spoke of him but why did he have children that are so dark? Have they been in the hot sun?"

Adakal spoke of King Solomon and the Queen of Sheba. He told Amon that the queen visited King Solomon and returned to Africa. He also told Amon that other Jews may exist in Egypt from the time of Moses, when the Israelites left Egypt so many years earlier. This was more than Amon could take in. Hour after hour they talked, and Amon did his best to understand new and different things that he had never heard of before.

"Do you believe that God made them that way?" Amon asked with childlike innocence.

Adakal responded, "I was unsure too until one of them asked me if I was sure that God did not have dark skin."

"The Hebrew God is not dark like that, is he?" asked Amon as he narrowed his eyes. "Adonai, Elohim, The Lord God is not black is he? Does the Books of Moses tell us about this? Moses should know because he spoke with God while they were in the desert."

"How do you know, Amon?" asked Adakal. "What makes you think that the Creator must look like me or you?"

Amon stared at the ground and shook his head from side to side.

"What if he is, Amon?" continued Adakal. "Remember that Moses' wife had dark skin. So what is wrong with extra dark skin?"

"But the Messiah looks like us for I have seen him."

"Yes, but you are talking about the Messiah. I'm talking about the Creator, the God of Abraham, Isaac and Jacob. It is He who made the world and all of us. I just don't know, Amon. I just don't know."

Chapter XXV

PONTIUS PILATE: GOVERNOR, PRAEFECTUS, PROCURATOR

In the province of Judaea, the city of Jerusalem was a political hub of Roman governance and military activity. Only the city of Caesarea, on the coast, housed more powerful officials and was larger in population. King Herod's palace jutted out from the coastline to become a major landmark. Governor, Praefectus and Procurator Pontius Pilate's primary residence was in Caesarea except when he traveled to Jerusalem to carry out his administrative duties.

Tiberius Claudius Caesar Augustus and the Roman Senate appointed Pontius Pilate to be the Governor and Praefectus. He was granted an exceptional amount of power to tax all commerce activities, create other tax initiatives to generate additional revenue, create and enact laws that would limit and control the general populace, and utilize the military to maintain civil order. Primarily his mandate was to preserve and maintain Rome's presence while generating vast amounts of revenue.

Pontius Pilate, born without influence or affluence, had an ability to speak with and make acquaintances with commoners, soldiers, officers and men of influence and power. His ability to manipulate and persuade, lured many a dignitary into accepting him as a friend, resource and advisor. His opinions, views and perceptions were intriguing, and were soon embraced by those of similar beliefs, eventually leading him into ever more powerful circles of authority. Over a period of time, he became friends with Sejanus, who openly endorsed anti-Jewish ideals and policies, and when Pontius became a friend of Tiberius, he was now within arms length of power which had become his idol.

Conspiracy With Malicious Intent

When Pontius Pilate had opportunity to romance and beguile Augustus Caesar's granddaughter, Pontius knew that opportunity lay ahead. There was no doubt that he loved her, but their marriage was one of convenience, especially for Pontius.

When Gratus left his eleven year governance in Palestine, Pontius was named as his successor. He was now willing to show his superiors that he was worthy of his designated position and purposed in his heart to rule with a strong and unforgiving hand.

Pontius Pilate's obligation was to Rome, to Caesar and himself. He had great influence on the Legatus and the officers under him, and governed with minimal cooperation from King Herod, who reigned throughout Palestine. Tact was the most important behavior Pontius should have demonstrated, however his arrogance and quick reactive temper put him into disfavor with the citizens of Jerusalem and ultimately with Caesar.

As Governor, he was appointed to ensure Rome's best interest by managing taxes and finances and maintaining the peace by suppressing special interest groups, including renegades, rebels and Zealots. Additional duties included the management of large sums of money, agriculture, citizen activities, enforcing Roman policy and the affairs of the province of Judaea and the cities of Caesarea and Jerusalem.

Pontius Pilate's influence and word was feared by many and challenged by few. In this province, Pontius Pilate was named Praefectus with additional responsibilities of managing resources, military power and ensuring that finances were accounted for and readily available, when needed.

He motivated staff and citizen, not with skilled leadership and gentle words, but with an iron hand. He ruled with unsympathetic feelings, accepted few requests and certainly did not entertain any recommendations. His offices and residences in Caesarea and Jerusalem, were lavish buildings that appeared more like small palaces rather than an extension of the Roman governance. Bribery, murder, conspiracy, deceit, theft and a fierce temper made him unpredictable, unapproachable and feared by everyone. Even King Herod, who himself was an eccentric despot, avoided Pontius Pilate whenever possible.

On rare occasions, Pontius used his jurisdiction to command soldiers to act according to his edict. The official Commanding Officer in Jerusalem was Tribunus Laticlavius Kadurra Senna, who acted under the watchful eye of the Legatus, who lived in Caesarea. However, Pontius was able to command and overrule him at any given moment.

Conspiracy With Malicious Intent

Positions within the Roman military structure were usually given to those, who had a history of power and wealth, which usually resulted in leadership displaying arrogance, affluence, overconfidence and lack of experience related to military issues. There were, however exceptions.

During the calendar year, Pontius would move to Jerusalem from Caesarea to attend to his administrate duties, and once his obligation were completed, he would eagerly return because Caesarea was a beautiful city, and because the citizens of Jerusalem were confrontational and resisted his powers. It was no surprise that he detested that city and its inhabitants, and they in turn, resented him.

His continuous confrontations with religious leaders and citizens of Jerusalem, was a continuum of disasters. On one occasion when the Jews were very angry at him for placing Roman symbols on and in the Temple, the Jews openly rebelled, and when he threatened to have all of them killed, they bared their necks and throats as they knelt before the Roman army. He never suspected that they were willing to die for their beliefs.

Arrogantly, he used sacred funds from the Temple to cover the cost of building an aqueduct to bring water into Jerusalem. Great unrest turned into a riot so he called for soldiers to dress as civilians and move among the crowd, and when a signal was given, they attacked the rioters and severely beat them.

****

A well dressed raven haired woman walked with confidence through the largest market in Jerusalem, and with her was an entourage of two very young women, an elder woman and six Roman bodyguards that were within three strides of her at all times. Her fine clothes and gold jewelry accented her beauty as she moved among the people. Most people avoided her, and it seemed evident that she had been to that market many times before.

She handled scarves, sandals, gold jewelry and trinkets. Occasionally, she would purchase something and hand it to the elder woman, who carried it for her. This regal woman purchased figs, pomegranates and dates. Again, she handed it to the elder woman, who eventually solicited the aid of one of the young handmaidens.

The youngest girl held an umbrella over this regal lady's head while she shopped. This woman of luxury wore gold jewelry and painted lines around her eyes, making her appear Egyptian. She had a presence about her that drew attention to her.

She walked confidently among the baskets, fine linens and well-crafted silver ornaments. She stopped to look at several rugs and tried to negotiate a fair price for sandals but shook her head and returned them to the table.

When she had completed her shopping, she waved her wrist at one of the bodyguards, who raised his hand to signal someone on the outer edge of the market. Immediately a chariot, with Roman symbols, moved carefully through the large crowd until it was directly in front of her. One of the handmaidens held her hand as she stepped into the chariot, and then the other women joined her. The chariot moved slowly to the edge of the market with other armed guards walking beside it. When they were a distance from the shoppers, six mounted cavalrymen rode up to the side of the chariot and all of them moved along a side street.

Some distance away from the eyes of the public, the entourage passed through an open metal gate and stopped at the door of a lavish building with Roman guards posted around it. The lady with her handmaidens walked up the granite stairs and entered the building as a guard closed the door behind them.

Some time later, another chariot arrived carrying a man of authority. Ten cavalrymen, who had escorted the chariot, waited as the man stepped from the chariot and entered the same building. Once inside, the man walked into the large parlor and was greeted by his wife.

"Pontay, I'm so glad that you're home," she said as she reached for his arm and placed her cheek to his. "A wonderful meal has been prepared for us. It is your favorite, roast lamb. Do hurry for its odor has made the children very hungry. Please hurry, Pontay."

"I trust that you had a wonderful day," he said as he waited for a servant to pour wine for him. He watched as the burgundy liquid swirled inside the tall and ornate glass goblet before removing his tunic and handed it to a servant.

"Pontay, I do enjoy it when you are home. I feel so much more secure when you are here with us, but I can hardly wait for us to return to Caesarea. You know that I love that city much more than Jerusalem. This city is so, so different, with its strange people, their strange customs and the extremely dry air. When do we return?"

Pontius smiled as he reached for his wine glass. "I like Caesarea much more than this place too. Here's to you, Claudia, my dear." He held his goblet high, sipped and savored it momentarily in his mouth as she smiled coyly at him.

Pontius walked down the granite hallway and opened a door to his children's play room. His son and daughter ran to him, anxious to tell him about the events of their day. He cast a glance at two nursemaids but said nothing to them.

When in the dining room, Pontius, his wife and two children sat at the long highly polished wooden table. A servant girl held a container of food as Claudia graciously placed food into her son's plate and then into her daughter's plate. When finished, she placed food into her plate and said, "Thank you Molinari."

Then Molinari carried the food to where Pontius sat and he watched as Molinari placed food onto his plate. Immediately after, she returned to the cooking room, Pontius reached for his wine and held it high as he wished Claudia, his son and his daughter good health.

After the evening meal, Claudia picked up her wine glass and made her way into a library where she reclined on a large pillow and sipped on the wine imported from Rome. "By the way Pontay," she said, "I have received an invitation for us to attend a party at King Herod's palace. Apparently, Herod and his wife will be in Jerusalem for the next few days. Tribunus Laticlavius Kadurra Senna, Tribuni Augusticlavii Emilio Caudoul and Tribuni Augusticlavii Phillo Pompados will be there with their wives or escorts. There is a chance that Legatus Sanndo will be there and I've heard a rumor that some Egyptian dignitaries will also be there. Do you wish to go?"

"Herod?" Pontius growled loudly. "I suppose that we should go, but I'd rather spend a quiet evening in the Praetorian than an evening with those arrogant men, lying about their wealth, their influence and their plans. Their arrogance froths my spirit and leaves an unsavory taste in my mouth. They revel in their own importance and reek of hypocrisy. As far as I am concerned, these contemptible fools should not be encouraged, let alone trusted."

"Kadurra Senna's wife is very nice to talk to. I do enjoy her company, but Herod's wife is . . ." she stopped and sipped her wine again. "Is he actually married or does he choose an escort moments before he attends parties and banquets?"

"Wife? He has the morals of a . . ."

Claudia interrupted, "Now, now Pontay, I know that his arrogance irritates you but it is only for one evening. How about it? Can we go?"

Conspiracy With Malicious Intent

"One evening is too much," said Pontius as he emptied his goblet. "Who can endure listening to, to braggers and fools for an entire evening? If it were not for the children and your smile, I would use stronger and uncultured language."

"Pontay dear, I do enjoy the banquets and parties in Caesarea, but it is the best thing that happens to us in this forsaken place." She smiled as she raised her goblet, "Ah here's to you Pontay. You were such a wonderfully rude man to Herod's last escort." She giggled as she emptied her goblet. "I believe her name was . . . Darlada." She covered her mouth with her hand as she silently chuckled.

"I have no idea what her name is or was, but I don't trust any of them," responded Pontius as he poured more wine into Claudia's goblet. "That woman with red hair has eyes and a mouth of a viper. When she is near, I always excuse myself." He reclined in his favorite chair to sip his wine.

"Ah Pontay, does she vex you because she could not keep her eyes off of you for the entire evening?"

Pontius narrowed his brows as he retorted, "Claudia, you know I have no interest in her so why are you taunting me with her name?"

Personally, I can't see you having any interest in her but I detect that she considers you . . . you to be a man of influence and power let alone . . ."

"Claudia," growled Pontius, "your smile warns me that you want to see my reaction but any comment about her irritates me."

"She does have an inviting body and displays it to everyone willing to look at her."

"Claudia that is enough."

"Pontay," she whispered as she sipped more wine, "when you defend yourself with anger, I . . . I'm sorry that I have overstepped my teasing. I'm sorry."

Pontius stared at the swirling wine within his glass goblet.

"Would you like me to have one of the servants tell them that we would be pleased to attend?" Claudia asked as she coyly smiled at him.

"I don't enjoy being forced into anything with Herod or any of his . . . his stable mates, but in the interest of neutralizing his political influence, I guess that . . ." He sighed loudly before completing his sentence. "I'll let you know tomorrow."

"But dear . . ."

"I will tell you tomorrow, Claudia. I do not wish to hear any more about this party. By the way, did you enjoy being in the market today?"

Chapter XXVI

THE PROMOTION

Thousands of pilgrims, from throughout the Roman Empire, descended upon Jerusalem to celebrate a major and critical religious rite known as the Passover Feast. Those with Jewish ancestry traveled hundreds of miles for a one time pilgrimage while others traveled every year for this solemn event. All roads that led to Jerusalem were filled with travelers from many nations and the streets were crowded with donkeys and camels, all laden with possessions that would be used during their travels. Every nation was represented. Men with their sons tried to move through the narrow streets and at times it seemed impossible to move among the crowds in the markets.

When Centurion Varrus Marcius Cassius de Lonnea arrived in Jerusalem four days before the Jewish Passover Feast, he was optimistic about rumors of a promotion, so when he was summoned to the office of the Commander-in-Chief of Jerusalem, Tribunus Laticlavius Kadurra Senna, he was expecting good news.

When he walked up the stone stairs to Senna's office, he had no idea that his life would change so radically that soon he would not recognize himself. His heart beat fast as he rounded the stone staircase to the top floor of the Military Planning Office and the Commander's office.

Kadurra Senna was the man assigned to maintain a firm grip on Jerusalem. His only obligation was to three men: first to Caesar, secondly to the Legatus Sanndo in Caesarea, and thirdly, to the wishes of the Governor and Praefectus Pontius Pilate.

Senna was a man born of Roman nobility, well educated and of considerable wealth. As a boy, he had his own servants from the day of his birth. He had never known want or discomfort, and now with unquestionable power, curbed only by the whims of Caesar, the Legatus and Pontius Pilate, lived a rather comfortable lifestyle envied by all citizens. His affluence included lavish meals and luxuries rumored to be beyond most men's dreams. His Achilles' heel was his arrogance, yet he never recognized his vulnerability because of his influence over people under his leadership and their fear of him.

Centurion Varrus Marcius Cassius de Lonnea arrived ahead of the assigned time and looked down at his shiny leather vestment, his new Roman sandals and the glistening hand grip of his gladius or short sword. He had to be sure that there was nothing that could be identified as insubordination or a careless attitude, which could be interpreted as a punishable offence.

Before knocking, he saluted the six guards at the door, who snapped to attention. Their eyes stared without blinking and their nostrils did not move as they held their breath, then slowly and silently exhaling.

Varrus nodded his head as the most senior of the six guards reached to the thick wooden door and knocked seven times, once for every person outside the door. The door creaked as it was opened from within and two guards with swords partially drawn, motioned Varrus to enter. As he stepped into the large room, the guards closed the door behind him.

Varrus looked straight ahead to the large desk full of maps, parchments and fancy feather quills, neatly placed beside various ink bottles. On the walls were tapestries and maps as well as oil paintings of Rome. An oil painting of Caesar was mounted behind a large wooden desk and at the end of the desk were several large flags on brass poles, one with a large eagle perched on the top of it. A small table to the right of the desk displayed several silver goblets and two flagons of wine.

Varrus did not recognize Tribunus Laticlavius Kadurra Senna for he had never met him before, so he saluted out of protocol and held his position.

Senna was standing by an open window and looking at the skyline of Jerusalem. His shoulders were rounded and his arms seemed short for his height, but his presence and stature commanded respect. His short grey hair was well groomed and his hands were exceptionally clean.

To Varrus' left sat another Roman officer, whose emotionless eyes matched his frozen face. His only movement was his chest as he breathed. Varrus remained rigid until told to stand at ease.

"Tribunus Laticlavius Kadurra Senna, Sir!" announced the senior guard, who paused a moment before continuing, "Centurion Varrus de

Conspiracy With Malicious Intent

Lonnea is here as requested, Sir!" A moment later, he stepped back to be in-line with the other guards.

Minutes passed without a sound in the room. Varrus and the other guards were well trained for such frozen moments, which could last well beyond thirty minutes.

After a long sigh, Senna turned his face from the open window to face Varrus. "Legatus Casso Sanndo has sent orders to Jerusalem that impact Roman Legion X," wheezed Senna. He looked down at the partially empty goblet in his hand before speaking. "My responsibility is to be sure that the Legatus is pleased with every aspect of our presence in Jerusalem and surrounding area." Senna cleared his throat and then continued. "By the way, you may stand at ease."

"Thank you Sir."

"Two major problems are before me. The first is the migration of thousands of fanatical Jews from all over the Roman Empire into this city, and from what I hear they come from areas outside of the Roman Empire. They arrive for a religious feast with their families, animals and servants. They crowd the streets and kill thousands of animals, paint blood on the doorposts of their houses and are highly irritable when they're faced with our presence in what they call their Holy City."

He motioned for a servant to pour more wine into his goblet and for the officer that sat silently near the flags and maps. Once his goblet had been filled, he sipped on the wine before continuing. "Each year we move cavalrymen and infantrymen to this city for more security, so this year I have ordered five hundred cavalrymen from Caesarea, three hundred cavalrymen from Scythopolis and two hundred from Jericho, just to keep this place from becoming the trouble spot of the entire Roman Empire. That means additional food for a thousand men and a thousand horses. Our task must be to gather and store provisions for all of them, and extensive plans have been made for additional patrols, which are needed to keep the peace."

He drank from his goblet and wiped his mouth on a lace cloth that lay on the table next to him. "Are you aware of these problems?" he asked as he motioned for more wine to be poured into his goblet.

"Yes Sir, I was the Centurion that escorted the three hundred men from Scythopolis."

"Oh yes, that's correct. None the less, my second problem needs to be addressed and that is why you have been summoned to my office." He sipped on the wine and placed the goblet onto the table. Squaring his shoulders before continuing, he narrowed his eyes as he began to speak. "It is my decision to fill a very important position that has recently been vacated, and that is why you are here."

Again there was silence.

"My plan," continued Senna "is to choose a worthy officer, who is known for his strength, leadership, discipline and ability to follow orders, regardless of the consequence. Your name, Centurion Varrus de Lonnea, has come to my attention."

The icy officer sitting next to the flags did not move as Senna continued to speak. In the silence that followed, Varrus remained focused on the tapestry behind Senna. He could feel the searing stare from the silent officer.

"Did you hear what I said?" asked Senna.

"Yes, Tribunus Laticlavius, Sir!"

"You are strong, for your voice does not fade or quiver when spoken to. That's good. Your next assignment is not for the weak or feeble. Your heart, voice and hand must be as strong and reliable as the blade of your sword." He paused for what seemed to be an eternity. "Your reputation in battle, utilization of resources, military maneuvers and decisions in times of stress are well noted."

"Thank you, Sir!"

"Step forward," he said in a commanding and arrogant tone.

Varrus stepped forward to face Senna, but did not crowd him for he knew the protocol and the consequences of violating that code of behavior. Now his back felt warmth from the unwanted stare from the silent officer seated behind him.

Senna sighed loudly as he tipped his head down slightly. His eyes were partially closed and the muscles in his cheeks twitched as he stood in silence.

Varrus continued to look forward and resisted the impulse to move.

"How many men have you killed?" asked Senna.

Somewhat surprised by the question, Varrus responded from impulse. "One hundred and sixty-two, Sir."

"Have you ever had second thoughts as you were about to slay anyone?"

"Only when they were without weapons to defend themselves, Sir."

"Hmmmm, honest. That's good." He did not change his position but continued to stare at Varrus. "When was the last time you killed a man, armed or unarmed?" he asked as his lips tightened.

"Twelve days ago, Sir!"

"Interesting. Has it been too long?"

Conspiracy With Malicious Intent

"Sir! I do not understand."

"You will," he said in a low tone as he turned and walked back to the open window to look at the view of distant hills surrounding the city. Again he sighed loudly and leaned on the stone sill to look down at the street below. After several moments, he turned to look at Varrus. He folded his arms across his chest as he began to speak. "How many have you wounded?" he asked in a monotone fashion.

"Hard to say, Sir, but I'd estimate several hundred or more, Sir!"

"When was the last time that you wounded a man, innocent or guilty?"

"I was forced into a confrontation in Sedden Valley a few weeks ago, where many cavalrymen and rebels were killed."

Varrus felt his face becoming very warm.

Kadurra Senna stepped up to be within inches of Varrus' face. As he did, he narrowed his eyebrows and momentarily tightened his lips. His breath smelled of garlic and wine, and his eyes were as emotionless as two blue opals. "You have been summoned from Scythopolis, where your rank is Centurion, is that true?"

"Yes, Sir."

"Because of your record of leadership and dedication, you will be given a new assignment. You will remain a Centurion with full responsibility of guards and prisoners in the Praetorian and be responsible for all executions. Your official title is Chief Executioner, which means you will ensure that all capital offences for crimes are carried out including floggings and crucifixions."

Varrus was unsure of what he had just heard.

Senna walked over to his chair behind a large desk and sat down. As he leaned back in his chair, it creaked loudly.

Varrus face felt numb and when he turned to look at Senna, he felt momentarily nauseated.

Once he was comfortable seated, Kadurra Senna placed his elbows on the armrests of the padded chair and folded his hands together under his chin as if in prayer.

A servant poured wine into his goblet and placed it in front of him, and then stepped back. Senna did not speak but swallowed loudly. "You'll curse me in my absence, but you will do what I tell you. Am I correct?"

"Yes Sir!" Varrus' voice was not as strong as it had originally sounded.

"Your new assignment is to work under the direction of Tribuni Augusticlavii Emilio Caudoul, who sits to your left. Allow me to introduce you to your new Commanding Officer."

Conspiracy With Malicious Intent

Varrus turned his head as Emilio Caudoul stood to his feet. He was taller and significantly older than Varrus or Senna, and his hands appeared exceptionally large. Varrus suddenly felt very warm, although the room was cool when he entered it.

Senna stepped between Emilio Caudoul and Varrus. "As Chief Executioner, you will manage the Praetorian that houses all prisoners and you will carry out all executions, and that include all floggings and crucifixions. Tribuni Augusticlavii Emilio Caudoul will monitor your decisions and activities." After smiling at Emilio Caudoul, Senna continued, "Just a warning. He is not easy to please nor is he patient with fools."

When Senna returned to his desk, Caudoul stepped close to face Varrus. He looked down at Varrus, but Varrus continued to look at Senna for he knew that protocol required that he keep his eye on the highest ranking officer, regardless of who spoke to him.

"You are now my property," whispered Caudoul. "I own you and your performance. You will have charge of many men, and you will deal with all of executions and anything else that is assigned to you in the death house. Are there ANY QUESTIONS?" His voice became gradually louder as he spoke.

Varrus felt nauseated and was forced to swallow several times and then whispered, "I don't know, Sir."

"It is an assignment that you will do. There is no negotiation. You will do an excellent job or you will . . ." he paused in the middle of his sentence to observe Varrus' reaction.

Varrus closed his eyes momentarily.

"Do you have any questions?" interjected Senna, in an icy tone

"Only two questions, Sir!"

"Very well. Choose them carefully," Senna said as he reached for the goblet of wine. After he finished his drink, he placed the goblet onto a lace cloth and looked up at Varrus.

"Sir! What is the minimum and maximum time that I will be on this assignment?"

Senna dabbed his lips with a red silken napkin that had been on the desk next to the wine container. "Are those the two questions that you wish to ask?"

"No Sir."

"Then choose them carefully," Senna said as he moved to stand near the large painted picture of Caesar. After a moment, Emilio Caudoul returned to his seat, without saying a word.

Realizing that he needed to carefully choose his words, Varrus asked, "What is my expected term of this assignment?"

"And your second question is?" asked Senna.

Varrus hoped that the answer to his first question would allow him an opportunity to reconsider what his second question would be, but the Tribunus Laticlavius had verbally outmaneuvered him. He was a shrewd man and a master of strategic planning with the ability to predict and measure the weaknesses and vulnerabilities of others.

"I have no second question, Sir!"

"HAHAHAHA. You are a wise man. Often the second question is more critical than the first one, but you are unsure of what the second question should be until you hear my answer to your first one. Am I correct?"

"Yes Sir!"

"He's the officer for this task," responded Caudoul as he attempted to smile.

"You're free to go. Your assignment begins immediately, so, you are excused to become familiar with your new obligation. You will be escorted to your new office as soon as you return to the street," said Senna in a dismissive tone.

Senna and Caudoul nodded and smiled at each other.

Varrus remained rigid.

Senna raised his goblet, "If you are waiting for the answer to your question, you will be disappointed," he said as he placed the goblet on the desk and folded his hands across his lower abdomen. "You will find out in due time. Good Day, Centurion Varrus de Lonnea."

Not since his first battle, many years earlier, had Varrus felt this shaken. His military career had its low points but this was similar to the wound he received from a spear thrown at him at close quarters during an ambush. Memories of those weeks of pain flashed through his mind like the speed of an arrow. He turned and walked toward a door that a soldier was opening. After acknowledging the guards with only a smile, he stepped in the cold hallway and started down the stairs.

His knees felt unreliable on each stair so he held the handrail as he moved down the staircase. The spiral stairway to the street seemed endless and each step tested his balance. Nausea mixed with anger and fear seemed to take his breath away, When he arrived on the ground floor, he closed his eyes to momentarily regain his composure.

When he stepped into the street, he found a chariot waiting for him.

The driver saluted and called his name, "Centurion Varrus de Lonnea?"

Varrus nodded.

"Tribunus Laticlavius Kadurra Senna's chariot is here to take you to your new assignment, Sir!"

Varrus stepped into the chariot and a moment later, the driver snapped the reins and two geldings quickly responded, for they too seemed to understand military protocol.

Chapter XXVII

CHAOS IN THE TEMPLE

When Jesus and his disciples approached the Mount of Olives, they stopped by the side of the road to rest. During their conversation, Jesus said to Andrew and Philip, "Go into the city and as you enter, you will see a colt tied there that no one has ever ridden. Untie it and bring it to me."

"What if the owner sees us and asks what we're doing?" asked Philip. "What shall we say for we don't have money to buy it?"

"Tell whoever asks, that the Lord needs it, and he will allow you to bring it to me," said Jesus as he patted Andrew on the shoulder.

So while the others remained with Jesus, Andrew and Philip entered Jerusalem and just inside the city gate, they saw a young colt tied at the side of a house. They approached it, and as they did, they saw a man standing nearby.

"What are you doing with my donkey?" asked the man when he saw Andrew untie it. "It's just a colt and too young to be ridden or to carry a load. Do you want to buy it?"

"No. We were told to say that the Lord needs it," to which the man replied, "If it's the Messiah who needs it, then yes, take it."

They led the colt out of the city gate and brought it to where Jesus and other disciples were waiting. When they arrived, Nathaniel put his cloak on the back of it and so did Thomas.

"What will you do with it?" asked Peter.

"I plan to ride it into Jerusalem," was Jesus' reply.

"It looks too young to ride," said John as he rubbed its soft ears.

"Strength and ability are not found in age or size, but in availability. God's plans will be accomplished, even when simple principles seem to be in question. It has been chosen to fulfill prophesy. Remember that all of my Father's creation has purpose. This colt's willingness is its strength."

As soon as Jesus was comfortably seated on it, John began to lead it toward Jerusalem and all of the disciples followed.

On the way, Judas asked, "Why are we doing this?"

Jesus replied, "So that the Scriptures will be fulfilled. Today you will see that all things have a purpose, even our journey. The time is now and the purpose will eventually be clear to you."

A rumor circulated that Jesus was on his way to Jerusalem, and as a result a large crowd began to gather in anticipation of his arrival. It was impossible to know how many people were there, but the crowd included men, women and children of all ages of various ethnic backgrounds and from various geographical locations because many had come to Jerusalem for the Passover Feast.

Several children, during their play, pulled down palm branches and were playing with them. They ran beside the crowd and waved the palm leaves in the afternoon breeze, and when some of the adults saw this, they joined in their play.

When the crowd saw Jesus and the disciples coming, they ran out to meet them, and began to wave palm branches and shout, "HOSANNA! BARUCH HABA B'SHEM ADONAI. BLESSED IS HE WHO COMES IN THE NAME OF THE LORD. BLESSED IS THE KING OF ISRAEL. HOSANNA! HOSANNA! BARUCH HABA B'SHEM ADONAI"

Some even put their cloaks on the roadway in front of the young colt, as it patiently plodded on its way into Jerusalem. The crowd ran alongside and continued to wave the palm branches. They also shouted, "HOSANNA! BARUCH HABA B'SHEM ADONAI. BLESSED IS HE WHO COMES IN THE NAME OF THE LORD."

When the disciples saw the enthusiasm of the crowd, they joined in by pulling down palm leaves and waving them as they moved along the street.

As the procession of reveling people with palm branches passed Adakal's shop, Amon stepped through the doorway. "Jerusalem celebrates more things than what we did in Nain. What is this one about?" he asked as he stood on a bench for a better view.

"I don't know what this is about. Maybe someone has returned from a long journey or plans to marry," responded Adakal as he continued to sweep the floor.

"Someone is riding on a young donkey. What does that mean?" asked Amon.

"A donkey? Many people ride donkeys. What is so different about this donkey?"

"I will go and see," said Amon as he elbowed his way into the moving and chanting crowd. He tripped over children and had several palm trees strike his face, but that did not slow him up. When he saw that it was the Messiah, he shouted, "MESSIAH! MESSIAH!" and Jesus looked over at him as he was riding by.

Amon raced back to Adakal's shop and shouted, "ITS THE MESSIAH! COME QUICK. HE'S RIDING A YOUNG COLT. WE'LL FOLLOW TO SEE WHERE HE GOES. HURRY!"

Amon and Adakal followed the crowd until it arrived at the Temple. Then Jesus stepped down from the colt and said to his disciples, "Return the colt to its owner. I have an errand to do in the Temple, so please join me later just outside the eastern gate."

None of the people or the disciples understood what he meant nor did they feel a need to ask, so the disciples returned the colt to where Andrew and Philip had found it.

When the crowd and the disciples had gone, Jesus walked into the Temple and looked around at the people, the moneychangers, the cages of animals and the priests, who were participating in the exchange of coins for sacrifices. He looked at the messy floor, the eagerness of the moneychangers and the dust in the air, and was repulsed by the odor. Then he took several long ropes and wove them into a cord as he walked into their midst.

A moment later, he knocked over several tables where moneychangers were sitting and coins rolled across the marble floor. Instantly, the surprised people stopped talking and watched as he kicked over cages and opened pens where lambs were being sold. Doves flew away when he opened several large cages. People began to run as they heard the loud snap of the cord that he was using as a whip. Lambs bleated, children screamed as men shouted, but Jesus did not stop his angry rampage.

As he moved across the courtyard, dust made it difficult to see all of his activities. Several priests hid in side doorways while others ran out of the main entrance. When Jesus happened to move to where Amon and Adakal were standing, they could see his angry face and the sweat running from his brow into his beard.

"MY FATHER'S HOUSE," he shouted, "IS TO BE A HOUSE OF PRAYER, BUT YOU HAVE MADE IT INTO A DEN OF THIEVES!"

People continued to run while others bent over to pick up rolling coins.

Then Jesus stood in the middle of the courtyard and held his clenched fists in the air and shouted, "A HOUSE OF PRAYER, THAT IS WHAT THIS IS TO BE, NOT A DEN OF THIEVES! THIS IS NOT WHAT MY FATHER WANTS HIS HOUSE TO BE."

The last few lambs ran out of the courtyard as the dust began to settle. Then Jesus threw the cord of rope to the floor and started for the exit. Dust swirled around his feet as he wiped his sweaty brow with his sleeve.

The Temple courtyard was in utter chaos. The Messiah had overturned the tables of the moneychangers' and had smashed the cages to free the doves and lambs. People returned to gather the lambs and children, who were calling for their mothers. Amon and Adakal left the Temple without saying a word. Both men were shocked and confused by what they had just witnessed. Their senses numbed, they walked as ones without sight or thought.

Around them the crowds continued to buy and sell, unaware of what had just happened. A camel bumped into Amon but he seemed not to care because he was in shock at what he and Adakal had witnessed.

"Why would a Messiah do that? Was not the Messiah supposed to come from God? He cared for people, heals them, but this make no sense," whispered Amon as he stood at the doorway of Adakal's shop. His eyes were wide with amazement.

"Should he not follow tradition and the sacrifices and the requirements and, and bring peace?" asked Adakal, sounding confused and disappointed.

Amon stepped into the street just as the chariot that Varrus was riding in rounded the corner and knocked down several people. It narrowly missed Amon, who lost his balance and fell backwards. As Amon hit the cobblestone street his eyes met Varrus' eyes.

"Hey you!" shouted Amon as he raised his fist, but the driver continued without looking back. Varrus may have looked at the pedestrians, but his mind was on his new assignment and not on the immediate comfort of Jewish citizens.

Moments later, the crowd moved back into the street and Amon stood on his tiptoes to see where the chariot that Varrus was riding in had gone, but it had disappeared down a side street. Instantly, he decided to follow, so he ran stiff-legged down the street hoping to see where the chariot was going. He was about to collapse out of breath, when he noticed the chariot stopping near a wooden door of a large stone building. Amon began running toward it and when he was within thirty paces from the door, he

Conspiracy With Malicious Intent

stopped to catch his breath. That is when he noticed guards standing at attention while Varrus entered the building.

He called to Varrus, who did not respond but disappeared behind a closed door.

Amon cautiously approached the chariot and moments later, several guards drew swords as they approached him. One guard placed the point of his sword against Amon's abdomen.

"I know Varrus," gasped Amon.

"Varrus, who?" asked the guard.

Varrus was nowhere to be seen and Amon had to deal with the immediate threat on his life. Out of breath he stammered, "The Varrus that, that . . . that just went in that door. I . . . I know him. He is . . . I saved his life."

"Who are you and what do you want?" asked the shortest guard.

"Wait! Wait! I have a parchment from the Roman's that will tell you that I saved Roman soldiers' lives. This will show you that I am a good citizen. See," he said as he reached for the parchment, hidden under his belt.

A soldier read the letter and narrowed his eyebrows. "This parchment means nothing to me. You have come into a place that is forbidden. This is the Praetorian. Now leave before I assign these men to cut your throat."

The guard crumpled the parchment and tossed it onto the ground and when the breeze rolled it away, Amon ran after it and picked it up. As he tried to remove the creases in the parchment, he mumbled to himself, "Gentiles. They need to be killed, that's what. Why did God make that sixth commandment?"

Later that evening, Amon told Adakal about how he had shown his parchment to the guards and how he had saved Varrus' life.

Adakal remained silent as he pondered Amon's stories and wondered if they could possibly be true?

Chapter XXVIII

THE PRAETORIAN AND THE EXECUTIONER

Laden with disappointment, apprehension and a heavy heart, the newly promoted Executioner entered the stone fortress, known as the Praetorian. It was heavily guarded as were all Roman buildings but this unsavory place housed societies most vile and violent criminals; thieves, murderers, extortionists, rapists, political prisoners and of course the innocent. Few if any were ever released. Escape was impossible and release only occurred at death.

Varrus was not surprised to see such precautions, but his mind was not on safekeeping but on understanding how and why he had been selected for such unsavory assignment. Nausea and anxiety threatened to invade his composure. Twice he fought the urge to vomit.

All guards saluted as the heavy doors were opened for him and he returned their salutes by instinct only. In the entrance, he was met by the Officer of the Gate, who introduced himself as Domina Salenus.

Varrus acknowledged him with a nod.

"May I show you to your office, Sir?"

Domina escorted Varrus up a stone spiral stairway, while two guards followed close behind. They marched in unison and their steps echoed an eerie and chilling cadence.

At the top of the stairs, Domina opened the door and after leaving the two guards outside, Domina escorted Varrus along a secondary hallway to a door with a Roman Seal and the word, Executioner, centered above it.

Varrus held his breath and closed his eyes for a moment while Domina held the door open.

In the room were several chairs, shelves with many parchments and a large desk with a wooden chair behind it. Varrus suddenly became aware that four strangely uniformed men were standing to his left. They wore long leather aprons and had red leather capes over their muscular shoulders. When he looked at them they cast their gaze to the floor and remained motionless and silent.

"Your office Sir," said the Domina Salenus as he stepped aside and waited for Varrus' response.

"Thank you," Varrus said as he looked around the room. A moment later, he walked over to the window and scanned the horizon of surrounding buildings from the second storey window. He cleared his throat and walked over to the chair behind his desk. "All of you may stand at ease."

"Thank you Sir," responded Domina Salenus. The four men with red aprons and capes nodded but remained silent.

After taking a long breath and exhaling slowly, Varrus spoke. "I am Centurion Varrus de Lonnea. My new assignment is to manage this portion of the Roman presence in Jerusalem." He paused to look at Domina Salenus and at the four caped men, who continued to gaze at the floor. "Tribuni Augusticlavii Emilio Caudoul is my immediate Commanding Officer and that means that his wish is my responsibility. I did not choose or request this unsavory assignment. I will expect you to do your tasks and assist me as I adjust to my new surroundings." He paused to lift several parchments from his desk before placing them gently back onto the drawer.

The room was silent as he closed his eyes and sighed.

"I will NOT pretend to be happy with this designated task. I will NOT tolerate in-fighting or signs of envy or jealousy. You will soon find that my words will either encourage you or challenge you. Your task is to assist me in learning all protocols. I will do what I can to make your stay with me more than tolerable."

All remained silent.

"What is that terrible odor?" Varrus asked as he lifted his nose in the air and then closed his eyes.

"We have not yet cleaned up the scourging cells from this morning's tasks," said the eldest of the men, who was wearing a red leather apron.

"Did I ask if there is an excuse? No, I asked, what that odor was? Now, is there anyone willing to answer my question?" His voice was strong, while skillfully hiding his apprehension, nausea and displeasure.

"Sir, we have had a very busy morning and have not yet cleaned the entire area. The odor is drying blood mixed with urine, vomit and . . ."

"Fine, I understand," interrupted Varrus. He turned to Domina Salenus. "You are excused."

Domino saluted and left the room.

Varrus lowered his gaze to the top of his desk and then raised his eyes to look at the four men standing before him. "I wish to see the rooms immediately, before you clean them. Perhaps I will have a better understanding as to why they emit such a foul and distasteful odor," said Varrus in a no nonsense tone. "Roman stables smell better than what is beneath me."

The eyes of the four men remained cast to the floor.

"Before we go to see the rooms, I want to know your names and what tasks are assigned to you," Varrus demanded as stepped in front of the men.

"My name be Haddesna and I be from Carthage," responded the eldest man. His bald head and hands exhibited many scars and ink markings.

"Haddesna? How long have you used your skills on prisoners?"

"I know numbers but have lost count, Sir. I start in Carthage when young, and care not to know, Sir."

"How many men have you scourged?"

"I know not, Sir," he answered as he tightened his lips and slowly shook his head.

Varrus then moved his eyes to the man standing next to him. He appeared to be much younger but he too had scarred hands and black tribal markings on his forehead and arms.

"I be Lammal and I be from Iberia. I too have lost count of the days, Sir."

Varrus nodded at the man to Lammal's left.

"I be Danniah and I be from Babylon. I be one with little experience. Eight years be my time, by Chaldean calendar. I care not to know how many I have lashed, Sir."

"What do you hate most about this . . . this chore?"

"The screams of men make my head not sleep at night, but I will soon not remember."

"And you?" Varrus said in a questioning tone as he looked to the far left.

"My name is Raelfa and Thebes be my home. I not know, Sir. I cannot count. If numbers be told to me, they mean nothing."

After standing in silence for some time, Varrus sighed and walked over to a window. Turning to face the four men, he asked, "Who was the previous officer that I am replacing?"

"Executioner Hakkoz be here for much time," said Haddesna. "He plan lashes, torture and crucifying."

"Where is he now?" asked Varrus as he shifted his weight to the other foot.

"Rumor he be stabbed at drunken orgy, and we now be under order of a man called Caudoul."

Varrus walked across the room to sit behind his desk. He opened the drawers and shuffled through some parchments before looking up at the men. "Do I have an assistant?"

"Yes, Sir. He be not here. He make a list of things we need. He bring the list of men, we reward for their evil, Sir," replied Haddesna.

"What is his name?" asked Varrus.

"Mabboodda."

"Well until he arrives, I want to know what you do, why you do it and when you do it. You will tell me everything and demonstrate every task so that I become fully aware of your chores."

All of them nodded as a sign of agreement.

"What is the task that you do?"

Raelfa spoke first. "My task be to clean and oil the whips afore they be hung in the well."

Varrus' icy stare caused Raelfa to add, "Sir."

"What is so important about the whips being oiled and then placed in a well?"

"Weights on them in dampness cause them to stretch to bring more injury when they be laid on a bare backs and legs of the men who come here."

"What does the oil do to them?" asked Varrus.

"It keep them from breaking while they be stretched," responded Raelfa.

When Varrus' eyes looked at Haddesna, he responded, "It be my task this week to clean floors and walls, Sir."

Varrus nodded.

"Sir, it be my turn to wash blood, urine, vomit and . . . from dungeon cells," said Danniah.

"And you?" asked Varrus.

"I am Lammal. My task be to deliver the lashes and floggings this week, Sir."

Varrus rose and moved to the door. "Show me the rooms where you ply your skills and by the way, I want to see the rooms that need cleaning."

When Varrus and the four men stepped into the hallway, the men immediately moved to stand with their backs against the wall.

"What is the problem?" asked Varrus.

"We be slaves and follow officers," responded Raelfa.

"Fine but this time, you will lead regardless of protocols, so lead."

Varrus followed the four men, who led him down the staircase and into the underground chambers of the stone fortress. As they passed through the large wooden doorway into the torture chamber, Varrus asked, "How many men are housed in this building?"

"I be told that the three floors have many cells," said Haddesna, "and have more than two hundred men. More evil men be in separate area that holds many more. Maybe five or six hundred, Sir. I know numbers when I listen to what is said, Sir."

"What about in this area?" asked Varrus, as he turned his face to hide his disgust with the odor in the chambers.

"Those to be flogged are in low part of the Praetorian," said Lammal as he pointed to the end of the dark hallway. "Two men waiting now for flogging, then they go back to cells."

Suddenly those waiting to be flogged began to shout and curse in a never ending stream of insults and threats.

"So all you are responsible for is these two men?" asked Varrus.

"It changes when new people be brought to us from other parts of Praetorian," responded Lammal.

"Who is the worse criminal in the Praetorian?" asked Varrus.

"Mabboodda, tell us he be a man named Bar Abbas and his sons."

"And who is Bar Abbas?" asked Varrus.

"Mabboodda say Bar Abbas be the worst man in all of Palestine."

"What made him the worst criminal?"

The men looked at each other. "Mabboodda tell you. He know more than we," responded Lammal.

Varrus wrinkled his nose at the strong odor as he looked down the hallway toward the torture chambers. The floor harbored an offensive odor of stale urine, blood, vomit and death. Varrus felt a chill pass through his body as he peered into one of the dungeon cells.

Large steel rings were built into the stone walls, ceilings and the floors which tapered to the center of each room. There a small drain carried away bodily fluids and the water used to wash the floor and walls.

As Varrus moved down the hallway, he discovered a very large room with several benches and a wooden pole with its base in the stone floor. Its top was securely anchored into the ceiling.

"Each room be used for men that be meted their sentence. The large room be for those who share in same evil. Here, prisoners watch as partner share in reward," said Haddesna as he nodded and attempted to smile.

"How long will it be until this, this Mabboodda returns?" asked Varrus.

"He be returning soon. Maybe he be in your room now, Sir."

Varrus was about to look into one of the holding rooms, when Haddesna stepped in front of him. "Sir, it be not safe for you to look. Just then shouts and saliva flew passed Varrus' face, expelled from a prisoner around the corner.

Lammal immediately slammed a wooden pole against wall of the cell where the two men were housed. The sound echoed loudly as Varrus stepped back.

"These men be here for scourging but they spit and throw their own waste . . ."

Varrus interrupted, "Yes, I understand, and by the way, thank you." Lammal smiled as he nodded.

"Tell me about these two men," asked Varrus.

"These men will be scourged and cold water will be splashed on their back and then they be returned to the other part of the praetorian," responded Lammal.

Varrus' eyes looked to the wall behind the entrance and saw dozens of whips, poles, chains and straps. "Take me back to my office and the rest of you will clean this area. I'll be back to inspect it, and I want to see it clean when I arrive."

"Anything else Sir?"

Before leaving Varrus asked, "Why do you wear those red capes and aprons?"

They looked at each other as Raelfa responded. "Capes keep blood from our bodies and face as we be scourging, Sir."

"I see, and the red is the color of blood."

All of them nodded.

When Varrus entered his office, a short overweight black man with several teeth missing, immediately erected his body.

"Who are you?" asked Varrus as he walked over to his desk.

"My name is Mabboodda, Sir!" he said with an unusual accent. "I am your assistant."

"Where are you from?"

"Ethiopia."

"Ethiopia? I might have guessed. By the way, how did you receive your invitation to join the Roman legion for such a rewarding life?"

"Before I was captured I saved the lives of several legionnaires near the Nile. Then they brought me here, Sir. First, I was one of the executioners but was given this job because I can read and write three languages, Sir."

"What languages do you speak?"

"The language of my birth, Egyptian and that of the Romans."

Varrus looked down at the parchment in Mabboodda's hand.

"This parchment is for two men for lashes," responded Mabboodda.

"Yes I met them downstairs." Varrus paused, "Thank you, Mabboodda. There is much you need to tell me. First, who is this vile man named Bar Abbas? Apparently, he is considered to be the worst. What has he done?"

"He has stolen, murdered, raped and insulted the Roman garrison by killing many soldiers, threatened the Governor, almost succeeded in kidnapping King Herod on one of his journeys from Caesarea, maimed and killed many Roman horses and has stolen much from the Jewish leaders in Jerusalem. Those that follow him are as skilled at killing as he is. A great bounty was paid for his capture, and he is now in a cell and six guards watching him all day long. His execution and those of his sons has been set. It will be very soon, maybe in two days."

"Have you ever heard of a rebel named, Athaliah?"

Mabboodda lowered his gaze for a moment, "The name is not familiar with me. Who is he?"

"Never mind. What else do I need to know about this place? Tell me everything even if you think I already know it."

"You, Sir, are responsible for this part of the praetorian. All lashing, scourging and flogging is my responsibility. The other part of the praetorian is under Centurion Ben Ahaza, a much hated Jew from the province of Samaria. He tends to those who will die in prison, and we will tend to those who will die on the stake. If they are not sentenced to be crucified, then we deliver the lashes and return them to the other side of the praetorian to be under Ben Ahaza."

Several hours passed as Mabboodda told Varrus about every part of the building. Mabboodda was thorough and patiently explained all aspects of Varrus' job, including parchments that needed signing, crucifixions and security. His words included the number of men who receive lashes every week as well as the number of deaths in the chambers and on Roman crosses. He drew pictures of how crosses are assembled and erected, and how holes were to be dug the day before a crucifixion. He described the route to Golgotha, where the crucifixions were carried out.

Mabboodda walked to a different desk as Varrus closed his eyes and shook his head in silence. "How did this happen to me? My father would understand but my mother," he whispered to himself. "My friend and servant, Pollus will not understand but I must . . ."

Suddenly, Varrus heard muffled screams. He closed his eyes and held his breath. When the cries subsided, he walked to the window for fresh air.

"Mabboodda, is that the sound of . . ?" Varrus asked as Mabboodda looked up from his desk.

"Yes Sir. Two men are now reaping their reward," responded Mabboodda. He approached Varrus' desk and poured wine into a goblet and carried it to where Varrus was standing. "Here be some wine, Sir. The smell of wine in your nose may help you."

"Can you accompany me into the dungeon? I need to see what the reward is to these men and . . ." he did not complete his sentence.

As they entered the scourging chamber, Varrus could hear the loud smack of wet skin being split, followed by a scream of excruciating pain of someone moving toward unconsciousness. Varrus momentarily closed his eyes as the cries diminished into irregular gasps and gut-wrenching moans.

Again and again the wet smacks continued until the feeble moan ebbed into silence. Eventually two final bone chilling wet smacks found its mark without a responding voice. After a long period of silence, Varrus could hear several irregular gasps and then, Varrus could hear a loud splash of water striking something.

Mabboodda whispered, "That be cold water striking the prisoner's back. It sometimes revives the prisoner so more lashes can be given, and if not, then the blood, vomit and urine be washed away."

Varrus and Mabboodda moved down the corridor. There kneeling on the floor appeared to be bloody raw carcass of a man with both of his arms tied to several metal rings above his head. The man was not moving and appeared to be lifeless. Blood flowed from his back to the floor, then toward the centre of the room where it disappeared into a drain.

"Will he live?" whispered Varrus.

"His stripes will be washed with cold water and he be laid on a wood bench. If he is alive in the morning, he will be taken back to his cell where Centurion Ben Ahaza and his men tend to him. If he dies, he will be buried."

Conspiracy With Malicious Intent

"What about him?" Varrus asked as he nodded his head in the general direction of a man lying in a fetal position on the cold floor.

"They have not dealt with him. He is to receive a minimum lashing."

"Minimum lashing? What is that?"

"Minimum is three lashes from a split whip with two tails on it. Maximum is seven lashes with a whip of seven tails."

"What is the average number a man can endure before he dies or goes unconscious?"

"It varies, Sir. I once saw a demented man from Arabia take the maximum and never fall to his knees or scream in pain, but that was only once Sir."

"What happened to him after that?"

"When we cut his cords, he attacked several floggers, killing two of them, so one of the guards killed him with a sword."

Varrus was overwhelmed by what he had just heard.

"Sir, if you don't mind me saying so, you will eventually get used to it."

Before Varrus left the chamber, he looked again at the small irregular streams of blood making their way down the sloped floor to the drain. A moment later, he moved his head from side to side and stepped into the hallway. There, he paused to take a large breath of stale air before he and Mabboodda returned to Varrus' office.

"Sir, I have checked all our stocks and we have plenty of lumber, ropes and spikes for crucifixions. We also have replaced some of the horses that were getting old, and I have ordered more salt to disinfect the floor and we will get new whips. Is there anything else you could think of that we need?"

"Are all of these men guilty or are some innocent?"

"All who arrive, claim they be innocent."

"I have killed in self defense and in battle, but I take no pleasure in this, this torture. Who gains from this? Do the men who send them here find some pleasure in this?"

"I know not, Sir."

"I cannot think of anything we need, except perhaps . . . fresh air and some compassion."

Just then Varrus could hear muffled screaming and knew that the second man was now receiving his lashes.

"How was I chosen for this assignment?" he whispered to himself again. "Could things be any worse?"

Chapter XXIX

A DEVASTATING MESSAGE

When Varrus arrived in his office the next morning, he called to Mabboodda. "I wish to inspect all of the men who are part of this insanity."

"Yes Sir."

Within the hour, eighty men were standing in formation in an inner courtyard. When Varrus entered the courtyard, all of the men snapped to attention as Mabboodda shouted, "CENTURION VARRUS DE LONNEA."

Instantly the men moved their hands to their chests, then to their swords and immediately responded in unison, "CENTURION SIR."

When Varrus and Mabboodda walked between the rows of men, Varrus paused occasionally to look at how the men were dressed and how they presented themselves.

Once the inspection had been completed, Varrus moved to the front of the assembly. "I expect that the next inspection I have with you will include some demonstrated changes. Swords and vestments will be polished, sandals will be cleaned and helmets will be placed properly on your heads. If not, I will choose one person out of every eighth man to receive one lash from a split whip. Do I make myself clear?"

"YES SIR," they responded in unison.

After dismissing the men, Varrus returned to his office with Mabboodda following close behind. "I want to see improvement and changes," Varrus said. "Just because they think they're tasks are filthy and work in terrible surroundings, they are allowed to become careless and sloppy. That will change, Mabboodda. See to it that they are prepared next time."

"Yes Sir."

"I take no pleasure in this new assignment," Varrus said as he ran his fingers through his hair, "but I must do as I have been told and so will they." He walked to the window and took a breath of fresh air. "I will need you to help me with this new protocol, however," he paused, "this will not allow you to gain an edge on my command. I will treat you fairly but that is all I will promise."

"Yes kind Sir."

"How long have you been here?"

"Many years Sir."

"How many men have you executed?"

"Don't know, Sir. I lost count and there be no need for me to know."

"Why do you not know?"

"If I not do this, then someone else would do it, Sir, so numbers mean nothing to me."

"Mabboodda, this position has not been my choice either, but that does not mean that I will not ensure Rome's expectations and standards."

"Sir, may I ask a question?

"You may."

"Have you ever been to a crucifixion?"

"I have witnessed twelve: three in the city of Nain but they were dead beforehand, four in Scythopolis, three north of Capernaum and two in Cana. Each time, I was at a distance. What I do know is that I will never enjoy them."

"Well Sir, you will get used to it. You learn to ignore the cries from the cells below. Your first crucifixion will be the worst. Your men know how to do their tasks. All you do is observe and sign the parchments. The men will do their best at the crucifixion, so they can regain your confidence." He paused and then continued. "Please do not be angry at me but . . . but I am your assistant, Sir. If you trust me, I will help you with all of your duties. When you appear in control and all goes well, then I too appear to be good at my duty."

"Thank you Mabboodda. I wish to be alone before my superior officer arrives. I expect him here at any time."

"One last thing Sir, if I may?"

"Yes, what is it?"

"Your reluctance to be part of this is not . . . I mean it be not a sign of weakness. These tasks are not what most people take pleasure in, Sir."

Varrus nodded as Mabboodda stepped into the hallway and quietly closed the door behind him.

Conspiracy With Malicious Intent

Varrus walked to the window to breath fresh air. Eventually, he moved to his chair behind his desk, only to be interrupted with a knock on his door. Before he could respond, it was opened and Tribuni Augusticlavii Emilio Caudoul entered the room. Varrus immediately rose to his feet and saluted.

"I see that you have settled into your new duties and I've heard that you have inspected your men."

"Yes Sir."

Emilio Caudoul walked over to a chair and before sitting down, he cleared his throat. "If you do your job well and there are no problems, you will see very little of me. If you are unable to keep up to your newly assigned tasks or make poor decisions, then you will see more of me than what you wish. Do I make myself clear?"

"Yes Sir."

"Do you have any questions?" he asked as he sat down.

"Yes Sir. The word, questions, means more than one, and I have several."

Emilio granted permission with a nod. "Continue," he said with an icy tone, knowing that he had left a verbal opening for Varrus to speak. "How long will my assignment be at this location, Sir?"

"You will know when you receive your orders to leave, and no sooner. What is your second question?"

"Why was I selected for this unsavory task?"

"By now you must have realized, that every position you have been selected to be part of, whether infantryman or officer, will always have unsavory tasks. Yours happens to be now."

"Thank you Sir."

Tribuni Augusticlavii Caudoul walked out of the room without returning Varrus' salute.

Varrus listened to the sounds of Caudoul and his personal bodyguard walking down the spiral stairway. When all was quiet, Varrus leaned back in his chair and stared at the ceiling. "The only way I will survive this insanity and these unsavory duties and . . . and this promotion is to consider what my father would do, and what Pollus my servant will say, when he arrives from Scythopolis."

Varrus remained in his office until darkness embraced the city, then he started for his quarters. At the front gate, Domina Salenus, Officer of the Gate motioned that he needed to speak with Varrus, so Varrus walked toward him.

"Sir, I just received word that you are to go to Tribuni Augusticlavii Caudoul's office, Sir. It sounds urgent."

Varrus returned his salute and thanked Domina.

When Varrus arrived at the Officers building, he told the guard at the gate that he was to report immediately to Tribuni Augusticlavii Caudoul for a very important message. When Varrus entered the private quarters where all the high ranking officers and their families lived, he waited in the lavish entrance. Some time later, Caudoul entered the room. He was not in uniform yet he walked with confidence and authority.

"Centurion, I take no pleasure in this conversation, but I have been notified that your servant, Pollus who was being escorted from Scythopolis to Jerusalem has fallen to thieves and murderers. Two legionnaires escorting him have also been killed. All clothing, weapons and your personal property have been taken."

"Pollus . . . Pollus has been killed?"

"I do not understand how a Centurion such as you would have a personal servant when only high ranking officers have personal servants. None the less, he has been killed and his body has been buried where he has fallen."

"Where is his body, Sir?" whispered Varrus as Caudoul turned to leave.

"That I do not know. If you wish to know more, speak to someone in Kadurra Senna's office in the morning. And oh, I certainly hope that this personal setback will not alter your performance as Executioner."

Varrus tried to control his breathing as Caudoul said, "Good night Centurion."

Varrus walked as though blind when he crossed the barracks compound. He entered the hallway to his room and opened the door. Before sitting on his cot and removing his sandals, he hung his gladius on the corner post of his cot and breathed deeply. Tears flowed down his cheeks as he remembered Pollus.

His memory, now blurred and numbed, made it difficult to recall the message given to him. "Pollus had been murdered on his way to Jerusalem," he whispered. "Pollus is dead and has been buried by the side of the road as a commoner. How can this be true? Killed by the side of the road like an animal," he whispered again as he laid his head on a pillow with his arm across his forehead. "Murdered and buried by the side of the road without words of comfort. How can this be?"

Varrus turned to face the wall and softly mouthed, "First, I am given this promotion with duties that I loathe and now . . . I find out that Pollus, my friend, lies in an unmarked grave, murdered by rebel Jews." He closed his eyes as his breathing became irregular.

As he lay there he recalled the many years of friendship and devotion he had received from Pollus. He remembered when the Messiah healed Pollus of palsy and the joy he had when Pollus had been restored to health.

Grief overwhelmed him as he lay in silence, wishing that the message was not true.

"What could possibly be worse?" he continued to say. "There is no position of comfort for what I feel. Am I to die of grief? Nothing could be worse than this. Nothing."

Chapter XXX

A VILE AND MALICIOUS AGREEMENT

Amon was disturbed by what he had seen the Messiah do in the Temple, and after lying awake for an extended time, he rose just as the sun was rising. Once outside he went to the market to find out what people were talking about and to hear their strange words. He was amazed at the number of black people that moved throughout the crowds and wondered where they had come from. While passing a vendor that sold silver pots and jewelry, he noticed some people with long black hair and unusual shaped eyes. Their skin was a golden brown and he stared at them for a long time and wondered if they were Jews. They wore strange symbols on their clothing and walked in strange shaped shoes.

Men with grunting camels, laden with large boxes, stood next to various colored donkeys while nervous flocks of sheep circled the troughs, anxiously waiting for their turn at the precious water. Children ran and played among the crowds and Amon found all of this activity to be overwhelming.

While he sat under the canopy of a large building, he overheard a conversation between three men, who appeared to be merchants. What caught his attention was the word, 'Messiah.'

"Some call him a Messiah, but I ask you, would a Messiah do such a thing in the Temple? Would he? I ask you."

"We can meet on the steps of the moneychangers building after we have eaten and then we can discuss what happened in the Temple yesterday," one of them said. "How can someone who claims to be from God do such things?"

Amon hurried to tell Adakal and then both of them raced to listen to the men's conversation. They found a large group of men discussing what

Conspiracy With Malicious Intent

they had seen and heard in the Temple, and what they thought about the Messiah.

Three men, who had been in the Temple during the debate between Jesus and the Sadducees, Pharisees, scribes and priests, were telling their story. They willingly shared what they had witnessed and added their opinions to every sentence. Some questioned whether Jesus was a prophet or a Messiah. Many wondered why he would disturb activities at the Temple. Others seemed pleased that he had asked questions that no one could answer. The debate lasted late into the evening and when Amon and Adakal heard that the Messiah was last seen in Bethany, they decided to go there the next morning.

While it was still cool, Amon and Adakal started for Bethany, and it was fortunate that Adakal was familiar with Bethany for he had been there many times. On their way, Amon complained that he was hungry.

Adakal was pleased to tell Amon, "There is a large fig tree on the side of the road, just outside of Bethany. That tree is known for its many tasty figs. No one owns the tree, but everyone stops to pick and eat them. When you get there, you can eat as many as you want. They're the best figs you'll find in Palestine."

"Are they that good because they are fat and ripe?"

"No, because they are free," laughed Adakal.

Amon smiled as he wagged his pointer finger at Adakal, "You've been with me too long."

Just outside Bethany, Adakal stopped by the side of the road and looked up at what was once a large fig tree. "This is strange," he said as he continued to stare at the dried branches. "This tree is dead. I don't understand. It looks like it has been dead for many years."

"What's the matter?" asked Amon as he crossed the road to look up at the dead tree. "Are you sure this is the tree?"

"This large fig tree has been here for many years and is known for its good figs. Everyone, who passes here, eats from this tree because no one owns it. Its figs have been known to be wonderful and sweet. I wonder what happened to it. It looks as if it has been dead for years, but I ate off this tree several weeks ago. I don't know what happened to it," he repeated several times.

Several men stood nearby, looking at the tree. "This tree was alive yet two days ago. I passed by here with my friend, and we ate many figs, and took some home but now there is not even leaves".

What happened to it," asked another man who was leading two donkeys laden with wood.

"How long has it been here?" asked another man, who was carrying a basket with small birds in it.

"Maybe you have found the wrong tree," said Amon.

"No. No. I was here not long ago and there were many leaves and it looked very healthy."

"This is very strange, especially since this is the season for figs," Adakal said as he scratched his head.

"If the Messiah can raise dead people, do you think he could make this tree have figs again?" Amon asked in an innocent tone.

"Maybe, if he walked by here. If he has walked on this road, he's eaten some of these figs too. I wonder if he knows about this tree."

Amon appeared disappointed when they arrived in Bethany for it looked like any other town in Palestine. The streets were full of people on their way to and from the market, all preparing for the Passover Feast. Large herds of sheep passed through the streets and legionnaires seemed to be everywhere.

"Sheep I like, but Romans, I like about as much as eating fish," said Amon as he shrugged his shoulders.

"Careful where you step," said Adakal. "Sheep have a silent way of letting you know where they've been," He quickly stepped to one side to avoid stepping in manure.

Adakal asked several people if they knew where the Messiah was, but no one seemed to have seen him. One person told him that the Messiah was last seen at Lazarus' house on the eastside of Bethany. After enquiring where the house was, Amon and Adakal walked to the eastside of Bethany to look for Lazarus' house.

****

While Amon and Adakal had been entering Bethany, the Messiah and his disciples were entering the Temple in Jerusalem. As they stood there, they watched as rich men placed their tithes and offerings into the Temple treasury. Most of them stopped for short conversations, and from a distance, they seemed pleased to see each other.

In the middle of this long line of rich men stood a poor widow with shabby clothes, and as she entered the Temple she placed a coin into the treasury container. Pushing her aside, one younger man, wearing beautiful clothing, moved through the doorway and nodded to a friend as he dropped his tithe into the coffers.

The Messiah turned to his twelve followers and said, "Listen to this truth. That poor widow," he motioned with his head, "has given more than all of them, for they gave out of their abundance but she has given all she has. She is now at the mercy of my Father, who will care for her."

"Why does the Temple need this money? It has many gifts, gold and precious stones. It's a wealthy place, so why does anyone need to give?" asked Judas Iscariot.

"My Father does not need their wealth, but desires their worship. Worshipping is not possible without giving, either of yourself, your mind or your substance. When you give, you show your appreciation. It is not to be payment for a debt, but showing that by your giving you are acknowledging your need and dependence on my Father to provide more when you need it. If you do not give, you are ignoring the generous hand of my Father."

Several minutes passed as they thought about what Jesus had just told them.

"This is a wonderful Temple, but the day is coming when not one stone shall be left upon another. All things will be changed," Jesus said as all of them looked at him, unsure of what they had just heard.

"When will this be?" questioned Andrew.

"Take heed that you are not deceived," continued the Messiah. "The time is coming when great and sudden changes will happen which you will not understand."

When he and his disciples entered the Temple several priests and their aides recognized Jesus and remembered that he was the one that chased people and animals out of the outer court. They wanted to challenge him but decided to watch and listen instead.

After teaching in the Temple, Jesus made his way to the Mount of Olives and though his disciples wanted to know more about why the Temple would be destroyed, no one dared ask him what changes he was speaking about.

****

Some time later, Amon and Adakal stood at front of a small whitewashed home. Adakal knocked several times before a man answered the door.

"Are you Lazarus?" asked Adakal.

Before answering, the man looked at Adakal and then at Amon. "That is what my name is but what is it that you want?"

"We," said Amon as he stepped closer to the front door, "we're looking for the Messiah. Is he here?"

Surprised by their question, the man at the door replied, "No. He left early this morning and must have gone back to Jerusalem."

"We have just come from Jerusalem and did not see him on the road," responded Adakal.

A dark eyed young woman came to the door as they spoke. She smiled, "Would you come in and have something to eat with us? My name is Mary and my sister, Martha, should be back from the market shortly. Please come in."

Both men agreed and entered the house, never suspecting that they would hear wonderful stories of what the Messiah had done for this family.

Amon told them of Hannah's son and how the Messiah had raised the dead boy to life. He was about to tell them of Zebedee and of his experience at the Sea of Galilee.

Lazarus raised his hand and interrupted. "I too was dead," smiled Lazarus as he nodded his head up and down. "Yes me, but Jesus raised me back to life." He looked at Mary, who became too emotional to speak.

Both men sat in silence as they listened to Lazarus.

"Yes, it's true," Lazarus said as he continued to nod his head up and down. "I was dead, yes dead and buried for four days," he said as he held up four fingers. "That is what they told me. Yes, four days, and when Jesus came to visit my sisters, he asked where I was buried. They showed him, and when the stone was moved away from my tomb, Jesus called my name."

"How did you know this if you were dead?" asked Amon.

"I was told this by my sisters," he said as he pointed at Mary. "When Jesus called my name, I heard it as clearly as I hear you and you hear me. It was so plain to me so I crawled out of the hole. Jesus' followers helped me take off my grave clothes."

"What was it like to be dead?" asked Amon as his eyes widened.

"I don't remember anything, not even being sick, but when I was freed of the grave cloths, I recognized my sisters and Jesus with all of the others who travel with him." His eyes twinkled as he spoke.

As he spoke, Mary left the room and returned with a tray of grapes, pomegranates and dates. "More food will be here when Martha returns from the market," she said in an apologetic tone. "We don't have much but what we have we will share with you."

Amon was totally engrossed in all of the stories that Lazarus spoke about. He wedged questions into each of the stories and Lazarus patiently answered every one of them.

Some time later a woman entered the house and Lazarus pointed to her, "This too is my sister. She's Martha."

The woman nodded and walked into a small room at the back of the house as the men resumed their conversation. While all of them ate, the women sat nearby and listened to the men's conversation.

It was dark when Amon and Adakal left Lazarus' house. Both men were concerned for their safety, but there was sufficient moonlight to travel and since the distance to Jerusalem was not very far away, they traveled as fast as they could.

Amon's mind was so full of stories of the Messiah that he slept very little that night.

****

While Amon and Adakal attempted to sleep, sixty-nine of the seventy members of the Jewish religious governing body, known as the Sanhedrin, met behind locked doors at the Temple to discuss their ever increasing frustrations with the Nazarene known as Jesus, who claimed to be the Son of God. The only one absent was Caiaphas the High Priest; however his assistant Hiddo, Vice Chief Justice, willing arranged, controlled and dominated the meeting.

As the flames flickered in the oil lamps on the walls of the Temple, so did the flames of jealousy flicker in the hearts of these men, who willingly attended to discuss what could be done to put the blasphemer to death.

After Hiddo raised his hands to silence the conversations within the room, his soliloquy began with, "We all know why we are here. If anyone is unclear, then leave the room now." There was a moment of silence as he looked around the room and then continued. "This Galilean from Nazareth has challenged us at every turn. He has made us to look incompetent and dishonest. Not only did he knock over the moneychanger's tables and scatter the animals to be sacrificed, he has divided the people against themselves. He has challenged lawyers, insulted every Pharisee and Sadducee and has questioned our knowledge of the Torah . . . and he has challenged our leadership and tradition. His actions suggest that we have little influence with what God has entrusted to us, the Mosaic Law. It is our responsibility to deal with this outrage. We have heard him forgive sins, claim to be the son of God and claim to be the king of the Jews. His very presence brings division to the people and among us. He challenges what we teach and disrespects our tradition. This must NOT continue."

"And what about all the things he does on the Sabbath?" responded an elderly man sitting near the door. "He challenges all decency and laws that are in the Torah. Moses gave us the Law and has required that we guard it, but he said he has come to destroy the Law that we try to keep and teach."

"And what about his blasphemy? This cannot continue," shouted a voice from the back of the room. "He claims to know God and tells everyone he comes from God, but would God tell us to keep the Sabbath and let him break it when he blatantly heals on that sacred day? He refers to himself as a king, but we have no king. King David and King Solomon were truly our kings but he is worse than the uncircumcised pagans that rule over us."

"All we need is for him to say something against Rome or the Governor, and disaster will occur. Pontius Pilate would love to put his hand to us again. We must do something to protect ourselves and our families from this, this outrage."

"What do you suggest that we do, Hiddo?" asked another voice.

"We've tried to catch him in a lie, but he has outwitted every lawyer.

He has made statements that challenge the knowledge of every member of this sacred place," said another angry voice. "It must be stopped."

"This cannot continue," two men said simultaneously.

"Our laws tell us that a blasphemer must be put to death," said another voice.

An old man's voice responded, "We must end his influence with the people or God will hold us responsible for not maintaining his Laws. God put to death those who did not obey his Laws, so we must act now to show God that we do not agree with this blasphemer's voice and actions."

Hiddo raised his hand. "That is what we must discuss tonight. Caiaphas, our High Priest, has requested that we devise a plan to end this evil and to deal with this blasphemer."

Turning to a table, Hiddo drew a large circle on a blank open scroll in front of him, then placing his fist into the center of it and he said, "The plot we agree upon must be complete as this circle. It must not have any loose ends and everyone must be shielded from blame when this is completed."

Silence momentarily gripped each heart and all eyes stared at the circle on the new scroll, except for Hiddo's, which scanned the eyes of those around him.

"All of you have agreed that we must stop this Galilean troublemaker, so to show your approval, you must place your fist in this circle as a symbol of your agreement. This is a sign of your agreement between us and God. I will be the first, so let me see your fists in the circle."

Within moments, dozens of fists reached for the circle on the scroll; however the final eight seemed rather reluctant but soon sixty-nine closed fists appeared into the circle.

A series of raps on the door of the inner temple caused all of the men to withdraw their fists from the circle. Hiddo nodded to a young servant who tiptoed to the door and put his ear against it. As he did, he held his breath.

Again the code was repeated.

Three long taps, two short taps, a pause that lasted a full breath and then the sound of a tiny tap from a metal coin.

Hiddo stood motionless and barely breathed.

Again the code was repeated.

Hiddo nodded and a young servant opened the door, and there stood three men. Two appeared to be Temple workers, and the third seemed strangely out of place. Hiddo motioned for them to enter, and then the door was locked behind them.

The two Temple workers walked confidently over to Hiddo, but the third man stood in the darkest corner of the room. His heavy eyebrows hid his eyes and his beard covered his mouth. His cloak of woven cloth hid his hands that were hidden in the sleeves of the garment. It was difficult to determine if he was an educated man or less than a commoner.

Hiddo leaned forward to receive a whispered message from one of the Temple workers, and then smiled as he walked to a large chair at the front of the room. The silence was uncomfortable for everyone. Initially all eyes focused upon Hiddo but eventually they moved to the stranger at the back of the room.

"Each person has his price," said Hiddo in a taunting tone. "What is yours?"

"Fifty pieces of silver," was the reply from the stranger, who stepped closer. The hood that he wore revealed only the lower half of his face.

"May I remind you that the price of a slave is only thirty pieces of silver, not fifty? Your greed is one of your weaknesses, is it not?" responded Hiddo. A sneer framed his face as he spoke.

"My price is fifty pieces of silver," repeated the man at the back of the room. "This man is worth more than a slave. No negotiation," he insisted in an unwavering tone.

"We'll pay you only thirty pieces of silver. If you are unhappy with that, perhaps I can have the Temple police arrest you, create some charges against you and turn you over to the Romans to be flogged for speaking against Caesar."

The silence was overwhelming.

"Did you hear what I said? We will turn you over to the Romans as a troublemaker for stirring up the people, and they will deal with you. Is that worth an extra twenty pieces of silver?" asked Hiddo whose face now resembled an asp.

The stranger brushed his beard with his right hand and after a long pause, agreed. "Thirty pieces of silver it will be."

Hiddo stood to his feet, "If you fail or tell anyone about this meeting, your tongue will be cut out by the Romans for cursing Caesar."

The stranger nodded and then asked, "Where's my silver?" Then he licked his lips and swallowed.

A moment later, Hiddo dropped a leather pouch onto a wooden table. The sound of silver coins echoed throughout the room and every eye was on the pouch, except for Hiddo's, whose eyes focused on the face of the stranger, who had stepped closer to the front of the room.

Hiddo picked up the pouch and shook it. After holding it above the table, he dropped it again, allowing the sound of silver coins to grasp the stranger's heart. Then Hiddo motioned for a servant to pick up the pouch and take it to the stranger. Reaching for the pouch of silver when the servant brought it to him, the stranger looked up at Hiddo and nodded.

"No need to count it. It's all there. We would never cheat anyone, especially someone as important as you," Hiddo taunted as he folded his arms across his chest.

Several moments passed as the stranger counted the coins and then placed them back into the pouch.

"How will we know when to act," asked Hiddo.

"When the time is right, I will notify you where the best place will be," responded the man with the pouch containing thirty pieces of silver.

"It must be away from the crowds," insisted Hiddo.

"I will let you know where to meet and who he is when I kiss his cheek." There was a slight hesitation in his voice when he said, "When you lay hands on him, hold him fast . . . then my task is done."

Hiddo nodded as a servant opened the door, but before the stranger went out into the darkening street, Hiddo asked, "You are Judas Iscariot, are you not?" His voice and words taunted the stranger, who was about to leave the room.

The stranger nodded and with a soft voice whispered an inaudible, "Yes."

When the door was locked behind him, the room reeked of betrayal and death.

Chapter XXXI

THE PASSOVER LAMB AND THE WARNING

The next morning, Adakal told Amon that he was going to the Sheep Gate, just north of the Temple, to buy a lamb for the Passover Meal. When they arrived, there were hundreds of people bargaining over thousands of lambs in dozens of pens. The lineup was beyond what Amon had ever seen or imagined. Eventually, Amon and Adakal moved into a position where they were able to lean over the fence to look at the lambs.

Amon reached over the fence and touched one of the lambs, and it looked at him. Its dark eyes sparkled as Amon tried to stroke its head. The bleating from the flock was so loud that Adakal and Amon could barely hear each other speaking.

"This is the one, Adakal. I have a silver coin," shouted Amon. "How much do they cost?"

"We'll have to wait until we get to the gate," said Adakal.

Amid all of the bleating and bargaining, Adakal and Amon eventually stood before one of the shepherds. Once the price was agreed upon, Amon paid for the lamb and after picking it up, they started for Adakal's house.

Amon felt so proud that he could afford such a perfect lamb. Sharing it with Adakal and his family gave him such a good feeling. He smiled as he carried it, and Adakal's three children constantly touched it as they walked beside him on the crowded streets.

Adakal said, with tears in his eyes, "I have never been able to purchase a Passover Lamb. We always go to my brother's place to share their lamb but this will be the first time that we will have our own lamb. Thank you Amon."

As they walked home they neared the same intersection where they had met the chariot that Varrus had been riding in, several days earlier. People suddenly rushed out of the way as mounted cavalrymen raced around the corner. One of the horses bumped into Amon, who tried to keep his balance but accidentally dropped the young lamb, which fell to the stone paved street.

Adakal immediately grabbed the lamb to avoid it being run over by another horse. Fortunately, Amon, Adakal and his children were not hurt but Amon's anger reddened his face as he reached for the lamb and began to stroke its head. Regretting that he had saved the lives of Roman soldiers some time ago, he raised his fist and shouted, "Someday, I will kill one of those Romans. They are pagans so I know God does not care about them and neither do I."

"What about the sixth commandment?" asked Adakal's eldest daughter.

"That commandment, it, it was given for Jews fighting Jews, but it has nothing to do with what we could do to Gentiles," stammered Amon.

Adakal's eyes narrowed as he looked at Amon, who grinaced and shrugged his shoulders.

After supper, Adakal's sons called, "Abba, come quick. The lamb we brought him is unable to stand."

Adakal and Amon rushed out to see the lamb struggling to its feet.

"The Passover Lamb is . . ." said Adakal as he looked at Amon. "The lamb has been hurt. It must have happened when it was dropped when the Romans knocked us over on the way home. We cannot use this lamb for the Passover Meal. It must be a perfect lamb without blemish and NOT be injured."

"What can we do Abba?" asked the eldest child.

"We must purchase another one," he said disappointedly. His heart pounded as he leaned over to touch its injured leg. The lamb bleated and Amon's heart experienced anger and sorrow at the same time.

"But I only have two more coins left from all the ones I received in Scythopolis. What do we do now?" asked Amon as he knelt beside Adakal to touch the injured lamb.

"Let's go back to the Sheep Gate, where we bought this one. There is yet time and maybe they will let us have another one," said Adakal as he stroked the lamb's injured leg.

Both men walked in silent sadness back to the Sheep Gate the next morning. Amon carried the injured lamb and as he walked, he closed his eyes and hugged it. "Baby lamb, I'm sorry. I didn't mean to drop you." Tears dripped down his cheeks as they neared the Sheep Gate. "It's that pagan's fault, not mine. Really, I didn't want to hurt you." Tears dropped into the lamb's wool.

When they arrived at the sheepgate, Adakal waved to the man, who had sold the lamb to them. "Simon, I know that you sell only perfect lambs for the Passover but," he said as he turned to look at Amon. "But we bought this perfect lamb, and now it limps from a hurt foot and leg. Now we can't use it for the Passover. Is there yet another we can have?"

Simon looked at Amon, who was holding the lamb. "What happened?" His dark eyes scanned Amon's face.

"Roman soldiers almost ran over us and when we jumped out of the way Amon dropped the lamb. He didn't mean to. It just dropped."

"Ah, so now I am supposed to . . ?"

Adakal interrupted, "Simon, you know that we cannot use this lamb. It must be a perfect lamb. It was not our fault and it is not your fault. I know that it is the Roman's fault."

"Then take it to the Roman who caused this."

"Simon, there is yet time to give me another one," pleaded Adakal.

Simon stepped closer to check the leg of the lamb. He inhaled slowly and then looked at Adakal. "Is it my fault that the lamb was hurt after you bought it?"

"No, Simon," he whispered, "but it is not our fault either."

"You realize that I will not be able to sell it to anyone else."

"I will buy another one . . . but since I'm new to Jerusalem maybe you could take this one back and sell another one to me," pleaded Amon.

"What will I do with it? We have many pilgrims and citizens, who buy lambs but this one . . . I . . . I don't know." He shrugged his shoulders as he closed his eyes.

"You must have more lambs, like all those over there," pleaded Adakal as he pointed to several pens nearby.

"Since all of the cages and pens were destroyed in the Temple courtyard, we lost many lambs and don't have enough to sell. Remember that during the Passover thousands of people come to Jerusalem from all over the world, and now you, now you want me to give another lamb to you." Simon rubbed the forehead of the injured lamb as it bleated loudly.

The three men stood in silence as they re-examined the lamb. Again, it bleated loudly as it tried to jump out of Amon's arms but he held it firmly in both arms.

"Give me the lamb," said Simon with a disgusted tone to his voice. "You are causing me to think that soon I will be too poor to buy food for my nine children. How much do you have and what coins will you give me?"

Amon handed Simon another coin. "This is all I have," he said sadly.

Simon reached for the coin and put it in his teeth to see if it was a hard coin before placing the injured lamb into the pen and returning with another. "Adakal, be sure that you tell nobody. No one must hear of this. I don't want others to hear that Simon took this lamb back. Did you hear me, nobody?"

"We will not tell anyone," Adakal assured him as he reached for the other lamb. "Why would we tell anyone?"

As they walked away, Amon could not help but look over his shoulder at the injured lamb that remained behind. It bleated and Amon quickly turned away.

****

When Varrus stepped into his office, Emilio Caudoul was sitting behind his desk. Varrus immediately snapped to attention and saluted.

Emilio sat in silence and stared at him. "You look like you have not slept. What's the matter? Are you sick?"

"Sir!" responded Varrus, surprised to see his Commanding Officer. "I have had no sleep because of the news you gave me last evening. I grieve because of the loss of my servant, Pollus."

Emilio lips were tight and he nodded his head from side to side as he looked at Varrus. "Did you speak with someone in Senna's office?"

"Yes Sir. That's why I wasn't here when you arrived."

Emilio stood to his feet and walked around to the side of the desk to where Varrus was standing. "I've heard good things about you. You're eager to follow orders, strong enough to deal with these murders and still make good decisions. That's good."

"Thank you, Sir but I . . ."

"Silence!" he said as he walked to the opposite side of the room, turned and looked at Varrus. "I may not have been here as often as you expected but I do know what's going on."

"I don't understand, Sir."

Emilio reached for the small container of wine and poured some into a metal cup. "Where are the colorful wine glasses that were here before?"

"I use only the metal ones, Sir. The others are in a drawer. If I knew that you would be here, I would have placed them on the table, Sir."

Emilio nodded and after several sips of wine, sat in a chair near the window. "Do you enjoy your new position?" Emilio asked.

"I've not been in it long enough to decide, Sir!"

"Well, three men will soon be here. One is the famous thief and murderer, Bar Abbas and two of his followers. Rumor has it that they are his two sons. Each of them is to receive forty nine lashes and then be crucified."

"Bar Abbas? Mabboodda has told me about him."

"Yes the famous Bar Abbas. We have sought him for years and now we will execute him. He's the prize catch of Palestine, you know."

"Is he a Jew?"

"Yes and that is what makes this crucifixion even more important." He shook his head from side to side again and sighed loudly. "I find interesting that these Jews, who all claim to belong to the same lineage, continue to steal from each other and kill each other, and here is what is even stranger, they want us to execute the guilty along with the innocent. They seem not to care, so why should we?"

Varrus remained silent.

"Here's something that you need to hear." Emilio motioned Varrus to a chair and then continued. "The only person that is meaner than these two young men is their leader Bar Abbas." He turned the metal goblet in his hand. "He has killed at least one hundred and sixty seven of his own kind, organized rings of thieves to loot businesses, houses and the Temple. His men have raped countless women and have threatened the lives of religious leaders, including the Governor and King Herod. They killed over one hundred legionnaires. Did you know that?"

Varrus held up the flagon of wine. "More wine, Sir?"

"This wine is terrible. It should be fed to hogs but they don't allow hogs in this country, do they? By the way, are there any hogs in Palestine?"

"No but in the country of the Gadarenes, on the eastside of the Sea of Galilee, there are large herds of hogs. One of the largest herds of swine is kept near a small town known as Gerges. A story that I recall hearing about, involved a massive herd of swine that were overcome with something and suddenly they rushed over a cliff and fell into the Sea of Galilee, and all drowned."

"I thought that was only a legend," responded Emilio as he narrowed his eyes.

"It happened a long time ago but people still talk about it. Some say that some evil raced the herd over the edge to drown in the sea."

"What a waste of good food." Again Emilio sipped wine from the goblet. "This is slop. Have you nothing better than this?"

"I'm sorry Sir, that's the only wine I have been given."

"Very well," he said as he held his goblet up for Varrus to fill. "Think of it Varrus. Bar Abbas has killed his own countrymen, Roman soldiers, and is believed to have attempted to kidnap and kill King Herod and Pontius Pilate. He is either brave or stupid."

"The only other man, who has caused Rome such difficulties is a man named Athaliah. We searched for him for many days but never found him. He was last seen in Samaria and Galilee," responded Varrus.

"What do you think of men like that?"

"I have no opinion, Sir."

"Don't play innocent with me," Emilio said but was interrupted by a knock on the door. He looked over at the door and shouted, "ENTER!"

Mabboodda entered the room. "Sir!" he said. "Two of the three men to be scourged and crucified have arrived. Bar Abbas is not here. Are there any special orders?"

Emilio responded. "Well, they've arrived. They must end their miserable lives with as much pain as possible. Forty nine lashes are not enough as far as I'm concerned. Just be sure that they remain alive for the crucifixion." Emilio stood to his feet and as he placed the empty goblet on the desk, he asked, "Only two are here? When will Bar Abbas arrive?"

"Sir, only two young men are here," Mabboodda said as he looked at Varrus. "I know not when Bar Abbas arrives."

"Be sure to treat these condemned fools accordingly," was Emilio's cold response as he started for the door.

"Permission to speak. Sir," interjected Varrus after Mabboodda left the room.

"What is it?" Emilio said as he belched loudly. "My god, this wine is terrible. How can you drink this slop?"

"This Bar Abbas," responded Varrus, "why has he not been crucified already if he has been found guilty of all these crimes? How has this man managed to evade execution this long?"

"He has been very difficult to find but the lure of gold has caused some citizens to cooperate because their greed is stronger than blood. He has been in prison for only a short time, but his sentence has not been carried out yet because . . ." he looked into the empty goblet, "I cannot drink this slop. I'm sure that you can find better wine than this."

Varrus waited for Emilio to continue.

"Varrus, why do YOU think Bar Abbas' execution has been delayed?"

"There is hope that his men will try to free him or be careless in some way, allowing for the capture of as many of his men as possible," responded Varrus.

"Very good. Seldom do legionnaires think. Now I know why you have been recommended for this position."

Varrus nodded. "If we wish to capture more members of his gang, we should find someone who looks like him and spread the news that he is to be transferred to Caesarea. Then when the look-alike is escorted to Caesarea, the gang may try to free him and the Legion could round up all of them.

"That is how we caught these two members of his group. So now take care of them. I'll be watching how efficient you will be, so do NOT disappoint me."

"No Sir! I will not," responded Varrus as Emilio left the room.

Varrus walked over to his desk, glad to have his office back. Just then Mabboodda entered the room.

"Sir!"

"Yes, what is it?"

"I have the papers for the two men downstairs. I need your signature to complete their sentence."

Varrus reached for the parchments and scanned what was printed. "Mabboodda, did you notice that these two men are brothers? And oh, when do you expect Bar Abbas to arrive?" he asked Mabboodda.

"I know not Sir, but when he does I'll tell you."

After signing the parchments, Varrus asked. "Where has Emilio been all this time?"

"I've heard he be at a drunken orgy. I'm surprised he returned so soon. He lives to die. Strange wish, but someday he be having his way."

"So I'm responsible to make him look good, am I?" asked Varrus.

"Yes Sir. Just remember if you disappoint him, he will have you flogged and maybe executed," responded Mabboodda. "He be a vile man."

"Crucifixion is not what I would want, so thank you for the warning."

****

Conspiracy With Malicious Intent

Judas Iscariot rejoined Jesus and the eleven disciples at the Mount of Olives. Only John was suspicious of his absence but said nothing. Eventually, Jesus and the twelve left the Mount of Olives and walked toward Jerusalem. When they were within a stones throw of the city wall, the Messiah sat on the stump of a dead tree and motioned for his disciples to sit down.

"Peter and John," said the Messiah, "go into the city and you will see a man carrying a pitcher of water. Follow him to his house and when he asks what do you want, say to him the Master needs the guest chamber for the Passover Meal. Then, he will show you a large room. Prepare for the Passover Meal and we will join you later in the day."

They left and as they walked through the streets, John pointed to a man walking with a large pitcher or ewer on his shoulder, so they followed him. When he was about to enter a house, the man turned to face them. "What are you seeking?"

Peter replied, "The Master needs a guest chamber to celebrate the Passover. We have been told to look for you."

The man showed them a large room on the second floor and asked no other questions. He even provided a Passover lamb for their celebration, so they eagerly prepared the meal and waited for the Messiah and the ten disciples to arrive.

****

When Hiddo arrived at the home of Caiaphas, a servant ushered him into the guest room and offered him some fruit, but Hiddo was not interested in food. He nervously paced the floor until Caiaphas entered the room.

"What is it, Hiddo?" Caiaphas asked as he ran his fingers through his hair for it appeared that he had just risen from sleep. "You're early. I hope that you have something important to say."

Hiddo looked at the servant, who left the room immediately and closed the door.

Nervously looking about, Hiddo stepped closer to Caiaphas and whispered, "We have found one from within the inner circle, who will betray the blasphemer."

"At what cost?" Caiaphas asked without showing any sign of emotion. He adjusted his robe as he waited for an answer.

"He requested fifty pieces of silver and . . ."

Conspiracy With Malicious Intent

He was interrupted by Caiaphas. "FIFTY! That is too much! The price of a slave is only thirty, so why should we . . .?"

"He has agreed on thirty," Hiddo interjected as he raised his hand to calm Caiaphas.

"Have you offered the silver to him?"

"Yes. The betrayer told us that we must pay the silver before the deed is done."

"Where are the blasphemer and his followers now?" Caiaphas whispered as his facial grin turned into a sneer.

"That we are not sure of, but we have our spies in the streets, and when we hear, we will follow and wait for the sign."

"A sign? What sign?"

"The betrayer's name is Judas Iscariot. He has agreed to let us know when and where to arrest Jesus. When we move in to arrest this blasphemer with the Temple Police, the betrayer will place a kiss on the cheek of the blasphemer, so that there is no doubt as to whom we have."

"A kiss? How c-l-e-v-e-r?" Caiaphas whispered.

"Yes, especially since it will be dark, we need to be sure we have the right man."

"Good, very good, Hiddo," Caiaphas said as he clasped his hands together. "I knew that I could count on you. Who is this betrayer? A man named Judas?"

"Judas Iscariot comes from Kerioth, the city where Edomonites live."

"Kerioth? He's from Kerioth?" Caiaphas' voice sounded optimistic and eager to proceed. "Is this Judas an Edomite?"

"He may well be. If he is from Kerioth it is possible but his name is Hebrew."

"Little is in a name. Edomites have often changed their names to gain the benefits of being a Jew. If he is willing to be a betrayer then he cannot be trusted with a name, besides few Jews will live among Edomites." Caiaphas wiped his mouth with the back of his hand as he paced the floor, then turning he asked, "Who is his father?"

"His father's name is Simon . . . but I guess he may have changed his name also to be thought of as a Jew." Hiddo smiled, pleased that their plans were now moving into place.

"So he may be a descendant of Esau and is NOT a Jew?" purred Caiaphas as he stroked his beard. "That is wonderful. So this betrayer is NOT from the House of Israel." He leaned back in his chair as a smile moved across his face and his eyes closed slightly.

"Yes, it is possible that his lineage is of Esau, but," whispered Hiddo.

"How wonderful?" interrupted Caiaphas. "So, he's an Edomite and not a Jew. E-x-c-e-l-l-e-n-t," whispered Caiaphas. "What else do you know about him?"

"He's the one that carries all of the money that the blasphemer's group owns, and we know that he has helped himself to the coins many times without their knowledge. He's perfect as a betrayer."

"It sounds as if he is not to be trusted. Are you sure that we can trust someone as greedy as him. I mean if we have already paid him thirty pieces of silver, do you think that . . ?"

"No, all will be well. You should have seen the look in his eyes when he counted the pieces of silver. His eyes were glazed, and his hands shook slightly when he picked up the coin pouch from off the table."

"You must leave now," Caiaphas whispered. "When the betrayal and arrest occurs, be sure to have the Temple Police there to make the arrest. I want to be there for the arrest so let me know as soon as possible. We must move quickly to a trial and sentencing. There must not be any errors. Do you hear? NO errors!"

****

Pontius sat at his desk, in his residence, reading the report that he had received from Tribunus Laticlavius Kadurra Senna. He suspected that some of the information had been fabricated, so he read the report a second time. When he had completed his reading, he turned the document over in his hand and reached for the goblet of wine that was on the table next to him.

Knowing that this report would be in the hand of the Legatus within two days, he moved the candle closer and scanned the report for the third time and when he realized that this report was overdue he carried it over to his desk and sat down. Reaching for a quill, he dipped it into ink and signed it. Moments later, he picked up the red wax, held it near a candle and allowed several drops to fall onto the parchment. Immediately after, he pressed his insignia ring into it, waited a few seconds before removing it.

There was a knock on the door and it opened slightly. Pontius looked up. His piercing eyes focused upon a young girl in the doorway.

"Kind Sir, your wife has requested your attendance. She is very upset and wishes to speak with you." The young handmaiden cast her gaze to the floor as she curtsied.

"Very well, tell her that I will join her in her chambers in a few moments."

The door closed and Pontius stared at the wall for some time, then left the room and walked down the hallway to the base of a curved granite stairway. At the top of the stairs, he moved down a hall to his wife's sleeping chamber. He was about to knock, when he heard sobbing from within, so he opened the door slowly.

"Claudia. What's the problem?" he asked in a soft tone as he entered the room and closed the door behind him.

She ran to him and grabbed both his hands. "Pontay, I have had several dreams during the night and today as I slept. I have . . ."

Pontius turned to the two young women and the older woman in the room. "All of you may leave," he said. "When we need you, we will summon you."

When the door closed behind them, he helped Claudia to her bed. Looking down on her, he took a long breath. "Now what is the problem? Is it about the banquet at Herod's palace?"

"No, no Pontay. My dreams have been about the man that the servant girls and I have told you about many times. He's the one that has healed the sick and is at odds with the High Priest and the religious leaders. My three handmaidens have also seen the miracles that the Galilean performs. His words are gentle but I have seen the eyes of those Temple vipers and I know that they are plotting to have him murdered."

"You rant like some woman that has been in the hot Palestine sun. What has this to do with me? Now please lie down and go to sleep. I have much to do this evening. I'll send for your maidens."

"No, no Pontay. Please listen to me," she insisted as she grabbed both of his hands. "I have told you many times that this Jesus is different. His words are different and I have . . . yes, I have considered them. He claims to be a god and, and the king of the Jews."

"A god and a king? What makes you think he's a god let alone a king?"

"No one can do the miracles that he does unless he is a god. The jealous religious leaders despise him for he claims to know god and he does things that they cannot do. Their jealousy is so evident, Pontay. I know that they plan to do harm to him."

"Claudia, why do you fret about some Jew? What has this to do with me? Are we Jews that we should care?"

"Because I have seen these religious vipers force you into assisting them with other problems. Now I am worried that . . ."

"Worried? About what?" he asked, sounding somewhat annoyed "Whatever you do, promise me that you will have nothing to do with the plans of those religious leaders."

"What plans?"

"They're planning to get rid of him and maybe kill him. They cannot be trusted," she insisted.

"Claudia, please lie down and do not worry about my duties. I have carried them out over many years without your advice or, or any of your dreams and . . ."

Again she interrupted. "Pontay, please do NOT do anything against this man and do NOT do anything for these religious leaders. They have a way of forcing their way . . ."

"They wouldn't dare," Pontius said as he raised his hand to touch her forehead. "They know that I have the final say on all executions, but if they murder him, then they will face me with conspiracy charges."

"What if he is a king? What if he is a god or the son of a god? Do nothing that would destroy this man. Pontay, p-l-e-a-s-e."

"He is NOT the king of the Jews. If he were, why would these Jews want to kill their king? And if he is a god . . .?"

"P-le-a-s-e Pontius."

"Now go to sleep, Claudia. It is late and I have much to do."

"I have had many vivid dreams about this man. I believe he is a god. Pontay, p-l-e-a-s-e have nothing to do with him especially since I believe they are trying to kill him."

"Claudia," his voice sounded irritated.

"Pontay, if you ever met this Galilean or spoke with him, you would find that his words would warm your heart. He knows what truth is."

"Truth? What is truth?" asked Pontius.

"Pontius," she whispered, "I a-m afraid."

"Claudia, has he beguiled you? Have his words begun to change you?"

"Pontay, his words would change even you. He is able to look inside of you, right into who you are. At first, I felt condemned when I listened to him but his words convinced me that there is more to my existence than comfort and ease."

"Claudia, you speak as a silly woman. What could he possibly do for me? I am the Governor and Praefectus? Have you forgotten that?"

"But he is a god, Pontay."

Pontius did not reply but shook his head as he closed his eyes

Before lying down, she gripped his hands again and looked up at him.

He nodded. "I'll send for your maidens." Then he pulled the lace covers over her. "Now sleep," he whispered as he kissed her forehead. "Worry leaves marks on the brows of anxious men and worrisome women. Please sleep for I have much to do before morning."

Chapter XXXII

THE MEAL AND THE BETRAYER

The pilgrims throughout the Roman Empire, who came to celebrate the Passover Feast in Jerusalem, numbered in the thousands and as a result of this massive migration, cavalrymen from Caesarea, Scythopolis and Jericho were temporarily relocated to Jerusalem to help maintain peace during this emotional religious celebration. It was an extensive undertaking that required significant planning regarding housing and food preparation, schedules for additional patrols and care of all horses.

The streets were eerily calm during the evenings prior to the Passover celebration. Only the hooves of several hundred horses could be heard as additional patrols moved throughout the darkened streets. Every cavalryman stared at the blood above the doors and on the doorposts of the houses, and wondered what kind of people would do this.

One person made his way among the shadows, following the misaligned streets that ultimately brought him to the High Priest's house. This obscure figure remained motionless while a mounted patrol moved by. Once they were out of sight, the lone figure rapped gently on the door of a luxurious home.

When the door opened, a small sliver of yellow light momentarily cast a glow onto the face of the man who knocked and the one who opened the door. It was closed as rapidly as it had been opened, once both men had entered the building. Once inside, the two men walked along a marble hallway and entered a library. The only sound that was evident to servants was the sound of feet on the polished floor, and the sound of the library door closing.

In the silence of the partially lit room, Hiddo waited for Caiaphas to appear. When he did, Hiddo whispered, "Everything is in place. The Temple

Conspiracy With Malicious Intent

Police and the spies are combing the streets of the city at this moment. The snare is being set. Now we wait."

Caiaphas started to pace around the room unconsciously scratching the palms of his hands. "You must keep me apprised of all that happens. If the Romans become involved too soon or in any way, other than to put the Nazarene blasphemer to death, this plan will fall apart," said Caiaphas in a hushed tone.

"We are ready, and now is the time to deal with this blasphemer. We must accept our responsibility to get rid of this evil. He must be stopped. His words have undermined our status and reduced the Law to nothing. We cannot tolerate this any longer. Our very tradition is being destroyed."

"Everything IS in place and it WILL go as planned," insisted Hiddo.

"It must go well. If Pilate finds out that we have . . ." he stopped and looked at the door. Instantly, he moved to the door and opened it, but no one was there. After closing it, he moved closer to Hiddo. "Nothing, I mean nothing must go wrong," he whispered, his eyes glowing intensely and his jaw tightly clenched.

"Caiaphas. Do you doubt our ability to carry out this plan? What would make you feel more comfortable?"

"When he is dead and the deed is done. Then and only then I will be at ease."

"It will be done, and so do not be vexed."

"Are there any, I mean any trouble spots or any dissenters among the Sanhedrin?" whispered Caiaphas.

"Several men were slow to agree but it will go well. Trust me," said Hiddo.

Caiaphas opened the door and called his senior servant, "MALCHUS." Moments later, a young man entered the room and bowed his head in respect.

"Malchus, you are to follow Hiddo wherever he goes. You must be within an arms length of Hiddo at all times. He has a very important task to do and when he tells you to come and tell me, nothing, I mean nothing, must hinder you from summoning me. Do you understand?"

Malchus nodded.

"Whatever message Hiddo has you carry to me, must be brought to me with the greatest haste possible. No one, not even a Roman soldier, must stop you. This is a matter of life and death. It is the most urgent message that you will ever carry."

Conspiracy With Malicious Intent

A moment later, Caiaphas moved to the door that led into the hallway. "Both of you must now leave, for I must return to the Passover Meal, but keep me informed. Nothing must go wrong."

Hiddo and Malchus disappeared into the shadows, ignoring the sound of hooves and snorting horses in the distance.

****

When the Messiah and the disciples entered the upper room, they were pleased that everything had been prepared for Pesach or the Passover celebration. Peter and John smiled and greeted everyone with a kiss and an embrace, and eventually they moved around the prepared meal to recline on pillows and rugs.

The original Passover Meal was simple and contained roasted lamb placed on a platter next to the unleavened bread, bitter herbs and several containers of wine as well as a container of bitter sauce. Additional food was prepared and placed in critical places for everyone to participate in.

When the entrance to the room was secure and the evening lamps had been trimmed, the Messiah and the disciples stood around the traditional **U** shaped setting as they waited to recline. Everyone knew that only two places were reserved: one for the guest of honor and one for the host of the Passover Meal. All other places were open to anyone.

One by one, the hungry disciples moved nearer to the prepared foods which were spread on a cloth on the floor in the centre of the **U** setting. They waited for Jesus to take his leadership and host position before they began to recline for the meal.

The significance of the seating arrangement and where the food was placed is cultural. The food is set in the centre of a large **U**, and where people sit is important. The first sitting position, **U*** is a place reserved for the honored guest or special friend of the host. Immediately to the left of the honored guest is where the host of the Passover Meal reclines, **U***. The remaining places around the **U** shaped sitting arrangement are now open to anyone.

When Jesus took his position as the host of the Passover Meal, all of the other disciples moved around the **U** shaped arrangement and reclined. As it happened, Judas Iscariot reclined to Jesus' right and as a result, sat in the position of the honored guest. To Jesus' left sat John the Beloved and to his left sat Nathaniel, and the others began to choose a place around the

Conspiracy With Malicious Intent

U setting. The final place for reclining was across from the Messiah and Judas Iscariot, ***U** and that is where Peter was forced to recline.

It was not an envied position because the person, who sat there, was expected to be the server, who was to attend to the needs of all guests. Peter was not impressed with his lowly position but reluctantly squatted down.

After they had reclined, they listened to reading from the book of Exodus which described their forefathers and the events that led to an opportunity to flee Egypt. This story included the details of all the plagues and terrorizing tale of the Death Angel, who passed over all of the houses, touching only the first born of families that did not place blood on the doorposts and lintel of the door of their house.

They sat in silence as they considered what had just been read to them. They ate and drank in a presubscribed order designated by the protocols of the Passover Feast. As they tasted the bitter herbs and ate the roasted lamb they considered the anxiety that families had as the Death Angel moved among the houses and the palace in Egypt.

None of the eleven men in the room with Jesus noticed how restless and nervous Judas Iscariot was during the Passover supper. They were too busy reminiscing all of the events of the past few weeks. They talked about the day that Jesus rode through the streets of Jerusalem on a young colt, and the people, both adults and children, who ran along side of him as they waved palm branches and sang.

Simon Peter remembered the encounter that Jesus had with the lawyers in the Temple and the poor woman who gave all that she had. Nathaniel spoke about the surprise he had when Lazarus was raised from the dead and James recalled seeing Jesus curse the fig tree just outside of Bethany. Judas Iscariot was the only one who remained silent.

After they had eaten the meal and completed the requirements of the feast, Jesus stood and removed his upper garment and wrapped it around his waist. They became silent, unsure of what he was about to do. He poured water into a basin and now all eyes were upon him. They watched as he picked up a towel and walked over to where Judas Iscariot sat. They gazed in silence, not understanding what he was about to do.

Jesus knelt down and began to wash Judas' feet. Judas' eyes widened as he looked down at Jesus who dried his feet with the towel. Then Jesus refilled the basin and moved to John the Beloved, and began to wash his feet. After drying them, he poured out the water and replaced it with fresh water for the next disciple, who happened to be Nathaniel. Jesus continued to move around the room to wash every disciple's feet. When he was about to wash Peter's feet, Peter stood up and said, "You will NEVER wash my feet."

"What I am doing you do not understand, Simon, but eventually you will understand," responded Jesus as he smiled and motioned for Peter to sit down.

"No, Master. You cannot wash my feet." His voice cracked as he spoke. "If you will not let me wash your feet, then you can have no part with me."

Looking around the room Peter whispered, "Well if you must, then wash my hands, my head and all of me." Peter looked at the others, for his conscience was provoked because he was the one designated to serve the guests and wash their feet when they arrived at the Passover Feast. He was humiliated so he refused to do what was expected of him.

Jesus replied, "He that is bathed does not need to wash every part, but not all of you are clean."

All remained silent, and when Jesus was finished, he emptied the basin and hung up the towel. Without a word, he walked over to where he had reclined for the supper, folded his legs under him and sat down. He reached for the food and began to eat as the disciples nervously glanced at each other. Moments later, they began to whisper to each other and eventually resumed their previous conversations.

When it was very late, Jesus raised his hand and all became silent. Every eye was upon him, except those of Judas Iscariot, who was staring at the plates that once held the food.

Jesus reached for the bread, raised it above his head and gave thanks. Then he broke it into pieces and handed to them so they could pass it around. Before Jesus handed a piece of bread to Judas Iscariot, he waited until Judas looked up at him. When he did, Jesus nodded.

Then turning to the rest of the disciples, he spoke with a strong yet sad voice. "This is my Body . . . which is given for you. Eat ye all of it." He paused before he continued. "As often as you do this, do this in remembrance of me." He appeared sad and greatly stressed.

Judas stared at the remaining Passover Lamb in the plate and then at the bread in his hand. He tried to eat the Bread that Jesus had handed to him, but could not, so he held it in his hand. Everyone thought he had eaten it, except Jesus, because Jesus knew that he was the one to betray him.

Solemn moments passed and everyone ate the Bread, and then Jesus reached for the large container of wine. They watched as he poured wine into a goblet and said, "Take this and drink ye all of it. For I say unto to you, that I will not drink of the fruit of the vine until the Kingdom of God has come."

The room remained silent.

Jesus raised the goblet and said, "This Cup is the Cup of the New Covenant and it is my Blood . . . which is shed for you." All of them looked at the wine container and found it difficult to understand how the wine in the goblet represented their Master's Blood.

When Jesus lowered the goblet, he handed it to Judas because he sat in the position of honored guest. Judas held it to his mouth but found that his lips could not embrace the wine, so he removed his lips from the cup and handed it back to Jesus, who turned and handed it to John the Beloved, who sat to Jesus' left.

As the goblet was handed around to each guest, they held the goblet and all looked at Jesus before drinking from it. When the goblet was handed to Peter, he looked at Jesus, who nodded, assuring him that this was acceptable. He drank from it and placed the goblet next to the plate that held the roasted lamb.

The silence was more powerful than they had ever experienced.

Then Jesus said something that distressed them greatly. It hit them with a force that they could not comprehend. He said, "Behold, the hand of him that will betray me is with me on the table."

The silence in the room became intimidating. Eleven pairs of eyes stared at the table but the remaining two pairs, those of Jesus and Judas Iscariot, looked at each other momentarily. Immediately, every hand was withdrawn from view and it was impossible to hear their breathing.

Jesus continued, "And truly, the Son of Man goes as is planned, but woe to the man by whom he is betrayed."

Immediately, they all began to discuss and question themselves as to who they thought it might be. Betrayal was unacceptable, so to cast suspicion away from themselves, they began to brag as to whom would be the most trustworthy. It escalated into an argument as to who would be the strongest follower, the most reliable and the greatest.

Judas was the only one, who did not participate in the discussion for he was not in any position to argue because he suspected that Jesus knew that he would be the betrayer. He wondered how Jesus could possibly know about the plan, and yet, Jesus allowed him to sit in the position of honor. Perhaps there was still time and maybe, just maybe, Jesus thought it was someone else. A chill ran up Judas' spine. He shrugged his shoulders in an attempt to relieve the tension.

As Jesus continued to speak, Judas reviewed his plan and reminded himself of his purpose. He reached to his waist to feel the leather pouch that contained the thirty pieces of silver. Feeling uncomfortable, he sighed and realized that his breathing had become irregular. At that moment, he began to experience shortness of breath and felt mild chest pain as his heart began to beat irregularly.

Simon Peter stood to his feet. "Jesus, I want you to know that I am with you. I am devoted to you. I will never betray you, regardless of what everyone else does. Surely it cannot be me. I will defend you and NEVER betray you."

"Simon, Simon," said Jesus in a calm and assuring voice. "Satan has desired to have you that he may sift you as wheat but I have prayed for you."

Simon Peter's heart seemed to stop beating and all eyes were now upon him. Judas was pleased that Simon Peter was taking all the attention for it made it easier for him to remain undetected.

Jesus continued, "I have prayed for you, Simon, so that your faith will not fail and when you are completely changed, strengthen your brothers."

Simon Peter protested. "But Lord, I . . . I am ready to go with you to prison or death! Surely it cannot be ME." As he spoke, he tapped his closed fist onto his chest.

"Simon, Simon," Jesus said. "Before this very morning and before the rooster crows twice, you will deny me three times. Yes, Simon you will deny me and say that you do not know me."

Peter was devastated and when someone in the group told him to sit down, acute anger griped his heart and he was without words. It sounded as if he was to be the one to betray Jesus. He wanted to protest and shout back but he was momentarily out of breath after hearing that he would deny knowing Jesus.

"That cannot be," whispered Peter to himself as he turned his face away from the table guests. "Whenever I try to do or say something good it all fails and I look like a fool. This cannot be."

Jesus continued to speak but Simon and Judas could not hear the words that were being said. After several minutes, Jesus began to be heavy hearted. John the Beloved, who was sitting to Jesus' left, leaned over and whispered, "Master, who is the one that will betray you?"

The others did not hear because they were too busy promising each other that they would be more reliable than the other.

Jesus turned his head slightly to the left so Judas could not hear, and whispered, "The one I give the bread dipped in meat sauce." At that moment, Jesus took a piece of bread, dipped it into the stew pot and handed it to Judas Iscariot, the honored guest. Their eyes met again and Jesus whispered to Judas, "Do what you must do, quickly."

The others, who saw Jesus handing the bread to Judas, considered it an act or sign that the Host, Jesus, was honoring Judas. Never did it occur to them that Judas would sell Jesus for thirty pieces of silver.

Judas immediately stood to his feet and grabbed the bag that contained the group's money and started for the door. Everyone, except Jesus and John, thought that he was going to pay for the food and use of the room. Once he was out of the room, they continued to debate and discuss their willingness and ability to defend Jesus at all costs.

Judas did not return and John became very restless but Jesus placed his hand on his shoulder and nodded 'no' so John remained silent even though he felt his heart bursting.

As the hour became late, Jesus and the eleven sang a Pesach or Passover song known as the Hallel: words from the Psalms.

It was the last song that Jesus sang with his followers but just before everyone left the room, several men called to Jesus. "Jesus, look we have two small swords to defend you and ourselves. We are ready."

Jesus said to them, "That is enough," and they believed that Jesus was confident in what they had to defend themselves, so they rose and followed Jesus into the dark Jerusalem streets.

They walked in silence for none of them asked Jesus where he was going, so they followed, confident in their ability to defend Jesus. The moon was bright enough for them to see the path they were on, so like a flock of sheep they walked on, having no concept or idea of what the night sky would bring.

****

Several hundred strides from the Upper Room where Jesus and his disciples were eating the Passover Meal, Judas Iscariot met two servants from the Temple. In the shadows of the buildings, Judas assured them that Jesus was on his way to the Garden of Gethsemane.

"It's a place he goes often. I know he will go there," whispered Judas.

Conspiracy With Malicious Intent

"Come with us," one servant whispered, and immediately three shadows hurried from the shadowed building toward the Temple.

****

A light rap on Pontius' home office door caused him to place the parchment, sent to him by Caesar, on his lap. After he called, "Enter" the door remained closed so he rose to open it.

"Sir," said the soft voice of an adolescent girl, "your wife is not well, for she cries in her sleep and awakens often and . . . and screams. Please come to see her, kind Sir," she said as she lowered her eyes to the floor and curtsied.

"Very well," he sighed. "You may lead. I will follow."

He placed the parchment on a shelf next to the door and followed the young girl down a long hall and up the flight of marble stairs. When they arrived at Claudia's room, the young girl stepped to the side to allow Pontius to enter the room first.

"What is troubling you now Claudia?" he asked as he walked toward her bedside.

As he put his arms around her, she gasped, "In Rome and in Egypt, there are many gods but this man, who heals the sick, bothers me. Pontay, I believe he is a god."

"Why this man? What makes him a god? I may not have seen or met him but surely he looks like every other man. What makes him a god? Just because he says he is a god?" Pontius stepped back and raised his arms. "It's late and I have much to do," he said, trying not to sound too irate.

"My servants and I have listened to him and what he says burns in my heart, and I am unable to sleep." She wiped her tears from her face and looked up at him, "Pontay my dear, I fear that you will be somehow drawn into some evil against this man by those vile religious vipers."

"Claudia, you are a gifted woman. You have always been able to meet people and understand them within minutes, so why do you fear this man? What has he done that vexes you so?"

"That's just it. I do not fear him for he has done nothing but good, but I fear that harm will befall him, this very night. And you," she stopped to take a breath, "you will find that the jealous religious leaders will somehow get you involved in putting him to death."

Pontius sat on the edge of her bed as she stood and nervously paced across the floor.

Conspiracy With Malicious Intent

"What do you mean put him to death? How can this be?" asked Pontius.

"They are planning to kill him, Pontay. Oh, they will not do it themselves but plan to talk you into doing it for them," she said as she stepped closer.

"And how do they plan to make ME kill this man?" He raised his arms and shrugged his shoulders, "I cannot send a regiment to look for him to see if he is well. Why should I care about him? He's just another Jew . . . so what makes him so important?"

"You've heard about the good that he does."

"He means nothing to me," interrupted Pontius. "If he meets with harm, it is his undoing for angering every religious leader in Jerusalem, even that pompous ass, the High Priest, who I, by the way, loathe. Now please try to sleep again. I will have the servants bring the children into your room to sleep with you, so you feel better."

"NO, NO, Pontay. I have had the same dream several times and each time there is a plot to kill this Nazarene they call Jesus. If I am dreaming this time and time again, it means something going to h-a-p-p-e-n." She purposely slowed the words of her sentence.

"Claudia, my dear," he sighed as he placed his hands over his face. "If I did not have so much reading to do, I would come and sleep with you, but this is a busy time for me and I wish to get as much done as possible so we can return to Caesarea."

"Pontay dear, did I not dream about our first son's death? And did I not dream about your assistant, Porcano's murder. I dreamed about my father's death two days before it happened, and this is one of those times, Pontay. I am fearful of what is about to happen."

"What do you want me to do?" he asked as he stood to his feet. He sounded irritated and deeply annoyed.

"Will you promise me that you will have nothing to do with this man's death?"

"Claudia. I will be careful, but nothing will happen. I AM in control and I AM able to make my own decisions. Remember, that is what I do."

"But if Gadia, our daughter, and Lassia, our son find out that you have dealt evil to this man, they will . . ."

"What do they care? They are still young and I am experienced at dealing with such plans, so please try to rest." He went to the door and called to the two young girls. "Bring the children to her. She needs the comfort of the children tonight."

"Yes, Sir," they said in unison as they curtsied.

As Pontius was about to close the door, Claudia called to him, "Whatever happens, do NOT have anything to do with that man, p-l-e-a-s-e Pontay."

He bit his lower lip as he closed the door and started for the stairs. He returned to his office and library to resume his reading. When he closed the door to his chamber, he poured himself a glass of wine and reclined in his favorite chair. Closing his eyes, he stretched, yawned and reached across the table to pull the candle closer so he could read what Caesar required of him.

Silence and solitude is what he craved. It was the only time he felt comfortable, confident and in control.

Chapter XXXIII

THE ARREST AND THE EAR

It was near midnight when Judas Iscariot and the two temple servants arrived at the Temple. When they rounded the last corner on their way to meet with Hiddo, they met Malchus and Hiddo. All of them jumped back in surprise but when Hiddo recognized them, he motioned for them to follow him. They entered the Temple and moved along a corridor to a large hall, where members of the Sanhedrin anxiously waited for news about the arrest of the blasphemer. Their discussions anticipated victory. There were; however a number of members that had voiced their opposition to trial with a predetermined outcome.

When Hiddo entered the room where the members of the Sanhedrin waited, all conversation ceased. Hiddo waited until the door was locked, then moved to a podium to address the group.

"Tonight," he said with a note of arrogance, "we will be arresting the Nazarene, the blasphemer and the troublemaker. The time has come for us to end his evil influence among our people. On the surface it appears that he may have done some good to some citizens, but when it is held up to his violation of the Mosaic Law and tradition, he is guilty of death because he blasphemes by claiming to be God, and he violates the Sabbath." He paused a moment to catch his breath before continuing. "As all of you know, both charges are punishable by death. These are laws given to us by Moses and then passed on to our ancestors. We are required to obey them and teach them to our children and he is required to respect and obey them also."

Several members began to whisper to each other and so Hiddo raised his hand to silence them. "This reproach must be stopped, and respect must once again be established. We cannot allow his behavior to change our people's beliefs and traditions. We have been given the responsibility to guard our children from this evil. It IS our responsibility to protect the integrity of the Tanakh. If we do NOT, then God will punish us for NOT being diligent and obedient."

When he paused, whispers immediately filled the room. He raised his hand again and members of the Sanhedrin became silent. "We now know where this troublemaker and blasphemer will be at this time of night. When we go to that place, it will be dark, and because we will have only lanterns, it may be difficult to recognize him among his followers." He cleared his throat and continued. "This man," he said as he pointed at Judas Iscariot, who was standing near the doorway, "will let us know which person is the blasphemer by placing a kiss on his cheek. We will grab him and hold him fast. Did you hear? We will hold him and he will not be able to escape. This time there will be no crowds to protect him."

"What if there is a battle? Are you prepared for a fight?" asked a voice from the front row.

"Yes, we have prepared for that. He has eleven disciples and we will have thirty Temple Guards all of whom will be armed with swords and staves. Any other questions?" responded Hiddo.

"What will happen after his arrest?"

"He will be brought before Caiaphas and all of you will be able to participate in his trial."

A lawyer known for his knowledge and experience, named Ehud, stood to his feet, "I must remind you that holding a trial by night with a predetermined outcome of guilty, and holding it during a feast makes it an illegal trial." He paused to allow his sentence to be fully understood. "Passing sentence before sunrise is NOT an acceptable procedure. It is i-l-l-e-g-a-l. Further to that, we do NOT have the power to pass a death sentence upon anyone, even if such a person is guilty. How do you plan to keep this from the Governor?"

Hiddo appeared irritated by the questions. "Thank you Ehud, but did you not place your fist into the circle as a sign of agreeing with us that something needs to be done? Are you recanting your vote? We know the law and have taken steps for Rome's judicial influence to become involved once we have completed our interrogation."

"Hiddo, if I may continue, the only one, who can sentence anyone to death in Jerusalem or Judaea, for that matter, is Pontius Pilate. We do NOT have the authority to sentence an offender to death even if we find him guilty. The Sanhedrin has no such jurisdiction. The only way that this can happen is if an offender is guilty of violating Roman law, and violating the Sabbath and blasphemy is NOT a violation of Roman law."

Suddenly, the room erupted into verbal accusations, threats and shouts of anger. After Hiddo calmed the angry participants he turned to Ehud. "YOU," he shouted emphatically, "dare to defend this blasphemer in our midst after what we all have decided. How dare you?"

Ehud raised his hand as the crowd continued to berate him, and after some time, Ehud shouted, "THE DEATH SENTENCE, I REPEAT THE DEATH SENTENCE FOR BLASPHEMY AND VIOLATING THE SABBATH IS NOT THE ISSUE HERE."

Several moments passed before the men became silent. Ehud began again. "If you wish to have this, this plan to continue, you need to determine if a Roman law has been broken and then appeal to the Governor, who ONLY has the jurisdiction to sentence a person to death. I ask you, how will you ensure that the Governor will enact a death sentence verdict upon this Nazarene?"

Again the room was engulfed in accusations, threats and angry words.

"I know that I placed my hand in the circle to show my support but and I must say but, we must be careful that what we have planned will not come back upon us. This MUST be calculated carefully to ensure that the Governor does NOT suspect that our request for the life of this man is misrepresented as punishment for violating our religious laws."

"Ehud," responded an elderly man seated in the front row, "we have all agreed, and I recall seeing your fist in the circle when we began our planning. Are you now standing against us? We have a responsibility to deal with this man who claims to be a god and our king. We have only one God and we have no king. Our only kings were David and Solomon. This man is not a king nor is he the king of the Jews. Our plan is to eliminate potential problems with Rome, especially if they hear that he claims to be our king. Whether king or not, we must get rid of him, and you agreed, did you not?"

Ehud raised his hands to request silence. When the room became silent, he continued. "I want to be sure that this is NOT perceived as a conspiracy. Conspiracy or the rumor of a conspiracy will never cause speculation and distrust to die, especially if the public hears about it. Once they hear about it, we will never be able to convince them that there was no conspiracy. Remember that all we wish to do is end this blasphemer's claim as being our king and being a god."

"Conspiracy to kill a king?" shouted several men at the same time. "How can that be when neither is true?" He is not our king, nor is he a god and as far as our intention to create a conspiracy . . . that is not true either."

Again Ehud waved his hands to calm the crowd. "The guidelines for an arrest, the charges and accusations filed against someone, an adequate defense and the time lines for a trial and the verdict must all adhere to our laws and Roman laws. If any of these are in questions, an illegal trial exists."

"Ehud, a lecture from you about what is required is not necessary," shouted someone from the rear of the room. "SIT DOWN."

Hiddo raised his hands and pointed to the back of the room as he spoke, "This is not a conspiracy nor is he a king nor is he a god. Let us not hesitate now that we are this close to dealing with this problem. All is in place and the man at the back of the room has agreed to specific terms that will allow this event to take place. We have already paid for his services."

"Whether we have paid for services yet to be provided or not," said a man from the region of Arimathea who's named was Joseph, "a man is considered innocent until a proper trial has been provided: one with a proper defense and an opportunity for the accused to defend himself three times. If even these basics are ignored, and as you know, a trial held at night and during a feast is unacceptable. You have now created an illegal trial."

Hiddo glared at Joseph. "You sound as if you wish to defend this blasphemer and troublemaker. He is destroying our tradition, our words and the laws of Moses. No SIT DOWN," he shouted.

"Hiddo, as Vice Chief Justice of the Sanhedren, your role is to ensure procedure and decorum, not to determine guilt before a trial has been held. Have you lost your focus in this matter?" asked Nicodemus.

"ARE YOU AND JOSEPH HIS DISCIPLES AND SECRET FOLLOWERS?" retorted Hiddo. His jugular vein in his neck pulsated as he shouted.

The crowd began to berate both Nicodemus and Joseph of Arimathea. Their insults were vicious and mean. If it were not for a man named, Isaac Ben Hadda, the crowd would have rushed Nicodemus and Joseph and expelled them from the room.

"Gentlemen, gentlemen," said Mannsaher Ben Hadaea. "Why are all of you so eager to break the law to preserve the law. You cannot sentence a man before his trial. You . . ."

Hiddo raised his hand as he spoke. "Sit down Mannsaher. We have heard all that we wish to hear from you and your . . . your sympathizers."

Conspiracy With Malicious Intent

Issac Tsad Ahala stood to his feet. "Have you lost your senses? You are speaking of a man, who has violated the Sabbath and I know that the Laws of Moses require a capital sentence to be carried out but you are passing it without holding a trial. We are in the Passover and a trial held during a feast is illegal. You MUST allow for legal counsel and an opportunity for a man to defend himself. If not you are violating the law to keep the law."

Hiddo pointed to the back of the room until all the members became silent. All eyes turned to Judas, who pulled his headpiece over his forehead and lowered his gaze to avoid eye contact with everyone in the room.

"All is in place. The moment we have made the arrest," continued Hiddo. "Malchus will hurry to Caiaphas' house. Then we take our captive to Caiaphas' place for trial. All of you will have opportunity to witness the trial."

Again Ehud stood to his feet. "In a trial such as this we need witnesses. Have you found reliable witnesses and, have you forgotten that the accused has three opportunities to make his defense? Next there needs to be deliberations and discussion. This will all take time and I warn you that deciding his guilty before the trial even begins IS conspiracy. What if he appeals to the Governor? How will we be able to explain our actions to the Governor?"

"What about the Roman soldiers? Will they be nearby and will they stop us?" a voice asked.

"We are using the Temple Police because it is a Temple issue. The Romans will have little to do with it, at least at the beginning."

Hiddo turned to Ehud, "Are you with us or have you become one of his disciples?"

Ehud responded with, "As a teacher of the Law, both Mosaic and as an advisor of Roman law, I have been part of many legal issues, so I caution you that if a trial is considered to be illegal, we run the risk of reprisals from Pontius Pilate." His voice became louder as he ended his sentence.

A young lawyer stood to his feet. "Ehud, we do not question your knowledge of the law. What we see is a man, who seeks to defend a blasphemer. He is no king. He is no prophet or Messiah but a man who is disrupting the people and challenging what Moses has entrusted to us. If we will not guard the law, then who will do it? I have been a student who has learned much from you but I am confused. Is this different than if we found a woman in adultery or captured a thief, who has stolen from the Temple? Using your words, 'The laws of Moses are more than ten in number, so how can you expect us to turn aside from his violation of the law of blasphemy, violating the Sabbath and speaking of destroying the Temple?"

Ehud closed his eyes and waited for the room to become silent. "I am merely suggesting something which all of you know and understand, and that, if we pronounce someone guilty before the trial begins, and we have not allowed for a proper defense or an appeal, all of our actions will be determined to be unlawful and illegal. If we proceed, we are in violation of the law ourselves. We cannot break the law to protect the law."

Hiddo walked over to the door and before opening it, looked back at the men in the room. "All of you have agreed to the necessity of this arrest and we need to do it now."

Ehud raised his hand but before he could speak, Hiddo interrupted, "It's too late to stop now. Ehud, thank you for your concerns but we must do it now."

****

Pontius reclined in his favorite chair next to his bed. He closed his eyes and took a long breath, held it for a moment and then exhaled slowly. "Palestine is such an abyss. The weather is terrible, the people are demented and I can't wait to return to Caesarea. It's so much better to be near the Mediterranean Sea. Oh, to feel the breeze as it crosses the water. It makes me feel free."

There was a soft rap on his door. "Enter," he said as he adjusted his bedclothes. He sounded somewhat irritated.

An elderly female servant entered, curtsied and set a flask of wine on his night table. "Your evening wine Sir. Will there be anything else?"

"Wine and a good sleep is all I need. I want to enjoy the next twelve hours in peace and quiet. This will help. Thank you." He nodded, "You are excused."

Just as she was leaving the room, Pontius called to her. "Lydia. How is my Claudia? Is she resting well?"

"I have not been in her chambers but I will check if you would like."

"No. I'm planning on a long sleep, so do not disturb me with breakfast. I do not wish to be bothered until midday."

"Yes Sir." She curtsied and closed the door quietly as Pontius cupped his hand around the flame of the candle and with a gentle puff, converted the room into darkness.

Conspiracy With Malicious Intent

****

Varrus lay awake for hours unable to deal with the loss of his servant, Pollus. Unable to find a position of comfort, he lay on his back with his forearm across his forehead. When he heard his name called, he sat up, lit the candle on the table and called, "Enter."

"Sir!"

"Yes, what is it?" he asked as he tried to adjust his eyes to the small flame in the hand of the man at his door.

"The two thieves who are to be crucified on the morrow are unruly. Would it be your wish that we flog them now to settle them down?"

"Give me a moment," Varrus said as he donned his uniform.

Neither of the men entered Varrus' room for they knew the protocol of privacy for officers.

"Does not Mabboodda deal with these things? Where is he?" Varrus sounded irritated.

"He's the one that sent me to you. He needs your approval, Sir."

When they arrived in the lower chambers, Varrus could hear several men shouting obscenities. He entered the room where the two men were being held. One of them spit at Varrus and narrowly missed him. Immediately, a guard standing next to the prisoner used his fist to punch the man's jaw, knocking him to the stone floor. He moaned loudly as blood ran freely from his mouth and nose. The second prisoner laughed loudly and taunted Varrus.

"Would you have him flogged? Sir!" asked Mabboodda, who was standing some distance from the condemned men. "They struck me and I am fortunate to be alive."

"No. Place them in separate cells."

"Yes Sir," said one of the guards.

"And he," Varrus said as he pointed at the one knocked to the floor, "will be flogged if he utters one sound or causes any more trouble."

"You will NEVER crucify me, you . . ."

His sentence ended abruptly when a long wooden pole slammed into his ribcage, taking out all residual breath from his lungs. He remained on the floor and began gasping for breath.

With only moans coming from the man, Varrus turned to Lammal, the executioner from Malta. "Any problems? Then flog him but be sure that he will be alive for his crucifixion tomorrow. He is sentenced to die tomorrow and dead he will be on the morrow. He must live long enough to be crucified," Varrus said as he looked at Mabboodda.

"Yes Sir!" replied Mabboodda with a smile on his face. "By the way are you alright, Sir? You appear to have no color and your eyes are . . ."

"It is my grief that drains my color and enthusiasm for life. My servant, Pollus was with me since a lad. His murder will not depart from me."

Varrus made his way back to his room, escorted by two soldiers. As he entered his room, he said to the men, "It must be the moon that makes this evening so strange. Nothing good can come from this. I've seen too many full moons and it seems to make evil more vile."

He closed the door and prepared for sleep that would not come.

****

Jesus and his disciples had been in the Garden of Gethsemane for some time when he became very grieved in his spirit. He motioned for Peter, James and John to follow him. The four walked deeper into the darkness of the garden, and none dared to ask where they were going. After they had walked twenty or more strides, Jesus said to Peter, James and John, "Stay here and pray. I will go over there to pray." He pointed to an area an additional ten strides down the pathway. "My soul is overwhelmed with sorrow to a point of death. Stay here and keep watch." Moments later, he walked a stone's throw into the darkness and the thick undergrowth.

There he fell on his face and prayed. "My Father, if it is possible, may this cup be taken from me. Not my will but your will be done." Great anguish gripped his soul and words did not come easily to him.

Some time later, he returned to the three disciples and found them sleeping, because it was very late. In an anguished tone, he asked them, "Could you not keep watch and pray with me for one hour? Please watch and pray. I know your spirit is willing but your body is weak. Please watch and pray with me."

He went away the second time to pray. "Father, if it is possible to have this cup to be taken away from me . . . unless I drink from it, but may I do your will." Again his spirit was so overwhelmed that words did not come to him. He remained there for some time and continued to commune with his Father.

Extreme stress and anxiety ravished his human body causing 'hematohidrosis', a condition where blood vessels around sweat glands constrict causing dilation and rupture, resulting in small amounts of blood to enter the sweat gland. When perspiration causes sweat to be secreted, drops of blood flow to the surface of the skin and as a result, sweat is mixed with blood droplets.

When he returned the second time, he found Peter, James and John sleeping because their eyes were very heavy for it was very early in the morning. Then Jesus turned away and prayed the third time, saying similar words. His soul was in deep agony.

When he returned, he found them sleeping again. "Look," he said, "the hour has come for the Son of Man to be betrayed into the hands of sinners. Rise, for I see lanterns in the distance. The betrayer is now here."

Peter, James and John rose in a stupor and began to follow Jesus, who walked toward the lanterns. When they met the other sleepy disciples, they were unaware of what was about to happen. In the confusion of seeing many lanterns and dozens of men approaching, the drowsy disorganized disciples did not recognize Judas Iscariot because they did not expect to see him, nor did they suspect him to be the betrayer that Jesus had spoken about.

John, however, knew and watched as Hiddo and Judas approached Jesus. When the mob confronted the disciples, Jesus walked into the midst of them and looked at their torches, swords and staves. Only John thought that he recognized Judas Iscariot but did not have time to say anything.

"Who are you looking for?" asked Jesus in an unwavering voice, knowing what their answer would be.

"We are looking for Jesus the Nazarene," said Hiddo.

"It is I that you seek. These with me have nothing to do with your intentions. Leave them alone for it is I that you seek."

At that moment Judas stepped close to Jesus, leaned over and kissed his cheek.

"Shall we smite them with a sword?" shouted one of the disciples and instantly there was confusion. Simon Peter drew a small sword and swung it, cutting off the ear of the High Priest's servant.

Malchus immediately dropped to his knees and screamed because of the pain, and the mob stumbled back to see what had happened. By the light of their torches, Jesus picked up the ear and gently returned it to Malchus' head. The crowd was amazed that it was completely restored and instantly healed.

In the confusion, Judas Iscariot vanished from among them. He ran through the trees because he knew the area well for Jesus and the disciples had been to that garden many times.

Conspiracy With Malicious Intent

Jesus turned to his disciples, "Put your swords away. He who lives by the sword will die by the sword." Then he turned to the mob, "Why have you come to me as to arrest a thief? You have brought your swords and staves. I was daily in the Temple, so why did you not arrest me there?"

Hiddo and the mob did not respond to his question but stepped forward as the Temple Police grabbed Jesus and tied his wrists together. At that moment, all of the disciples feared and fled, and so did Malchus.

The mob led Jesus away to Annas, the father-in-law of the High Priest, Caiaphas. Meanwhile, Malchus ran as though blind. His heart pounded, his lungs ached and his legs burned as he ran. When he arrived at Caiaphas' house, he pounded on the door until it was opened.

Covered in blood, Malchus stumbled into the room as he gasped for breath. Caiaphas, seeing the blood all over Malchus' face and clothing, instantly feared that a battle had occurred and many had been slain. His heart grew weak with fear as Malchus fell to his knees, gasping for breath.

"MY EAR. IT WAS CUT OFF . . . OFF I TELL YOU . . . DURING THE ARREST," he gasped loudly. "SOMEONE HAD A SWORD . . . AND THERE WAS CONFUSION. JESUS STOPPED THE CONFUSION . . . AND PICKED UP MY EAR AND PUT IT BACK ON MY HEAD. LOOK AT MY EAR." Again he gasped for breath, "SEE THE BLOOD ON MY CLOTHES!"

"YOU ARE MAD!" shouted Caiaphas as he stepped back.

"NO! LOOK AT THE BLOOD ON MY SHOULDER AND ON MY CLOTHING AND FACE. THAT BLOOD IS FROM MY EAR THAT WAS CUT OFF. LOOK, LOOK . . . JUST LOOK," he shouted as he stepped closer to Caiaphas. "LOOK MY EAR IS BACK AS IT WAS BEFORE." He tugged at it to show Caiaphas.

"IF YOU SPEAK TO ANYONE ABOUT THIS, I'LL HAVE YOU FLOGGED. DO YOU HEAR ME?" shouted Caiaphas.

"BUT MY EAR! JESUS HEALED IT. LOOK! LOOK!"

"SILENCE! I COULDN'T CARE LESS ABOUT YOUR EAR," Caiaphas shouted as he slapped Malchus with the back of his hand, sending Malchus sprawling to the floor. "ALL I WANT TO KNOW IS ABOUT THE ARREST. HAVE ANY OTHERS BEEN INJURED OR KILLED. DID THEY ARREST THE NAZARENE? WHERE ARE THEY NOW?"

"I think they have Jesus but I'm unsure of where they are going. I ran when my ear was put back on my head," he gasped. LOOK! LOOK, IT HAS BEEN RESTORED!"

"SILENCE!" screamed Caiaphas as he leaned over and slapped Malchus a second time. "IF YOU TELL ANYONE OF THIS, I WILL HAVE YOUR

TONGUE CUT OUT AND BOTH EARS CUT OFF! SILENCE FOR I DO NOT WANT TO HEAR ANYMORE OF IT."

Other servants stood at the door and listened to Malchus words.

"WELL, FIND OUT WHERE THEY HAVE TAKEN HIM, YOU FOOL AND DO IT NOW!" shouted Caiaphas.

Malchus ran from the room with the side of his face and all of his clothing covered in blood.

Chapter XXXIV

THE HIGH PRIEST AND THE BETRAYER

Orange and yellow flames on countless torches, in the hands of anxious and nervous men, cast quivering streams of light on everyone and everything within twenty strides of Jesus. The kiss, the arrest, the confrontation between the mob and disciples, and the personal injury to Malchus, provided Judas Iscariot with an excellent opportunity to step into the trees and foliage, where no one could possibly see him.

Once on the footpath to Jerusalem, Judas ran in early morning twilight, as quickly as possible, taking every calculated opportunity to avoid detection. His plan was to enter the city and later in the day leave through the north gate to Jericho. Once he was within the city walls, he was forced to wait at the back of a stable, while a mounted patrol passed within several strides of where he hid.

His heart pounded and his chest yearned for more air but he managed to keep his composure. He overheard the officer of the patrol tell his men that several people had been beaten and robbed on the road to Jericho, so Judas decided to remain in the stable and delay his departure to Jericho. As he slowed his heart and breathing, he counted the money he had taken from the disciples and the silver pieces he had received for the betrayal. When he was sure that all coins and silver pieces were there, he placed them back into his leather pouch. Waiting there for some time, he considered other routes of escape from the city. Perhaps Jericho was not the place to be, and Bethany offered little in the way of security, however if he decided to return to the town of his birth, Kerioth, it would be easy to travel southward into the province of Idumaea.

When all was silent, he left the stable and rushed down several narrow streets that led to the Sheep Gate at the north end of the Temple. He reasoned that the disciples would not likely be in that area, nor would any other people be there for the pens were now empty because all of the Passover Lambs had been sold for the Passover celebration.

His escape plans were altered when he was within a few strides of the main gate of the sheep pens because he suddenly recognized a familiar voice. He immediately stepped behind a two-wheeled cart to listen. As he turned his ear to the soft voice, he recognized that it was Andrew and he was speaking to someone. Holding his breath, he listened to their whispers and recognized Matthew's voice when he responded to Andrew.

"All of the lambs are gone so no one will come here. This should be a safe place to hide."

"We can wait until evening," responded Matthew in a nervous whisper. "Then we can leave. By tomorrow the excitement will have died down."

"But what about the Master? Where will they take him?" asked Andrew. "What will they do to him? Will they kill him? I thought we could defend him but we needed more swords and . . ."

"But we were outnumbered, so what could we? What do we do now?"

Judas decided to make his way to the south end of the city to hide where all the city refuse was taken. He cautiously made his way through the streets and exited through the Dung Gate and rushed across the field to a small ravine. Gasping for breath, he sat under a tree. "What a place to end up," he mumbled to himself as he looked around at the piles of unwanted refuse. "No one will come here during the Passover Celebration," he muttered to himself. "This will give me time to think about what I can do next."

He considered going to Bethany but was worried that someone in that city would recognize him, especially since he had been there when Lazarus was raised back to life. As he sat there, he realized there was no one to help him. It was the first time in his life that he felt truly alone.

Traveling to Kerioth was an option but the longer he sat there the more difficult it became for him to make a decision. Eventually his conscience began to vex him. His heart pounded in his chest, sweat formed on his brow, and when his ice cold hands reached up to wipe his brow, he became anxious about what he was experiencing. He moaned loudly. Again, he counted his money along with the silver pieces, but when he tried to return the coins to the leather pouch, his hands began shaking so badly he dropped several coins and two pieces of silver. As he picked them up, his breathing became more irregular, his chest began to ache and he could hear his heart pound in his ears.

Conspiracy With Malicious Intent

Eventually the odor of his surrounding prompted him to enter the city. There, he managed to find an old building that was being repaired, and knowing that no one would be working during the Passover, he stepped into the inner shadows of the structure. As time passed, he recounted his money and looked at the pieces of silver again. The memory of Jesus honoring him by handing him the sop or bread dipped in the stew, and washing his feet at their Passover supper gripped him. "Jesus knew who would betray him, but how did he know? If he knew, why did he honor me by washing my feet and giving me the sop?" he whispered to himself. His mouth was dry, making it difficult to swallow.

After sighing several more times, he put the silver and coins back into his pouch and mumbled, "When did Jesus begin to suspect? Was I careless? Maybe one of the others warned him about me? Yes, that was it. It must have been Peter. He always has his nose into everyone's affairs."

He remained in the shadows of the building for a long time when he realized that all of the coins and the pieces of silver were of little value for he had no place to safely keep them. Indecision plagued him. Again he considered returning to Kerioth, but remained hidden in the city. Several moments later he was sure that going to Jericho would allow him to escape but when he recalled the words of the legionnaires that passed near him, he thought about going westward to Joppa located on the coast of the Mediterranean.

As he sat in silence in the broken down building, his conscience gnawed at his very existence. Finding it stressful to sit, he stood to his feet and was surprised that his legs were so weak that they could scarcely bear his weight.

Small streaks of light started to reach across the eastern sky. Judas recalled the day when Jesus fed the five thousand, walked on water, raised Lazarus back to life, fed four thousand, spoke to many on the hillside, cast demons from the lives of others, hugged children, put his arm around him to encourage him to remain in the group, washed his feet and then offered honor to him by handing him sop at the Passover supper.

He wiped his mouth with the back of his hand. "After doing all of that, he must be the Messiah that is to come. Maybe I made the biggest mistake of my life," he admitted to himself. "What if they kill Jesus? It makes no sense. Why would Jesus honor me if he knew it was I that would betray him," he reasoned to himself.

Judas felt as if his chest would burst. Tears formed in his eyes when he recalled the day that Jesus sent them out in pairs to heal the sick and proclaim the good news of the Lord. "Those were better days," he admitted to himself.

Eventually, he could not contain himself. A loud groan gushed from his throat and he dropped to his knees, gripped the dry soil with both hands and began to sob. His vision blurred and he became nauseated. After vomiting, then reeling back to the corner of the building, he dropped to his knees as he continued mumbling to himself and wiping saliva from his nose and mouth. Little did he know that his complexion was changing from a healthy looking person into an ashen colored shadow of a man.

Anxious to escape his memories, he decided to go to Jericho, so he slowly and cautiously made his way toward the eastern city gate. He narrowly escaped detection at the city well and when he staggered down a side street, several soldiers saw him and laughed at him because they thought he was drunk. Little did they know that he was incoherent with grief, regret and on the verge of a total emotional and physical breakdown.

****

Annas, a rich Sadducee and powerful man, always used his influence and his son-in-law, Caiaphas the High Priest, to achieve his goals. He was visibly pleased with Jesus' arrest and certainly was delighted to have Jesus standing in front of him in the privacy of his building rather than in public. His smile mimicked that of an adder pondering its prey.

"So, you are the Galilean from Nazareth, who claims to have the power to forgive sins? Are you God?" His mouth tightened as he spoke. "Your brazen words also claim that you are a king, a king of the Jews?" He leaned back as he narrowed his eyes as he folded his arms across his chest.

Jesus remained silent and his unblinking eyes stared at Annas as though he knew Annas' next words.

"Your blasphemy includes forgiving sins and claiming to be the son of God. You are the one who has caused people to scorn us. You have cast doubt upon our knowledge, respect, and public status, and have attempted to destroy our traditions. Not only are you guilty of blasphemy but you have broken many Mosaic Laws such as disrespecting the Sabbath. Now you will be judged for your lack of respect." His lips were tight enough to cause them to lose color.

"What must we do now?" a voice called out.

"I'm glad that I have had the pleasure to meet you, especially in this unique moment of time." He cast his eyes to the floor as he spoke. Then shaking his head slowly from side to side, he continued, "Your words have irritated everyone: Sadducees, Pharisees, priests, lawyers, rabbis and those who study the Law. How did you expect to escape? If you know the Law as well you claim you will know that blasphemy is a capital offence that requires your life. The Law demands that we put you to death by stoning."

Jesus remained silent.

"This violation is most serious because it violates the very words of God. You know the Ten Commandments and the Mosaic Laws. How do you expect to avoid punishment?"

"It's the blasphemy that condemns him," a voice shouted.

Annas nodded in agreement. "Take him to Caiaphas' place. He can deal with this, this blasphemer. Once again we see that nothing good comes out of Nazareth. You are worse than a thief and a murderer. Our worst lawbreaker, Bar Abbas is better than you. Take him away," he shouted as he stood to his feet.

On the way to Caiaphas' house, plans were made to hold a trial for Jesus even though they knew they were breaking the law, but their anger and jealousy blinded them, so they cared little about the potential of wrongdoing.

Meanwhile, the morning twilight made it easy for Simon Peter to follow the crowd as they took Jesus to Caiaphas' house. No one seemed to notice or question him as he drew near, so he made an attempt to blend in with the unruly crowd.

When they arrived at Caiaphas' house, the mob crowded through the main gate. Peter, however, lost his courage when he saw how many people were entering so he stood outside as he tried to decide how he may enter.

At that moment, Elias one of the house servants of Caiaphas arrived at the gate and walking beside him was the disciple, John who was a personal friend of Elias.

John's eyes met Peter's and when Peter motioned to him, John nodded his head for Peter to step near. When he did John whispered to Elias, "This is a friend of mine." Elias nodded his approval and the three of them entered the Caiaphas' courtyard. Once inside, John followed Elias to a side door and Peter moved near a window to see and hear what was unfolding.

Inside the house, there were scribes and elders waiting, for they had heard that Jesus had been arrested and would soon be there for a trial. When the illegal trial began, every attempt was made to present witnesses against Jesus but all of them contradicted themselves and each statement that was made was inconsistent and contradictory.

Abdar, the first witness, stated that he remembered that Jesus forgave the sins of a woman who was known to be a prostitute but when he was asked to clarify when this happened, he was unable to remember the time, the date, the place and the name of the woman. After further examination and questioning, he was told that he was free to sit among the crowd.

The second witness, Jesher, claimed to have heard Jesus claim to be god and the Messiah, but when asked if Jesus forgave sins, he was unsure of where this had occurred. Further questioning produced confusion so he was told to sit with the crowd.

A third witness responded to the question: 'When did this Nazarene break the Sabbath?' His response given was found to be a date that was not a Sabbath, so he was asked to give his opinion about Jesus as a Jew.

"He claims to be a Jew and . . . and I saw him heal a blind man and speak with tax collectors. Once I saw him speaking with a harlot at the well near the east gate but I am unsure if he is a Jew."

Six additional witnesses were unable to answer questions or to confirm rumors that Jesus forgave sins. It became evident that all witnesses perjured themselves with their statements. Finally, two witnesses were found to give evidence against Jesus and it became apparent to even the unlearned that they had been coached regarding what to say.

Ehud, a leading authority of the Law and legal procedures, and three others attempted to speak but they were told to, "Sit and be silent."

Finally in frustration, Caiaphas walked up to Jesus and asked, "Are you the Messiah, the Anointed One, the Christ and the Son of the Blessed?"

"You have said it and I am. Soon you will see the Son of Man sitting on the right hand of power and coming in the clouds of heaven," responded Jesus.

Immediately, the High Priest tore his clothes as a public sign of great distress and anger. "What further need have we to hear his words or find witnesses? His very words have condemned him. YOU HAVE HEARD THE BLASPHEMY. THIS BLASPHEMY IS WORTHY OF DEATH ACCORDING TO THE LAW!"

As they hurled insults at Jesus, Jesus continued to stare at Caiaphas. His unblinking eyes intimidated Caiaphas, who shouted, "BLINDFOLD HIM." Without further discussion, Caiaphas condemned Jesus to death. Someone struck Jesus with their fist and he turned away. Then they began to spit upon him, but he remained silent.

Someone shouted, "IF YOU ARE THE CHRIST AND THE ANOINTED ONE, TELL US WHO STRUCK YOU?" and they all laughed and jeered him. Their verbal assault and physical contact continued for an extended amount of time until Hiddo raised his fist. "All of you placed your fist into the circle, agreeing with this trial, you must step forward and use that clenched fist to strike the face of this blasphemer. There will be NO exceptions."

One by one the members of the Sanhedrin, except for Ehud Bar Jabal, Joseph Elishama from the town of Arimathea and Nicodemus Ben Arod, stepped forward and struck the blindfolded Nazarene. Hiddo wanted to verbally identify them when they refused to strike the Nazarene but Ehud raised his hand and stared at Hiddo, so Hiddo remained silent.

Finally when all of the participants had struck his face, several grabbed his beard and jerked until hair and flesh was ripped from his face. Immune to his pain, they watched the blood freely flowing to his chest onto the floor. Stepping back so that no blood would mark their hands or end up on their clothes or sandals, they watched as Jesus shivered from the pain.

They continued to say many blasphemous things about and to him, but he held his peace. Their words were cruel, malicious and unkind. Their venom flowed from their mouths as vomit. When they became tired of their evil actions and words, the group prepared to take Jesus to Pontius Pilate, the Roman Governor.

Meanwhile, Simon Peter moved toward a small fire that had been started to warm the participants because of the cool morning air. Peter cautiously stepped closer for a better view and when he did, he heard them talking and laughing about the arrest and what happened to Malchus' ear.

As they laughed, Peter squatted next to the flames to warm himself, when a girl next to him looked at him, and in the orange flickering glow of the fire, said, "This man was with the Nazarene blasphemer when they arrested him. I recognize him. HE WAS THERE," she shouted as she pointed at him. "HE WAS THERE," she shouted as she stood to her feet.

"Woman," Peter said in a low gruff voice, hoping to silence her, "You don't know what you are talking about and I certainly do not know him. You're wrong, so sit down and shut up."

Several minutes later, someone else pointed at Simon Peter. "She's right. This fellow was with the Nazarene when he was arrested. He's the one who cut off Malchus' ear. Yes, you were there and are one of his followers," he insisted as he pointed at Peter.

"Man, I don't know what you are talking about," responded Peter in an angry and confrontational tone.

In the glow of the flames and the morning twilight, a cock crowed some distance away indicating that sunrise was nigh.

At that very moment someone said, "Your very speech and accent betrays you. You're Galilean. You're one of his followers. You were with him and YOU'RE ONE OF THEM!" he shouted as he also pointed at Simon Peter.

Peter cursed and swore in an attempt to divert attention away from himself, only moments before the cock crowed the second time. At that moment, Peter felt a dart go through his heart. As he turned to leave, he looked at the side door just as they were leading Jesus from the building. That is when his eyes met Jesus' eyes. Peter ran blindly to the entrance gate into the darkness as tears running down his cheeks. John the Beloved, who had helped Peter enter the courtyard, stepped back into the shadows as Peter disappeared into the morning light.

The turmoil within the High Priest's jurisdiction and circle of influence scattered the confused and frightened disciples, who happened to be nearby. They ran through the darkened streets. Some remembered Jesus' words that Peter would deny him three times before the cock would crow twice. The confusion and mayhem in their hearts and minds was minor in comparison to the turmoil in the heart and mind of the two betrayers: Simon Peter and Judas Iscariot.

****

Since Varrus could not sleep, he dressed and walked down into the dungeon to see how the two thieves had acted during the night watch. All was silent when he arrived in the chambers. Danniah, the executioner from Babylon, stood as Varrus entered the dungeon.

"Is all well?" inquired Varrus as his eyes darted around the darkened corners and down the hallway.

Danniah nodded, "Yes Sir."

"Was flogging necessary?"

"No, Sir! They realized that they be not long here. I think they decided that more pain has little value."

Varrus returned to his office and stared at the records of the two men, who were scheduled to be crucified. He picked up the first parchment that listed the charges of theft and murder against the man, and noticed that in the lower corner of the parchment were the words: 'Known member of rebels led by Bar Abbas.' Then he read the second parchment and saw the same words written on the bottom: 'Known member of rebels led by Bar Abbas.'

He closed his eyes and mourned the loss of his servant. Pollus had not been granted dignity but was buried in the Judaea countryside as a commoner. Varrus' heart ached and he wept until there were no more tears.

Several hours later, he moved to the shelf near the window and reached for the Records Book and began to read the large document. He was surprised that nine hundred and thirty-six men had died, while in the dungeon, one thousand two hundred and forty-seven had been flogged and four hundred and nine had been crucified. Closing the Records Book, he turned to the window for fresh air and silently wished that he would not have to supervise his first crucifixion on the morrow. It was a task that he did not look forward to. The fresh air that he drew into his lungs was all that provided relief.

****

Waking early, Amon chose to sit on the porch and when Adakal found him, he sat next to him. Both remained silent, not daring to look at or speak with each other.

After a long period of silence, Amon whispered, "Passover is both a good time and a bad time; a good time for us to remember but a bad time for lambs."

"I wonder who the Messiah ate the Passover with," whispered Adakal.

"Do Messiahs celebrate the Passover?" asked Amon as he wiped a tear from his eye.

"If he is a Jew, then yes, he will celebrate the Passover. All Jews celebrate the Passover, even Messiahs. You should know that."

"We should have waited at the Sheep Gate to see if he and his followers stopped to buy a lamb. Then, we could have seen him," said Amon as he stared at a beetle scurrying from under his sandal.

"Jerusalem will be very quiet during the Passover," said Adakal. "Nothing ever happens in Jerusalem."

"Even in Jerusalem?"

"Yes Amon, especially in Jerusalem. You'll be surprised how quiet it will be in this city."

Chapter XXXV

THE GOVERNOR AND THE KING

A gentle rap on Pontius' bedchamber door caused him to stir. Again, he heard the gentle rapping, so he turned his face to the wall and pulled his bed covers over his head, but the tapping continued. In anger, he tossed back the covers and sat on the edge of his bed and shouted, "GIVE ME A MOMENT."

After he rubbed his eyes, he responded in anger. "THIS HAD BETTER BE IMPORTANT." He brushed his hair with his fingers, blinked his eyes before lighting a candle and stood to don his clothes. He opened the door and was about to berate whoever was at the door, but held his temper when he looked down upon a young servant girl, who paused to make a curtsey.

"Sir, please Sir. Many men are in the courtyard and will not leave. They are calling for you."

Surprised by her words, he stepped back and narrowed his brows. "Who are they? What do they want?" He was surprised and angry, yet gentle.

"I know not, Sir, but they sound angry."

"WHERE'S MY BODYGUARDS?" Pontius shouted. At that moment, the Captain of Security and personal bodyguard, Lanapous, appeared at the end of the hallway. Running toward Pontius, he called, "Sir, I know it is early and still dark but the city seems to be in an uproar and some men from the Temple are here and will not leave until they speak with you. What do you wish me to do?"

"KEEP THEM FROM THE DOOR. If any of them dare touch the door or enter, THEN KILL THEM," Pilate shouted, sounding extremely irritated. He stepped back into his room to wash his face and brush his hair. Some time later, he appeared on the balcony overlooking his courtyard to face his early morning uninvited guests. They became silent when they saw him. His angry eyes scanned their faces as he inhaled slowly. "What are you doing here? The sun is still rising and already you Jews are agitated. NOW, what are you unhappy about?" he asked in an icy tone. "This had better be worth my loss of sleep."

"Caiaphas is in desperate need of meeting with you!" someone shouted.

"Caiaphas? What does that pompous ass want? Why should I meet with him this time of day or listen to his Hebrew ranting? His arrogance irritates me to no end. I have yet to hear something from his vile and despicable mouth that is worthy of my time. WHAT DOES HE WANT?" His words echoed within the courtyard and several doves flew off into the morning air.

"It is a matter of great urgency. He needs to speak with you."

"WHAT DOES HE WANT? Why should I listen to his requests?" asked Pontius in a slow and deliberate way.

"The Temple Police have arrested a Nazarene, who is a blasphemer, and they are about to pronounce a sentence of death on him but they . . ."

"They do NOT have the jurisdiction to sentence anyone to death, especially during the night. Actions like that are illegal, besides only I, the Governor have that power." He shook his fist at them as he spoke. "What makes Caiaphas think he has power to declare such a judgment?"

"But the man they have arrested is a troublemaker and has caused much trouble among our citizens. We are trying to deal with him but need your help."

"Caiaphas is the troublemaker. Who will arrest him? Perhaps someone should pass a sentence of death upon him. It would not take me long to approve of that."

"He has requested that you come to speak with him."

Pontius turned as a servant brought him a glass of wine. He sipped on it and rolled it around the inside of his mouth to refresh it and then spit into a large vase of flowers nearby. After clearing his throat, he continued, "I will NOT be told what to do, NOR will I go to see him. If he wants to speak with me, then HE must meet with me at MY building at Six Corners. Do you understand me?"

"But he's too busy right now and wants to speak with you at the Temple," replied one of the men in the front row.

"Sleep makes me busy too, besides I do NOT obey Caiaphas." His voice sounded very irritated. "By the way, who is this . . . this troublemaker that you have arrested?"

"Jesus the Nazarene," someone called out.

Pilate stopped for a moment as he remembered Claudia's words to him. Then he replied, "Very well, I will be in my building when I am dressed. Now leave or I will have all of my guards show you the way out." He turned and walked back to his room. The uninvited guests knew what he meant so they left the courtyard immediately.

As he was walking back to his room, Pontius shouted, "LANAPOUS! HOW DID THESE PEOPLE ENTER MY COURTYARD? WHERE WERE YOU? ANSWER ME. HOW DID THEY ENTER WITHOUT YOUR KNOWLEDGE?"

"I don't know, Sir!"

"I want answers to those questions. I WILL DEAL with whoever let them in, so tell me how did this happen?"

"Yes Sir!"

Pontius entered his private chamber for some personal matters and then started for the dining room. "BRING ME SOMETHING TO EAT," he shouted. He appeared to be in no rush and when he was finished eating, he stepped outside and walked down the stairs to his waiting chariot. Just before stepping into the chariot, he motioned for Lanapous to come near.

Lanapous stepped closer as Pontius stared at him. "Who let that mob into my courtyard? I WANT TO KNOW." His jaw was tight and his lips lost all color as he spoke

"I'm still trying to find out, Sir!"

"Have an answer for me when I return or you will be flogged. Do you understand me? FLOGGED!"

Lanapous momentarily closed his eyes as the driver snapped the reins of the geldings that pulled the chariot.

When Pontius arrived at his administrative office at Six Corners, he could hear many voices on the other side of the building. He stepped from his chariot and six guards escorted him up the stairs and through the front door of the building. Once inside, he strode confidently across the marble floors and down the hall to his large and opulent office. Two guards opened his office door and once he was inside, a guard removed Pontius' tunic from his shoulders and handed it to a servant, who was standing nearby.

"What is all the noise that I heard so early in the morning? It is still dark outside. Have these Jews started another riot?" asked Pontius. "It must be what they eat or the sun that makes them so irritable. If it were not for Caesar, I would have all of them slain and their blood put onto the doorway of my office. They do that to innocent lambs so why not do it to these . . . these fools? Death is all they understand."

When he stopped ranting, one of the servants said, "There are several hundred people in the courtyard and they are extremely restless. There's no telling what will happen, Sir."

"Send a message to Tribunus Laticlavius Kadurra Senna and tell him that I want, do you hear, I WANT THREE HUNDRED MEN IN MY OFFICE COURTYARD, NOW," shouted Pontius as his assistant helped him with his judicial robes.

"Yes Sir."

A moment later Pontius left his office and walked to his balcony that overlooked a large courtyard at the side of his administrative building. When he stepped into view, the crowd eventually became silent. All eyes were upon Pontius, so he slowed his pace and stopped for a moment to glare at the mob. "How many people are here?" he whispered to the bodyguard next to him.

"Originally there were less than a hundred but at last count, there were more than three hundred. That is my guess, Sir. They keep increasing in number and their milling around makes it hard to count and . . ."

"Order another hundred soldiers to stand by. When these Jews start ranting, who knows what they will do? This time of the year with the Passover Feast, thousands arrive in this city and this may be a major confrontation, so call for more men. When they arrive, tell them that when I raise my hand above my head, they are to draw their swords and wait for my signal. When I drop it suddenly, they shall clear this place, even if all of these, these crazed fools die by the sword! If we must, then let us fill this courtyard with Jewish blood."

"Yes Sir," replied his bodyguard.

Pontius turned to face the crowd and stepped closer to the front of the balcony to lean on the elaborate railing. He turned to one of his aids, "Where is Caiaphas?"

"He's not here yet, Sir."

"When he arrives, call me. Until then, I will be in my office." He left the balcony and walked down the hall to his office.

Irritated by the delay and wait for Caiaphas, Pilate ranted loudly, "WHERE IS THAT POMPOUS ASS? He calls for me because it is important and now it is I that must wait." He picked up a glass goblet, emptied it and then hurled it across the room. "If he is not here soon, I will return to my . . ."

A guard entered the room, "Sir, it will take more time for the additional legionnaires to get here, so do . . ?"

"When they arrive let me know. Surely they can assemble three or four hundred men at a short notice." His anger was evident. He sat at his desk and gritted his teeth and his jaw muscles twitched as he stared at the window.

Moments later his bodyguard returned. "Sir, Caiaphas has just arrived."

"He shall wait until I am ready to see that pompous ass. Besides, I want to have the legionnaires in position before I begin," was Pontius' angry reply.

Pilate turned his head when he heard Caiaphas shouting, "I AM HERE PONTIUS. I AM HERE. COME OUT SO THAT I CAN SPEAK WITH YOU."

An aide stepped into the room, "Sir, three hundred cavalrymen have arrived and have surrounded the mob."

When Pilate was told that they were in position, he motioned for his servant to open the large drapes that separated his offices from the courtyard, and then he called loudly, "CAIAPHAS, THIS HAD BETTER BE IMPORTANT."

Caiaphas made his way through the crowd and approached the steps to the terraced balcony, which was double the height of a man above the courtyard floor.

The crowd became silent as Caiaphas stepped to the bottom of the stairs. "May I come up to where you are?" Caiaphas asked.

Pontius said nothing but narrowed his eyes. "Keep your eyes on this asp and if he shows any sign of threat to me, kill him," whispered Pontius to another bodyguard, who slowly drew his sword. "Be sure to cut off his head and open his abdomen so that his entrails can be seen. I loathe this man."

Once on the balcony, Caiaphas turned to the people and raised his hands as he slowly moved toward Pilate. From the back of the crowd a dozen Temple Police pushed Jesus through the crowd toward the stairway. It took them some time to make their way through the mob, and Pontius could see that Jesus had difficulty walking.

As Jesus stumbled up the stairs of the balcony, Pontius looked down at him and could see that both of Jesus' eyes were blackened, his cheeks marked with bright red blood and most of his beard had been ripped from his face. Blood dripped from his nose and from his chin, and he appeared in great discomfort and crippling pain.

Caiaphas turned to Pontius. "We found this man," he said as he pointed to Jesus with an open hand, "perverting the nation and being negligent in paying tribute to Caesar, plus, he said he was a king. We all know that Rome has no king, only Caesar. We need no king since Caesar is the leader."

Pilate folded his arms across his chest, "When you speak, I become more resentful of you because I know that your words are hollow, deceitful and confrontational. There is no truth in them. THE SUN HAS NOT YET RISEN AND YOU CALL ME OUT TO THIS . . . THIS RIOT AND INSURRECTION. YOU JEWS ARE IRRITABLE, ARROGANT, INSUBORDINATE, SPITEFUL RUDE AND . . ."

Caiaphas interrupted Pilate. "We have reason to bring this blasphemer to you. His very actions are a threat to Caesar and to Rome. I would think that you, especially you, the Governor, would be concerned about that, or are you becoming less concerned about issues that threaten Rome?"

Pontius took a long breath and looked at Jesus. "Bring him here so that I may speak with him." They began to push Jesus to the top of the stairs and as they did, Pontius motioned for a chair to sit on.

As Jesus stumbled across the balcony, he looked at Pontius and then back to Caiaphas.

Pontius tightened his lips and narrowed his brows when Jesus was standing in front of him, he asked, "Caiaphas, who has beaten this man?"

"He resisted arrest and we were forced to subdue him."

"How many did it take to subdue him?"

"We needed many Temple Police to ensure that he did not escape."

"A man of God such as you . . . involved in bearing false witness against his neighbor? Is that not a violation of your Mosaic Law and one of the commandments that you so carefully claim to be a core to your religious code? That must be one of the Ten Commandments that you have overlooked or is it a habit of yours to ignore the ones you don't like?" taunted Pontius. Casting his eyes back at Jesus, Pontius continued, "Caiaphas, I find it hard to believe that this man resisted arrest. Did you gain any pleasure in seeing this man beaten?" A moment later, Pontius continued. "Resisted arrest, huh . . . I don't believe you."

Caiaphas' face reddened with anger but he held his peace.

"Caiaphas, did you order the arrest of this man and were you there when they arrested him and were you the one that passed judgment on him? If you were, then you have violated the law because a judge cannot order the arrest AND attend the arrest AND then pass judgment on a trial that was held by night, let alone during one of your feasts. Your procedures violate your own laws and Roman laws. Your actions have created an illegal trial."

Caiaphas cast a glance to Ehud and those that questioned the process and procedures of the trial.

"What else has this man said that has angered you?" asked Pontius.

"He claims to be the king of the Jews, but we have no king but Caesar."

"How long did it take you to create that phrase?" mocked Pilate.

"We know that Caesar and Herod do not want another king to be in this region, so we bring this critical issue to you, or are you not interested?"

Pontius turned to Jesus. "Are you the King of the Jews?"

Caiaphas nodded and smiled at Pontius.

"What have you done?" Pontius continued, but Jesus did not reply.

"You heard him," said Caiaphas.

Pontius tightened his jaw muscles and after a moment of silence, turned to Caiaphas. "What are you charging this man with?"

"He is a threat to Rome with . . . with all his talk about a kingdom and we have heard him speak of buildings being destroyed. He said that the Temple will be destroyed and not one stone will be left upon another. That sounds like a violent rebellion, does it not?"

"Since when is distorting the truth a difficulty? Perhaps he learned how to distort truth listening to you and your brood of vipers," mocked Pontius.

"He is turning citizens away from us. Claiming to be God is an offence according to our Mosaic Law, for he said, 'Your sins are forgiven.' Only God can forgive sins."

"Your religious law is different than Roman law. I care not of your religions laws. Am I a Jew? If this is a Temple issue and something between you Jews, then you deal with it, and may I remind you that if you put him to death, you will have to deal with me. I AM THE GOVERNOR, NOT YOU." Pontius' pointer finger was only a shadow away from tapping Caiaphas on the chest. "This sounds to me like a conspiracy of some kind. How can you hold a trial without my knowledge and how can you pronounce a man guilty and how can you sentence him to death during an illegal trial that convened during the night? Did he have three opportunities to present a defense or rebuttal against the charges that you fabricated?"

"He must be stopped . . ."

"Caiaphas, you have not presented any indications, facts or proof that he is a threat to Rome. All you have done is speak of issues that irritate you. I find no fault in him. He has not broken any Roman law, especially none that requires death, let alone a beating. But since you have already completed the beating, I will overlook your assault on him. Remember that you cannot sentence a man to death for some, some Temple or Jewish religious law. Rome has no obligation to punish anyone because of a violation of your Jewish laws."

Caiaphas leaned over and said, "Others have been sentenced to death for less and that was by your hand, so why are you declaring him innocent, when we all know that you care less?" His eyes glared at the Governor.

Pilate raised his hand in anger and all of the legionnaires drew their swords. The sound of blades brushing the metal cuffs of the scabbards emitted an eerie sound, causing the mob to turn and fearfully look at the legionnaires.

Caiaphas moved closer to the railing of the balcony as several people shouted, "AWAY WITH HIM. AWAY WITH HIM. AWAY WITH HIM."

"He is teaching throughout all Jewry from Galilee to Jerusalem that he is the Christ and Anointed One from God," continued Caiaphas. "We all know that he is NOT the Anointed One from God. He is NO Messiah but a blasphemer that needs to be executed."

Pontius slowly lowered his raised arm. "Where is he from?"

"Nazareth."

Pontius continued to lower his hand. "So he's from Galilee, is he?"

The guards remained poised for an attack to clear the courtyard.

"Well, if he is from Galilee, then he is from Herod's jurisdiction, so take him out of here and go see Herod. He happens to be in Jerusalem at this time. Go and see him and LEAVE ME OUT OF THIS PLAN TO HAVE SOMEONE EXECUTED. ALL OF THIS IS OF NO CONCERN TO ME. NOW LEAVE OR I WILL HAVE THE LEGIONNAIRES WASH THIS COURTYARD WITH YOUR BLOOD."

"But we . . ." said Caiaphas.

"I have spoken, Caiaphas," snarled Pontius as he turned to leave. "By the way, you have only moments to be out of my courtyard or I will have my soldiers show you the way out."

Caiaphas tightened his lips and glared at Pontius, who once again raised his hand. Three hundred mounted legionnaires waited for Pontius' signal. The crowd reluctantly dispersed.

Caiaphas and his followers went to Herod's summer palace, and with the use of bribery planned to present their case to Herod through an advisor, named Bilhan. It was well known that Bilhan was interested only in three things: money, power and prestige, so with a sizable bribe, Bilhan promised to arrange for King Herod to consider Caiaphas' concerns.

Bilhan entered Herod's chambers and convinced a young servant girl to wake Herod for it was still early. "Tell him that an urgent matter awaits his decision," he said. "High priests from the Temple are here to seek his advice."

When Herod appeared in a state room, Bilhan stood to his feet. "Great King," he said. "I have a request from the High Priest of Jerusalem to meet with you on an urgent matter. Caiaphas knows that the hour is early but it is a matter of great urgency. If you would meet with him it will bring additional recognition and status to you."

Herod grunted as he reached for a handful of fruit from a nearby tray and then drank an entire goblet of wine before placing the container on the table next to him. As he wiped his mouth with a silk napkin, he belched loudly and then shook his head from side to side.

"Caiaphas wants you to meet Jesus of Nazareth. He's the one that does miracles among the people from Galilee to Jerusalem. Apparently, this Jesus has violated some rather important decorum and Jewish laws. As a result, Caiaphas admits that he needs your advice as what to do. It is an urgent matter."

Herod's mood changed when he heard that Caiaphas wanted him to meet Jesus for he had heard many things about him. As Herod continued to eat, he asked, "Is this the Galilean, who performs all of these miracles I have heard about?"

Bilhan nodded, "Yes, your majesty.

"Is this the man that, that John the . . ." He paused as though he was uncomfortable saying Baptizer, because it was he who had John beheaded.

"Yes, your majesty."

Herod remained silent for a long time before responding, "Fine, summon Caiaphas and I will listen to him."

When Caiaphas arrived, Herod was comfortably seated on his large leather chair that was decorated in pure gold. When he nodded, Bilhan motioned to Caiaphas to enter the room. Caiaphas bowed before Herod as Bilhan had recommended, and waited until he was granted permission to speak.

King Herod placed his wine goblet on the table next to him and raised his hand. "It is extremely early in the day for me to listen to you. I have heard that it is an important matter, so please do not disappoint me. I plan to return to my bed with three of my partners, so do tell me what it is that is so important. You may begin."

"Your Highness," Caiaphas began.

Herod smiled at Bilhan and looked back at Caiaphas.

"I appreciate your gracious acceptance of my request to commune with you at this early hour about a difficulty that we have been facing with a Galilean."

Herod looked at Bilhan again and smiled.

Caiaphas continued. "This man that we wish to present to you has challenged all of our valuable religious tradition, blasphemes openly in public and in the Temple, does not pay taxes to Caesar and stirs up the people to be disrespectful to all in leadership including you. He's . . ."

He was interrupted when Herod raised his hand. "Your words are many and your plans are transparent. If you have aught with a man from my jurisdiction then bring him in and present your case. I have much to do this day and I do not want my time wasted with hollow words and placating gestures."

Disappointed by the disruption, Caiaphas turned and motioned for several people to bring Jesus into the judicial room.

Herod narrowed his eyes and leaned forward as Jesus was ushered into the room by the Temple Police. A servant placed another tray of fruit next to Herod and then poured more wine.

When Jesus arrived in their midst, Caiaphas began to speak again. "Please allow me to introduce to you to this Galilean, who we have determined to be the troublemaker and guilty of violating our religious laws, all of which are punishable by death. He has stirred up the people and claims to be God, which calls for execution according to our Mosaic Law."

"What else irritates you about him?" asked Herod as he reached for the goblet of wine. "You've said all of this before. You're wasting my time."

"He claims to be the king of the Jews. He is NOT our king. We have no king and we are not willing to have anyone be a king, except for you, your highness."

"Your tongue is incapable of using truthful words, so chose them more carefully," responded Herod. "You refer to a king. What kind of king? If he plans to oust me, I am not upset or want to put him to death. He appears to be vanquished by someone who has beaten him beyond immediate threat."

"But he has violated our laws and stirs up the people."

Conspiracy With Malicious Intent

Herod raised his hand again. "Silence Caiaphas, I can see better when you are not talking." Then Herod stood to his feet and walked over to face Jesus. "Why is he blindfolded and why is he bound? There are thirty men in this room and a dozen soldiers with swords. What will he do that is so dangerous? Release him so that I may speak with him."

Moments later, Jesus blinked his eyes and massaged his wrists where the ropes had been.

Herod stepped closer. "Who has beaten this man?"

"He resisted arrest and so the Temple Police were forced to deal with him to subdue him," responded Caiaphas.

"He must have been very resistant, for his eyes are swollen, his lips are bleeding and parts of his beard are missing. Are there protocols written for the Temple Police to maim anyone resisting arrest or are all people maimed even if they do not resist arrest?"

"It was necessary for us to be sure that he would not escape," replied Caiaphas.

"Fine," Herod said as he turned to Jesus. "So, you're the one I have heard about. My servants have told me that you heal people of all kinds of diseases and injuries."

Jesus nodded as he wiped the blood from his mouth.

"They also tell me that you fed several thousand people on what, two or three occasions? Impressive, very impressive."

Jesus nodded, said nothing, but wiped blood from his mouth and nose again.

"I've heard that you have cast out devils and actually raised several people from the dead. Is that true?" Herod continued as he walked around Jesus to view him from behind.

Jesus nodded in silence.

"I can see by your face that you seem to have run into some difficulty or did you actually receive these marks when resisting arrest?"

Still Jesus did not respond to Herod's questions.

Herod motioned to his servant to bring him the goblet of wine. "I've heard that you were born in Bethlehem and were a carpenter in Nazareth. How can someone like you do all of those miracles?"

Jesus did not respond.

"Did you happen to know a man named John, John the Baptiser?" Herod turned his head slightly to one side and listened for a response.

Jesus raised his gaze from the granite floor to look into Herod's eyes.

Conspiracy With Malicious Intent

"What happened to John was . . . was quite unfortunate. I want you to know that I always wanted to see a miracle, something that is unusual. Can you do a miracle for me?"

Jesus held his peace.

"Anything will do, so do something or does there have to be a special need?" He turned to look at Caiaphas, who shrugged his shoulders.

A few moments passed and Herod walked back to his throne and sat down. He reached for some grapes and after putting several in his mouth he said, "I'm disappointed. I thought that you would do something to impress me." He chewed and swallowed. "I am getting old," he said as he looked around the room, "and would like to be made young again. You know, more virile and more hair and smoother skin. Can you make me young again?"

There was no reply.

"Bilhan, maybe we should bring in some blind beggars or several mutes into this room so he will have something to work with. What do you think?"

Bilhan shrugged his shoulders as Jesus wiped the blood drops off his nose and chin again.

"I can see why you would consider yourself a god if you can do all of these things, but Caiaphas, ah Caiaphas seems to be insulted by your actions and wants to have you put to death for doing all of these . . . I guess they're called miracles?" His tone taunted Jesus.

Jesus kept looking directly into Herod's eyes.

"Do you understand that Caiaphas has been deeply insulted and wants you dead?" He paused to drink more wine and handed the goblet back to his servant. "Yes, I said dead," he continued as he nodded his head up and down. "Do you think that it is jealousy that has made Caiaphas so angry?"

Caiaphas' face reddened as he tightened his jaw.

"Caiaphas, you have chosen to execute a man that has been helpful to the general population and disrespectful to you, and that is NOT a crime worthy of death. He has not responded to my questions, in fact he has not been confrontational, so I am not ready to sentence him to death."

"But he's a blasphemer and disrupts all activity around our Temple and challenges all of our laws and traditions. He perverts people and now citizens are against us."

"Caiaphas, he has done nothing worthy of death. So you have been insulted but that's not crime. I'm sure that there are many within the walls of Jerusalem, who would gladly insult you if they were sure that there would be no repercussions. You may not be as well liked as you think you are. In fact, I have heard our Governor refer to you as pompous ass and I do not see him standing here with charges that you feel would defend your, your dignity, if there is any."

Caiaphas looked at Bilhan and Bilhan closed his eyes and subtly moved his head from side to side.

"Before I send him back to Pontius," concluded Herod, "let me send him off as the royalty he alleges to be part of. I find no fault or disrespect in him, despite what you say."

Caiaphas' face reddened with anger but he held his peace.

Herod called to a servant. "Bring us one of my royal robes; the red indigo seamless one with the gold threads and tassels. Put it onto this Nazarene's shoulders so we can send him back to Pontius looking like the king he claims to be."

When they put the robe on Jesus, Herod laughed as he looked at Caiaphas. "He actually looks like a king, don't you think?"

Caiaphas was so angry that his neck veins bulged but he said nothing. Just as they were about to leave, the Temple Police bound Jesus' hands again and then led him away.

Herod laughed as they walked out of the room. "Oh and by the way, do NOT take that robe off of him. I want Pontius to see it. And oh, if I hear that you removed that robe before he arrives at Pontius' chambers, I will personally have my body guards find you and you will not be happy with what I will ask them to do to you."

Once they were gone, Herod muttered to himself, "Caiaphas what an incompetent religious leader he is. Just because he has been insulted, he wants to have someone put to death." Then turning to Bilhan he said, "Oh, by the way, Bilhan, don't you think that sending Jesus to Pilate with one of my special robes was a nice gesture?"

"I'm sure he'll be impressed to see it your Highness."

Chapter XXXVI

ANGER, ACCUSATION, DISTRUST

When Ehud closed the door to a small room in the Temple, it was clear to him and his colleagues that they were very concerned about what had occurred under Caiaphas' leadership. After sitting down at the head of the table, Ehud called the meeting to order.

"It is evident to me that an evil has taken place. Caiaphas' anger has blinded him to misguide the Sanhedrin into conducting an illegal trial. All of us have agreed that what has happened leaves the Sanhedrin open to reprisals from the Governor, particularly because only he has jurisdiction to sentence someone to death. I do not say that the Nazarene is not guilty of violating the Mosaic Law and I am not saying that he should not be punished but what I am concerned about is that this has been an illegal trial with many violations."

Ahadu raised his hand, "I have considered the inconsistencies too but what do we do about it for Caiaphas and Hiddo will not recant their decision and will not admit that the trial was wrong, according to the law?"

Mannsaher began to speak. "Ehud, you warned all of them that forging ahead was not acceptable and there was no reason to abandon a legal process to bring about a legitimate verdict."

Ben Hadda raised his hand. "I am willing to document the violations to show that the Sanhedrin has made in grave error. Let us make a list of the violations.

Quite some time later, Ben Hadda folded his hands together, under his chin before speaking. "Now that we have made a list of violations of the law, I am fearful that all of us are as guilty as the condemned Nazarene."

"What should we do now, Ehud?" asked El Hatzar, the oldest man in the room.

"I know that all of us placed our fist into the circle, indicating that we, yes we were in agreement with the arrest but . . ."

"What bothers me, is that when this betrayer was paid . . . that was blood money paid for a man assumed to be guilty."

"If only he had not violated the Sabbath."

"And his blasphemy, remember that he claimed to be God."

"Is he really our king?" asked Mannsaher. "I am beginning to think that we are in agreement that he . . . he is the Messiah but . . . I am very uncomfortable with putting this Messiah to death."

"Claiming to being a king is not worthy of death," responded Ehud.

"If he is the Messiah then what he said is not blasphemy."

Their discussion continued for several hours and eventually Sandtza, the scribe, handed a parchment to Ehud to read. On it was a list of procedures that indicated an illegal trial.

Ehud read the parchment out loud and asked, "Are there any other items that should be added to our discussion?"

After an extended period of silence, Ehud began to read the list of items again and then signed the parchment and handed around the table for the signatures of those in the room.

TRIAL VIOLATIONS

We, the undersigned, provide notice that procedural irregularities exist, bringing into question the validity and legitimacy of the trial of the Nazarene. We do not suggest that the Nazarene is innocent of the charges or has not violated Mosaic Law, but this court has not ensured quality standards because the presiding judge has not remained distant from the accused or his accusers, creating a serious breach and violation in procedure, formulating an illegal trial. These noted violations and irregularities have invalidated the effectiveness of the court and may have tarnished the reputation of the Sanhedrin, who have always attempted to provide honourable deliberations and ensure ethical results:

A trial must NOT be held by night
A trial must NOT be convened during a Feast or on a Feast day
The High Priest must NOT conspire or contribute to the arrest
The accused must NOT be bound before he was condemned
No witnesses were ever called for the defense
Witnesses were sought during the trial to testify against the accused
An accused cannot be convicted on his own evidence
The High Priest did NOT allow for questioning from other lawyers
The use of violence during a trial is illegal
The High Priest did NOT insure the safety of the accused at all times
The High Priest has NO jurisdiction to pronounce a legal and binding death sentence
A civil court had NO jurisdiction to pronounce a death sentence
A sentence of death was declared in the High Priest's house.
An acquittal can be proclaimed at any time but a guilty verdict MUST be announced the following day and in the Temple in the Hall of the Hewn Stone.
Caiaphas rent his priestly clothing in public: a violation of his role and position
Caiaphas is NOT allowed to place anyone under oath once he has rent his Priestly garments

These blatant violations and irregularities have made this an illegal trial which MUST therefore be declared a mistrial.

We, the undersigned, request a meeting to discuss these issues following the Passover.

Agreeing as signed:
Ehud Bar Jabal
Ahadu Mortica
Mannsaher Ben Hadaea
Isaac Ben Hadda
Hashem Bar Yoseph
Tzandtza Ben Lalamada - Scribe

Nicodemus Ben Arod
Joseph Elishama
Isaac Tsad Ahala
Yoseph El Hatzar
Telebha Atazda

The parchment was delivered by the scribe to the Caiaphas' office.

****

One of Pontius' aides knocked several times before entering his office. Waiting until Pontius looked up from the parchment he was reading, Manduri remained silent.

"What is it, Manduri?" asked Pontius without looking up from his desk where he was dipping a quill in an inkwell.

"I've been just notified that Caiaphas has taken Jesus the Nazarene to King Herod, as you suggested. Apparently, King Herod spent some time trying to sort through the allegations and accusations against him, and in frustration, King Herod has referred this case back to you."

"DAMN HIM!" he shouted as he looked up at Manduri. "He gives the impression that he is so thorough but now he has a chance to do something with a Galilean from his jurisdiction and fails to follow through. He's passing this on to me as a joke of my leadership." Pontius slammed his fist onto the desk so hard that the quill fell from the inkwell.

"If I may Sir, King Herod is sending Jesus back to you, wearing one of his royal seamless robes, and insists that you are the one to deal with this case."

Pontius slammed his fist on the desk again as he stood to his feet. "Manduri, it is still early in the morning and I should not be here, but I've been disrupted from my sleep, called to come and listen to Caiaphas' ranting, and now Herod is, is adding to the chaos of my day. I should be at home at this time of the day. I can't wait to get back to Caesarea. I detest this city and I detest these people and I detest Caiaphas even more. Were it within my wish, I'd, I'D LEVEL THIS CITY AND ERASE ALL MEMORY OF THIS INFERNAL PLACE." The veins in his neck bulged and saliva drops sprayed from his mouth as he shouted.

"I'm sorry Sir. What do you wish for me to do?"

"Herod is trying to make a fool of me by making me deal with these Hebrew laws that mean nothing to me or Rome. CAN THERE BE ANY OTHER REASON?" He began to pace across the room as he spoke.

"I don't know Sir, but maybe it's because Jesus said that he was a king," responded Manduri in an apologetic tone.

"Manduri you may be correct but I suspect that King Herod is too lazy to do anything so he goads me with this, this irritation. I have other things to do. It is still early in the day and I fear what is yet to come." He walked

Conspiracy With Malicious Intent

to the window and took a breath and exhaled slowly as he looked at the eastern sky. "The only comfort I take, in all of this, is that Herod had to get out of his bed to speak with Caiaphas . . . yet I still wonder why Herod does nothing to deal with this vexatious issue. The case is simple. A man from Nazareth vexes these insolent religious leaders with things like claiming to be their king or some kind of a god and they respond with violence. It is I that would like to react to their violence with violence of my own."

"If I may, Sir, did you not send him to King Herod because he is from Nazareth in the province of Galilee?"

"YES and Herod, the fox, is supposed to rule Galilee and all of the citizens from that region. Besides, I do not want to deliberate on one of his citizens, so why doesn't he deal with it?"

"Sir, if I may, maybe he is unnerved by his hasty act of beheading John the Baptizer. Remember that John the Baptizer said a Messiah was coming and when Herod had him killed, maybe, just maybe he's now afraid to put someone to death, especially if this Jesus is the Jewish Messiah."

"You may be right. Herod had John the Baptizer beheaded and is fearful of dealing with another Jew."

"Sir," interjected Manduri, "and it has been rumored that this Nazarene and John the Baptizer are related to each other. Some kind of cousin, I have heard."

"Manduri, there are times I suspect that you are a Jew."

"Well Sir, I suspect that Herod is fearful of making another error in judgment."

"Manduri, you are clever and yes I agree with you that Herod is afraid. That's it Manduri. You've done well."

"Remember Sir, Herod, in one of his orgies saw his stepdaughter dancing and was aroused with passion for her and promised her anything even up to the half of his kingdom, and she asked for the head of John the Baptizer."

"Yes. I was glad that I didn't attend or participate in that debauchery; a man's head for a dance from a young girl. What kind of fool would fall for that or make such a promise? Only a leacherous depraved man with fading sexual drives would stoop to such insanity."

"Apparently, Herod's wife detested John and told her daughter to ask for that human prize."

Pontius closed his eyes and shook his head before running his fingers through his hair. "Herod: what a fool. He has no morals. Think of it Manduri, passion for his step-daughter."

"What do you wish me to do, Sir?"

"Bring me something to eat and also call for my chariot and eight of my best bodyguards to accompany me to King Herod's palace."

Manduri immediately sent for Pontius' chariot and when it arrived, he returned to Pontius' office. "Sir, your chariot is now here. Do you wish to eat before you go, Sir?"

Grabbing several things to eat, Pontius walked down the hall toward the front door. Calling back over his shoulder, "Manduri, you have done well."

"Thank you," whispered Manduri as Pontius left the building.

When Pontius arrived at Herod's summer palace, he had his speech prepared. He was angry that Herod would play this political game with him. He was convinced that Herod had intentionally avoided this case for personal reasons.

The guards opened the gates of the outer courtyard of King Herod's summer palace when they recognized Pontius' chariot. The two black geldings that pulled his chariot, nervously danced across the cobblestone courtyard to the front of the marble stairs of Herod's palace. Eight bodyguards dismounted and positioned themselves next to the chariot as Pontius stepped down and adjusted his robe. Attallo and Demino, two of Pontius' best trained bodyguards, known for their dexterity with the sword, stepped to his side while the remaining men stood next to the chariot.

Pontius did not wait for an invitation to use the marble stairs but walked up to the large wooden doors and stared at the four guards. There was a moment of silence before one of Herod's guards stepped inside but not before Pontius growled, "Open this door. I'm here to see King Herod and I want to see him NOW." His lips were tight and his voice was strong and confrontational.

When the door was opened, Pontius and his two bodyguards, Attallo and Demino, stepped into the inner courtyard and confidently crossed the marble floor to where long branched palms and lush vines hung between two giant white granite columns. Pontius had been to this palace several times before, so he walked directly to the brass door and stared at the guards, who recognized him and reluctantly opened it. Pontius walked through the doorway with an air of confrontational arrogance. Attallo and Demino, with their hands on their swords, followed close behind.

Pontius walked directly to the marble stairway but two guards, at the top of the stairs, drew their swords, signifying that Pontius had come far

Conspiracy With Malicious Intent

enough. Attallo and Demino immediately drew their swords and it appeared as if there might be an unsavory confrontation.

Risking a major altercation was not a concern to Pontius for he was angry and it showed on his face. His jaw was clenched and his eyes narrowed as he said, "I am Pontius Pilate the Governor and Praefectus and I am here to speak with King Herod and I intend to see him . . . NOW."

The two guards at the top of the stairs did not move and neither did Attallo or Demino. After a few tense moments, Bilhan appeared on a balcony overlooking the stairway and called, "Why, if it isn't Pontius Pilate or should I say Governor Pontius Pilate? You're early. The invitations for the party have clearly stated that the party is next week." His tone was taunting and had an air of insult.

"I am NOT here for a party. I demand to speak to King Herod. I know he's here so find him. I need no appointment and I will NOT leave until I have spoken to him."

"I will see if he is willing to see you."

"He is available. He spoke to a Nazarene and Caiaphas not long ago, so I know he is available."

After a few tense moments, Herod stepped from behind a heavy curtain on the third floor of the inner courtyard. "Well, well if it isn't Pontius Pilate." His voice echoed in the cavernous open foyer. "I hear that you may be too busy to attend my party next week, but think nothing of arriving when it suits you."

"You know full well why I'm here," challenged Pontius as he looked up at Herod.

"It's early in the day and I . . ."

Pontius interrupted. "You have already been up this morning and speaking with Caiaphas and his prisoner, so do not pretend that you were sound asleep. If you had time for Caiaphas then you have time for me."

"Well, if you insist, come up. My men will not harm your bodyguards," he said as he disappeared behind the velvet drape.

Pontius and his bodyguards walked up the stairs, past the two guards, who stepped back but did not put their swords away. Bilhan smiled and turned to usher Pontius along the marble walkway that curved around the courtyard. When they arrived at the second spiral stairway, Bilhan met Pontius. "Is it possible to have your bodyguards put their swords away?"

Pontius said nothing but continued to walk up the stairs. Bilhan opened the door and Pontius stepped into a lavish room with a small pool, several comfortable chairs and ornate wooden tables containing trays of fruit

Conspiracy With Malicious Intent

and drink. Colorful velvet drapes were on every wall. Long golden tassels hung from each drape and every embroidered chair was made of silver and brass. The padded seats and backs were made of hand woven tapestry. On the tables were colorful lace tablecloths, burgundy napkins and tall multi-colored wine glasses. The marble floor shone as if it had just been polished.

"Come in Pontius," Herod said as he raised his goblet. "Your men seem to be somewhat uneasy about this visit, but do come in." Herod raised his glass of wine to Pontius' bodyguards.

"They know their duties and the most important one is to keep me from insolent guards like those at the top of your stairs."

"Pontius, Pontius. Come now. If I entered into your residence uninvited, your men would also draw swords to protect you, wouldn't they?" he queried in a mocking tone.

"Herod, you know why I'm here. It's about the Nazarene from your Galilean province, and you . . ."

"Now, now Pontius," he said in a slow and taunting tone. "Have a seat. I think better with a glass of wine in my hand. It relaxes me. I can see that you need to have a moment to recover from your anger. Anger leads to regret, so have a seat, take a breath and sip some wine."

His tone irritated Pontius who responded, "It's too early for wine. I'm here to speak to you about one of your Galilean citizens; the one Caiaphas brought to you."

Herod snapped his fingers and a scantily dressed servant girl poured red wine into two tall glass goblets. Then she carefully approached Pontius and placed one of the wine goblets on the table next to Pilate and then walked over and placed the other glass next to King Herod.

"Pontius, please have your men wait outside. You can trust me. I have no intention of dealing evil to you, after all this meeting was your idea, remember?"

Three young very beautiful dark eyed women stepped from the pool and slowly covered their nakedness before moving behind a curtain. Herod adjusted his robe and pointed at them as they disappeared. "There are many benefits to royalty. You should have a pool at your home, Pontius. Those maidens have a way of keeping me young."

Pontius momentarily closed his eyes.

"Young flesh is so wonderful, Pontius. Oh, I forgot, you have but one wife. A lovely lady indeed but I . . . I enjoy variety."

Pontius stared at Herod as he spoke. Rings were on every finger and the large golden bracelet on his wrist reflected a glint of light. "Please have a seat and a sip of wine. It will calm the beast in you," Herod said as he smiled and moved his hand to point to a chair next to Pontius.

Pontius looked at his bodyguards, who placed their swords back into their scabbards and moved to a position behind him. Attallo stood to Pontius' left and Demino to his right.

Herod looked up at them and then to his six bodyguards and cleared his throat. "Pontius, we have had our differences in the past but they are of no significance in this issue. Both of us have our duties, our jurisdiction and our pride, so why are we suspicious of each other?"

"I am here to discuss the man that Caiaphas brought to you this morning. He's from the province of Galilee and is your responsibility, not mine. I deal with people in the province of Judaea and not Galilee," insisted Pontius in a confrontational tone.

"Caiaphas. Ha. He's a fool. I recall you calling him a pompous ass. Am I correct?"

Pontius remained silent as his jaw muscles continued to twitch.

"Well I've never trusted Caiaphas and have no intention of trying to like him. Now Pontius, have some wine so we can discuss the purpose of your, your impromptu visit. I have no hidden motive. I'm visiting Jerusalem and work is not what I wish to do, especially this time of the day."

Pontius held the goblet in his hand and stared at Herod. His jaw muscles twitched slightly and his face reddened.

Herod held up his wine goblet to toast Pontius and said, "Go ahead and drink from it. My Wine Taster has had some and so have I. Go ahead," he insisted as he emptied his goblet and placed it on the lace tablecloth.

"Why are you sending that Galilean back to me? He is from your province and is your responsibility, not mine."

"Pontius, my visit into Jerusalem is just that; a visit. It's an opportunity for me to visit neighboring regions. In fact, I may go to Egypt to visit Pharaoh in a week or two. When was the last time you were in Egypt? By the way, your wife is from Egypt, isn't she?"

"NO, SHE IS NOT," responded Pontius in obvious anger. His voice echoed in the cavernous atrium and vestibule.

"Pontius, you're easily angered. Sip the wine for it will calm your troubled spirit."

Conspiracy With Malicious Intent

Pontius lifted the goblet to his lips and took a small sip. He could feel his anger abate and was frustrated to think that Herod could so easily defuse this situation.

"Now listen, Herod," Pontius responded, as he lowered his glass and raised his pointer finger.

"Now, now Pontius please don't raise your voice for the servants will think little of you. And as for your pointer finger, it's of little value to you or me." He grinned and adjusted his robe.

"Why have you sent this Galilean back to me? I think you knew it would irritate me."

"I have sent this Jesus back to you because I found no fault in him. If I sentenced him to death, then he would have been brought back into my region to carry out the sentence, and that would be too much work for my court and I would have to return to Galilee prematurely. Besides, I respect your judgment, so I will let you decide what to do with one of my citizens."

"Now listen, Herod . . ."

"Death is far too severe for someone who seems to have broken some obscure Hebrew law. You know how radical that jealous Caiaphas is. It's he that should be on trial."

Pontius felt his cheeks redden.

"If you're truly that angry at me then I will have this Nazarene transferred to my district, but if he comes to me I may not even put him in prison, for he has not broken any law that requires death." Herod snapped his fingers for his goblet to be filled. "What do you think, Pontius?" He watched as a servant girl poured more wine into his goblet.

"I declared him an innocent man," said Pontius as he adjusted his weight in his chair.

"More wine, Pontius?" Herod purred as he stood to his feet.

Staring at the lace tablecloth in front of him, Pontius cleared his throat and watched as the servant girl poured more wine for him.

"How can I put this man to death since he has done so much good for our citizens? He does not deserve death. That is a Caiaphas idea," said Pontius.

There was pause and Herod winked at Pontius. "Pontius, you handle this. You can handle it, can't you?" he said in a taunting manner as he raised his goblet.

"What do you mean by that," asked Pontius in a confrontational tone.

"Well, I heard about the Kaffnal trial that you mishandled some time ago. I heard that your soldiers raided the wrong house and killed eight innocent people and then a week later you had another man executed because he looked like a rebel named Kaffnal. That doesn't make you look very competent but in this case, I will still trust you."

Pontius stood to his feet as Herod continued, "I heard that even Caesar sent you a letter regarding that event. By the way, has Caesar responded to any more of your irrational acts?"

Pontius watched as Herod walked over to the pool and lowered his foot into the water. "Pontius, I'm willing to let you handle this case. You may not believe it but I will trust whatever your decision is."

Pontius pushed his goblet to the centre of the table. "Well, what about the trial of John the Baptizer? I heard you offered half of your kingdom to your stepdaughter but she chose instead to have John's head on a platter. By the way, how is your stepdaughter? Is she happy that you kept your word? What did she do with such the prize, especially since John was also an innocent man?" asked Pontius with a sardonic grin.

"Pontius," snarled Herod as he pointed his finger at Pontius, "you've gone too far. You come into my palace and then insult me and expect me to consider you an ally. I'm willing to overlook your indiscretion of forcing your way in here, uninvited and . . ."

Pontius interrupted, "You told me to relax and now you're the one upset or did I stumble upon the reason why you really do not want to sentence another innocent man to death?"

Herod's eyes narrowed in anger and his lips tightened. "Pontius, you will handle this case with Caiaphas. I detest Caiaphas and want nothing to do with his petty quarrels. He is a despicable fool that cannot be trusted. If the truth be known, I despise that man and would sooner sentence him to death but he does not live in my jurisdiction."

"Very well, I will deal with it but you will owe me a favor which I will collect in the future," said Pontius as he reached for the goblet that he had pushed into the centre of the table. "Remember that I plan to collect and collect I will." He emptied the goblet and placed it back onto the table.

"I thought you would see things my way," smiled Herod. "By the way, will you and your wife be coming to my party next week? We have more in common than you may think." He smiled as Pontius turned to leave the room.

Moments later, Pontius' chariot was on its way back to his office. As it traveled through the streets, Pontius shouted at the driver, "STOP AT MY HOUSE."

"Yes, Sir!" responded the driver as he veered down a narrow side street. When the chariot stopped at Pontius' house, he stepped down from the chariot as he growled to the driver, "Stay here. This will not take long."

"Yes Sir!" said the driver as he looked at the eight mounted bodyguards, who nodded and one shrugged his shoulders.

When Pontius entered his home he was visibly angry. His cheek muscles tightened as he moved up the stairs and through an open door. Once inside, he ignored the salute from two guards as he walked confidently down the hall.

"WHERE IS LANAPOUS?" he shouted, his dark eyes glaring with rage. As he approached the guard's room, the door suddenly opened and Lanapous stepped into the hallway.

"I demand that you tell me who was responsible for allowing that mob into my courtyard this morning. WHO WAS RESPONSIBILE?" Pontius shouted. His pointer finger tapped the chest of Lanapous as he spoke.

Trembling, Lanapous stepped back into the room and with dilated pupils tried to explain to Pontius what happened. "While you were away I tried to find out who might be to blame. No specific person was responsible, Sir. It happened at the changing of the guards. That's when it must have occurred."

"What do you mean, IT MUST HAVE HAPPENED? EITHER IT DID OR IT DIDN'T. WHICH ONE WAS IT?"

Lanapous swallowed as he looked at three other guards in the room. "Sir, I will personally see to it that the changing of the guards will be in increments to cover this possible weakness and vulnerability."

Pontius took a long breath, held it a moment and exhaled slowly. "The gate is to be locked so who opened it?"

"That I do not know, Sir."

"How long have you been my Chief Bodyguard?"

"Six years, Sir!"

"You will be disciplined for this breach of security. I will arrange for you to have one lash for every year that you have served me. Do you understand?"

"Yes Sir!" Lanapous said as his knees trembled.

"I will not allow incompetence to be found in my home, especially with the security of my family. The lives of my wife and family are more valuable than an incompetent fool such as you."

"I'm sorry Sir, but it may not be my fault that . . ."

"Fault is your responsibility. It is you, Lanapous and you will pay for this. No further discussion or pleading. If you beg or plead your case, I will double the lashes.

Pontius walked out of his house, stepped back into the chariot and he shouted to the driver, "MY OFFICE. AND I MEAN, NOW!"

Chapter XXXVII

THE TRIAL, THE NOTE, THE BASIN

Amon and Adakal decided to go to Bethany to see if the Messiah was at Lazarus' house. It was very early when they walked along the narrow streets of Jerusalem, which were quiet because of the Passover Feast, but when they heard a noise in the distance, they decided to find out what was happening. As they neared the sound, they could tell that a crowd was shouting.

They walked past the Temple and as they neared one of the wells, they could hear the crowd chanting a phrase, "CRUCIFY HIM. CRUCIFY HIM. CRUCIFY HIM." Their chanting echoed among the buildings and both men began to run, anxiously anticipating some confrontation. The noise became louder and louder as they neared the Roman Administration Office located at Six Corners. When they entered the open courtyard, they were amazed to see so many people and mounted cavalrymen, but did not understand why the crowd was so incensed. They remained at the fringe of the mob and kept their backs to a wall.

****

When Pontius arrived at his office, he could hear the sound of a large mob on the other side of the administration building at Six Corners. As he stepped from his chariot and he asked, "Manduri, what is that noise I hear? What is going on?"

"Sir, that noise is from the mob which Caiaphas brought with him. They have returned from Herod's palace, and have gathered while you were at King Herod's. The unruly crowd has been shouting and ranting and demanding a crucifixion. They are in a frenzy and out of control. Their shouts have created a fury of, of angry people. There is no telling what they will do."

Pontius carefully measured his steps on the marble stairs as he entered his office. After walking to the window, he pulled the curtain aside to see several hundred people jumping and chanting in the public judicial courtyard below him.

"Find out if the three or four hundred soldiers I asked for are still here."

"When the mob went to King Herod's palace, the legionnaires were not needed, so they returned to the barracks."

"WELL GET THEM BACK, NOW," growled Pontius. "When they arrive, I want to know, because I'm not going out there without military presence," insisted Pontius.

"Yes Sir."

"Be sure that there are at least three hundred more legionnaires. I have no intention of losing this battle."

"Yes Sir!"

Manduri assisted Pontius with his judicial robe and when it was on his shoulders, he tied the golden tassels around Pontius' waist and adjusted the epilates on his shoulders. Meanwhile, the mob continued to shout, "CRUCIFY HIM. CRUCIFY HIM. CRUCIFY HIM. CRUCIFY HIM. CRUCIFY HIM. CRUCIFY HIM."

"The one that needs to be crucified is Caiaphas. He's the devious viper that has caused all of this. If I ever have a chance to deal with him, I will not forget this. He will eventually pay for this," snarled Pontius.

Manduri returned some time later, "Sir, three hundred cavalrymen have returned as you requested. Should I request another one hundred legionnaires to be sure Sir?"

"How many fools are in this crowd?" asked Pontius. His voice sounded stressed and extremely agitated.

"The courtyard holds five hundred and it appears to be much more than that, Sir."

"Then order another three hundred cavalrymen and two hundred infantry. I do NOT intend on failing with this confrontation with Caiaphas and his murderous mob. If we have a battle, I want Caiaphas and his assistant, whatever his name is, to be killed first."

Time passed as Pontius waited for additional soldiers to arrive and when Manduri entered the room, he called, "Sir, Caiaphas is calling for you to appear. What shall I do?"

"Make him wait. Waiting will not hurt that arrogant fool."

Manduri left the room and returned a second time. "An additional four hundred legionnaires are here as you requested and are now in place. Do you have any orders that you wish me to pass to the Cohort Centurion?"

"Tell him to watch for my signal. If I raise my left hand into the air, prepare to battle and when I lower it quickly, engage all of these Jews. If they all die, be sure that Caiaphas dies but do not scar his face. I want to be able to identify him so I can bury him in a pit of manure at the Roman stable."

Pontius started for the courtyard but waited out of sight of the crowd to listen to the mob and their endless chanting. He whispered to himself, "If this is the worst mistake I ever make, I want it to be bathed in the blood of these fools. They put blood on the doorposts of their houses so blood on the cobblestones of the judicial courtyard will be acceptable."

Manduri waved to Pontius to indicate that all infantrymen were in their place.

"This is my courtyard, not his," whispered Pontius as he stepped from behind the large curtain.

The fevered crowd had been chanting for a long time, and their anger did not seem to abate and when he appeared it intensified.

"CRUCIFY HIM. CRUCIFY HIM. CRUCIFY HIM. CRUCIFY HIM. CRUCIFY HIM. CRUCIFY HIM," they chanted endlessly.

Caiaphas piously strutted toward Pontius and then turned to face the mob. When Caiaphas stopped in front of Pontius, he leaned over and said, "Now you know how serious this is."

Pontius responded with, "I will do nothing while this mob continues to shout, so silence them or I will have those soldiers," he pointed at the mounted cavalry moving into the courtyard, "wash this place with their blood."

"You have tried this before and when we bared our necks to your soldiers, you changed your mind for you knew that Caesar would not approve of your murderous injustice."

"And the injustice you desire against this innocent man is not murderous?" asked Pontius. "Come, come Caiaphas. Don't lecture me on what is murder. Doesn't one of your commandments prohibit murder?"

Caiaphas raised his hand to speak but Pontius continued.

"If this issue was a matter of civic security or some matter of Roman law, then I may consider your words, but you are so determined to have this man put to death to save your reputation, despite the injustice of convening an illegal trial. You are wrong and you know it."

Conspiracy With Malicious Intent

Caiaphas turned to the mob and raised both hands and after some time the mob stopped shouting. Turning to Pontius he smiled and moved the palm of his hand toward the crowd.

Pontius sighed as he moved closer to his judicial seat. Though not totally comfortable, he felt secure that the mounted cavalrymen and infantrymen were in position, should a confrontation occur.

Caiaphas motioned and several men brought Jesus onto the platform and when Jesus stood before Pilate, Caiaphas began to speak. "Pontius, the day is early but there is much to do. You have heard our case against this Galilean from Nazareth and why our Mosaic Law requires his death. Herod has heard our case against him and has referred it back to you and now, the final decision is in your hands."

"May I remind you that Herod did not sentence him to death because he, like I, find no fault in this man."

Caiaphas waved his hand and the crowd began to jump and chant again. "CRUCIFY HIM. CRUCIFY HIM. CRUCIFY HIM. CRUCIFY HIM. CRUCIFY HIM. CRUCIFY HIM."

Caiaphas lowered his hands and the mob eventually became silent.

"I will NOT sentence him to death because you ask for it. This is NOT a Roman issue but a Temple issue. If you insist, I am willing to have him flogged, but then I will release him.

"That is NOT what we require," insisted Caiaphas.

"My mind is made up and that is all that I will do," said Pilate. "He does not deserve death. He is innocent of the charges that YOU have created," he said as his pointer finger pointed at Caiaphas' face. "Roman law is about dealing with civic issues and NOT about abstract religious whims. If I belonged to a belief that did not tolerate fools and believed that they should be put to death, then you Caiaphas, would have been executed some time ago. Religious laws and belief do NOT require capital sentences and this man, does NOT deserve to die because you and these fools request it."

"Rome has killed thousands of innocent citizens so what is one more?"

"This execution that you seek will be on your hands, so how will you live with violating your precious sixth commandment?"

Again, Caiaphas raised his hand and the crowd began to chant. "CRUCIFY HIM. CRUCIFY HIM. CRUCIFY HIM. CRUCIFY HIM. CRUCIFY HIM. CRUCIFY HIM." Caiaphas eventually lowered his hand and the mob became silent again.

Conspiracy With Malicious Intent

Pontius looked around to see that the cavalrymen and infantrymen were in key positions. He knew that an order from him would instantly bring an attack upon the crowd, regardless if they were armed or not. He rose from his judicial chair and the crowd waited for his words.

"Each year at this time, someone is released from prison during this religious time you call the Passover, so I will release the Nazarene to you. To demonstrate my cooperation, I have decided to have him flogged and then released."

Caiaphas stepped closer to Pontius and leaned over. "We do not want Jesus released. You heard what the crowd wants, so do it, or will you show everyone that you are fearful and inept." His lips were tight and he appeared extremely angry.

Pontius lowered his eyebrows to stare at Caiaphas, and felt red-hot anger deep in his chest. Again he was tempted to motion to the legionnaires to clear the judicial courtyard so he kept his left hand below to his waist. Several cavalrymen breathed a sigh of relief when Pilate did not give the signal to clear the courtyard.

"You have given all of us the impression that you are ruthless and care not for anyone. So prove to us that you are in charge of Roman issues in Jerusalem. Remember that your record in Jerusalem is marked by poor decisions, greed, bribery and injustice, so now you can make up for it. Give the crowd what they want," insisted Caiaphas. His eyes were angry and his lips were colorless.

"This is NOT a Roman issue. The charges that you have created are NOT worthy of death. Caiaphas, this is about you and your pride and I believe that you have in your Torah a phrase that states, 'Pride goes before a fall.' Well, a holy man such as you is filled with pride, and it is evident that you ignore all other laws. That is what I see."

"You would think nothing of turning your soldiers upon hundreds of our unarmed people, so why are you so concerned about another Jew?" goaded Caiaphas. "How can the death of this Jew impact this whole nation of Israel, the Roman empire or the entire world? So put him to death. What does it matter to you?"

"You claim to have held a trial, well you and I know that it has been an illegal trial for it was held at night and I doubt very much that you allowed the Nazarene to adequately defend himself. You pronounced sentence before it was daylight. What you have done is legally wrong. It was an illegal trial and this is a conspiracy to commit murder: a conspiracy to kill a man claiming to be your king."

"We need no lecture from you. Your courts are less than adequate and often decisions are made before the trial begins," Caiaphas argued. "Who are you to tell us what is legal let alone moral?"

"Was your trial any different? You intentionally set up that illegal trial for the sole purpose of executing or having this man executed," retorted Pontius. Your very commandments forbid that or have you conveniently forgotten that bearing false witness and murder are a violation of TWO of your precious laws?"

"He has violated our laws and will corrupt our nation."

"You have no nation. You are a captured people or have you forgotten?"

"We want this man executed."

"So why did you not execute him after his illegal trial? You had him in the early morning darkness. We would not have known and probably not cared but now you have created this . . . this frenzy and now you wish for Rome to do your murdering. Are you afraid of the sixth commandment? If you plan and abet the process, then you are as guilty as the one who sheds the blood."

"We want him put to death."

"Then I will release your worst nightmare into the city," said Pontius.

"Who might that be?" asked Caiaphas as he placed his hands inside the sleeves of his priestly robe.

"Bar Abbas."

"Bar Abbas? Ha. We don't care about Bar Abbas. We want Jesus to be put to death for his blasphemy. It's Jesus that we want crucified."

Pontius stormed off the platform when the crowd began chanting, "CRUCIFY HIM. CRUCIFY HIM. CRUCIFY HIM. CRUCIFY HIM. CRUCIFY HIM."

In his chambers, Pontius displayed his fury when he threw a flagon of wine across the room and shouted, "THE SUN HAS HARDLY RISEN, AND CAIAPHAS HAS ALREADY CONDEMNED A MAN TO DEATH IN AN ILLEGAL TRIAL. KING HEROD HAS INSULTED ME. INSANE JEWS ARE SHOUTING IN MY COURTYARD AND I HAVE NOT YET HAD TIME TO PLAN MY DAY."

Manduri stepped closer. "Sir," but Pontius was in no mood to listen to Manduri. He turned away and walked to the window and placed his elbow on the sill and tipped his forehead into the palm of his hand.

"Pontius, Sir," Manduri said again.

Conspiracy With Malicious Intent

"What is it Manduri?" Pontius asked as he returned to his desk and drank some wine. Then wiping his mouth with a linen cloth, he asked, "What is it Manduri?"

Manduri stepped nearer and whispered, "Sir, there is an urgent message from your wife. It arrived while you were arguing with Caiaphas. Do you wish to see it now?"

"Give me a moment to think, Manduri. I am torn between slaying all of these Jews and . . ."

"Sir, the note from your wife. Do you wish to see it, Sir?"

Pontius rubbed his forehead and closed his eyes. "Manduri, the life of an innocent man is in the palms of my hand and . . ."

Holding out the parchment for Pontius to see, Manduri whispered, "Sir, it seems to be important."

Pontius nodded before reaching for the parchment and opened it.

> **'Pontay, my dear.'**
> **Do not have anything to do**
> **with this man called Jesus.**
> **I have had many**
> **dreams about this man and**
> **I feel evil is nearby.**
> **If you participate in any way,**
> **then something terrible**
> **will befall us.**
> **Please, Pontay**
> **have nothing to do with him.**
> **Claudia**

As the crowd continued chanting, Pontius read the message several times before folding it and handing it back to Manduri. He motioned for more wine and then, when he had emptied the goblet, he walked out onto the balcony.

When Caiaphas had silenced the crowd, Pontius shouted, "WHAT EVIL HAS THIS MAN DONE? HE HAS DONE NOTHING WORTHY OF DEATH. EXECUTING AN INNOCENT MAN IS A VIOLATION OF ONE OF YOUR TEN COMMANDMENTS, SO WHY DO YOU WANT HIM CRUCIFIED?"

"CRUCIFY HIM. CRUCIFY HIM. CRUCIFY HIM. CRUCIFY HIM. CRUCIFY HIM. CRUCIFY HIM," the insane mob continued to chant.

Pontius motioned to Caiaphas to come near and once beside him, Pontius leaned over and said, "I want to spend a few moments with this Nazarene. You will wait here. Did you hear me? Wait here."

Caiaphas nodded in agreement as the crowd continued chanting.

Jesus was ushered into a smaller room next to Pontius' office and there, Pontius chose to speak with Jesus. Only eight armed soldiers, Manduri and Jesus were allowed in the room.

"Why is this man wearing this lavish robe in my judicial court? Is someone mocking me because he is some kind of king? WHERE DID HE GET THIS ROBE?" he shouted folded his arms across his chest.

Manduri stepped forward and in a whispered tone said, "Sir, it's a robe given to him by King Herod."

"HEROD? Damn him. He's trying to make me out to be a fool."

"Perhaps it's Herod's attempt to ease his conscience, Sir," said Manduri.

Placing his nose near Jesus' face, Pontius changed his voice into a low monotone. "Are you or are you not the King of the Jews?"

"Are you asking on your own behalf or have others told you this?" responded Jesus. Blood continued to drip from his chin and nose.

Pontius raised his hands above his head and shouted, "AM I A JEW? Your own nation and High Priest have delivered you to me to be executed. WHAT HAVE YOU DONE? TELL ME! WHAT HAVE YOU DONE THAT IS WORTHY OF DEATH?" he shouted in rage.

Jesus remained silent.

"If you're a king, where is your kingdom," continued Pontius, "and where are your subjects?"

"My kingdom is not of this world. If my kingdom were of this world, then my servants would fight for me and would ensure that I would not be delivered to the hands of Jews or Gentiles."

"You're sure of that, are you?"

"My Father has tens of thousands of angels standing by, and if I were to call, they would descend upon all of you and the entire world, but that is not my Father's wish."

"Angels . . . tens of thousands of them . . . all waiting for you to call?" For a brief moment, there was silence and then Pontius stepped back, scratched his head and paced back and forth before stopping in front of Jesus. "Legions upon legions and they're waiting nearby? They would follow you into death?"

"None of them would perish or be injured or wounded."

Pontius sighed loudly as he paced with his hands behind his back. "Are you their King or are you the King of the Jews?" His voice was now softer and reflected true concern.

Jesus answered, "You said that I was a king. To that end was I born and for that cause I came into the world that I should bear witness onto the Truth. Everyone that is of the Truth, hears my voice."

Pontius walked over to his chair and when he slumped into temporary comfort, he folded his arms across his chest and his eyes did not leave Jesus. It was easy to see that he had difficulty deciding what to do. He moved his head from side to side and responded with, "Truth . . . truth. What is truth?" he asked in an unassuming tone.

Jesus said nothing.

Outside the crowd continued to chant in an ever increasing fevered pitch.

"Truth does not prevent nor does it avoid confrontation but seems to invoke anger. Is that why Caiaphas and that mob are so angry?" asked Pontius as he stood to his feet. "I know that you have not done anything worthy of death . . . but you can see my dilemma. They want you dead and you say very little to defend yourself. By Roman law, you are able to deny or respond to charges three times, did you hear, three times, but you say little. I have the feeling that during their illegal trial you were never allowed to defend yourself and if I know Caiaphas you were not allowed to bring witnesses in your favor."

Jesus did not respond to Pontius' question but wiped blood from the corner of his mouth.

Pontius placed his left hand over his face and then rubbed his forehead. "I know that the trial that Caiaphas provided was an illegal trial. First, it was convened during the night and secondly, you were not allowed any defense or chance to deny the charges. Thirdly, Caiaphas does NOT have the jurisdiction to sentence you to death. What bothers me is as that I have the impression that you are accepting your fate without a word. Don't you know that I, yes I, Pontius Pilate the Governor have the power to free you or condemn you to death?"

"You have no power except that which has been given to you," responded Jesus in a gentle voice.

Amazed at Jesus' demeanor, Pontius narrowed his gaze and stroked his chin, before continuing. "You stand and look at me as if this is a problem that is easy to solve, but their anger," he said as he pointed in the direction of the chanting, "and your demeanor makes this impossible to solve. Why not defend yourself?" Pontius continued to pace the floor. "I hear that you have healed many people and have fed thousands, so what is wrong with that?"

Jesus stood in silence but did not take off his eyes off of Pontius.

"You give me the impression that you know what is going to happen and act as if this unsavory event was planned. If it was planned, then who's the one on trial, Caiaphas . . . or is it I?" His voice suddenly became a whisper.

Manduri poured more wine and as Pontius reached for goblet he said, "Even my wife believes that you are innocent." Placing the goblet on the table after he drank from it, Pontius returned to the courtyard and when the crowd was sufficiently silenced, he shouted, "I FIND NO FAULT IN THIS MAN! THERE IS NOTHING THAT HE HAS DONE THAT IS WORTHY OF DEATH."

Caiaphas responded, "You know what to do to calm this crowd."

"I have two options. One is to have all of those mounted legionnaires clear the judicial courtyard, even if it means the slaughter of hundreds of your ranting Jews or . . ."

"An incident like that will not please Caesar and you know that or you would have already acted, so do what they ask. After all, Jesus means nothing to you and he means nothing to Herod, but to us, we want him crucified."

"But why crucifixion?" Pontius' face began to show signs of intense stress and vulnerability.

"You Romans invented this type of execution and we are accepting it. How many other Jews have you Romans executed without caring, so why not execute one more?"

"But this man is innocent. He has done more for your people than you or your Sanhedrin. Name one thing that you have done. Have you fed these people? Have you cured them of diseases? Have you raised their dead? YOU should be crucified for doing nothing. You walk about as some, some exalted person and by doing so you act as if you are a god. IT IS YOU THAT SHOULD BE EXECUTED, NOT HE. HE IS INNOCENT OF ANY CHARGES

Conspiracy With Malicious Intent

THAT YOU CREATE. I HEARD THAT YOUR WITNESSES COULD NOT KEEP THEIR STORIES STRAIGHT."

"These people will stay here until you act. Did you hear me?" His grin irritated Pontius to a point where Pontius reached into the folds of his clothing and felt the handle of his dagger but he turned to face the crowd.

As the mob chanted, Pontius raised his voice, "ACCORDING TO YOUR CUSTOM, I WILL RELEASE SOMEONE TO YOU. IT IS EITHER BAR ABBAS OR THIS NAZARENE."

The mob began to chant, "NOT HIM, BUT BAR ABBAS. NOT HIM, BUT BAR ABBAS. NOT HIM, BUT BAR ABBAS. NOT HIM, BUT BAR ABBAS."

Caiaphas spoke slowly to Pontius. "If you will not crucify Jesus, then you are not a friend of Caesar. When Caesar hears of your defiance to maintain the peace, HE WILL NOT BE PLEASED." He smiled and Pontius could see a viper in his eyes.

Returning to the rear chamber where the guards, Jesus and Manduri were waiting, Pontius walked over to his desk and sat down. His eyes fell upon the parchment that his wife had sent and momentarily closed his eyes.

"Herod knew this would happen and he knew I would be squeezed as a grape. Caiaphas is the one that should be crucified!" he said as he stood and began to pace across the floor in front of Jesus.

Outside, the frenzied mob continued their chant.

Eventually Pontius stopped in front of Jesus. "I have heard of all the things you have done. I'm beginning to think that you are who you say you are and that's why Caiaphas is so incensed. He's jealous."

Jesus said nothing.

"Tell me one more time, are you the King of the Jews."

Jesus did not respond but continued to look directly into Pontius' eyes, and moments later Pontius looked away. Raising his hands above his head, he said, "It seems as if I . . . I'm the one on trial. What have I done to deserve this? You look at me as if you have hidden powers to free yourself, yet you stand there, accepting your lot. Don't you care about what will happen to you?"

Jesus remained silent.

Before motioning for the guards to bring Jesus out into the courtyard, Pontius whispered, "Tens of thousands of angels . . . huh . . . waiting and watching? Now that is something I wish Caiaphas could see."

By now, the crowd was in such an uncontrolled frenzy that Caiaphas could barely calm them.

"Very well," said Pontius. "We will scourge him." Then he motioned to several soldiers, who took Jesus and tied him to a column that supported the overhanging roof. After removing the robe that King Herod had placed on him, they began to lash Jesus with fine cords and a leather whip, while the crowd continued to chant.

At first Pontius watched but eventually looked away and shook his head. "These Jews are mad," he whispered to himself. "My hate for them is beyond what I can describe. I can taste my hatred for them. If I were Caesar I would wash this country with their blood."

Someone in the front row of the crowd shouted, "He claims to be a king so place this crown of thorns on his head."

At that moment someone handed a soldier a crown made of thorns, and the soldier pushed it down upon Jesus' head. Everyone watched as the blood ran down Jesus' forehead, face, shoulders and chest. Then the soldier untied Jesus' arms that had been bound to the granite column. Jesus quivered and shook from the pain as another soldier replaced Herod's robe back onto his shoulders.

One of the Temple Police shouted, "HAIL TO THE KING OF THE JEWS!" Then a soldier stepped up and punched Jesus, knocking him to one knee. Another soldier pulled on the remaining tufts of his beard until blood ran down his face and created a puddle at his feet. Still, he spoke not a word nor did he cry out but accepted the abuse and pain.

His silence inflamed his tormenters, who intensified their cruelty.

Pontius finally raised his right hand to call them to cease their beating. "I give him to you but I want you to know that I find no fault in him. I declare him innocent of your charges."

Caiaphas shouted, "WE HAVE A LAW AND BY THAT LAW, HE MUST DIE BECAUSE HE MADE HIMSELF TO BE THE SON OF GOD!"

The crowd started to shout, "CRUCIFY HIM. CRUCIFY HIM. CRUCIFY HIM. CRUCIFY HIM. CRUCIFY HIM. CRUCIFY HIM."

Suddenly, Pontius' heart was filled with fear so he called to have Jesus brought back into the small judicial room where he had initially interviewed him.

Jesus stumbled as he was being pushed and almost fell to the floor. Once inside, Pontius approached Jesus again, "Who are you?" His voice was soft and barely audible.

Jesus did not answer but grunted loudly as blood ran from his nostrils, lips and back, and pooled on Pontius' marble floor.

"You do not speak with me. Do you not know that I have the power to crucify you and have the power to release you? Do you NOT understand?"

Jesus tried to swallow and Pontius could hear blood gurgled in his throat. "You have . . . no power at all against me," he whispered. "You have no power except that it has been given to you; therefore the one who delivered me to you has the greater sin."

After hearing those words, Pontius found it difficult to speak. It was the first time that Pontius had experienced guilt in a long time. His chest tightened as he gasped for air.

Again Jesus tried to swallow and at that point Pontius knew that he was forced to make a decision, so he stepped out into the courtyard.

Before he could speak, someone shouted, "IF YOU RELEASE HIM YOU ARE NOT A FRIEND TO CAESAR. WHOEVER MAKES HIMSELF A KING SPEAKS AGAINST CAESAR. WE HAVE NO KING BUT CAESAR."

Pontius looked at Manduri and then back to the Centurion standing in the doorway. At that moment, Pontius saw the large pool of blood that Jesus was standing in, and when he heard the mob chanting outside, he motioned for them to bring Jesus out to the courtyard again. As they walked toward the outer balcony where the mob was chanting, Pontius said to a servant, "I am going to take him out to the crowd and when I get back I want his blood off my floor," he said, as he adjusted his judicial robe.

When Pontius appeared in front of the crowd, they became silent. They watched as he walked to the Judgment Seat, called The Stone Pavement or in Hebrew, Gabbatha. It was about the sixth hour and Pontius announced to the crowd, "BEHOLD YOUR KING!"

"AWAY WITH HIM. CRUCIFY HIM!" they shouted.

Pontius shouted back, "SHALL I CRUCIFY YOUR KING? BOTH KING HEROD AND I HAVE FOUND THIS MAN INNOCENT OF DEATH. HE HAS NOT BROKEN ANY LAWS. HE IS INNOCENT."

Caiaphas and several priest shouted, "WE HAVE NO KING BUT CAESAR!"

At that moment, Pontius knew that he had no control of the situation, so before he turned Jesus over to the mob, he called for a basin with water. When Manduri filled the basin with water, Pontius pulled up the sleeves of his robe and placed his hands into the water.

As he washed his hands, the courtyard became eerily silent. Then Pilate said, "I WASH MY HANDS OF THIS MATTER. HE IS AN INNOCENT MAN AND I PASS ALL GUILT ON TO YOU. I WILL NOT TAKE ON ANY OF THIS

GUILT." Then, Pontius dried his hands on a royal blue towel, and when he had finished, he handed it back to Manduri.

Caiaphas said as he looked at Pontius, "Place this guilt upon our children's children, but crucify him."

Pontius nodded in agreement and they led Jesus away to the Praetorian, where he was to be scourged before his crucifixion.

Chapter XXXVIII

A PRISONER NOW FREE

"That man they're going to crucify looks like someone I have seen before," said Amon as he leaned over to speak with Adakal. "How can you see who he is? It's a long way from here and his face has been beaten, so how can you say you know him?"

"I've seen that man before," insisted Amon. "I think I know him."

"If you're so smart, who does it look like?"

"Adakal, I'm not sure and I am afraid to say, but that looks like the, the Messiah." His last word was a whisper.

"It can't be. How can the Messiah be here? Who would beat such a good man? Why would they beat and then want to crucify such a good man? Amon, you're meshugga."

Amon turned to a man standing next to him. His face was partially covered so Amon leaned over to look into his face. "Do you know that man?" he asked as he pointed in the direction of Jesus.

"Yes," whispered the man.

"You do? Is he the Messiah?"

"Y-e-s," responded the man in a whisper.

"Really! How did he get here? I thought he would be busy today healing people or raising more dead people. Are you sure that is the Messiah?" Amon's eyes studied the face of the man he was speaking to.

The man groaned as he breathed, "Y-e-s." He coughed and when he removed his hand from his mouth, Amon realized that the man appeared to be very ill for his lips were blue and his eyes appeared as though the had not slept for days.

"Say, you don't look so good. Did you eat some bad goat cheese or too many new olives?"

The man coughed again and wiped the saliva from his mouth.

"I think I've seen you before too," said Amon. "You . . . you were with the Messiah near Jericho when I was . . . a . . . when the blind man, named Barta something was blind and was made well. Jesus made him to see. You were with a man that spoke to me. His name was Andrew. Do you know him too?"

The man remained silent. His jaw sagged slightly and his complexion was cyanotic and ashen.

"Who are you?" asked Amon.

"It's not important."

"Well what's your name?" insisted Amon.

"Judas," the man whispered.

"Jerusalem has many Judas' but which one are you?" asked Adakal.

"Judas Iscariot," he whispered as he turned and staggered away, as a man without sight.

"I don't think he feels too good," responded Amon as he turned to Adakal.

****

As the mob began to disperse, Pontius walked into this office and sat down. His eyes focused upon the small parchment that Claudia had sent him. He commanded the guards and Manduri to leave the room, and when he was alone, he closed his eyes and hung his head in silence.

"I have been squeezed as a grape. Caiaphas initiated this and Herod knew what would happen," he whispered to himself. "Claudia was right. This was a conspiracy with an illegal trial and all of this to kill their king and I . . . I was unable to stop it," he said to himself. "How did this happen? I tried to stop it but . . ."

Some time later, Pontius called Manduri. "Bring me a large sign so I can write something on it. It must be a large sign so all will be able to read what I will write."

****

In the dim light of the halls and cells of the Praetorian, an unkempt man was summoned to his cell door. He sat up and looked at the guards, who unlocked his cell door, grabbed him by the arms and dragged him into the hallway, without any explanation.

"If you were outside and didn't have your friends and a sword, I would cut your throat, you pagan pig," he said in a gruff voice as he tried to free himself from the guard's grip.

The guards said nothing but pushed him down the damp corridor until they came to an Iron Gate. After it was unlocked, the man was ushered up several flights of stairs and past three guarded checkpoints before stopping at an outside gate of the Praetorian.

"What is this all about? Have you brought me out here to execute me?" asked the prisoner as he tried to shake off the grip of the guards that held both his arms.

As the key opened the Iron Gate leading to his freedom, the guard said, "Bar Abbas, you're free to go, so leave before I am tempted to use my sword to gut you."

"Go? Why? So you can hunt me down and kill me or use me as bait to lure my followers?" Bar Abbas snarled.

"You're free, now go."

"Why?" Bar Abbas asked as he glared at the faces of his guards.

"Someone has paid for your freedom, now go."

"Paid? How and with what? The only way someone can pay for my freedom is with their own life. Now who would do that?"

"They have. Now go. You're free."

The guard pushed Bar Abbas through the gate and locked it from within.

"What's the name of the man who paid for my freedom? Who is he?" asked Bar Abbas as he stepped back from the Iron Gate. "Why would anyone be foolish enough to do that?"

"It was your life for someone named Jesus from Nazareth."

"Nothing good comes out of Nazareth, so who is this fool?"

"Apparently good does come out of Nazareth. His life for yours, now go. You are free," said the guard as they turned to walk away, leaving Bar Abbas standing on the street alone."

"Someone named Jesus? Why? What does he get out of this?" Moments later, running footsteps faded into silence, as Bar Abbas disappeared from sight.

****

Pontius remained in his lavish office with the drapes drawn. His eyes could not avoid the small note, which Claudia his wife had sent him. It lay

Conspiracy With Malicious Intent

on the corner of his desk, next to three inkwells, his official seal and red wax.

"What will I tell Claudia when she asks what happened to Jesus?" he whispered to himself as he poured some wine into his goblet. "I know she'll ask if I received her note and . . ." he sighed as he began to sip the wine.

"Caiaphas, all of the Sanhedrin and Herod have conspired against this man. What was I to do? Caiaphas that detestable pompous ass . . ." His thoughts and words were interrupted by a knock on his door.

"Enter," he called. His voice seemed weaker than before.

Manduri entered the room with a narrow, irregular piece of roughly sawn wood. "Is this acceptable, Sir?"

"Bring it here. Aw, yes Manduri this will do. Now bring me additional ink and a narrow brush so that I may write on it. I will call you when I need you. I wish to be alone. Be sure to open the drapes so I can see when I write."

"Yes Sir," responded Manduri. When the drapes were opened, Manduri left the room and closed the door behind him.

Pontius sat for a long time and stared at the piece of wood. "What should I write that will tell the truth about this Nazarene?" he asked himself as he poured more wine. "My words must say . . . they must say who this Jesus is and something about him. I cannot say, 'innocent of all charges' or everyone will question, why was he crucified?"

He closed his eyes and after sipping on the wine until the goblet was empty, he picked up the small brush and dipped into the ink container that Manduri had brought to him. Pausing momentarily to consider what he should write, he began to relive the events of the day and in frustration set the brush back onto the table and rose to his feet to pace around the room.

"Perhaps I should say, Jesus a prophet who claims to be the King of the Jews. No that is not what should be said. How about: Jesus the Nazarene who claims to be the King of the Jews?" Again he dismissed his former words. "What about Jesus from Nazareth and Galilee. No, that will not do. People know that Nazareth is in the province of Galilee."

He considered other words but seemed displeased with any of the words that crossed his mind so he returned to his chair and leaned back and closed his eyes, not to sleep but to consider what the sign should have written on it.

****

Amon and Adakal followed the crowd as they moved out of the courtyard where the trial of Jesus had been held. Many of those that had cheered and chanted were pleased with the verdict and argued openly with others, who questioned what had been accomplished.

Unable to fully comprehend what had just take place, Amon and Adakal walked in silence and when they arrived at Adakal's home, they sat on the porch. Words did not come easy, so they remained silent.

Amon broke their silence. "Adakal, that was the Messiah, I'm sure of it. We were going to Bethany to find him, but now they're going to crucify him." Amon wiped several tears from his cheeks.

"Messiah's are not supposed to be killed. What do we do now?" asked Adakal. He reached for one of his children who was standing nearby.

"Since I have come to Jerusalem, there are too many things I don't understand. Maybe that is why rabbis say they don't know. Maybe they say that because they really don't know."

"I don't know either," whispered Adakal, "but if you're sure that it was the Messiah that we saw, what can we do now?"

Chapter XXXIX

THE BETRAYER AND THE EXECUTIONER

When Judas realized what he had done, he was on the verge of a physical and emotional collapse. He staggered through the streets and at one point did not know where he was, or where he was going. Blinking his eyes to regain the ability to see more clearly, he shook his head as he reached for the building next to him. Gasping for breath, he tried to ease his memory but deathly fear suddenly gripped him, making his chest feel as if it were about to burst.

Later he collapsed near one of the city wells, and someone offered him a drink of water but he staggered to his feet and made his way to the side of a building where he collapsed again. His loud moaning frightened those who offered assistance, so they fled from him, thinking him to be deranged.

When Judas sat up, he appeared as a dead man. His face lacked color and his lips were cyanotic and saliva dripped from his mouth. His eyes were glazed and unable to focus. When he groaned, several people backed away, fearful of what he might do.

Unable to determine where he was, he rose to his feet and wobbled down the street. He fell onto a set of stairs that he momentarily recognized as the Temple where, hours earlier he had accepted the thirty pieces of silver for a betrayal of a friend. He fell several times at the entry of the Temple but once inside, he began to shout, "HIDDOOO, HIDDOOOO. WHERE ARE YOU? HIDDOOO, DO YOU HEAR ME? HIDDO, HIDDO. HIDDOOOOOOOooooooo."

From a side door, a bearded man watched him and when he thought that he had been seen he immediately closed the door. As Judas shouted, a priest entered the room and told him to be silent but he shouted all the

Conspiracy With Malicious Intent

louder. Finally the priest asked what he wanted to which Judas replied, "I needs to sthpeak wiff Hiddoooooooooo, NOWwwwwwww!"

"Hiddo is not here."

"WELL, FINE himmmm!" Judas words were slurred as a drunken man. Saliva continued to drip from the corner of his mouth and found its way into his beard and onto his chest.

Caiaphas entered the room at that moment quite unaware that Judas was there. "Who is that unruly creature? Mad men are not allowed in the Temple," he growled in a disgusted tone.

"I AM JUDATH. JUDATH ISCARRRRIOT . . . AN I BROWK BACK THE THRITEEEEEE PIEETHESTH OF SSSLIVER."

Unsure of whom Judas was, Caiaphas responded, "I don't know what you are talking about. Now leave or I will have the Temple Police arrest you."

"Hiddoooo, paid me to be bethtray Jesuth and . . . and I'm here to return the ssssliver."

Shocked by this meeting, Caiaphas moved to the opposite side of the room. "Sorry, we cannot take it back," replied Caiaphas. "It's yours. It's what you wanted and we have received what we wanted, so keep it, and oh, I would prefer that you leave immediately."

"I wanna return thith to you," slurred Judas as he fell to the floor and then tried to regain his balance while on his hands and knees.

"A deal is a deal. You received what you asked for and we received what we wanted," responded Caiaphas. "Now GET OUT!"

In desperation, Judas opened his leather pouch and took all his coins, including the thirty pieces of silver, and threw it across the Temple floor. They bounced loudly across the marble floor and several pieces struck a table, near the veil that hid the Holy of Holies.

Caiaphas stood motionless, watching the money and silver bouncing and sliding across the floor.

Judas stood up and staggered forward, fell to his knees and sobbed loudly, but Caiaphas and the servant did not move.

Then Judas shouted, "I HAVE BE . . . BETRA . . . YED AN INNOTHESS MANNNN, AND YOU . . . YOU WILL KILL AN INNOTHESS MAN!" He eventually got to his feet and tried to run from the Temple but his legs folded and his eyes failed him because he ran into a wall and again fell to the floor. Blood ran from his nose and mouth. When he rose, he moved as a man without strength or sight, and when he tried to leave, he knocked over a table with Temple utensils on it. Moaning as he stood unsteadily to his feet, he staggered out of the Temple, leaving behind a bloodied handprint on the wall near the entrance.

****

When the Temple Police and mob brought Jesus to the Praetorian, he was unrecognizable. His face was bloodied, most of his beard had been torn from his face and both eyes were badly swollen. He was taken into the dungeon and was about to be fettered to a wall, when Mabboodda arrived and asked, "Who has beaten this man?"

One of the Temple Police responded, "I think he was beaten at Pilate's courtyard."

"Why did they not complete the job? There be little left for us to do. He be a rag of a man."

Several moments passed as Mabboodda read the parchment. "This man is to be scourged and crucified," he mumbled as he continued to read. "This is not Bar Abbas as we expected so who is he?" After rereading the parchment, Mabboodda pointed to the cells down the corridor and said, "Well whoever he be, the other two will be pleased that they do not have to suffer and die alone."

Mabboodda motioned to the Temple Police, who then pushed Jesus into a side room, where he fell to the cold floor.

Eventually Varrus appeared at the top of the stairs. "Did you call for me?" he asked.

"Yes. The other man to be crucified has arrived. He's to be scourged and crucified but he has already been beaten in Pilate's courtyard, so we may not need to flog him again."

Varrus continued down the stairs and when he arrived, Mabboodda said, "Sir, this man has already been severely beaten and adding more to his back will accomplish nothing. If we add more, he may die before he reaches Golgotha."

As the Temple Police left the dungeons, Mabboodda stepped into the cell where the Nazarene had been pushed. Varrus remained in the hallway and closed his eyes as he mumbled to himself, "This will be the worst day of my life. What else can descend upon me?"

Mabboodda stepped back into the hallway. "Sir, he has been severely beaten, but he appears to be strong. He needs to be scourged also. It is part of his sentence, so we will do as we have been told."

"Is this Bar Abbas, the one we have been waiting for?" asked Varrus.

"I don't think so. The parchment say a different name but I will look again to see who he be."

"By the way, who is the executioner on duty?" asked Varrus.

"Danniah, and he be here soon."

Hinges creaked on the door at the end of the corridor, and Danniah entered the cellblock. "You call me?"

"One more has arrived to be crucified, so now we have three. You may start," was Mabboodda's response.

"Oh this man," he said as he pointed to Jesus kneeling on the cold wet floor, "has already be flogged and beaten afore he arrive.

"All need to be scourged and you can start with any one of them,"

Danniah reached for his red leather apron, placed it around his waist and started for the room where the damp well cured the whips.

Mabboodda followed Varrus to his office and when they entered the room, Mabboodda said, "Sir, here be advice to you. Do not take this task to your person. It is a job that someone will do, and it just happens to be you and me. We have no power to stop this."

Varrus sighed loudly as he reached for the parchments that needed to be signed.

"Sign them later, Sir. Since this is your first crucifixion, I recommend you stay in your office until we be ready to leave. You need not witness the flogging. The sound be hard enough to endure but seeing it will change you."

"It's not that I have not killed men or wounded others, but it was in battle, where . . . where they are able to resist or run. Killing those without weapons or killing those tied to a post is different," said Varrus as he tried to swallow.

Suddenly, Varrus could hear the crack of the whip and the sound of leather smacking wet skin followed by a crazed cry of inconsolable pain. Again and again the whip found the tender skin of its victim, and the subsequent screams began to ebb until they became increasingly difficult to hear. After some silence, the crisp smacking sound continued and then suddenly abated.

Varrus asked, "Is that it?"

"No. That be twenty-one lashes. There be more to come."

Varrus wanted to wait outside but realized that his men would see him as a weak link, so he started down the stairs to force himself to witness the last of the lashing. What he saw caused him to stop in his tracks. Blood was running across the floor to the center drain. On the walls were thousands of blood droplets. It looked as if someone had used a brush to hurl blood against the walls. He took an extended breath and looked at Danniah, who nodded as he made his way to pick up a pail of cold water. There he washed himself and then splashed the water onto the walls and across the floor, removing the evidence of pain. Suddenly, Varrus detected the odor of death.

"They will now welcome death," said Danniah.

Varrus fought the urge to bend over to help the beaten man to his feet. "Is it . . . I mean have you finished?"

Danniah walked past Varrus without saying a word, washed the whip and hung it on the rack. Then turning to Varrus, he said, "They be ready, Sir. My job be finished. Now I follow you to do my duties at the hill."

Varrus looked at the two men who lay in one corner and was amazed at how much flesh had been removed from their backs and ribs. Sinew and bone was exposed causing the men to shiver uncontrollably. On one of the wooden tables lay the man who had just arrived. His body was almost unrecognizable and Varrus needed a moment to recognize where his head was for it too had been viciously beaten.

Varrus stepped back into the hallway just as Mabboodda opened a side door and moments later thirty soldiers stepped into the cellblock. Six of them grabbed the three beaten men and forced them to their feet. Two of the men moaned and pleaded for death, while the one who had just arrived wobbled unsteadily on his feet and gasped for breath. Deep within him there was a gurgling sound and his shallow breathing sounded as though he was near death. Blood continued to flow from his back and sides. Dried blood caked his cheeks and chin.

As they were about to stagger out of the dungeon, Mabboodda grabbed the royal robe that lay on the floor and draped it over the shoulders of Jesus. "There, you be ready to go," he said.

"Why is that man wearing a royal robe? It looks like something very costly. What does that mean?" asked Varrus.

"He came with it on. Where it came from I not know but he leaves with it, if it be acceptable with you," responded Mabboodda.

Varrus reluctantly gave his approval. "Yes I, I guess so," he whispered.

Mabboodda looked at Varrus. "We usually tie the crossbeams on their shoulders and make them carry it to Golgotha before we spike it to the upright beam. Then we raise it and drop the entire cross into a hole in the ground. Other times, we make them carry and drag the entire cross out to

Golgotha, and then we bind them to the cross. Which way do you want us to do it, Sir?"

Varrus was at a loss for words and only shrugged his shoulders.

"Would you rather that I make the decision since this be your first time Sir," asked Mabboodda.

Varrus nodded his approval.

"Fine, these two men," Mabboodda shouted as he pointed to the two thieves, "will carry the crossbeam and this new man will carry the entire cross." Turning to Varrus, he said, "Our task be to keep them alive until they arrive at Golgotha. If they die on the way, the man who is in charge of Jerusalem will be very angry. The trick is to make them suffer without dying. The cross is what kills them."

Two soldiers lifted the crossbeam onto the shoulders of the first thief and tied his arms securely to it. He dropped to one knee from the weight but was forced to stand. He staggered under its weight.

Then two other soldiers placed a crossbeam onto the second thief's shoulders and secured his arms to it. He also dropped to his knees from the weight of the wooden beam.

In a soft whispering sound, one of the prisoners turned, "Please kill me. I cannot . . ." He did not finish his words for he was immediately struck in the face with a fist from one of the soldiers. Moments later, he was lifted to his feet. "If you wish for me to strike you again continue to talk. Now be silent or we will cut your tongue out before we leave. I know you can't talk without a tongue."

Varrus watched as the crossbeams were tied to the shoulders of the two thieves.

"Death is death. Soon they care not," Mabboodda said as the two thieves were forced to pass in front of him.

When they brought Jesus from the side chamber, the entire cross was placed on his shoulder. He slumped to his knees and leaned forward so that the blood in his mouth could fall to the floor. A moment later, he was forced to stand. His knees wobbled and his jaw quivered as if he were cold. He grimaced from the weight of the wooden cross but said nothing and blinked his eyes to clear the blood from his eyelashes. He groaned loudly as he erected himself to adjust to his wooden burden.

The Nazarene was forced to wait until the two other men were lined up in front of him and then the soldiers opened the wooden doors leading to the street. Varrus was amazed at the number of people that were waiting outside. He looked at Mabboodda, who shouted, "Now be the time, MOVE!"

Just outside the doors, eighty cavalrymen waited for the procession to begin. As the condemned stepped into the street, the cavalrymen immediately cleared a path for the procession. Their horses forced children out of the way and occasionally, a legionnaire used a whip to force adults to move away from the condemned men.

Mabboodda motioned for Varrus to mount his horse and then walked over to the two-wheeled cart that carried the ladder, spades, ropes, mallets and spikes.

The mounted escorts surrounded the three condemned men as they began their painful journey to Golgotha. The cavalrymen's duty was to protect the condemned from the crowd and keep the path open for continuous movement. Ten mounted legionnaires followed those that cleared the path while eight others rode on either side of the two thieves. Behind them rode six more cavalrymen, followed by the man with the royal robe. At the rear of this procession of death, six cavalrymen followed. Twenty additional legionnaires walked beside the condemned, continuously urging them to keep moving. Several strides behind the procession, the cart followed.

Before leaving, Mabboodda had given the execution parchments to Varrus and told him to sign each page but Varrus decided to sign them later so he put them into a saddlebag.

Once the cadence of death began, Varrus rode next to the cart, but Mabboodda motioned for him to ride ahead of the two wheel cart. "Oh, by the way, Sir, you must ride at the front of the procession not back here. The cavalrymen want a leader, not a follower, Sir."

Varrus nudged his mount with his heels to force his way to the front of the line. The noise from the crowd was deafening and Varrus was surprised that the crowd had to be restrained. Some people in the crowd threw objects at the condemned men as others spit upon them. Varrus was sure that, had it not been for the cavalrymen, the citizens would have rushed in and killed them. For a moment, he considered drawing his sword to protect himself.

Varrus remembered hearing someone saying, "That doesn't look like Bar Abbas. I have seen him and he has more muscles in his arms and shoulders."

"I heard that he and two of his men are the ones who are to be crucified," responded a man beside him.

The slow march continued and when Varrus looked up, he saw many people perched on top of buildings to watch the procession. Some watched in silence, while others shouted insults and waved their fists.

As they neared the Temple, Varrus was surprised to see several priests standing on a platform to watch as the condemned passed by. Hearing cheers from the crowd, Varrus turned to see the condemned man, who was wearing the robe, drop to his knees. Varrus reined his horse and rode it over to where soldiers were helping him to his feet. Again, the procession of death moved along the dusty cobblestone street.

Unable to comprehend the emotions of the crowd, Varrus shook his head in disbelief. "How can these people be so angry and take such pleasure in their pain?" he muttered to himself.

Cavalrymen knocked several people to the ground because they were interfering and blocking the pathway. There were shouts of insult and anger, but it did not stop the condemned men as they plodded toward their appointed death.

Again, the man with the royal robe dropped to one knee and appeared to be unable to carry the cross any farther. Varrus moved his mount closer just as one of the soldiers lifted the cross, so that the condemned man could rise to his feet.

Several people received blows from cavalrymen's whip because they were standing too close to the condemned men. One child was knocked to the ground and a horse stepped on it but the death march did not stop.

Varrus decided to remain in the centre of the procession where he could watch all of the activities more carefully. His gelding moved with precision and when someone came too close to him, the horse turned its chest to keep the person from reaching for Varrus. Its long legs began to strike out at the man and eventually forced him back into the crowd.

When the man with the robe dropped to his knees again, Varrus moved closer, and when he was next to him, Varrus thought he recognized him. He leaned over the horse's mane and withers for a better view. Just then the man with the robe raised his gaze, and in that moment, his swollen and blooded eyes met Varrus'. Nausea instantly overcame Varrus, and for a moment, he thought the condemned man wearing the robe was Jesus, the man who had healed his servant, Pollus.

Varrus immediately sat upright. Dazed by what he thought he had seen. He reined his mount to a stop and reached for the parchments in his saddlebag. He began to read the names of the condemned.

Asiel Jodiahia Nassa Bar Abbas, member of a Zealot group led by Bar Abbas. Guilty of theft, murder and violence against Rome and common citizens. Minimum forty nine lashes, condemned to death by crucifixion.

Conspiracy With Malicious Intent

Hilkah Aheem Kassna Bar Abbas, member of a Zealot group led by Bar Abbas. Guilty of theft, murder and violence against Rome and common citizens. Minimum forty nine lashes, condemned to death by crucifixion.

Jesus the Nazarene, guilty of blasphemy, forty nine lashes and condemned to death by crucifixion.

Varrus eyes returned the words, 'Jesus the Nazarene.' "This cannot be," he said as his hand trembled slightly. "This was the man that healed my servant Pollus and . . . and whose words I have listened to in Capernaum, Nain and along the Jordan River. This cannot be. This cannot be."

Varrus chest felt such pain, he was sure it would burst. "How could it be that I would bring death to a man, who has healed so many people including Pollus?" He turned his face away to draw a large breath to avoid the urge to vomit. His heart continued to pound in his chest, and he found himself leaning forward to look more closely into the face of the man wearing the robe. Blood continued to flow from his face and mouth, and patches of dried blood were pasted to his hair and forehead.

"It looks like him," whispered Varrus, "but how can it be? His name is on this parchment and it looks like him but . . . but this cannot be happening. If this is Jesus as the parchment tells me . . . oh no, but what can I do? I'm unable to stop this."

Varrus tried to sit erect in the saddle. His eyes looked off into the distance. "He looks similar to Jesus but that face and beard. I cannot be sure. He's almost unrecognizable," Varrus whispered as he tried to take a large breath. "How can the parchment be wrong? This must be Jesus the Messiah," he said to himself.

Again he leaned forward to have another look, but Jesus fell to his knees. In a moment, one of the soldiers lifted him and that is when Jesus' eyes looked at Varrus again.

Instantly, Varrus felt weak and almost fell from his saddle. He grabbed the mane of his gelding as he looked away for his next breath. Turning his face back to Jesus, he saw the pain and stress on his bruised and swollen face. Nausea continued to overwhelm Varrus and he quickly turned away again to control his emotions and preserve his dignity. He closed his eyes and breathed deeply and with each breath he felt his stomach heave.

The crowd continued pushing and swaying from side to side, and one of the soldiers drew his sword to force the crowd away from the condemned men. The crowd scrambled back for they knew that the soldiers had orders to kill anyone, who tried to stop or interfere with the crucifixion.

When Jesus fell to his knees again, Varrus saw a black man standing at the front of the crowd, so he moved his horse toward him. "YOU," he shouted as he pointed at the man, "YOU CARRY THAT CROSS FOR HIM AND DO IT NOW!"

The black man was unsure of what to do until another cavalryman reached down and grabbed him by the hair. "YOU HEARD THE CENTURION. CARRY HIS CROSS AND DO IT NOW."

Jesus seemed unable to continue. The frightened black man reluctantly stepped forward, knelt down and placed his shoulder under the beam and began to bear the weight of the cross. At that moment, Jesus wiped the blood from his mouth and stumbled forward.

Varrus almost leapt from his saddle. His eyes were witnessing agony, his heart was aching and his mind felt as if it would unravel.

The sound of a whip started the procession again and it moved another hundred strides closer to Golgotha. Varrus was forced to turn his back to the condemned men and in a moment of personal determination forced his horse to the front of the procession, so he did not have to look at Jesus. No one in the crowd noticed his tears as he rode without seeing.

In the crowd stood two men, who watched in silence as the legionnaires and thieves passed by. When Jesus staggered by, both of them could not believe their eyes.

"THAT'S THE MESSIAH!" shouted Amon. He tried to move with the procession but the crowd was too tightly packed.

"WHERE ARE YOU, AMON?" shouted Adakal, but Amon did not hear for the noise of the crowd.

Amon tried to force his way to the front of the line, but when he saw a cavalryman, he decided that he should find another route, so he tried to run ahead for a better view.

When Amon reached the front of the line, he noticed the gelding and who was riding in the saddle. He shouted, "VARRUS," as he pounded his chest with his fist. "DID YOU KNOW THAT IS THE MESSIAH? YOU MUST HELP HIM, QUICK."

Varrus turned his head so he did not have to look at Amon. He had never felt so empty, not even when he was told of Pollus' death. Even if he wished to, he could not have spoken for his senses and throat were now paralyzed.

Chapter XL

THE PLACE OF THE SKULL

A rap on the door of Pontius' administrative office caused him to look up from his desk. Moments later he responded, "You may enter."

"Sir, it has been some time since I left you. Is there anything you need? More wine or something to eat?" asked Manduri.

"Here is the sign I have made. As you can see it's written in Greek, Latin and Aramaic. What do you think?"

Manduri looked down at the sign that had the words, 'Jesus the Nazarene, King of the Jews' printed on it. "Where do you wish this to be taken, Sir?"

"Manduri, have this taken to Golgotha where they will crucify the Nazarene. Tell the Centurion in charge to be sure that this sign is to be posted above the head of Jesus. If he questions it, point out my signature and my seal."

"I will see to it that it is sent immediately."

"NO Manduri. YOU will deliver it, personally."

"Yes Sir."

"I want everyone, who is able to read, to see this, especially the Jewish religious leaders and Caiaphas."

"Very well, Sir. I will attend to it immediately."

"Manduri, before you leave, please bring me more wine and shield me from further intrusions for I wish to be alone."

"Do you wish for me to check on you when I return from Golgotha?"

"That would be fine, Manduri. You are excused."

"Thank you Sir."

****

Conspiracy With Malicious Intent

On the north and western side of the Jerusalem, the condemned made their way to Golgotha, known as the Place of the Skull. Its origin is the site where the head of the warrior Goliath had been placed on a lance after the shepherd boy, David, defeated the Philistine giant. Over the years, the word Goliath evolved into Golgotha, and as a result it became known as the Place of the Skull.

The cavalrymen continued to force people away from the condemned men. When they arrived at the crucifixion site, the two thieves were forced to lie on their backs on a large and crudely cut wooden beam. Moments later, the cross pieces were tied and spiked to the larger piece that would become the erect piece of the cross. Once secured, ropes were attached and the cross, along with its human cargo, was raised into position so it could be dropped into the hole in the ground which had been dug the day before.

When the first thief was being raised, he tried to scream but his breath was taken from him, when the weight of his body paralyzed his diaphragm and intercostal muscles. When the cross was dropped into the hole, the combined weight of the wooden beam and its human cargo produced a solid thud that it could be felt ten paces from the hole.

The condemned man pushed on his legs to reduce the pain in his shoulders and to allow him to take a breath. His trembling throat emitted a deathly moan and a fading gasp. He opened his mouth to inhale and soon grimaced because of the tremendous pain in his shoulders, chest, back and abdomen.

The second thief was raised and he also tried to scream when the cross was dropped, with a loud thud into the hole, causing him to stop breathing. He tried to shake his head so air could enter his nostrils, mouth and lungs but his attempted gasp ended suddenly when his chest was unable to move.

Varrus needed every ounce of discipline to remain in his saddle. His heart was pounding, his mouth was dry and his hands were ice cold. He whispered, "Jesus. How could it be that I, Varrus had to repay you by crucifying you?" Tears ran down his cheeks and he wondered if anyone in the crowd or his men saw how upset he was. It was pain that he could not endure. To him this agony was equal to the pain experienced by the condemned men.

He moved his horse so people near him could not see his face and then he watched as Jesus was laid on the cross that he had carried to Golgotha. When the first spike was driven into Jesus right wrist, a cold shiver ran through Varrus' body and he turned away. He almost vomited when he heard the mallet strike the long spike a second, third, fourth and a fifth time.

The loud 'ping' of the mallet striking the metal spike could easily be heard thirty paces away and as the spike challenged the hard dry wood, audible and painful moans from the Messiah increased with every ping. The spike continued to pierce the metacarpal bones of the wrist, radiating intense pain up the radial, ulnar and medial nerves in the arm and up toward the brachial plexus and the ventral branches of the cervical and thoracic spinal nerves.

Varrus closed his eyes and took several quivering breaths as the mallet began to drive the second spike into the crudely cut wooden beam. The sound caused Varrus to move his horse to a different location but the mallet continued pinging again and again. When the executioner stopped using the mallet, Jesus moaned loudly as he attempted to adjust to the pain.

Danniah began to drive a spike into Jesus' feet. The sound of bone and flesh being ravished by the spike was something Varrus would never forget. Even the crowd became silent as the sound resonated among the observers. Eventually, the cross was raised and dropped into the hole with a thud. For a brief moment, there was silence.

Jesus tried to raise his head but when the cross dropped into the hole in the ground, his blooded chin bounced off his chest.

A mounted rider carrying a large piece of wood from Pontius Pilate's office approached Golgotha. Suddenly four mounted soldiers intercepted the intruder and after some discussion, they escorted the man, with the piece of wood to where Varrus was sitting on his horse.

"Pontius Pilate has given orders that this sign is to be placed on the cross, above the head of the Nazarene."

Varrus nodded his approval and said, "Give the sign to Danniah."

When the sign was given to Danniah, he called, "Bring a ladder from the cart so I can put this sign above the head of the Nazarene."

After Danniah had nailed the sign to the cross above the head of the Nazarene, he climbed down the ladder and turned to Varrus, "What be written on this sign?"

In a voice that was barely discernable, Varrus whispered, "Jesus the Nazarene, King of the Jews."

"It has many symbols that I have never seen before," said Danniah as he wiped perspiration from his brow.

"It is written in Aramaic, Greek and Latin," said Varrus.

Members of the crowd looked up at the sign and wondered what it said. Those that mocked and jeered Jesus pointed and laughed even though they were not able to read or understand what it said.

ישוע נצריא מלכא דיהודיא

IHCOYC NAZWPAIOC O BACIAEYC TWN IOYAAIWN

INRI

IESVS·NAZARENVS·REX·IVDÆORVM

Varrus nudged his horse to the outer edge of the execution zone and turned his back to the crucifixion site. His heart ached for the Nazarene who had healed his servant, his mind swirled with despair over the loss and death of his trusted friend, Pollus.

His spirit was bruised beyond repair. He was unsure of his future for all he could feel was hopeless anguish.

When he turned his face to the crosses, his eyes blurred and with all senses numbed, he grasped at the mane of his mount to prevent falling to the ground.

He had never experienced such chest pain and his extremities were as cold as ice. Eventually, he became aware that Danniah was gathering the tools, ropes, shovels and ladder to place them into the two-wheel cart. Then he looked up at the three men and wiped sweat from his brow.

When Varrus' horse pawed the ground, bobbed its head and snorted, Varrus lowered his gaze and shut his eyes. When he looked up, he watched as a legionnaire, who was walking by, spit at Jesus.

"Why me?" he asked himself. "All of this authority, yet I am helpless to stop this terrible deed. I was helpless when they selected me for this insane assignment and I was helpless when Pollus was murdered. How could all of this happen to me within only a few days? My life has ended and I am no more."

It was hard to believe that the trial and crucifixion had taken place and it was only the third hour: nine a.m.

****

While the cross of the Messiah was being lifted to be dropped into the hole, Amon slumped to the ground. His heart was numb and he stared in disbelief. The Messiah whom he had hoped to meet was now dying before his very eyes. He thought of Hannah's son, and the days that he had traveled through arid countryside to Galilee to find the Messiah. He remembered seeing a blind man healed on the way to Jerusalem. He had been only a few strides from the Messiah as he tried to carry the cross along the street, but now he was near death.

Even though Amon was some distance from the crucifixion site, he could hear the guards and priests mocking the Messiah. Anger equal to a red, hot piece of iron lay in the pit of his stomach. He closed his eyes. "Now I hate Romans more than ever. First they killed Asa and now the Messiah. We may never have another Messiah. God sent us one and they killed him. Why would God ever send another Messiah, if people did this terrible thing to him? Maybe God will get mad and come back and kill all of us for what they did." He closed his eyes and remained silent for a long time.

Laughter could be heard not far from the foot of the cross, so he raised his head and watched as the soldiers started to cast lots for the blood stained seamless robe the Messiah had received from King Herod. They knew it was a very valuable robe even though they did not understand where the robe had come from. They turned it over in their hands and kept feeling the blood soaked velvet fabric with the gold threads and tassels. An experienced eye noticed the reflection of sunlight off the threads, and silently coveted its ownership.

Once the soldiers agreed that casting lots was the way to establish ownership of the robe, they took turns casting the octagon shaped cubes. Occasionally, there was a cheer from a soldier that remained in the game, and swearing could also be heard from someone who had been eliminated from possible ownership.

Casting lots for his seamless undergarment or vestment and his robe, was fulfilling prophesy written in the Tanakh (Psalms 22) that said, 'They divided my clothes among themselves and gambled for my robe.'

As the condemned gasped for breath, those that gambled for Jesus' vestment and robe cheered and laughed at the possibility of winning such valuable prizes. Thirty soldiers stood guard; some leaning on their spear, others sitting on rocks, while the remaining continued to cast lots.

Though casting lots was a forbidden activity to legionnaires while on duty, Varrus was unwilling to deal with their indiscretion. He maneuvered his gelding among the men and stopped momentarily near a group of women, who were sitting on the ground and mourning the condemned. He silently wondered who they were as he rode by them.

Amon turned his head to look at the women, who were sobbing, and he also wondered who they were. That is when he saw the officer move his horse to an isolated spot to view all of the activities at the crucifixion site.

Thoughts of killing a soldier surfaced when memories of Asa ran through his mind. Amon watched as the horse bobbed its head, snorted and pawned the ground. Then his anger overwhelmed him and he began to walk toward the mounted officer on the horse. When he was within twenty strides of the officer, he realized that is was Varrus.

"Varrus! Is that you?" His final words became a whisper as he approached. He was surprised to see Varrus' face. It appeared as a face that had visited death. His eyes were somewhat swollen, his mouth was partially open and his color was that of a dead man.

"Varrus, you're the one, who . . ." He paused. "I thought that was you back in the city, but I never thought that you would do this to our Messiah." Varrus acknowledged him with a nod but said nothing.

Amon stopped several strides from Varrus and raised his hands to the sky, "Varrus, why you? Why you? I thought that you were a friend to the Messiah and . . ."

"I did not choose this Amon. It was chosen for me and since I was assigned to carry out these orders, I must do what is expected of me." He sighed before continuing, but words did not come easy. "Amon, I did not know that this would be our Messiah."

"What would happen if you refused?"

"I could NOT refuse or there would be four crosses for you to look at. I did not know Amon and. . ." his voice trailed off to an agonizing whisper.

"But Varrus, you . . ."

Varrus' horse adjusted its footing when Varrus changed position in the saddle. Amon could hear the leather of his saddle creaking and when he stepped closer, the gelding turned its head toward him.

Momentarily Varrus closed his eyes, "Amon, my heart has died a thousand times today. I am unable to even think about tomorrow. My servant Pollus has died too, and today I have died. Do not look upon me anymore . . . for I am a condemned man."

"But he's the Messiah," pleaded Amon.

"He's your Messiah, Amon, but he cannot be mine. Look at what I have done." Then he turned his head, nudged the gelding with his heels, and it moved down to where the soldiers were casting lots.

****

Mary the mother of Jesus, Mary's sister, Mary the wife of Cleophas and Mary Magdalene continued their painful vigil. The disciple, John the Beloved, knelt among them, sharing in their deep pain and trying to comfort them.

On the ground not far from the crosses, Amon sat in silence. He could not understand how this could have happened. As tears ran down his cheeks, he whispered, "I have come so far to find you and now you are dying in front of me. Why? Now I have no Messiah and my life has no purpose. Why? Why?" He tossed dirt into the air and it swirled around him as it fell to the ground.

"I cannot go back to Nain so where do I go now?" He grabbed a hand full of dirt and tossed it into the air again and again. The dust responded to a breeze and scattered on the ground some distance away from him.

The Sadducees, Pharisee and scribes continued to berate Jesus. They shouted, "If you are a god or the son of God, come down from the cross. Then, we will believe you."

Someone shouted, "He saved others but he cannot save himself."

Suddenly, Jesus moaned and uttered with his dry throat, "Father, forgive them for they know not what they do."

The two thieves called to each other but few cared what they said. One of them mocked Jesus and said, "Aren't you . . . a Messiah. Save us . . . and yourself. If you are . . . a god, then get us out . . . of this terrible . . . death."

The other condemned man rebuked him. "Have you no fear . . . of God? You're . . . getting the same punishment as he . . . but we deserve it, but . . . he has done nothing wrong." Turning to Jesus, he said, "Remember me . . . when you come into your kingdom."

"Today . . . you will be with me in paradise," whispered the dying Nazarene.

Others continued to mock the one who claimed to be the king of the Jews. "He saved others yet he cannot save himself. He's the king of Israel is he? If he is, let him come down from the cross and then, we will believe him."

By now the Nazarene's pain was beyond a human's ability to bear. He was dying of severe dehydration from massive fluid loss. His body was now in systemic, hypovolemic, neurological and cardiogenic shock; each being potentially lethal.

He was suffering from hemorrhagic shock, which is the loss of massive amounts of fluid and plasma. It is a medical crisis because the body has no remaining oxygenated blood for the vital organs of the body: heart, brain and lungs, resulting in death to tissue, known as necrosis. This irreversible injury destroys tissue, contributing to death. The Messiah had lost almost all of his blood and body fluid.

This hemorrhagic shock began in the Garden of Gethsemane when blood mixed with sweat appeared on his brow and body just before the Temple Police arrested him. Then when he was taken to meet the religious leaders, responsible for the conspiracy, they slapped him, punched him and called to him, 'If you are a prophet, tell us who struck you?'

This was more than a general 'roughing up' but a serious beating where his eyes are blackened, where blood shifts from veins and arteries into the tissues around his eyes, known as ecchymosis. Then his beard was viciously ripped from his face; an extremely painful act of brutality. Now the blood begins to flow unimpeded because facial tissues are very vascular and any attempt to slow or arrest the flow of blood will be all but impossible, so hemorrhaging continues to be a major issue. This blood loss continued unchecked while Jesus was taken to meet the Governor and Praefectus Pontius Pilate. Bleeding continued while he spoke to Pilate, while he was transported to meet King Herod and while he was returning to Pilate's Judicial Seat.

He is also in 'Cardiogenic Shock' because the heart is unable to provide oxygenated blood to its own muscle, and so its beat begins to race, not because of fear but because it is trying to provide much needed oxygenated blood through the cardiac arteries to blood starved cardiac muscle. This cardiac muscle and the electrical impulse generating cardiac muscle contraction becomes irregularly rapid, foretelling impending death.

The condemned Nazarene was now in 'Pulmonary Shock' because the lungs were not able to oxygenate the small blood that passed through the lungs because there was, literally no more blood to circulate. There is little residual volume of air in these lungs and what is there, cannot adequately oxygenate the small amount of fluid, which cannot flow through the alveoli of the lungs.

He was in 'Neurogenic Shock' because the nerves of the body are so starved for oxygen from the severe trauma and blood loss that they do not function and now initiate numbness. All extremities become cyanotic or blue and are extremely cold to the touch because of lack of circulation.

His renal and gastrointestinal system has long since shut down in an attempt to conserve blood for the vital organs. It is now a matter of time; measured in the number of attempted breaths taken.

This loss of blood and vital fluids began, not on the cross but in the Garden of Gethsemane, where he prayed to his Father to have this vile and malicious event taken away. Hematohidrosis, though extremely rare, is a serious medical condition contributing to blood of fluid loss. Blood vessels around the sweat glands constrict and are ruptured, allowing blood to ooze into the sweat gland so that when a person perspires because of stress, the sweat is mixed with blood, causing further fluid loss.

Lack of oxygenated blood to the mucosal membranes of the mouth causes his saliva glands to cease functioning, resulting in thick and sticky mucous saliva which causes his tongue to stick to the roof of his mouth making swallowing and speaking almost impossible.

With peripheral shutdown and all systems failing, his body was now in irreversible metabolic acidosis. His ribs, pelvic and knee joints ached when muscle tone ebbed, resulting in dislocation of wrist, elbows, shoulders and ribs so that intercostal muscles are stretched and torn. The weight of his lower body stretches his diaphragm so breathing becomes impossible. Every fiber of his body burns and his lungs are now afire, and he is about to hallucinate as extreme vertigo taunts his memory and reasoning.

Psalms confirms that he became disjointed.

In his fragile humanity, he moans and with his swollen tongue, he speaks in a barely audible voice, "I thirst."

A legionnaire dipped a sponge into sour wine mixed with myrrh to deaden the pain and prolong death. Then he placed that sponge on a long stick and raises it to Jesus' lips, but when he savored it he recognized what it was and refused to take any of it.

Chapter XLI

DARKNESS, THE EARTHQUAKE, THE SPEAR

No one paid attention to an unkempt man leading a donkey to the edge of the crucifixion site. Legionnaires were busy casting lots for ownership of the expensive robe and other clothing that had been worn by the condemned. Women sobbed openly and religious leaders berated the three, now hopelessly impaled upon roughly hewn stakes. Those unsure of the reasons for the crucifixion wagged their heads and whispered questions to others, who cared less.

The disheveled man paused some distance from the three crosses for a long time. As he leaned across the back of his dusty donkey, he nervously cast his gaze from one end of the crucifixion site to the other. No one considered his importance or his motive for being there, so he continued to watch all of the activities.

Realizing that no one was paying attention to him, he placed his hand on his dagger and cautiously moved down the knoll toward the inner circle of activity. He stopped next to one of the larger rocks on the rim of the killing circle and gripped the donkey's tether as he sat on a boulder.

The long rest helped slow his heart rate and allowed him to control his breathing, for he was now within one hundred strides of the three leaning crosses. When anyone came near, he turned his face and moved his scarf over the bottom half of his face, so he would not be recognized.

In the distance, he could hear the arguments between the soldiers who were vying for the expensive robe and he heard the shouts from the religious leaders, so he decided to move to the other side of the knoll. As he moved along, his donkey stumbled and several children laughed at him. Ignoring their insults and taunting, he continued walking until he was within fifty strides of the impaled men. There he narrowed his gaze and sighed as he turned his head slowly to see if anyone was near him. He tightened his lips as he heard interrupted moans of the dying and watched as the falling droplets of blood were carried aside by the soft breeze touching the open wounds of the condemned.

The man stared so intently at the faces of the two thieves that he was not aware that a legionnaire was approaching him.

When next to him, the legionnaire asked, "And what is your interest in all of this? Do you want to see what death is like?" asked the legionnaire as he drew his gladius and pointed at the man.

The untidy and messy man nodded and then mumbled, "Nothing . . . just looking. I want to see if I know any of these men."

As he turned his face away, the legionnaire said, "I know you. I've seen you before. Who are you?"

"No one important," responded the unkempt man. "There are many such as me."

"Look at me so I know who you are," demanded the legionnaire as he motioned to several other legionnaires that were several strides away.

Looking coyly at the guard the man whispered, "I'm just passing by and thought that . . ."

"I have seen you before. What's your name?" the legionnaire demanded.

"I'm nobody. I was just passing by and . . ."

Placing the blade of his gladius at the throat of the scruffy man, the legionnaire interrupted with a demanding voice, "WHAT IS YOUR NAME?"

As the messy man was about to respond, the legionnaire again interrupted, "I know you. You're Bar Abbas; the one that was released by the Governor today. Why are you here?"

"I have come to see . . ."

"You've come to see the man that is your replacement, didn't you?"

Bar Abbas did not respond except to swallow and step back.

The legionnaire continued, "That man is your replacement," he said as he pointed with his free hand at the Nazarene. "Why he would do that for you is beyond me. As for me, all I'd like to do is slash your gut to see what your intestines look like."

The man was clearly uncomfortable with the conversation and tried to back away but the impatient legionnaire said, "Well now you've seen him so be gone. Killing you would be easy, but you were declared free by the Governor, so leave before I change my mind."

"I have come to see . . . my two sons," whispered Bar Abbas.

Conspiracy With Malicious Intent

"Those two thieves are your sons?" said the legionnaire as he narrowed his brows and looked up at the two thieves.

"I have come to see them die," whispered Bar Abbas.

"Well now you've seen them, so leave before I forget that you are a free man," responded the legionnaire.

After one last look at the three on the crosses, Bar Abbas led his donkey from the crucifixion site and was soon out of sight.

****

Confusion and regret ravaged Judas' spirit. He lay on the ground next to the gate through which people carried their refuse and garbage. Unable to think properly, he played with lumps of dirt that lay next to him and eventually stared at his dirty fingers and hands. His blurred vision also added to his confusion for he tried to determine what his sandals were because he removed them and began to play with them.

Looking at his hands through tears he momentarily remembered who he was and began to regret his betrayal. Rising to his feet, he walked through the city gate and on toward a grove of trees in the distance. When he arrived he looked up at them, and choosing one that was easy to climb, he gripped the first branch and then reached for the second and third. There he removed his rope sash from around his waist. Then looping one end around the branch he placed the other end around his neck and leaned forward.

The rope abruptly ended Judas' fall and life. His struggling for breath and his life ended in a desperate convulsion and a momentary shiver. Shortly after his convulsions had ebbed, the rope sash broke and he fell to the stony ground rupturing his abdomen so that his entrails flowed out onto the ground.

****

Shortly after Pontius Pilate's sign had been nailed to the top of the Nazarene's cross, there was a knock on Pontius' office door. Manduri slowly opened it. "Sir, there are some men outside. They are from the Temple and wish to speak with you."

Pontius did not respond.

Again Manduri whispered, "Sir there is a delegation for the Temple to speak with you. What do you wish me to do?"

Conspiracy With Malicious Intent

"The Temple? What do they want?" Pilate's voice was subdued, yet angry.

"They did not tell me, Sir." He paused and then repeated his question. "What you like the guards to do to them?"

"I would prefer that all would be slain."

"I understand Sir."

"Ask them what it is about. If they don't tell you, then throw them out. I want my privacy."

"Yes Sir."

Minutes passed before Manduri returned to knock and open the door. "I asked them, Sir. They want to know, who wrote the sign that was put above the Nazarene."

Pontius sat up and rested his elbows on his knees. "How many of them are there?" he asked.

"Six, Sir."

Pontius rose to his feet and started down the hallway to the courtyard where the trial had been. By his strides, it was easy to tell he was extremely angry. As he neared the door, one of the guards opened it and quickly stepped back.

Pontius strode out onto the balcony and looked down at them. "WHY ARE YOU HERE?" he shouted. "YOUR VERY FACES REVOLT ME. HOW DARE YOU COME HERE AGAIN? I AM A BREATH AWAY FROM HAVING YOUR THROATS SLIT. NOW WHAT DO YOU WANT?"

"We beg your pardon, but we are here to inquire about the sign above the Nazarene."

"What is that to you?"

"Who wrote it and who gave permission for it to be put there?" asked Hiddo.

"I DO NOT NEED YOUR PERMISSION TO WRITE IT OR TO PUT IT THERE," responded Pontius in anger. His hands were on his hips. "MANDURI CALL MY GUARDS AND TELL THEM I WANT ALL OF THESE PEOPLE SLAUGHTERED IF THEY DO NOT LEAVE MY COURTYARD IMMEDIATELY."

"All we want to know is who decided what to write on that sign," continued Hiddo.

"I WROTE IT AND IN MY OWN HANDWRITING. DID YOU NOTICE THAT IT IS IN ARAMAIC, GREEK AND LATIN? You can read those three languages, can't you?" taunted Pilate.

"Yes, but we do not like what you have written."

"Really?" asked Pontius in a sarcastic tone.

"If it must say something, then rewrite it to say, he said he is the King of the Jews."

"You have your man and you have had your crucifixion but you will NOT tell me what to write! WHAT I HAVE WRITTEN, I HAVE WRITTEN. DO YOU HEAR ME?" His neck veins bulged and his face reddened as he shouted.

In the momentary silence that followed, Pontius shouted, "MANDURI! I AM NOW COMING DOWN TO THE TERRACE STEPS. IF ANYONE REMAINS THERE WHEN I ARRIVE, HAVE THE GUARDS KILL THEM. I DO NOT WANT TO SEE THEIR FACE ANYMORE. KILL THEM IF THEY REMAIN IN THIS COURT WHEN I GET DOWN THERE. I WANT TO SEE THEIR BLOOD ON THE STAIRS OF THIS BUILDING."

A moment later, Pontius left the balcony and started for the stairs of the balcony just as the soldiers watched the Temple delegation rush from the courtyard.

****

The crowds stood and watched the three condemned men. Some wagged their heads, while others sobbed openly. They were sad when they remembered the wonderful things that Jesus had done in that region. It seemed so sad that the one, who was helping the unfortunate, was dying for doing so much good.

Nearby, all of the horses suddenly became restless and several of the cavalrymen found it impossible to manage their frightened mounts. Varrus' grey gelding suddenly surged forward, raising both front legs, snorting and trying to throw him but he managed to maintain control.

All conversation within one hundred strides of the three crosses suddenly stopped when a loud and throaty moan from the Nazarene, gurgled the words, "**Eli! Eli! L'mah Sh'vaktani**!" interpreted; 'My God My God. Why have you deserted me?'

Moments later, his extended and deep moan faded into silence. The last words audible to those nearby were, "It is finished. Into your hands, I commit my spirit."

The Nazarene's head drooped forward so that his chin touched his blooded chest and his last breath rattled deep in his throat. With bones out of joint, the rag of a man was now dead.

Instantly, there was a violent earthquake with sounds that were deafening. Many people were screaming and hundreds ran for safety. Others fell to the ground, while dozens dropped to their knees. When the earth stopped moving, it suddenly became dark as midnight. Not even stars could be seen. People were terrorized and found it difficult to find their way back to the city.

Varrus shook his head and said, "Truly this was an innocent man and the Son of God."

At that moment a strange and bizarre phenomenon occurred in the Temple which frightened the priests and scribes even more than the earthquake and darkness. It was the loud continuous sound of heavy fabric being torn; a sound that lasted for several minutes. Those that heard the sound now feared what had occurred even though they did know the seriousness of that event.

This was the sixth hour: noon, and the darkness remained until the ninth hour or three p.m.

****

When sunlight returned to the city of Jerusalem and the province of Judaea, priests began to walk through the Temple seeking what that ghostly sound was that mimicked fabric being torn. It was a very long and extended sound; familiar yet foreign.

One of the priests was terrified when he discovered that the three inch thick (8 cm) Veil, a linen curtain which separated the Holy Place from the Holy of Holies in the Temple, was torn from top to bottom, exposing the Arc of the Covenant that contained the Ten Commandments, the Rod of Arron and a Pot of Manna. On the top of the Arc of the Covenant were two gold Cherubim with their wings above and covering the Mercy Seat. This was a room with objects that were not to be viewed by anyone except the High Priest, and that only but once a year.

The Holy of Holies was a sacred room, ten cubits (15 feet or 4.57 m) long by ten cubits (15 feet or 4.57 m) wide and ten cubits (15 feet or 4.57 m) high. A linen Veil, three inch (8 cm) thick, surrounded this room and hid all contents including the presence of God from human view or contact. The Veil was therefore sixty feet long by fifteen feet.

It was made of fine linen and included blue, purple and scarlet yarn. On it were embroidered figures of Cherubim or Angels. The Veil was exceptionally heavy and not to be touched by anyone except the High Priest.

Its purpose was to shield sinful man and his gaze from viewing the Almighty. The Mercy Seat was where God rested upon glory and righteousness. Into this special veiled room, the High Priest entered only once a year to offer a blood sacrifice and incense. He would don a priestly robe and before walking, without sandals into this room, he had a rope tied around his ankle and a bell placed upon his chest. Those that waited outside would listen to the bell ring and knew that he was alive. If God was angry and put him to death because he was displeased with him or the offering he brought to the Mercy Seat, the bell would stop ringing. Since no one dared enter the Holy of Holies for fear of death, those outside could use the rope that was attached to his ankle to drag him out of the Holy of Holies. This was truly the most fearful yet sacred place for all Jews.

Immediately after knowing what happened to the Veil, all priests, rabbi, scribes as well as Temple dignitaries such as lawyers, Sadducees and Pharisees were greatly troubled. After summoning Caiaphas the High Priest, the area was sealed off until a decision could be made regarding what needed to be done.

****

After the extreme darkness had abated and sunshine returned, only twenty four soldiers, five women, John the Beloved, Amon, Mabboodda and Varrus remained near the three crosses.

Listening to Mabboodda's prompting, Varrus rode down to where the soldiers were and said, "Now is the time." Several soldiers took their spears and walked over to the crucified men. With one great swing of the spear handle, the first thief's legs were broken. He gasped and tried to cry out but lost all ability to breathe. Instantly, he became silent.

Then a second soldier walked over to the other thief and swung the handle of his spear with all his might. The sound of broken bones in his lower legs could be heard at fifteen paces away. The condemned man tried to scream but only gasped for breath, before he became silent.

Amon watched as they moved toward Jesus and again he wanted to say something but sat as though paralyzed and dazed with shock and grief.

When the soldiers saw that Jesus was already dead, one of them used a spear to pierce his left side to puncture his heart. The spear entered his abdomen in an upward motion, severing the lung, and puncturing the heart and the diaphragm. Water and separated blood instantly rushed out and down the spear handle and onto Jesus' legs and onto to the ground.

The combination of blood and tissue fluid flowing from the large opening of the body cavity combined with the jaundiced and deep mauve coloring of the body fluid proved to be a sure sign of death.

The soldier who had thrust the spear into the Nazarene's dead body, stepped back, surprised when he was covered in the mauve watery fluid that gushed from Jesus' corpse. Instantly several soldiers laughed at the inexperienced soldier.

Nearby a soldier chuckled, "Next time you'll remember to stay to the side."

"Yes," responded another. "Now that you're covered in that blood, you'll never be the same."

Varrus commanded, "Stay here 'til the bodies are removed from the crosses."

Varrus could not look up at the battered, limp bodies of the condemned men, but it was the gaping tattered wound from the spear wound on the body of Jesus that caused him to swallow so that he could retain dignity and decorum. He turned his horse to ride some distance from the crucifixion site, and there he sat motionless on his horse and looked at the three impaled men. In disbelief, he tried to make sense of the pain within, and marveled at how quickly his life had changed. It was an emptiness that could not be fathomed let alone described. His irregular breathing mimiced the gasps and moans of a dying man. He had no future for his world had suddenly ended, leaving an indelible scar on his soul. He remained there until the ragged bodies had been removed from their wooden stake.

****

By the ninth hour: three p.m. Jesus was dead and so was Judas Iscariot, his disciple and betrayer.

Chapter XLII

THE REQUEST FOR THE BODY

"The Messiah is dead, Amon. You saw him die. If he was a Messiah, he would have done something and not just died," said Adakal as tears streamed from his eyes. He hugged Amon as he spoke. "What kind of Messiah is that? Messiahs should live and not die. Now we may never have another Messiah. Why should God send another Messiah, if our people kill the one he sent? They have killed prophets and now . . . now they have killed the Messiah."

"Maybe this one was NOT the Messiah," said Amon. "Have you thought about that?"

"Amon, this was the only one we will have." He placed his hands over his face and sighed loudly. "When our forefathers killed prophets and disobeyed, God sent us into exile to die. What will He do now?"

"I too am disappointed and my heart feels like it has been squeezed, and at times I am sure that it will not beat again," replied Amon as he wiped the tears from his face.

"What I do not understand is how they could just kill him. Look at all the good he did, and . . ." Adakal stared at the ground as he spoke.

"Maybe," interrupted Amon, "it's because he knocked over their tables at the Temple. Have you even thought about that?"

"He did heal on the Sabbath and said he was a Son of God. Is that blasphemy? Maybe it was his fault, Amon. Maybe he was not a Messiah and, and God decided to let him be killed," whispered Adakal.

"I remember in the Torah that God does get angry, and maybe, just maybe you're right. Maybe God let him get killed."

"There is something strange about this. The Pharisees and Sadducees don't get along and yet, and yet," he raised his pointer finger, "they worked together to have him arrested. They sent him to a trial, and on top of that, the priests talked the Roman pagans into killing him, and they are not friends. Why did they not do it themselves?" Adakal leaned back and placed his head against the wall of his house.

"Jews sometimes do things that are inside out, and this might just be one of those times."

"No Amon, they don't want to be guilty of murder. Remember the sixth commandment? If they killed him then . . ."

"But they were part of it," interrupted Amon. After a couple of moments, Amon began to pace from one end of the porch to the other. "And," he said as he raised his pointer finger, "what about that man we saw in the crowd. He said his name was Judas something. Why was he not with the other followers of the Messiah? He knew the Messiah, didn't he? So why did he not help the Messiah?"

"I don't know, Amon."

"What about that, that Pilate man? Who is he?"

"He's the Governor. What he decides is what happens."

"But he said at that trial in the courtyard, that there is no fault in the man, who we thought was the Messiah, so why did he yet kill him?"

"I don't know, Amon, but these are good questions, but who knows those answers? That Pilate man must have believed that the Messiah was innocent and remember, yes remember, he washed his hands in front of everyone to show that he was sure that the Messiah was innocent."

"Yes, and," continued Amon, pausing for a moment to rub his forehead, "I still think that the Judas man, who was standing beside us in the courtyard when the crowd was shouting . . . he knows something too. I've seen him before when he was with the Messiah. Why did he look so . . . so bad and why did he stay there to watch?"

"Don't call him a Messiah anymore, Amon. He's dead and whoever heard of a dead Messiah?" asked Adakal. "What good is a dead Messiah to anyone? Only a live one can help us, not a dead one."

"Well, when he was alive he was the Messiah and this Judas man was with him when he used to be a Messiah. He seemed to know so much but why did he do nothing?"

"Yes and . . ." agreed Adakal.

"And Varrus, he was there and the one in charge of the crucifixion even though Jesus healed his servant. What about him? Why did Varrus not stop it? Maybe Varrus doesn't believe that the Messiah is the Messiah." Amon's voice softened at the end of his sentence.

"What did he say?" asked Adakal.

"It was the first crucifixion he was in charge of, but he said he could not stop it. He was very upset because it was Jesus, but," he raised his pointer finger into the air as he spoke. "I tell you, he still had his men crucify Jesus. Why did he not stop it?"

Before entering the house, Adakal turned and said, "Amon, who do we believe in now? Where do we find another Messiah? The person we thought was the Messiah is dead. Dead, Amon, dead, just like the lamb we ate for the Passover. God will never give us another Messiah."

"Maybe we should ask the men, who traveled with the Messiah. Maybe they know," said Amon. "There was a Andrew man and, and he knew Zebedee and, and maybe they know." His eyes opened wide as he spoke. "They will know, Adakal." For a brief moment there was a hint of optimism.

"They weren't even there," said Adakal as he moved to his favorite chair to a shady place on the porch. "He's not a Messiah, Amon, just like he is not alive."

Amon sat in a chair and leaned his head against the wall. "I remember another man, who sat with the women where the Messiah was put onto that wooden stake. Strange, so where did all of the others go? Where are they now?" asked Amon.

"I guess it would be nice to know but where do we start to look for them?" His voice tapered off into a whisper.

"What about the ground shaking so hard that I couldn't walk. Has that happened in Jerusalem before?" asked Amon as he adjusted his position in the chair.

"No."

"And what about the sky getting dark in the middle of the day? I could not even see the stars when I had my eyes wide open. Has that happened ever before in Jerusalem?"

"No."

Both men could not hide their sorrow. They began to relive the events prior to the earthquake and the darkness that had fallen upon the land.

After supper, they returned to the front of Adakal's house, where they were joined by two neighbors, Jaasha and Soloma. Regardless of the words they used, they were not able to comfort each other.

Jaasha asked, "It's getting dark and I would like to know, where is the body of the Messiah going to be buried? Maybe we should go to Golgotha to see if he is yet there. Even the priests do not want to leave the bodies on the cross for the night, so we should go and see where they will bury him."

****

Several hours before darkness, Caustas, one of Pontius' bodyguards, knocked on Pontius' office door.

"Enter," responded Pontius.

"Sir! There are two men here to speak to you about the crucifixion."

"If it is a priest or someone from the Temple, throw them out. I don't want to see any them, let alone speak with them."

"They said it is very important."

"I do NOT want to speak with any of them," repeated Pontius, sounding irritated.

"They are NOT priests, Sir."

"Tell them I have nothing to say."

"I know Sir, but they insist. They assured me that their words are not complaints or confrontational, but a request for the body of the Nazarene. They seek your approval to take it and bury it before nightfall."

"I have had a day I wish never to remember. Tell them that I do not want to speak with them. I want nothing to do with these, these Jewish fools. I loathe the sight of these people and would love to slay all of them. Rome would be better without these, these troublemakers and complainers."

Some time later, there was another knock on Pontius' door. Waiting for his call, Caustas stood patiently at the door. When he was about to knock again, he heard, "What is it now, Caustas?"

Caustas entered and saluted. Pontius did not look up from his desk but continued to write on a parchment. As he dipped the quill into the ink, Caustas cleared his throat. "Sir, a man named Joseph from Arimathaea and someone named Nicodemus want permission to take the body of Jesus before nightfall."

Without looking up, Pontius asked, "Why? What do they plan to do with it? Who could possibly want what's left?"

"They want to bury it, Sir."

Pontius stopped writing and placed the quill on the desk. He nodded, "I can see that they will not leave, so bring them in."

"Yes Sir."

Joseph and Nicodemus were ushered into Pontius' office and when the door closed behind them, they bowed respectfully. Knowing that speaking first may jeopardize their chances of receiving permission to remove and bury the body of the Nazarene, they stood in silence and waited for Pontius to address them.

Pontius continued to dip the quill into ink and write, so they remained silent. When Pontius put the quill onto his desk, he reached for his glass of red wine and sipped slowly on it. Looking up, he asked, "So you want the body of the Nazarene, do you? What will you do with it?"

"I have a personal burial plot in the Garden of Gethsemane, and it is there that I will be placing the body once it has been prepared." Joseph paused for moment to clear his throat. "And I must bury it before sundown, according to our tradition."

"Tradition? What is tradition?" Pontius asked as he sipped wine from the goblet. "Your people have strange traditions and customs. You crucify your king, hate people who do good to others even if it is on the Sabbath, you put blood on the your doorposts and make rules that are impossible to remember, let alone to keep."

Joseph stepped cautiously forward. "Please kind Sir. I must bury this man before it is dark. Your permission is requested and would be greatly appreciated. I have come knowing that this has been a very unsavory day for many people including you. We mean no harm. We seek only your approval and permission."

Pontus stood to his feet and stretched before walking over to where Joseph stood. Stopping within a hands width of him, he exhaled. His breath was warm and smelled of wine. Joseph wanted to step back but remained motionless.

"What is your name?" asked Pontius.

"I am Joseph Elishama."

"Where are you from?"

"Arimathaea."

"Fine, I want to ask you a question and your answer will likely make a difference if I grant this request or reject it."

Joseph swallowed as he nodded, fully accepting the conditions.

"Was this man you wish to bury the King of the Jews as he claimed to be?"

Joseph looked unblinkingly into Pontius' eyes. "He was more than that. He was the Messiah that we have all been waiting for so many years, but very few recognized him. They did not recognize him nor honor him. I am afraid that God will cause great calamity to our nation and maybe Rome because we have slain him."

Pontius returned to his chair and scribbled something onto a parchment with the quill, reached for the wax and placed his seal on it. Several minutes later, he walked over to Joseph and squared his shoulders and asked, "Who is this man with you?"

"His name is Nicodemus Ben Arod and he is a ruler in the Temple."

"He is very young to be a ruler, is he not?" asked Pontius.

"He may be young but aged in knowledge and graciousness," responded Joseph.

"Is knowledge truth?" asked Pontius.

Neither of the men responded to his question.

"What about truth. Is it something that does not change?" continued Pontius as he narrowed his brows and rubbed his chin.

Nicodemus responded, "Truth in the hands of evil men changes all too frequently, but truth in the hands of God is of great value and can be trusted."

The room became instantly silent as Pontius looked at the floor and tightened the muscles in his cheeks. "Tell me Nicodemus, if this man is the Son of God, why did he allow himself to be put to death?"

"There are many things that I do not know especially what God plans, does or thinks. Some of those things only he knows. Who am I to speculate or be impatient with his decisions and actions?"

"If he raised others back to life and healed others, why did he not interrupt his own death?" asked Pontius. "He apparently has the power to do that from what I have heard."

"That we do not know nor understand," responded Nicodemus. "There are many things in our lives and within our influence that we do not fully understand, yet we must accept them. Often a choice does not exist."

"I recall him looking at me as though he had the power to change everything and yet . . . I had the feeling that he was willing to allow this . . . crucifixion."

Joseph and Nicodemus said nothing.

Pontius sighed before continuing. "I have the feeling that he possessed power beyond anything mere man could have. If he had power to raise some people from the dead, why did he allow himself to be put to death? If he healed many ill people and was able to do so many unusual things, where did he get his power from, if not from a God?"

Joseph and Nicodemus nodded but did not speak.

Pilate continued, "He did not defend himself and I began to have the impression that he knew exactly what would happen and accepted it, as if this event had been planned. When he and I were alone, I knew that there was something inside of him more powerful than Rome. I have never met a man like him before." Pontius reached for wine and sipped on it loudly before speaking. "I am sure this man was a God and that any power I had was limited and not to be compared to his."

After pacing across the floor several times, he stopped and said, "He told me that legions of angels were watching and for a moment I wanted to look up and see if what he said was true. Was he who he said he was?"

"We believe he is the Son of God, alive or dead," said Nicodemus.

"Every country has its gods, some have many of them and they always seem to be made of silver, gold or stone, but this is a god with sinew and bone not like a piece of carved stone. When I looked into his eyes, even though they were swollen and he was in great pain, there was such power inside of him, and I had the feeling that anything I said would mean nothing to him. He was a man of purpose and of great strength."

Joseph nodded in agreement.

"No wonder he had many people following him and my wife and her maidens listened often to what he had to say. They told me of his miracles but I did not understand until today."

The room remained in silence as Pontius stared at a tapestry on the other side of the room. Manduri, Pontius' aide, entered the room and silently poured more wine but did not disturb Pontius who appeared deep in thought.

Walking across the room to stand in front of Joseph, Pontius said, "I washed my hands before the mob to show that I proclaimed him innocent and they agreed to have their children's children bear the brunt of his fury if he returns to earth. My wife was right." Then he snapped his fingers and said, "Manduri would you bring me that parchment on my desk?"

When Manduri handed the parchment to Pontius, he turned to Joseph, "Yes you may have the body. Treat it well. If anyone asks, show them this letter. My seal is on it. It's yours to keep."

Joseph and Nicodemus bowed.

"Caustas," said Pontius as he turned to his bodyguard. "Take several men and escort these two Jews to the crucifixion site and assist them in whatever way you can to remove the body of the Nazarene from the cross, and one more thing, once the body is on its way to be buried, return to barracks. We will have officially completed our responsibilities. It will be their choice how and where they bury it. We'll have nothing more to do with it," responded Pontius.

"Yes Sir. Is there anything else, Sir?"

"Once you have returned to the barracks be sure to inform Tribunus Laticlavius Senna about this."

"Yes, Sir."

****

Varrus watched as men on horseback, and several men with a cart approached the crucifixion site, so he nudged his mount and moved the reins to the right to see who they were. Several infantrymen intercepted the riders and the group with the cart.

Varrus moved his gelding toward the riders and the cart and when he pulled on the reins, he asked, "Who are you?"

"I am Caustas, Pontius Pilate's bodyguard and these people with the cart have permission to take the body of the Nazarene."

Varrus turned to look at the men next to the cart.

"I am Joseph Elishama from Arimathaea and this is Nicodemus Ben Arod and the other young men are servants. They will assist us in transporting Jesus to a tomb that is available for him. We have written permission from the Governor and Praefectus."

Varrus leaned over to take the parchment from Joseph's hand and after reading it, nodded his approval and rode ahead of them to the base of the cross.

Varrus called to six guards, "Assist these men in removing the body of the Nazarene from the cross, and HANDLE HIM WITH DIGNITY, for these men have written permission from the Governor to take and bury him."

When the body was lowered, it was immediately wrapped in a long and expensive piece of linen and bound as if he were a wealthy man. Then it was laid in the cart and cushioned for the ride to the Garden of Gethsemane.

As they were about to leave, Hiddo arrived, along with twenty members from the Sanhedrin.

Varrus rode to meet them. "What do you want?" he asked as he shifted his weight in the saddle.

"Who is taking the body?" asked Hiddo in a demanding tone.

"It is of no concern to you," responded Varrus.

"We want to know."

"Pontius Pilate has granted written permission for it to be taken and buried. It is a decision that does not require your approval. If you are unhappy, speak with him."

"We insist on knowing who is taking the body."

"The man, with the black cloak, is Joseph and that other man is Nicodemus," responded one of Hiddo's servants. "They're taking the body."

"At this point, Jesus is dead and the body is going to be buried by those men and that is final. The Governor has provided written permission, so there is little that you can do," said Varrus as he motioned for them to leave.

Disappointed, Hiddo and his followers turned and walked several paces from the execution site and watched as Joseph and Nicodemus walked ahead of the cart that carried the body of the King of the Jews.

****

The heavy drapes kept all natural light from Pontius' room so he did not know that was late afternoon. His conscience provoked him greatly and he was unable to find a position of comfort in his favorite chair, so he paced the floor for a long time. One thing pleased him and that was that he had written the sign that was posted above Jesus the Nazarene.

Hunger reminded him that he had not yet eaten for the entire day but he was reluctant to go home for he knew that he would have difficulty telling Claudia about the trial.

A gentle tap on his door interrupted him and he jumped slightly when he heard it. "Yes, what is it?" he snarled.

The voice was that of Pastolla, one of his bodyguards.

"Sir, I need to speak with you," he said as he pushed the door open.

"Yes. Come in."

Pastolla saluted. "Sir, there is a group of men at your front door, who want to speak with you."

"WHAT? Is there no end to these Jews and their . . ? WHO ARE THEY AND WHAT DO THEY WANT NOW?" His voice was icy and confrontational.

"They said that it is important to speak with you, Sir."

"According to them, it is always important. WHAT DO THEY WANT?"

"It's about the body of the Nazarene that you granted permission to be buried."

Pontius' face reddened and his jugular veins in his neck bulged as he slammed his fist on a table. "I AM GREATLY VEXED AND TIRED OF THESE TROUBLESOME JEWS. First, they want a man dead and when he is dead they want something else. TELL THEM THAT I DO NOT WANT TO MEET WITH THEM."

"But Sir, they insist."

"Pastolla, find Manduri and tell him to bring me some food. I have not eaten all day."

Shortly after Pontius had eaten, he opened the door to the veranda and looked down on the Temple delegation that had been waiting for him.

It was late afternoon and darkness was fast approaching and recently lit lamps cast eerie shadows on the walls of the courtyard and on ten guards that kept the uninvited guests at a safe distance from the door.

"What do you want this time?" asked Pontius in a mocking tone.

"The body. It was . . ."

"Yes, what about the body?" interrupted Pontius as he leaned on the veranda railing.

"They have taken it away and are about to bury it, but if someone steals the body then . . ."

"Then what?"

Someone called out, "This blasphemer said that he would come back to life within three days, and if the body is stolen then . . ."

"Ahhhhh, then all of you will look foolish and that is why you are here. Am I correct?"

"Yes," another uninvited guest called out.

"So what do you want this time?" asked Pontius.

"We would like you to assign guards to sit by the burial site to be sure that no one will steal the body during the next three to four days."

"So why don't YOU sit there? There appear to be enough of you or are you afraid to guard the dead?"

They began to mumble among themselves.

Pontius taunted them, "Why not use your Temple Police. They made the arrest and assaulted the Nazarene so let them set the guard. You do trust them, don't you?"

Again they whispered among themselves.

"Better still, go to Tribunus Laticlavius' Kadurra Senna and ask him to set a guard," Pontius said as he chuckled to himself.

"Senna does not allow anyone to meet with him nor make requests."

"So you come t-o m-e?" responded Pontius, as he deliberately stretched out his words. "Am I your friend that you can come here and freely make requests?"

"This is our last request. If you send a guard to watch the burial site, we will grant the respect that you richly deserve," said Hiddo.

"I need nothing from you and what I may need, none of you will be able to provide. I gave you your trial. I gave you the execution and now I am supposed to give you a guard? You want me to set a guard by the tomb for how long . . . three days? What about a week or a month?"

"No, Sir, just three days."

Pontius inhaled as he straightened his body to appear taller. "Let me ask you several questions. If you can answer them, then you will have your request for guards to tend to the burial site."

They remained silent, waiting for Pontius' next words.

"What are you going to do or say when you discover that this man was the Messiah that you have been waiting for all these years?"

The group began to discuss the question and eventually Hiddo responded. "What is your second question?"

"And what will you do if this Nazarene turns out to be the King of the Jews?"

They did not respond.

"I am still waiting for your answer to my first question and now you stall on the second one," taunted Pontius. "I thought you would have thought through these questions before you arrived at my door."

The Temple delegation discussed what their response should be.

Pilate waited for some time and then continued. "During the earthquake and the darkness, I heard that the thick veil in your sacred Temple, next to the Holy of Holies was torn or ripped from top to bottom by an invisible hand. Was that all coincidence or is it possible that this indicates that God was telling you that the Nazarene was the Son of God?"

Again there was silence as the Temple delegation were unable and unwilling to respond.

"Perhaps this God has escaped from the Holy Place that you hallow, and maybe he is looking for you at this time."

The group in the courtyard continued to whisper to each other. Finally, Hiddo responded. "We do not know the answers to your questions, so please consider our final request."

"A deal is a deal. No answer then no request. Answer my questions or leave."

Hiddo and those with him whispered to each other for a long time, before Hiddo raised his hand to speak. "We have already said that his blood would be upon us and our children's children, so you have been absolved."

"Absolved of what . . . breaking the sixth commandment and murdering an innocent man? I have heard that you have over six hundred laws but how can you deal with them when you break one of the original ten?"

"We know that you have granted our . . . ah request to have this Nazarene crucified and all we want now is for guards to tend to the place of his burial for three days. There will be no more requests, I can assure you."

Pilate considered Hiddo's comment. "Fine I will assign thirty men to guard the tomb under one condition, that none of you or anyone from the Temple comes near my door ever again. Not you, not your servants, nor your sons or daughter. If they do, I will assign Tribunus Laticlavius' Kadurra Senna to arrest and sell you and your families into slavery a-n-d," he paused momentarily, "anyone who we find on the streets of Jerusalem on Passover of every year hereafter will be sold into slavery. Is that understood and agreed to?"

Again there was silence before Hiddo reluctantly agreed. "We fully understand."

"But do you agree? Understanding and agreeing are significantly different. DO YOU AGREE TO THESE CONDITIONS?" said Pontius.

"We have agreed to bear responsibility of this man's death and you have washed your hands. Do you wish to wash your hands again? That is not something Caesar would do for he would comply to keep peace and peace has a way of giving the impression that all is well."

Pontius was enraged with their attitude so he turned away to allow his temper to cool. When he returned he said, "I will tend to this, not because I fear you or owe you anything, but that I will have the pleasure of not speaking to or seeing any of you again."

When they had gone, Pontius shouted, "MANDURI, CALL FOR A CENTURION TO PLACE A GUARD AT THE BURIAL SITE OF THE NAZARENE. They must remain for three days."

"Thirty men and three days Sir?"

"I suppose thirty men should be sufficient, after all where will a dead man in such a deteriorated condition go and who would want to steal that body?"

As Pontius signed the request, Manduri melted red wax for the official seal and had it delivered immediately to Tribunus Laticlavius Kadurra Senna's office.

Chapter XLIII

GUILT, REMORSE AND EXHAUSTION

Varrus watched as a cavalryman cut the rope that held the dead thieves to the cross. One by one their bodies tumbled to the ground as heavy torn rags. Each time one of them struck the ground, dust puffed up around them as they lay in a disjointed position. Two guards grabbed the second body and tossed it, along with the first body, disrespectfully into a Roman cart. Now loaded with the dead bodies, the cart made it way to a ravine nearby where the thieves were buried in shallow graves.

The second cart was loaded with tools, ropes, whips and the wood from the crosses that had been disassembled. Mabboodda supervised all of the activities. When the cart was loaded, Mabboodda motioned to Varrus, who reined his horse to lead the procession back to Jerusalem.

Only one cavalryman rode with a smile on his face, for he won the prized indigo seamless robe. It was Herod's royal robe worn by Jesus. The guard did not care that it was stained with the blood, for its value was even more than he imagined because the lining was sown with pure silk from the East and with threads of pure gold woven into its rich colored fabric. He rode with this prize across his lap and saddle.

Next to him, one of the cavalrymen cast an envious glance at it as he asked, "What do you plan to do with it?"

"Buy my freedom from Rome."

When Varrus arrived in his office, he closed the door and lay on his cot without removing his gladius. A few moments later, he began to shake as though he were having a seizure. When his body could not shake any more, he moaned as a wounded animal breathing it last. He gasped several times and seemed to lose consciousness.

Varrus stirred when there was a loud knock on his door. He stood unsteadily to his feet and stumbled to the door. When he opened it, Thetis saluted. "Sir all equipment has been . . . are you ill Sir? You look like those we have just . . ."

"What is it Thetis?" Varrus managed to whisper as he ran his fingers through his hair, blinked his eyes and tried to comprehend how long he had rested.

"The tools and the crosses have been washed and all has been taken care of, Sir. Is there anything else you wish for me to do?"

"Thetis, please notify Mabboodda that I am ill."

When Mabboodda entered Varrus' room some time later, he was surprised by what he saw. "Sir, I heard that you are ill. Is there anything I can do?"

"Mabboodda, I do not feel well. I feel as though . . ." he said as he slumped to the floor. Mabboodda immediately helped him into his cot and after removing Varrus' gladius, he helped him recline.

"The sun has been very warm today, Sir. Do you need some water? Perhaps some cold water will make you feel better."

"Oh, Mabboodda, the murder of my servant and . . . and the events of this day have ruptured my soul. One of the men we crucified was a friend of mine and I knew him well. I did not know that I would supervise his death. The death of these two friends has . . . taken away my will to live."

"Sir, how can this be?"

"There is no life within me. I have nothing left to give," whispered Varrus as he closed his eyes and rested his arm across his forehead.

"Rest and I will bring you some cool water and something to eat, Sir." He quietly left the room and hastened his return.

After Varrus had eaten and sipped cool water, he returned to his cot. "Thank you Mabboodda I do feel better."

"Rest, and I will only bother you if something very important requires your attention," said Mabboodda as he started for the door.

"Mabboodda, please check on me later."

After Mabboodda closed the door, Varrus lay on his cot and closed his eyes but when he did, the eyes of Jesus appeared before him and the sight of blood running down his badly beaten face caused Varrus to sit up. "NOOOOOOOOOO!" he shouted and then slumped back onto the cot and wiped his brow with the back of his hand. Pollus' face appeared before him, and then the eyes of Jesus again. He staggered to his feet and rushed to the window for fresh air. His mind experienced every emotion that he could possibly have. In the midst of his moans, he called his mother's name and then wiped the tears from his face as he lay on the stone floor.

"ME. WHY ME? WHAT HAVE I DONE TO DESERVE THIS? WHY DID IT HAVE TO BE ME THAT SUPERVISED HIS CRUCIFIXION? Why me?"

His words faded into a whisper. Nausea brought on vomiting and when the violent spasms and gastric convulsions ceased, he returned to his cot and lay as though dead.

Some time later there was a knock on the door. He moaned as Mabboodda entered the room. "Sir, you've been ill. I'll have this vomit cleaned up immediately."

While a servant was cleaning the floor, Mabboodda helped Varrus to his desk. "Sir, a parchment from Tribuni Augusticlavii Emilio Caudoul has arrived that originated with the Governor. Thirty men are to go to the Garden of Gethsemane and remain there for three full days to guard the tomb of the Nazarene. The reason this came to us is because we were the last to deal with the Nazarene."

"Mabboodda, I care not who goes. Who do you recommend?"

"Well the parchment lists a newly promoted Centurion named Calacius Barruna to complete the assignment. Apparently, Cohort Centurion Aquello has selected Calacius for the duty and your signature will release the body from our care."

After signing the parchment, Varrus returned to his cot. When he closed his eyes, the two images that troubled him most were the face of Jesus and the face of Pollus his servant.

Some time later his sleep was interrupted by a knock on his door. Mabboodda pushed the door open, "Sir, Centurion Calacius Barruna is here for his orders to guard the tomb of the Nazarene. Do you feel well enough to speak with him?"

"Please assist me with this, for I am weak and I . . ." he did not complete his sentence.

Mabboodda reached for Varrus' gladius and put it about his waist. "Sir, perhaps you should brush you hair. I know that you do not feel well but you are speaking to another Centurion."

"Thank you, Mabboodda. Is there anything else I need to know?"

"Yes Sir. He arrived moments ago so all you have to do is hand the orders to him."

"Thank you, Mabboodda."

Mabboodda left the room and returned followed by Centurion Barruna.

Conspiracy With Malicious Intent

Calacius Barruna snapped to attention and saluted when he entered the Varrus room.

"At ease," whispered Varrus. "It's been a very long day and I have been ill." He paused to take an extended breath. "Tribuni Augusticlavii Emilio Caudoul has notified me that the Governor wishes to have a Centurion and thirty men guarding the tomb of the . . . the Nazarene, who we have just crucified." Varrus paused to lean against the wall and momentarily closed his eyes. "He's the Jew that claimed to be the King of the Jews. I understand that your . . ." he hesitated and took another labored breath.

Mabboodda completed his sentence, "Your assignment is to take thirty men and guard his tomb for three full days. No one is to be near the tomb, which is in the Garden of Gethsemane. Here are your written orders. You will be met by several people who will bury the body before nightfall so make haste."

"Yes Sir," responded Calacius Barruna.

"Do you have any questions?" whispered Varrus.

"No Sir."

When the door was closed, Varrus stood at the window and breathed deeply, hoping to feel better. After vomiting again, he made his way to his cot, removed his gladius, lay on his cot and closed his eyes.

He mourned Pollus and whenever he saw the beaten and bleeding face of Jesus, he moaned loudly and convulsed as though he were having a seizure. "My life is over," he mumbled to himself. "I have no reason to live, yet suicide is not an option. But it was I . . . I that crucified the Messiah, who was kind enough to heal Pollus. Why have I been chosen to do such a shameful and immoral deed? My name will forever be dishonored but why should I care when I die and enter the pits of Sheol."

Varrus' soul had been damaged beyond repair and the spirit that once had purpose had become dormant, unable to rise again. With the face of Jesus deeply seared in his mind, Varrus found it hard to rest. In the recess of his immeasurable anguish, he tossed and turned several times before falling into unconsciousness and eventually into a deep sleep. Often he gripped his abdomen as though in great pain and occasionally pulled his knees to his chest. Saliva ran down his cheek onto his pillow and from a distance he appeared as a madman.

Mabboodda opened the door quietly to see if Varrus had fallen asleep but found him thrashing about on his cot. Momentarily, he considered waking Varrus but when he moved closer to the cot, he could not believe his eyes for Varrus suddenly sat up and called out, "POLLUS! IS THAT YOU?"

When Mabboodda did not answer, Varrus fell back onto his cot and tried to cover himself. "Pollus, Pollus I did not know. How could I know? Those eyes and, and . . . that face . . . oh that face with that jaw . . . and the beard torn from it. How could I know Pollus? Oh Pollus, how could I know?"

Shaking his head, Mabboodda slowly backed into the hallway and closed the door. The last words he remembered hearing were, "Pollus, oh, Pollus I did not know. How could I know? Tell me? Will I die as you? I do not deserve to live."

Chapter XLIV

SECURING THE TOMB

After leaving Varrus' office, Centurion Calacius met his Optio, Marcolis, at the front gate. Calacius read the parchment so he clearly understood his assignment, mounted his horse and turned to Marcolis and another assistant, Appalus. "Our orders are to secure a tomb in the Garden of Gethsemane for three days. An official document will come from the Governor and it will be delivered to us when we are there." He reined his gelding and the two men followed him to his office.

"Marcolis, select thirty men to accompany us to the Garden of Gethsemane. Arrange for a team of horses and a two-wheel cart. We'll need wood for fire and food for three days, shovels, ropes, powdered mortar and whatever else you think we will need, and when you're ready, send someone to notify me."

Calacius entered his office and found items that had fallen to the floor during the earthquake, so he spent time cleaning his room. As he moved around the room, he noticed several new cracks in the walls and one crack across the floor, and wondered what other damage may have been done to other buildings, including the Praetorian.

A cavalryman arrived at Calacius' office some time later, to let him know that the supplies were loaded and everyone was ready for duty. He and the cavalryman walked across the combat yard toward the courtyard and found all cavalrymen, as well as Marcolis and Appalus waiting next to their mounts.

"All of the supplies that you listed are in the cart and the men are ready for duty, Sir," said Marcolis.

"This is a rather unusual assignment," Calacius said as he reached for the reins of his mount. Before stepping into the saddle, he turned to the

Conspiracy With Malicious Intent

legionnaires. "No doubt Marcolis has told you all about this assignment. We are to place a guard in the Garden of Gethsemane for three days and three nights. Our duty is to prevent grave robbers from stealing a body. The Governor has issued this order and our commanding officers have selected us to do this task. Are there any questions?"

Appalus raised his hand. "Sir, if I may, who is this person that we are to watch over and who would want to steal a dead body?"

"I have no idea but I think this is the body of a Jew, who was crucified earlier today."

"Sir, if I may, taking the body of a crucified man . . . there is usually little left to bury, so who would want it?"

As Calacius climbed into the saddle, he considered Appalus' question and suspected that the men also wanted to know, so he turned his gelding to face them. "This is the body of a Nazarene, who was executed earlier today. His body will be placed in a tomb in the Garden of Gethsemane, and we will do as we have been told. We can discuss this when we arrive." He adjusted his weight in the saddle and called out, "MOUNT UP."

Initially Calacius rode beside the cart that carried the supplies while Marcolis and Appalus led the procession, northward to the Garden of Gethsemane. The young man driving the cart looked at Calacius and said, "Sir, may I ask, why someone would want to steal the body of a crucified man? From the crucifixions I have seen, there is little left after a man has died. The last crucifixion I was at, I could see the man's ribs because all the flesh was torn from his back."

"Why anyone would want to steal the body of a crucified corpse is unclear to me too, but this is a task that we were assigned to do. May I remind you that since the Governor signed and approved of this assignment, it carries with it a sentence of execution should we disobey or fail? If someone actually steals the body, we will have to answer for it with our lives. This is far more serious of an assignment than any of these legionnaires realize."

"How long will we be on guard, Sir?" asked another soldier.

"Three full days, so let's just get this over with." Calacius nudged his gelding with his heels and Satcho, his mount, cantered to the front of the line so he could lead the military procession toward the northern gate. As they were traveling along the quiet empty streets, Calacius wondered how long they would have to wait at the designated burial site for the body to arrive.

They moved past houses, shops and through two markets. Calacius stared at the blood marks on the doorposts of every house and wondered what made these people carry out such a strange practice. The streets and the markets were empty and it was eerily calm.

As they neared the city gate, Calacius looked over his shoulder to see if the legionnaires were following in formation. As they rode, he considered how unusual it was to have such a Roman procession for a dead Jew. He recalled hearing that this man claimed to be a god. Those that requested his execution must be happy to know the Jew was dead and that's probably why they wanted the tomb to be sealed; he reasoned to himself.

When they neared the city gate, Calacius thought of Varrus and how he seemed so shattered and distraught. He remembered hearing that Varrus knew one of the men, who had been crucified, and wondered if this was the man that healed his servant. He recalled Varrus speaking of a man, who claimed to be god. If this was the same man, no wonder Varrus was so destroyed. How could he have done this and, how could he have stopped it if he wanted to?

Many questions ran through Calacius' mind. Why did the tomb need to be sealed? Were the dead man's accusers fearful of who he really was. He recalled hearing a rumor that this man's death was related to illegal trial. Rumor of a conspiracy to kill this man spread among the legionnaires during the crucifixion. Maybe the accusers were afraid of his followers.

As the procession passed through the city gate, Calacius nodded at the guards who saluted their passing.

Since the garden was quite close to the city wall, it did not take long for them to enter the garden. Following one of its major pathways, they rode several hundred strides until they could see two men standing next to a rock wall in the distance. When Calacius pulled on the reins, he raised his arm and called, "Halt."

"Is this where the executed Jew is to be buried?" Calacius asked as he looked down at two men, and then to a hole in the rock wall. The younger man stepped behind the older men as Calacius spoke.

"Yes. He is to be put into that tomb," the elder man said as he pointed to an entrance that resembled a cave with a small entrance.

Calacius looked at the large stone next to the entrance. It was designed to roll over the entrance of the cave and drop into a rut that has been chiseled into rock. "Someone had spent a significant amount of time and money, chiseling this grooved rut that will seal the cave," said Calacius.

Turning back to the two men, Calacius explained to them, "We do not bury anyone. We only guard the tomb, so whoever brings the body will have to place it inside. We will not touch the body."

Both men nodded as though they understood and agreed.

"By the way, who are you?"

"I am Ehud, a member of the Sanhedrin, and this is Nathan my servant. We were asked to wait here until Joseph and Nicodemus arrive with the body of the Messiah."

Calacius looked back to the entrance before speaking. "Just remember that we do NOT touch or move the body. We are here only to guard it."

Ehud nodded, indicating that he understood. "Those who are bringing the body will place the body into the tomb, but we will need your help moving the stone over the entrance," he said in an apologetic tone.

After dismounting, Calacius stepped closer. "How long will it be before they arrive?"

"I do not know," Ehud responded as he shrugged his shoulders. "All I am to do is to show you where the burial is to be. Joseph and Nicodemus should be here very soon because the body needs to be buried before sundown."

"Fine," Calacius said and called to the men. "DISMOUNT and secure your mounts, and set up camp. Marcolis, establish a safe area around this tomb of fifty strides. Establish three fires so we are ready when the night air arrives."

The horses were unhitched from the cart and a safe area was prepared for the three day watch. Calacius neared the entrance of the tomb to view the unique design of the stone that was to cover the entrance. It had been carefully designed and created in a way that he had never seen before. "Someone very wealthy must own this tomb. Much thought and money has gone into its design," he said to Ehud.

The stone that was placed to cover the entrance intrigued Calacius so he knelt down to better examine how it was designed. It was a specifically shaped stone that was placed into a roughly fashioned trough or rut so it could be rolled to fall into a permanent position over the entrance, virtually sealing it and making entry impossible. The stone was almost chest high, almost two strides long and a cubit in width, making it very heavy. A stone wedge was placed to prevent it from rolling over the entrance prematurely and a large wedge was placed behind the rock so that it would not fall backward. In front of the entrance was a depression where the rock would eventually come to rest. Moving it once it was over the entrance was impossible. The entrance was not very large but the stone certainly was more than many men could move, if they desired to reopen the tomb.

"Someone had spent a significant amount of time and money, carving out the tomb and shaping the stone to fall into permanent position," Calacius said to himself again. "The one who planned this was very intelligent and skilled."

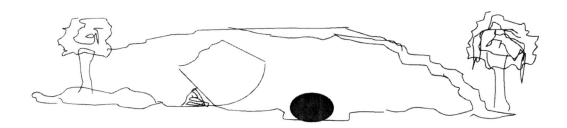

Moments later, Calacius could hear a cart approaching. The cart swayed slowly from side to side as it responded to the many potholes in the roadway. Three men appeared to be leading a small procession with four followers, who were pulling the cart up the gradual incline to where Calacius stood. Not far behind the cart, five women and a man followed, who seemed to be comforting them in their grief. They moved slowly and appeared unable to walk much farther.

When the cart stopped next to the entrance of the tomb, Calacius stepped to the side of the cart and looked inside and saw what appeared to be a body wrapped in costly white linen. There were several traces of blood near the hands, the head and the feet. On the linen were flower petals and spices to preserve the body. Calacius wondered why the body needed to be preserved for it was destined to decay.

The man, who had been leading the procession to the tomb, spoke first.

"I am Joseph and this is Nicodemus a ruler from the Temple."

Calacius acknowledged their presence with a nod.

"I have donated this burial site, "said Joseph, "and we need to bury this man before sunset. I understand that you have been sent here to assist us by sealing the tomb."

Calacius nodded.

"Pontius Pilate has agreed with our request and signed this parchment," Joseph said as he showed the parchment to Calacius.

Conspiracy With Malicious Intent

"Yes," Calacius said as he looked at the parchment, "but we will not touch the body or carry it into the tomb. We will only close the entrance and seal it, but nothing else."

"I want you to know that it was not I or any of these people who requested this Roman presence and the three day watch, but it was Caiaphas, the High Priest."

Calacius handed the parchment back to Joseph, "I have heard of him."

"I know that those who have requested this watch want no one to steal the body or tamper with it."

Calacius raised his hand as he narrowed his brows. "Tell me, who wants to steal a body that has been beaten so badly and then crucified? If they do, what will they do with it?"

"This man," Nicodemus said as he stepped closer and pointed at the linen wrapped form on the cart, "is the Son of God and the King of the Jews. He has been very influential in this region. He has healed the sick, raised the dead back to life and is known for his many good deeds among the people. He claimed that he would come back to life in three days, and this has many of his adversaries concerned and fearful. That is why they want to be sure that he remains in the tomb and as a result they have insisted on a three day watch."

"Why three days?"

Nicodemus responded to Calacius' question. "There are several reasons. First this man we consider to be our Messiah predicted his own death and said that he would rise from the dead in three days. Secondly, Jews believe that even though death has occurred, a man's spirit remains with his body for three days. And after three days he will be considered to be dead. So, if you guard the body for three days and no one tampers or steals the body, then his adversaries will consider him to be truly dead."

"So that's why we . . ."

"Exactly. The High Priest is afraid of two things. First, he is afraid that this man WILL come back to life as he said he would, and secondly, if he doesn't, the High Priest worries that if someone steals the body, the myth of his resurrection will be believed because there is no body." He turned to look up at the sun that was nearing the western ridge. "It will be dark in a few moments so will you allow us to begin?"

"Remember that we will not touch the body. It will be your responsibility to place it in the tomb. How long will you be until you are finished?"

"We have one hundred pounds of spices, balms and herbal flowers to prepare the body for burial, so when we are ready, we will call you," Joseph said as he turned to the servants. "You may begin."

The servants moved the cart next to the entrance and carefully carried the body and the embalming spices into the tomb. Calacius followed the servants into the tomb and watched as they placed the body on a stone slab. He marveled at the inside of the tomb, particularly how it had been hollowed out and that someone had made the stone slab for a body to lie on.

He watched as a linen cloth was wrapped around the head and liquid ointments were poured over the body and then flowers were placed next to the face, abdomen and under the arms. Eventually the servants stepped out of the tomb and Joseph, Nicodemus and Ehud moved into the tomb to view the body. Before leaving, they knelt down to give their respect to the dead man, and then moved to the exit.

Once outside, Joseph said, "We have now completed the burial. Please seal the tomb. You will find that gravity will help you roll the stone, but it will not move easily. It will need to be controlled as it moves into the closed position."

Calacius motioned for several men as he said, "Remove the wedges and guide the stone as it moves over the entrance."

After removing the wedges, the stone did not move so the legionnaires used levers, but it still did not move.

Joseph stepped closer, "I'm sorry, but it will take more than five or six men to move that stone. I suspect that you may need your horses."

Ten men pushed on it, but it did not move, so ropes were attached to it and twelve men pulled on it while several others used a wooden pole as lever but it did not move.

Joseph raised his hands, shrugged his shoulders and smiled.

Calacius was surprised at the effort it took for six men and two mares to move the stone. Slowly it began to roll and once it was moving, it needed only to be guided into position, and landed with a loud thud. Dust swirled up from its base and the vibration of it landing could be felt several strides away.

With the tomb closed, Calacius turned to Marcolis, "It will be impossible for someone to steal this body. They would need several horses and many men to move the stone, just to enter."

Calacius cast his eyes toward a group of mourners, twenty paces away. A man was comforting a group of women, who appeared to be in great distress. One distraught woman dropped to the ground and sobbed loudly. Her dark eyes were washed with tears and her hands were clenched with anguish. She seemed to age before everyone's eyes. The woman that knelt by her side was deeply wounded with grief. Lines across her face caused her cheeks to recede and her appearance became gaunt and she appeared as though she was near collapse.

The other women embraced each other and sobbed loudly on the shoulders and backs of those that knelt on the ground. Their weeping, momentarily caused Calacius to envy the dead man, for it appeared that he was much loved and greatly mourned over, not like those that had tasted death in battle. He was suddenly gripped with the realization that no one would mourn for him when he died.

The man, who tended to the grieving women, appeared to be strong and his eyes showed kindness and compassion.

Joseph motioned for the servants and mourners to step near and when they did, he uttered some words which sounded as a Hebrew prayer. The men consoled the women and each other as they watched the guards mix the sand, lime powder, mortar powder and water to make the material that would seal the tomb. By now it was dusk and a torch was needed to see where the mortar was needed to seal the tomb.

While the mortar was being applied, Calacius noticed a group of Jewish priests, approaching in distance. "Who are they?" Calacius asked Joseph.

"That is Hiddo, the High Priest's assistant, and the others are from the Temple. They are the ones that wanted Jesus dead and are the ones that requested this three day watch."

"Why did they hate this man?" Calacius asked.

"Jealousy and pride will erode character to a place where personal judgment does not exist," whispered Joseph.

Once the entrance was sealed, Joseph, Nicodemus, Ehud as well as the mourners and servants returned to Jerusalem. As they moved onto the pathway with their empty cart, Calacius walked to where Hiddo and the members from the Temple stood, and in a taunting tone asked, "Why are we doing all of this for a dead man? Do you expect him to go somewhere?" When they did not reply, he added, "After all, he is dead isn't he?"

"We do not want to have this body stolen," Hiddo replied. "Your task is to guard the body and not to taunt us."

"Why steal a destroyed body?" Calacius asked. "These people had it before it arrived here, so maybe they have already stolen it, and have replaced it with another body. Have you thought of that?" They looked at

Conspiracy With Malicious Intent

each other as Calacius smiled. "So why bury it and seal the tomb if you are not sure who is in there?" he asked as he pointed to the sealed entrance.

"It is the same body for we have kept contact under our watch since it was removed from the stake," said one of the priests. "We know this is the body of the blasphemer."

Another priest responded, "Just follow orders. Just guard the tomb. Do you understand? You're not here to taunt us." His voice projected an icy and confrontational tone.

"We have been watching for some time. We saw them taking the body, wrapping it and transporting it here, and we saw them placing it into the tomb. Now that the stone is sealed, guard it as you have been told to do," said the eldest man with a long white beard.

Moments later, a rider arrived on horseback and presented Calacius with the Roman seal from the Governor. "This," he said, "is to be placed on the entrance of the tomb. No one must tamper with it. It came directly from the Governor and has his signature and seal on it."

Calacius read it as the messenger turned and rode back toward Jerusalem. Then Calacius walked over to where Marcolis was standing, "We need to put a seal onto the stone. It's from Governor Pontius Pilate."

Once the parchment was secured to the stone, Hiddo walked over to look at it. "Be sure that the body is safe. Pilate and your Commanding Officer will not be pleased if you are careless," he sneered. "Your life will not be worth much if you fail in your duty."

Calacius glared at him and resisted an urge to draw his gladius. Suddenly the priestly delegaion turned and started to walk back to Jerusalem.

It was now dark and torches were necessary to see the surrounding area.

Appalus approached Calacius. "Sir, should we begin to dig safety trenches to defend our position because we will be here for three days?"

"No. There is no need to dig trenches in this garden. We can secure the area next to those trees and from behind those boulders over there. We can use that ridge, that row of trees and that rock ledge," Calacius said as he pointed at each object.

"Yes Sir. I will see to it that the camp is secure for the night. Oh, and Sir, is there anything else?"

"Secure a fire, thirty paces from the entrance. From there all the men will have full view of what can or will happen at the tomb. They will be able to warm themselves as they remain on guard. Start a second fire by that ledge and another one next to the path, near those two sycamore trees."

Conspiracy With Malicious Intent

"Yes Sir."

Eventually, everything seemed to be in place. Men were evenly distributed among the trees, the fires glowed some distance from the tomb and the written order from Pontius Pilate was secured to the entrance of the tomb. Calacius wondered if they were guarding the body or the parchment.

Some time later Calacius walked over to the cart that had been used to carry their tools and supplies, and placed his foot into the spoke of the wheel. Staring at the entrance of the tomb, questions began to enter his mind. Why were there so many people involved in this execution? What about Varrus? He seemed so destroyed. Was this the man that Varrus spoke about? Was this the man that had healed his servant? If it was, no wonder he looked like he had tasted death. How could he have put to death, the man whom he thought was a god?

"Sir," someone said, abruptly bringing Calacius back to his immediate responsibilities.

"Yes, what is it?" responded Calacius.

A young soldier tipped his helmet back. "Sir," he began, "why do you think so many people are interested in this, this dead man? Who was he?"

"Men are strange. Some plan the killing, while others do the killing. This man was some kind of god and he claimed to be a king." He reached up to rub his chin as he spoke. "Some people didn't like what he claimed to be and arranged for him to be crucified."

"Who were all of those men?"

"Some were enemies of the man who is buried here and some are his friends."

"Are they all Jews?"

"I suppose but I don't really know."

"Do you think he was a god or a king?"

"I have no idea but it must have been true enough to irritate enough people to want to kill him."

"I know what a king is but what is a god?"

As they spoke, several soldiers, one of them with a burning stick in his hand, walked over to view the parchment on the stone, and so Calacius and the young soldier joined them at the entrance.

One of them asked, "Is this order from the Governor?"

Calacius responded, "Yes."

Several moments passed before the youngest soldier turned to Calacius. "Why guard a dead man?" The sound of his voice was innocence woven with sincerity. "Who wants this dead body? If someone stole it, what would they do with it?"

Another legionnaire asked, "Sir, could you read this to me? I can't read." Calacius began to read the edict out loud.

BE IT KNOWN TO ALL WHO PASS THIS SECURE AREA

Jesus the Nazarene, King of the Jews is buried here
under the approval of Pontius Pilate, Governor and Praefectus.
Roman soldiers will secure this tomb and remain on guard
for three days. There must not be any interruption to their duty.
No one will be allowed to touch or tamper with this tomb.
If anyone, Hebrew or Gentile, male or female,
violate this order, they are to be put to death.
Soldiers will control access to this tomb.
It will remain intact and this seal must NOT be broken.

[signature]

Approved *[seal]*

Pontius Pilate
Praefectus & Governor
of Judaea

After Calacius had finished reading the edict, he turned to the legionnaires and said, "I don't particularly understand why someone wants this body. All I know is that I must be sure to do as Pontius Pilate has ordered. It may not make sense to me or you, but we must do what we've been told to do."

"Who would claim to be a god unless he really was one?" asked a second soldier as he adjusted his helmet.

"From what I have heard, he may have been a god. He said that he would return from the dead in three days. He raised some dead people back to life, and these religious leaders are afraid that he will raise himself back to life," said Calacius.

The youngest soldier turned to Calacius. "Can dead people become alive again?"

"I've heard strange stories of a man, who raised dead people back to life near the Jordan River. If it was him who did that, maybe he can raise himself."

"Well if he raised others back to life, then he can raise himself," whispered another legionnaire.

The oldest soldier, who was holding the stick with the small flame on it said, "So what's wrong with raising dead people? Is that against some law?"

"I guess it is if you want the dead person to remain dead," responded Calacius.

"That's what's strange about this place. If this dead man wants to come back to life, how will they be able to stop him?" asked the soldier with the burning twig.

"I agree," said Marcolis.

"That I don't know. I'm not sure it is our duty to try and stop him. We were told to guard the tomb to be sure that no one steals the body, but if he becomes alive again then," he shrugged his shoulders, "I don't know what we'll do," said Calacius. "We'll have to wait and see."

"I don't believe it can happen. That's the most . . ."

"If it won't happen, then don't worry about it," said another legionnaire, "but if it does, you'll never forget it."

Chapter XLV

ANGELIC BEINGS AT THE TOMB

Marcolis designated three separate watches, allowing ten soldiers to sit some distance from the tomb, ten to sit near the fire, while ten stood near the tomb entrance. After the food had been prepared, the men ate in alternating shifts.

Small pockets of conversation could be heard among the men, and off in the distance, jackals called to each other during the early evening darkness. Overhead several small clouds temporarily hid the yellowed moon as it crept across the sky.

The first hours were peaceful and uneventful. Guarding a body in a tomb for three days seemed rather unimportant. Irregular shadows moved across the stone that covered the tomb entrance whenever a soldier passed between it and the fire. The evening air was cool and often Calacius would sit near the fire to warm his back to prevent chills. Near midnight, he looked up at the moon and marveled how slowly it seemed to move. Occasionally, clouds hid its yellow shape as it moved from its overhead position toward the distant horizon.

Years of practice taught experienced soldiers to nap as they stood motionless, but awakening at the slightest sound. If it were not for the crackling of the dry wood being devoured by the yellow orange flames, there would not have been any sound. Hour after hour they guarded a silent and sealed sepulcher.

Calacius stared at the entrance and wondered who the man was that lay in there and why he had been put to death. Had he really healed sick people and raised some people back to life? Could he return back to life within three days?

Calacius remembered Varrus and how sad and exhausted he appeared to be. Calacius recalled Varrus' story about a man that had healed his servant and wondered if this was the man he had put to death.

The men took turns sitting by the fire and some time during the night, Calacius moved to the base of one of the trees and laid his head against the trunk and closed his eyes. Moments later, he slowly opened his eyes to look at the men leaning against other trees and large boulders. None of them dared squat or kneel for sleep would have quickly overtaken them, resulting in dire consequences.

Next to the cart, ten soldiers with wraps around themselves, lay on their sides and tried to rest for soon they would be called to relieve ten others. The night breezes were cool and so was the ground.

When morning drew near, Calacius was surprised that there were no birds singing, especially since this was a garden known for its many song birds. It was extremely quiet and seemed rather eerie.

When daylight arrived, the men were noticeably tired but they understood their orders, so they carefully placed themselves in comfortable yet strategic positions. Hour after hour, they remained vigilant, waiting for the assignment to end. During the day, the hot sun made it uncomfortable, so many of the men remained in the shade of the trees. It made no sense to anyone, but orders are orders, especially ones signed and issued by the Governor.

Calacius wondered what they would do if this dead man came back to life. Would he be able to move the stone on his own or would he have others come to help him? If he came back to life, he would likely die in the tomb for lack of air. The soldiers certainly would not help him, but maybe, he did not need their help. How could they possibly stop him?

Soon the soldiers began casting pebbles into a small bucket, five paces beyond the fire. It was primitive entertainment but certainly helped the legionnaires pass the time.

Gambling while on duty is forbidden but Calacius was willing to allow this activity, for who among his officers would come to a burial site to check on them. Hour after hour, they played and when they looked at Calacius, he smiled and nodded, granting his approval.

At noon, Calacius looked for Marcolis so he could speak with him about documenting their activities but found him chastising a soldier for leaving his post to relieve himself behind a tree.

The second evening was colder than expected. Were it not for the second fire, it would have been quite uncomfortable. Hour after hour, Calacius

Conspiracy With Malicious Intent

walked among the trees and men. Some of them spoke to him and others only nodded. One soldier was not found at his post so Calacius waited a few moments and when he returned, Calacius asked him to explain where he had been. The soldier was apologetic when he said that he had stepped away to relieve himself.

Eventually Calacius sat near one of the fires. Turning to his Optio he asked, "Marcolis, have you been documenting all of our activity?"

"Yes Sir."

"What do you think of this assignment?"

"I have no feeling either way but if you are asking what I think of the evening, it is a rather cool night, Sir."

The second morning arrived and again Calacius noticed that no birds were singing. "Strange but this place is known for its many birds, yet there is not a sound," he said to a legionnaire standing near him.

Again the day was hot and the men used trees to shelter themselves from the heat. By evening, the men seemed restless and Calacius suspected that they would have sooner been in a battle than in this garden guarding a body in a tomb.

Evening approached and once again fires were lit. Calacius moved from man to man, reminding them that soon they would be returning to the barracks. All of them seemed pleased that this assignment would soon be over.

Overhead, the moon moved slowly across the navy blue sky, and Calacius remembered that they were about to enter the third day. What if this dead man would actually rise from the dead? Who would help him out of the crypt? What would they tell their superior officers? Who would believe them? Strange thoughts plagued him during the night and eventually Calacius admitted to himself that he could not think of any way to stop this man, should he come out of the tomb. He continued to stare at the stone that blocked the entrance.

The night was long and Calacius was pleased that the assignment would soon be over. As morning approached, he saw something moving among the trees. Initially, Calacius suspected that it was an animal and decided did not pursue it.

The soldiers were tired and eager to complete their watch, so Calacius spoke to each of them, reminding them again that they would soon be packing the equipment and returning to the barracks at high noon.

In the early morning glow of the fire, Calacius saw one of the younger guards place his spear against a tree and then remove his helmet. Placing it on the top of a boulder, he stretched and yawned. Calacius was about to call to him about it, but saw that he was scratching his head in an attempt to remain awake. As he was replacing his helmet on his head, Calacius thought that he saw a narrow ribbon of light boring its way through the granite stone that sealed the crypt.

After blinking his eyes several times, Calacius narrowed his eyes as the light seemed to gain intensity, causing him to shield his eyes with his hand. It was then that Calacius realized that the light penetrated his hand and created no shadow. Several men stirred but seemed unwilling and unable to engage the light emitted from inside the crypt.

The light became frighteningly white, far beyond molten silver, yet it produced no noticeable heat. Finding it difficult to breathe, Calacius tried to turn from the light but lacked strength. Though the large granite boulder weighed a great deal, it appeared to be transparent as opaque glass. The light intensified to a point where Calacius found himself closing his eyes. It became apparent that the light penetrated everything, including the radial and ulna bone in his left arm which he held in front of his face. Then he realized that his eyelids could not protect and keep light from his eyes. He remembered feeling sluggish, as though he had just awakened from a deep sleep.

Then Calacius heard a helmet falling to the ground and its sound seemed so weak and insignificant. Seconds later, several metal spears fell to the ground and they sounded brittle and fragile. The few guards, he had seen moments earlier, had fallen to the ground and were not moving. They seemed so unimportant, like dry and brittle leaves being blown across a stone roadway.

Then an eerie sound began. It was the sound of granite rubbing against granite. That is when Calacius realized that the huge stone that blocked the entrance of the tomb was moving, not rolling but sliding as though a large hand had gripped it. The fire that had been devouring the logs danced wildly as though it was frightened by the light, for it leapt from side to side as though it was trying to escape its tether.

It became difficult to breathe because the air seemed to be as thick as smoke, yet it was clear and odorless. All of the men were now lying on their sides or back, like men who had just been cut down by a giant sword. As the light from within the tomb intensified, Calacius noticed that it passed through everyone and everything, including trees and boulders, yet it created no shadows.

The grinding sound continued and when the entrance was partially open an Angelic Being, double the height of an ordinary man, appeared at the entrance with a sword in his hand. The sword was easily three cubits long. The eyes of this Being were as molten bronze and the blade that he carried was covered in red and gold embers with what appeared to be small yet intense flames. The Angelic Being had large precious stones across his chest in the shape of a symbol Calacius had never seen before. The Being's long hair was that of silver, yet tinged with charcoal and amber, and his feet were shod with metal shoes. The sash around his waist was black as pitch and his wrist cuffs were studded with sparkling gems.

A soldier near Calacius started to shake as though he was having a seizure, but no sound escaped his shuddering body. Small puffs of dust rose from his quivering feet, and after falling to the ground, he remained silent as though dead.

Calacius was unable to make sense of all of these activities and it seemed to him that everything moved in slow and deliberate increments. He blinked his eyes as he tried to adjust to the intense light.

When the stone that covered the entrance eventually stopped moving, a second Angelic Being emerged from the tomb and in his hand was a spear, the size of a weaver's loom. The spear appeared as if it had just been removed from a blacksmith's forge, for it was red, yet a yellow orange in color. One of these Beings sat on the granite stone and the other stood beside it. They stared, as adders, at the fragile human forms on the ground, viewing them as prey.

Calacius tried to breathe but his throat remained closed. He flared his nostrils and opened his mouth as he gasped for breath. His chest ached and his heart pounded in his chest.

It was then that a man, yes a man emerged from the tomb. He wore no shoes but had a linen cloth around him and it fit as a priceless robe. The sash around his waist was as blue as the morning sky. He looked down at his hands and knelt on the ground, then raised his hands as if in prayer. Moments later he stood to his feet, nodded at the Angelic Beings and walked into the garden foliage. The Angelic Beings remained motionless as a Centurion receiving orders from the Legatus or Governor.

Time had no significance and reality did not seem to exist. Lying motionless was not optional, but a must. Eventually, the Beings entered the tomb and by the light that they cast in the garden, Calacius helped guards to their feet to escape into the dark undergrowth of the garden.

Conspiracy With Malicious Intent

Some distance from the tomb, Calacius managed to account for twenty-four legionnaires as well as Marcolis and Appalus. He wondered if the six missing men were dead. Those with him were mumbling phrases that made no sense. They were mentally shattered and emotionally exhausted.

Marcolis suggested that they flee in different directions for they knew their fate was now cast as dye to virgin wool. Death would be their reward for witnessing this unexplainable event. They had been disarmed and prepared for death by allowing the body of this Jew to walk out of the tomb and into the garden. If Pontius Pilate found out about this, all of them would be executed.

Reaching out and gripping several men near him, Calacius ordered them to be silent and remain there until the other six men could be found. "We cannot leave six men behind."

"But they're dead," whispered Appalus.

"You men follow me back to the tomb and we will return with those that are missing. The rest of you stay with Marcolis, and that is an order," Calacius demanded as he pointed at a group of them. "If they try to flee, slay them," he said to Marcolis.

"The six are dead! Why return?" insisted Marcolis.

"You will stay here until we return and that is an order!"

Six men followed Calacius back to where the fires were, and seeing no one including the Angelic Beings, they searched for the missing men and found them lying motionless on the ground. When they lifted them to their feet, Calacius realized that they were blind and unable to see a hand in front of their face.

Once all of them were together, Calacius said, "Now that all of us are here, we'll make our way to the Temple, where Caiaphas the High Priest and Hiddo will be. I heard that he and his assistant were the ones that wanted this man to be dead, so let us go and tell them what has happened," insisted Calacius.

They did not saddle their horses but returned to Jerusalem on foot. The blind and the mentally frayed were led by those who could see.

When they arrived, Calacius knocked on the side door of the Temple for some time before it was opened. The young man, who opened it, immediately stepped back when Calacius forced his way into the Hebrew building. The servant dropped the candle he was carrying and ran down the dark hallway as Calacius and his men followed.

Conspiracy With Malicious Intent

"WHAT IS THIS?" shouted an elderly man, who was sitting in a library. "GENTILES IN A SACRED HEBREW BUILDING? HOW DARE YOU? PONTIUS WILL HEAR OF . . ."

"WE HAVE BAD NEWS!" Calacius shouted. "ANGELIC BEINGS HAVE COME TO THE TOMB AND AWAKENED THE BODY OF THE MAN THAT WAS LEFT IN OUR CARE!"

"ANGELIC BEINGS? ALIVE? HOW DARE YOU?" the elder man scoffed as he tried to close the door of the library.

Calacius drew his gladius and placed it under the man's chin. "If I am to die and my men be put to death for this event then we will kill you to keep you silent," he responded in a threatening manner.

Immediately, several of the legionnaires, including Marcolis, drew their swords and stepped forward.

A larger door opened and a servant holding a candle above his head entered the room. Behind him walked another man, who was wearing a priestly robe.

"Who are you?" Calacius asked.

"I am Caiaphas, the High Priest and this, this is Hiddo my assistant." Hiddo stepped back and hid himself behind Caiaphas.

"We have news that you need to hear. It's about the crucified Jew that was placed in the tomb. All of us saw Angelic Beings with weapons with flames on their blades. We would have challenged them, but they were giants, double the size of an ordinary man, and when they walked, they cast no shadows."

The legionnaires began speaking at the same time and Calacius motioned for them to become silent.

"These Angelic Beings . . . had we engaged them, we would have been cut down as doves before a falcon," said Calacius. His voice did not indicate any sound of weakness.

Caiaphas narrowed his eyes. "Put those swords away and tell us more," he whispered as he motioned for them to follow him along the hallway.

"All of this is true," Calacius said as he followed Caiaphas. "Why would we, Roman soldiers come to you this early in the morning, force our way into your building and make up such a story were it not true? We saw all of this with our own eyes. Six of my men are blind because of the intense light coming from the tomb where the dead man had been laid. That dead man is now alive. We saw him walk out of that tomb and into the darkness of the garden. What purpose would we have in coming to you, if this was not true? Why would we create such a story?" insisted Calacius as his voice became louder by the moment.

The room they were in was filled with religious utensils and many scrolls on several desks. The door was shut and locked.

"We must know all of the details. Leave out nothing." Caiaphas' eyes appeared dilated and glazed with excitement and his voice waivered slightly.

By candle and morning light, Calacius repeated his story many times. Unable to fully comprehend what had happened and what they had experienced, all legionnaires began to speak at one time.

"SILENCE," shouted Calacius as he repeated his story. "By some strange and unexplainable event, the tomb opened, the body became alive and disappeared among the trees and bushes of Gethsemane."

"All of you are meshugga," insisted Caiaphas. His words were strong and confrontational and it was easy to feel the undertone of urgency in his every words.

"YES, it is true. That is what we saw." insisted Calacius as he lowered his gladius.

Caiaphas spoke to Hiddo in a language that Calacius could not understand, and Hiddo immediately left the room and ran down the hallway as Caiaphas motioned for Calacius and the legionnaires to follow him to a larger room. Once inside the room, Caiaphas left the room and closed the door. In the room were manuscripts, books and long tables with inkwells and writing utensils.

Calacius, Marcolis and Appalus did not put their swords away but waited as precious time elapsed. Calacius was visibly shaken but remained silent and when the legionnaires became restless he pushed his pointer finger to his lips, "SHHHHHHH," he said. Eventually, they heard people coming down the hallway.

When Caiaphas entered the room, Calacius counted fifteen men including Hiddo. They carried no weapons, so Calacius moved his free hand toward Marcolis and Appalus signaling them to hold their positions.

"These men," Caiaphas said to the men that had just entered the room with him, "have told us a strange and unbelievable story of light coming from within the tomb where the blasphemer was buried. They tell us that Angelic Beings held swords with flames to prevent them from engaging in a battle. It is obvious that they feared for their lives or they would NOT have come here, SO we MUST deal with this to protect ourselves and," he paused and looked over at the legionnaires, "do something to prevent their story from finding the ears of Jerusalem. If people think this blasphemer is alive, we will NEVER be able to control the crowds."

The legionnaires looked at Calacius, who responded, "Let him speak."

Moments later an old man entered the room. After he looked around at everyone, he cleared his throat and asked, "What is this that Hiddo has told me?"

After Calacius repeated his story again, the elderly man responded with, "Strange, yes, strange indeed. If what you say is true this is a serious matter. We must deal with it. Our challenge now is to make sure that this story does NOT leave this room and if it does, we must be sure that the people, who hear it, think that the body of this blasphemer was stolen by his followers. They must NOT hear or believe that this . . . this Nazarene is alive."

Caiaphas tried to interrupt but the elderly man raised his hand. "Caiaphas, you're the High Priest and much respect must be granted to you but under your authority this blasphemer was arrested, under your authority this crucifixion was carried out and under your authority a guard was set at the tomb and now, under your authority we have to deal with this problem. All of this was under your authority and now this problem must be solved outside of your authority, SO BE SILENT."

Caiaphas' neck and jaw muscles tightened but he said nothing.

"You," the old man said as he pointed at Calacius, "I do not seek to take away your influence but I request that you wait here while we seek a solution for this problem in another room."

Calacius nodded in agreement as all of them left the room.

Again the men became restless and Calacius pointed his sword at them and said. "I command you to be silent. If you will not, I will kill you."

Calacius and the legionnaires waited and watched small streaks of daylight move across the marble floor of the Temple. Sunrise was now upon the city.

Caiaphas and the members of the Temple eventually returned. He was noticeably shaken and seemed very angry because his authority had been usurped by an older man, whom someone called, Annas.

Annas began to speak. "We have had a strange thing happen and we, as you, do NOT want this story to be spread among Jerusalem or to Pontius Pilate or any other Roman official. This MUST be an event that is silenced. This discussion MUST remain in this room."

"Each soldier will be given two gold coins," said Annas. "If anyone asks why the tomb is open, tell them that you were outnumbered and someone stole the body. You will tell them that you were lucky to escape. Say nothing about these Beings or the light, but tell them that you did not have a chance to defend your position and whoever organized the attack surprised you during the night. I cannot stress this enough. Just be sure that you do NOT tell them that you think the Nazarene is alive."

Hiddo approached Calacius and whispered, "Remove these men from our Temple. Be sure that they know what to say. These events must not become public or Roman knowledge. If any questions are asked, then and only then, tell your story of being outnumbered at the tomb. Here is an additional two gold coins to help y-o-u-r memory. Be sure that you keep these men silent. By the way, use your coins wisely for they may be your last."

"This story is NOT acceptable," interrupted Calacius. "If we were overpowered, they will say that we slept or were too afraid for confrontation. We will say that the body was taken after we left the garden. That is the only way our lives will be spared. WE WILL NOT SAY THAT WE WERE OVERPOWERED."

Annas stood to his feet and his face was noticeably red and his jugular vein protruded. "YOU WILL SAY WHAT WE TELL YOU!" he shouted.

"WE WILL NOT. We will say that the body must have been taken once we had left the garden," said Calacius. He pointed his sword at Caiaphas as he spoke.

"THEN WHATEVER STORY YOU CHOOSE MUST NOT CHANGE," shouted Annas, "JUST BE SURE THAT NO ONE KNOWS ABOUT THE BEINGS OR THE MAN YOU SAY CAME OUT OF THE TOMB."

Calacius and his men left the temple, apprehensive and fearful of their future.

Chapter XLVI

THE GARDENER

In the home of Alkan a distraught and grieving believer in Jesus the Messiah, Mary his mother, Mary Magdalene, Mary the mother of James, and Salome remained behind locked doors because they feared the religious leaders and fellow Jews. They consoled each other the best they knew how, even though indescribable pain ravaged their hearts and emotions. Their pain and sorrow was so deep that it robbed their physical strength and threatened to take away their will to live. They found little comfort in the fragile words they whispered to each other, yet in a strange way each word became a balm and salve to their bruised spirits. With faces bathed with tears, they remained behind locked doors, not knowing what to expect or what to do next.

There were no minutes or hours in that room, only endless emptiness saturated with mental confusion, physical pain, emotional chaos and spiritual numbness. There were no positions of comfort and no words to express the loss they shared.

On the first day of the week, while it was still dark, restlessness overcame Mary Magdalene, who suggested that they go to the place where Jesus had been buried.

Alkan advised against it. "The streets are dark and the Romans have put additional patrols on the street because of the many pilgrims and if you remember, Romans were guarding the tomb. It's too dangerous to leave this place," he insisted. "Your safety is in this place."

"We can make our way to the garden where they've buried him. I need to be near him," insisted Mary Magdalene. "Besides, Romans will not likely be confrontational with any women walking through the streets or in the garden."

"You can do nothing for him even if you reach the tomb. You can't place anything next to him because of the large stone over the entrance. Why risk meeting Roman soldiers or spies from the synagogue?" pleaded Alkan's wife.

"Wait until daylight. Don't go now, for all of us have suffered great loss and I cannot endure the loss of any one of you," pleaded Alkan.

Mary Magdalene tried to convince the others. "Jesus has raised the dead and he can raise himself. Besides, it has been three days since the crucifixion. Maybe what he said about three days will come true." She sounded optimistic and eager to be near Jesus.

Mary the mother of James agreed with Mary Magdalene. "Jesus did say that in three days he would return and three days have passed. That's what he said, so now could be the time."

Alkan tried to reason with them but it was evident that Mary's mind was made up. "Please wait until light. Maybe we can convince Simon Peter and James to go with you. Let the men go first," he insisted.

Salome reminded them, "The disciples are hiding behind locked doors for fear of the Jews, and Roman soldiers are in the garden so why go now? If we go, then let's wait until it is light."

Joanna silently agreed.

Mary Magdalene felt an urgency to go to the tomb of Jesus, so she gathered spices and ointments to anoint the body of Jesus in an effort to bring some closure to her great loss. She convinced the other ladies to come with her and as they slowly made their way through the quiet streets of Jerusalem, they listened to every sound and watched for shadows near them.

They were not harassed by the guards at the city gate, so they continued down the hillside and eventually started up the gradual slope that led to the entrance of the Garden of Gethsemane.

"How will we move the stone that covers the tomb? Remember it took several horses and many guards to close it, so how will we ever open it?" asked Mary the mother of James.

"We have come this far and I don't want to go back. If we can't place it on the body then I would like to leave these spices next to the stone," responded Joanna.

Unsure of how they would move the stone, they continued in silence toward the tomb and were surprised, when they came to the area where the tomb was located and found no legionnaires, only the fires, horses and a cart. Mary Magdalene moved forward while the others remained behind several large trees.

She carefully selected her path toward the entrance. First, she stepped out from behind a sycamore tree and moved toward the cart and when she saw no one, she tiptoed toward the entrance. When she arrived at the tomb and saw that the stone had been rolled away, she waved frantically for the others to come near. They cautiously bent down to look into the tomb and saw that it was empty. Only several folded strips of linen and a folded napkin lay on the stone slab where the body had been placed.

Unsure of the significance of what they saw, they began to speculate what had happened and where the body of Jesus was, when suddenly two men dressed in bright robes appeared before them. The women immediately bowed their faces to the ground as fear paralyzed them.

"Do not be afraid," said one of the angels. "Why do you seek the living among the dead? Jesus is not here. He has risen from the dead as he said he would. Remember how he told his disciples, while he was in Galilee, 'That the Son of Man must be delivered, into the hands of sinful men, be crucified and on the third day be raised.' Remember what he told you?" The voice was strong and strangely comforting.

They were unable to move for fear.

The second angel said, "Now go and tell the disciples, and Peter, that Jesus is going ahead of you to Galilee. There you will meet him and see him."

Immediately all of them, except Mary Magdalene, turned and ran from the tomb until they came to the hedge that encircled the garden. Gasping for breath, they stopped when they realized that Mary Magdalene was not with them.

"What should we do?" asked one of them. "Should we return to look for her?"

Meanwhile at the tomb entrance, the angels disappeared before Mary Magdalene's eyes, and she finding it difficult to comprehend what had just happened and what had been said, remained within several strides of the tomb entrance. As she blinked her eyes she turned when she heard footsteps behind her. There before her was a man, whom she assumed to be the gardener coming toward her.

"Why are you crying?" the man asked.

"OH," she responded, "they have taken away the body of Jesus and I don't know where they have laid him. If you know, please tell me so I might go to him."

The man she assumed to be the gardener, said, "**Mary**."

She instantly recognizing the voice of Jesus and whispered, "Rabboni." Shaking, she reached for Jesus, but he stepped back and said, "Do not touch me for I have not yet ascended to my Father."

She fell at his feet to worship him and when she looked up, he was gone. Moments later, she hurried off and found the others at the hedge that circled the garden. With great excitement, she shared with them what had happened to her and the conversation she had with Jesus. Together, they rushed down the narrow pathway that led from the garden to Jerusalem. After rushing through the city gates and along several streets, they rounded a corner to the side door of a stable, and rushed up the stairs to the loft where they pounded on the door.

After hearing a wooden slide unlocking the door, Mary Magdalene called out. "WE HAVE BEEN TO THE TOMB OF JESUS AND I SPOKE TO HIM."

Another called out, "HE'S ALIVE!"

The door opened slowly, and immediately the women rushed into the room to tell the disciples what had happened in the garden. Once inside the room, all of the women began to speak at once, telling them that Jesus was alive.

When the disciples heard the story, they were speechless and awestruck. The women repeated their story several times before any of disciples believed what they heard.

"How can this be?" Nathaniel asked, as his eyes widened.

"We don't know," responded James, "but if the women were there and Mary Magdalene spoke with him, he must be ALIVE."

Simon Peter and John raced from the loft, and ran down the street to the city gate and out to the garden. The morning sun was now lighting their path and when they arrived in the immediate area, they could see horses tied to trees and Roman equipment lying everywhere.

Even though John arrived at the tomb first, he waited for Peter. Out of breath but eager to look into the open tomb, Peter stooped down and entered the tomb. When he came out, he had the linen wrap in his hand and the folded napkin. "He's not in there," he whispered. "He must be alive because these linens are neatly folded. If someone had stolen the body, they would have taken these grave clothes and not taken the time to fold them. This folded napkin is a sign that he will NOT be back."

Moments later, the other disciples arrived out of breath and Andrew knelt down to look into the tomb, and then reached out to touch the napkin. "Peter, this means that he will not be back."

Tears of joy ran down their cheeks as they danced together next to the tomb entrance.

"We'd better leave in case the Romans return for their horses. I wonder where they've gone," whispered Andrew.

****

Calacius insisted that he and the legionnaires return to the Garden of Gethsemane. "We need to pick up the horses, the cart and supplies. We cannot leave them in the garden. I know that many of you feel that you are not able to return, but you WILL obey or I will personally slay you. Do I make myself clear?" asked Calacius, showing them that he was in command.

The legionnaires approached the garden with great fear, but when they did not find anyone there, they picked up spears and weapons that had been left behind. The fires had long since burned out and the food remained in the two-wheeled cart where they had left it. The horses were still tied to trees and when Calacius cast a glance at the entrance of the tomb, he could see that it was wide open. A chill ran the full length of his spine and onto his arms, and suddenly he became aware of birds singing.

Eight legionnaires had lost all memory and reason, and six were blind because of the intense light, but Calacius commanded the remaining men to gather all equipment and place it into the cart. Once their task was completed, they started back to the military barracks, fearful of what would happen to them.

Just after they were entering at the barracks, Calacius reminded the men, "Keep your mouths shut. Do not speak of this event and if you must answer any questions about our duty, say that the body must have been taken after we left the garden."

As they were tying up their horses, Calacius immediately assigned Marcolis to take the six blind men and the eight confused legionnaires to see the physicians. He assigned Appalus to supervise the others who returned all of the equipment to the storage buildings. Once they had departed, Calacius returned to his office and locked the door.

Chapter XLVII

BROKEN HEARTS AND GOOD NEWS

The events that Amon had witnessed overwhelmed him. He slept little and continuously reviewed his memories of what he had witnessed and what Jesus had done. He recalled the healing of blind Bartimaeus, Zacchaeus in the tree and the incident in the Temple but the image that caused him to weep was his memory of Jesus dying on the cross. Anger raged in his chest when he remembered the legionnaires and their brutality, Varrus' participation and the mocking religious leaders. His anger was much stronger than his remembrances of Asa. Again he vowed that if given a chance to kill a Roman pagan, this time he would not hesitate like he had in the past.

A feeling of great disappointment came over him when he considered that his search for the Messiah was over. He understood why Adakal was disappointed and had abandoned his hope for a Messiah. Unsure of where to go or what to do next, he decided to go to Bethany to speak with Lazarus and his sisters.

He ate figs, cheese and flat bread with Adakal and his family before giving him several coins for all of the food that he had eaten during his stay with the family. Adakal was sad that Amon was leaving and the children hugged Amon as he stood on the porch.

Amon knew that Adakal's faith had wavered when he saw the beaten and crucified Messiah. He hugged Adakal before saying, "Adakal, some day, another Messiah will come into Jerusalem. By that time, I will be ready. Maybe your children will be grown and you will be an old man, but," he raised his pointer finger, "but until then, I want you and God to know that this prophet came close to being the Messiah we needed. That was the closest anyone came to being a Messiah. Someday, Adakal, there will be another Messiah."

"Shalom Amon. Maybe I will see you yet again."

Amon walked through the streets and eventually was on his way to Bethany. Other people were on the road too, but Amon did not stop to speak with any of them for he walked as a man with a purpose. He passed the dead fig tree near Bethany and confidently entered the city.

From his memory, he was able to walk through the marketplace and down the narrow street past the moneychangers building and the butcher shop, and when he arrived at Lazarus' place he rapped on the door. Martha opened it.

"Shalom. I am Amon. I was here some time ago with my friend Adakal and we were looking for the Messiah."

"Yes, yes." said Martha as she began to cry. "They have killed Jesus. Did you know that?"

"I know that the Messiah is dead. My chest hurts about it too, but I have come to talk to someone because my head hurts and my heart doesn't want to feel good either. I don't know where to go and . . . and you are the only people I could think of," said Amon he lowered his head and tears began to wash his cheeks and beard.

Lazarus came to the door and motioned with his hands, "Come, come," he said. "We are very sad too because Jesus has been killed and now he is dead. Dead like I was, but I am not able to raise him as he raised me."

"Yes, I know and I was there," said Amon as his voice cracked with emotion. "It was terrible. His face was so badly beaten and there was much blood and . . ." After Amon gained control of his breath, he continued, "I almost did not recognize him. Most of his beard was ripped from his chin and his eyes were swollen so he could not see."

Mary immediately left the room because she was too overcome to listen to the remaining details of Amon's story.

"Where have they laid him?" asked Martha as she wiped tears from her eyes.

"Adakal's friend told us that he overheard someone saying that he was buried in a garden just outside of Jerusalem."

During the silence that followed they grieved loudly.

"I heard," said Amon, "soldiers guarded where he was buried. You would think that killing him was enough but no, they waited to be sure he was dead." Tears continued to run down his cheeks and speaking became very difficult.

Their sobbing and grieving could be heard from outside.

"Yes, we heard," responded Martha. "Many of the disciples had to flee. Only John was able to be there during the crucifixion and I heard he helped Jesus' mother." Martha became too emotional to speak and then after she gained control of her emotions, asked, "Have you seen any of the disciples?"

"That garden that you are talking about must be the Garden of Gethsemane. It is north of Jerusalem," said Lazarus. "I know that place. It is where Jesus and the disciples would often go to."

Moments passed and Martha asked, "Why have you come here?"

"I don't know," admitted Amon, sounding like a lost man. "I guess this is a place I could speak with people, who believed in him. My friend, Adakal doesn't believe in Messiahs anymore and I well . . . well I need to speak to someone who does. I need to be someplace with people, who knew him. Will we ever have another Messiah?" asked Amon as he buried his face in his hands.

"He cannot be replaced," said Lazarus.

Late in the day, Amon returned to Jerusalem because he had no where else to go. He was out of money, had no food and no place to stay. As he made his way to Adakal's home, a Roman chariot passed him with a Roman officer riding next to the driver, and that is when Amon remembered Varrus. He decided to find Varrus.

When he arrived at the Praetorian, he asked several guards if they knew of Varrus, but they did not answer him. When they told him to leave, he returned to the city square where he had spoken to several people, but no one admitted knowing who Varrus was or where he might be found. By late evening, he was very hungry and found himself begging for food. Unable to find a place to lie down, he trudged back to Adakal's house. When he knocked on the door, Adakal's wife opened it.

"Please, may I speak with Adakal?" Amon whispered apologetically.

When Adakal came to the door, he looked at Amon and opened his arms. "You're back. Did you not find anyone else besides us who is sad about the Messiah being dead?"

"You remember Lazarus and his two sisters? They heard about Jesus and are very sad too, but no one knows what to do now," replied Amon as he stared at the floor.

"Well come in," said Adakal, trying not to sound too disappointed that Amon had returned.

"I'm sorry, but . . . can I sleep here one more night because I need help finding that Varrus man."

"How will he help you?"

"I want to speak with him before I go back to the Sea of Galilee."

"You're going back to the Sea of Galilee?"

"If the Messiah's men came from Galilee, then maybe they have gone back there and, and I can work for Zebedee again. I have nothing else and no place to work, so there I will live until the next Messiah comes along."

The next morning, Adakal and Amon walked to the Praetorian. As they stood and looked at the rock walls, two soldiers stepped out from the gate and shouted at them. "What do you want, you Hebrew dogs?"

"I have come to see my friend, Varrus."

"Varrus, who?"

"He was the Centurer with a grey horse and the one leading the men to be killed."

A guard drew his sword.

"May I show you this?" asked Amon as he unfolded the letter he had received from Marcus while in Scythopolis.

The guard leaned over to look at the parchment. "I do not read but I'm willing to kill you if you do not leave."

"Wait! Just wait!" a familiar voice said from a window above. It was Varrus. "Bring him up to me."

Amon looked up and waved at Varrus, and when Amon entered the building, Adakal was forced to wait at the front gate.

When they met at the top of the stairs, Amon smiled and tipped his head to one side as he looked at Varrus. Meanwhile, Varrus excused the guards and then closed the door.

"Amon, I am a tormented man. How could I know that I would be the one assigned to crucify the Messiah, and after he healed my servant Pollus?" Walking as an old man, Varrus moved to a chair and sat down. After placing his hands over his face, he said, "Amon, I have done such a great evil and was unable to prevent it. It was I who killed the Messiah. Think of it Amon. It was I who did this thing."

"I too have come a long way and all I found was a dead Messiah. He helped everybody but himself. I too have a hurt in my chest and my head cannot understand why he would not help himself." Amon sat in a chair next to Varrus' desk. "Maybe this Messiah could only help others and not himself. Maybe the next Messiah will come and be able to do everything and not die."

"I wish that I could have freed him but every time I was near him I could do nothing. I am a tormented man. I was the one that executed him, Amon. Think of it. I was the one that signed the death parchments. Amon, I . . ." he shook his head from side to side.

"I can see your hurt on the outside so the inside must feel as bad as mine. It must be the Jewish inside of you that hurts because Gentiles don't care about our Messiah."

"Amon, the other thing that has destroyed me was news that Pollus the servant whom Jesus healed was murdered on his way to Jerusalem, and I was not able to bring him here for burial. Now he lies in a ditch by the road as a common thief."

"That is not good Varrus. Nobody should have that much trouble. We Jews have troubles too. My brother was killed and left to lie beside a burned shop and nobody cared. I know what it is like to hurt."

After an extended amount of silence, Amon spoke. "Varrus, I was in Bethany to speak with Lazarus, the man who the Messiah brought back from the dead. I wish that your servant and my brother, Asa, could be made alive again by the Messiah."

Varrus said nothing but sighed loudly.

"My heart," said Amon, "is in much pain and everything I think about is upside down. Maybe he was not the Messiah. Maybe he came to show us what a Messiah should be like when the real one comes along."

For some time they tried to console each other but nothing they said eased their anxiety. During their conversation, Varrus learned that Amon was staying with a friend and had no means of support, so Varrus gave Amon six coins.

Amon returned to the street where Adakal was waiting and they walked away unsure if they would ever see Varrus again.

The next day, Amon returned to Bethany again to speak with Lazarus. Mary invited him in and they spoke of the many things Jesus had done. As they were eating, there was a sudden knock on the door and when Mary answered it, Andrew stepped into the room. When Mary recognized him, she called to Martha, "It's Andrew!"

Out of breath, Andrew stumbled into the room and leaned against the table to catch his breath. "THE MASTER IS ALIVE! THE MASTER IS ALIVE! he shouted. "We saw him and he appeared to us and spoke with us."

Unsure of what he had just said, Lazarus, his sisters and Amon stared at Andrew, who nodded, "YES! YES! IT IS TRUE. We've seen him and, and

Peter entered the tomb where he was buried. It's true! Now, we know what he meant when he said he would suffer much and rise again in three days."

Mary slumped to the floor as Martha closed her eyes and turned away. Lazarus leaned back in his chair as Amon stood to his feet and moved closer to Andrew.

"You're the man that I spoke to when a blind man named Bartama something was made to see again."

"Yes, I remember you. Yes, I remember you," responded Andrew.

"So this Messiah, we saw killed, you're talking about IS ALIVE? That's what I heard you say . . . so he raised himself by himself back up again?"

"YES, YES," said Andrew as he nodded his head up and down with tears running down his cheeks.

"So, why did he let himself get killed?" asked Amon.

"JESUS SPOKE TO ALL OF US. THOMAS TOUCHED HIM. HE ATE WITH US. HE'S ALIVE!" He threw his hands into the air and spun around as a young person dancing with exuberant joy.

Amon begged for the chance to go with Andrew, but Andrew told him to stay with Lazarus. When Andrew was gone, Amon hurried back to Jerusalem, eager to tell Adakal that the Messiah was alive.

When he arrived at Adakal's house, he was out of breath as he knocked loudly on the door. After sitting down to rest and catch his breath, called to Adakal. He was still puffing loudly when Adakal opened the door.

"Amon! Why are you . . . ?"

"ADAKAL!" Amon shouted as he stood to his feet and started to shake Adakal. "THE MESSIAH . . . THE MESSIAH HE IS ALIVE. I SPOKE TO ANDREW, WHO IS HIS FOLLOWER AND HE SAID THAT THE MESSIAH SAT AND ATE WITH ALL OF THEM. ADAKAL, HE'S ALIVE! DID YOU HEAR ME? ALIVE! THE MESSIAH IS ALIVE!"

"Amon. The sun has hurt your brain. How can a person be dead and alive after three days?"

"Lazarus was dead for more than three days . . ."

"But Amon . . ."

"How was Hannah's son dead and then made alive? I don't know about dead people and these things that can be, but he's alive again. THE MESSIAH MADE HIMSELF TO BE ALIVE AGAIN!"

"Amon, are you sure? Did you see Him?" His words were barely audible.

"No, but Andrew told us and I believe him. I believe." His words turned into a whisper as tears flowed down his cheeks. "Adakal, Adakal . . . dead but now alive, I tell you. We don't need another Messiah. This is the real one just like my father, Beno said." His voice faded into a whisper and he dropped to his knees.

Adakal sat down and placed his hands over his face. "Where do we go to see him? When can we see him? Are you sure Amon? Are you sure?"

"I must see the Messiah. My heart has burned inside since I saw him in Nain. When I saw him heal the blind man, I was so glad to be near him but when I saw him beaten," he paused to wipe tears from his cheeks, "I did not know what to think. All my thoughts were inside out and when . . . when I saw him on the wooden stake, I wished . . . I wished I would die too. Adakal, my heart hurts so much but now it feels free. Adakal, he's alive!" He nodded and smiled so that all of his teeth were clearly visible.

"Amon, are you s-u-r-e?"

"Yes. I believe and you must believe too. Now I will go to find Varrus and tell him so his heart will heal. Maybe now your heart will heal too and you will be happy again."

"Amon, there is no Messiah. He is dead. No one can be killed that badly and then . . . then be alive." His voice reflected sadness, disappointment and profound doubt.

"But Adakal, he's THE MESSIAH!" Amon's head moved up and down so fast that he became dizzy.

"Amon, you want that man to be alive so you believe he's alive. If he could not stop being killed how can he make himself alive?" Adakal turned and walked to the end of the porch and folded his arms. "Amon, the man we thought was the Messiah is dead and we were wrong. There is no Messiah."

Chapter XLVIII

THE MIRACLE AND THE MANDATE

When Amon and Adakal arrived at the Praetorian, one of the guards remembered that Amon met with Varrus the day before, so he entered the building to tell Varrus.

"Sir!" he said as he saluted. "There be a man outside, who be here to see you yesterday. He would like to speak with you again."

Varrus looked out of his window and saw Amon, so he turned to the guard, "Yes. Bring him in."

"Yes Sir. But there are two of them."

"Yes, bring both of them in. I will take responsibility."

"Yes Sir."

When Amon entered the room, he could not contain the news any longer. Before the door was closed, he stretched his hands as far apart as possible and shouted, "VARRUS. THE MESSIAH IS ALIVE!"

Varrus cocked his head to the side and narrowed his brows.

"Yes Mr. Varrus. It's true," he said as he started to dance around the room and hold his hands above his head. "THE MESSIAH IS ALIVE. THE MESSIAH, I TELL YOU HE'S IS ALIVE, MR. VARRUS, HE'S ALIVE. YES, YES ALIVE, LA LA LA LA DA DA ALIVE LA LA," he sang until Varrus raised his hands for him to stop. Varrus looked at Adakal, who grinned and shrugged his shoulders.

"Mr. Varrus," said Amon, as he gasped for breath after his dance, "you know that not even the Roman's could kill him. The Messiah is alive, Mr. Varrus, we thought he could only help others and not himself, but and I must say BUT, I tell you he made himself alive again. It's true," he said as he moved his head up and down so fast that he almost lost his balance.

Varrus seemed unsure of what he was hearing.

"I tell you, Mr. Varrus. The Messiah that healed your servant is alive, even though you, I mean he was killed and now he's alive."

Varrus interrupted, "Who told you this?" He appeared overwhelmed by the concept that the Messiah, who was so badly beaten and had a spear thrust into his side, may be alive.

"I was in Bethany and one of the Messiah's men, Andrew, came and told us that he ate with the Messiah and spoke with him."

"But I saw him die. I saw the death fluid flow from his side when the spear was thrust into him. Why did you come to tell me this?" asked Varrus, sounding confused. He reached for his chair and sat down.

"So you can live again! I'm living again and now I have hope and so does Adakal." He smiled showing all of his teeth.

Adakal shrugged his shoulders and raised his hands to his waist. "I heard it too, but I still think the man we thought was the Messiah is dead."

"Where is the Messiah now?" asked Varrus as he slowly stood to his feet.

"I don't know, but he's alive. He might come back to Jerusalem or maybe go back to the Sea of Galilee," said Amon as he sat down to take a much needed breath.

"He will not come back to Jerusalem after all we did to him. Why would he come back here?" responded Varrus, sounding confused.

"If he is not here in a few days, then Adakal and I are going to Bethany to find him," said Amon, "but if he's at the Sea of Galilee, I will go there." Again he nodded his head up and down.

Varrus sat back into his chair and thought about what Amon had said. "He will not want to see me after what I did to him," he whispered. "I cannot expect to see him or . . ."

"I don't think he'll be angry at you so you can come with us when we go to find him."

"But I am a Centurion and the Executioner with duties to perform. I cannot go with you Amon."

"Tell one of your men to do your job until you get back," said Amon confident with the advice he had just given.

Sounding very discouraged, Varrus asked, "How will I know if he is willing to see me?"

"If the Messiah is not here in a few days, Adakal and I will go and find him and maybe bring him to see you."

"Your words are hard to understand Amon. I would like them to be true . . . but I am unable to make sense of them."

Conspiracy With Malicious Intent

While Amon and Adakal were returning to Adakal's house, Adakal expressed his doubt about the Messiah being alive. Amon tried to convince him but Adakal refused to believe Amon's stories. "Amon," he said, "you have been my best friend and the words that you have told me gave me hope but now I find them hard to believe. I saw the man who I thought was the Messiah die and . . . and now my head does not want to think about a dead Messiah."

"Adakal, come with me and we will find that Messiah. Why would his disciples lie about seeing and eating with him if it wasn't true?" He smiled and shrugged his shoulders.

For the next week Amon and Adakal walked through Jerusalem and asked many people about the Messiah but no one seemed to know if he was alive or where he might be. Days passed, causing Amon and Adakal to be concerned that the Messiah may not be returning to Jerusalem. Eventually both of them began to doubt that the Messiah was actually alive. They tried several times to speak with Varrus, but each time they asked about him they were sent away. On their last visit to the Praetorian, they were threatened and chased away.

Amon could not stand it any longer and decided to return to Bethany. Adakal insisted that he had a family to support and wasting time looking for a dead Messiah was foolishness. Several times he said, "If the Messiah is alive, then we would have heard about it. Amon there is no Messiah. He is dead. You saw it and so did I. My mind does not want to think of a Messiah anymore."

When Amon arrived at Lazarus' place, he called from outside and when Lazarus opened the door, Amon opened his arms as wide as he could and asked, "Have you heard if the Messiah is yet alive?"

Lazarus invited him in and told Amon that the Messiah and his followers, including his sisters were at the Mount of Olives. He explained that it was too far for him to go but his sisters had left moments before Amon had arrived.

Amon was unable to contain his excitement when he heard that others were going to see Jesus. After Lazarus explained where Amon was to go, he ran as fast as he could.

When he neared Jerusalem, he asked several people where The Mount of Olives was and a man leading a donkey told him that it was a ridge near the outer wall of Jerusalem. When he pointed in the general direction, Amon started to run. When he arrived, he could see a crowd gathered in the distance, so he hurried even though he was out of breath. As he approached the crowd, his heart was beating faster than it had in years. Standing on his tiptoes on the outer rim of the group, Amon recognized the Messiah voice when he was speaking.

The Messiah said, "Remain here in Jerusalem and wait for the promise of the Father, which you heard about from me. For John truly baptized with water, but you shall be baptized with the Ruach HaKodesh (Holy Spirit) in a few days."

Several people asked him many questions and he answered all of them except for, 'When will you restore the kingdom of Israel, and when will you return?'

Jesus response to the last question was, "It is not for you to know the times or the seasons, which the Father has appointed. But you shall receive power, after the Ruach HaKodesh has come upon you, and you shall be my witnesses in Jerusalem and in Judaea and in Samaria and unto the uttermost parts of the world."

While all of them were looking at Jesus, he started to rise above the ground and continued rising upward until a cloud hid him from their sight. They stood looking up, hoping to see him but he was gone from their sight.

Two men stood near them and one said, "You men of Galilee, why do you stand here gazing into heaven? This same Jesus that has been taken up from you into heaven shall come in the same manner as you just saw him go."

The crowd, the disciples and Amon stood awestruck for a long time before returning to Jerusalem.

Amon grabbed Andrew's arm as he walked by. "Mr. Andrew, two of my friends don't believe that the Messiah is alive, but now that he is gone to, to that place called the sky, they will never believe that he is alive. What shall I tell them?"

"Tell them the truth, Amon. Tell them the truth."

Amon rushed back to Adakal's house and found him sitting on the porch playing with his children.

"I have news about the Messiah. This time I saw him, yes me," he said as he came near. He beat his chest as he spoke. "I, yes Amon, I saw the Messiah. Many people saw him. My heart is free. Now I know for sure he's alive. I saw him Adakal. Yessssss I did." He nodded his head up and down as he spoke.

"Where is he now?" asked Adakal as folded his arms across his chest.

"He's," Amon paused, "Adakal, can I sit with you? I will tell what happened, but first you must trust me. Do you trust me, Adakal?" He used his fist to pound his chest as he spoke.

Adakal shrugged his shoulders, "Sometimes, but your stories are . . . they seem so hard to believe and . . ."

"You will find this hard to believe," insisted Amon, "but and I, yes me Amon saw the Messiah is alive. I saw him lifted into the air and a cloud covered over him and he's gone to the sky that someone said is . . . heaven." He spoke the last word in a whisper. He smiled and leaned over to look into Adakal's eyes.

Adakal opened his arms, exposing his palms, "Amon there is no Messiah. If I cannot see him then I will not believe. When you talk about clouds and, and the sky and, and heaven, my head does not believe in what you say. I do not want to hear about a Messiah that is dead or one that went up into the clouds. I need a sign, not a dead man or someone rising off the ground and hiding behind clouds like those," he said as he pointed upward. "A Messiah like that, I don't need. He is dead Amon. Goodbye Amon," Adakal said as he reached for his children and stepped to the door.

Amon stepped closer to entreat his friend but Adakal stepped back, lowered his gaze, entered his house and closed the door.

Amon raised his hands, but the sound of the door closing held a note of sadness and finality.

"But he is alive, Adakal," whispered Amon. "I saw him. I really did," he repeated as he heard Adakal lock the door.

"But Adakal . . ."

From behind the door, Adakal said, "I need a sign, not a dead man. Not rising off the ground and hiding behind clouds. A Messiah like that, I don't need. Goodbye Amon."

Chapter XLIX

DOUBTERS, DECEIVERS AND BELIEVERS

Adakal's faith wavered when he saw the Messiah crucified. It was beyond his comprehension that the Messiah would allow himself to be beaten, berated, brutalised and the placed on a wooden stake. If he could raise the dead, why was he powerless to stop this terrible event? When Jesus was known to be dead and removed from the cross, all hope was gone. In Adakal's mind, he was not the Messiah and questioned if another Messiah would ever come.

Amon's enthusiasm could not convince Adakal that the Messiah was alive, nor would Adakal go with Amon to hear Simon Peter, who spoke to large crowds on a daily basis. Adakal not only doubted that a Messiah had been in their midst, but he doubted Amon's eyewitness accounts, especially when Amon told him about seeing the Messiah slowly rising off the ground and disappearing behind a cloud. He referred to Amon's eyewitness accounts as 'stories, just stories' and so he isolated himself from Amon. His disappointment was too great to overcome.

His last words to Amon were, "I need a sign, not a dead man. Not rising off the ground and hiding behind clouds. A Messiah like that, I don't need. Goodbye Amon."

Amon never saw Varrus de Lonnea again. Legionnaires at the Praetorian were unwilling to speak about him. Amon was unsure if he had been sent to another city, or worse. Amon worried that he may have become overcome with disappointment, grief and guilt. He remembered his last visit with Varrus, and found him to be devastated, overwhelmed and defeated with his role in the crucifixion. The death of his servant and the promotion to Executioner was too much for him to bear or overcome.

Varrus remained in Legion X in Jerusalem for only two months until he received his requested transfer to Italy. Ultimately, he became a Cohort Centurion based in southern Italy. Subsequent promotions made him a Tribuni Augusticlavii and then a Tribunus Laticlavius under Legatus Gais de Bonda.

Roman military records document an officer with the rank of Imperator listed among the dead in a battle in Macedonia, but the spelling and clarity of his surname casts some doubt as to whether it was the Varrus de Lonnea that Amon knew. The officer's name was Imperator Varrus de Lonnae, a slight variation in spelling of the last name.

Joseph Caiaphas, son-in-law of Annas, was the High Priest for approximately twenty years, with responsibilities related to the Temple Treasury, managing temple personnel as well as the Temple Police, and was called upon to perform religious rituals and ceremonies. He enjoyed additional duties and acted as a liaison between the Jewish leaders and the Roman government. Caiaphas served during Pontius Pilate's entire tenure and shared a mutual disrespect for each other. Many people questioned the relationship that the High Priest had with the Roman leadership of Legion X.

Joseph Caiaphas lived in affience and used his powers and influence to his advantage and not for the general population. He was in power during and after Pentecost, and was the one that questioned Simon Peter and John about the healing of a man. He was a strong leader and Head of the Sanhedrin, and is believed to be responsible for sentencing Stephen, the first martyr, to death by stoning.

Lucius Vitellius, the Syrian Governor in 37 AD, removed Caiaphas from office and replaced him with a brother-in-law named Jonathan, a son of Annas.

Caiaphas' sarcophagus is believed to have been located south of Jerusalem, in the last part of the twentieth century. The inscription on the side of the ossuary, or bone box, had his name written in Aramaic. In it, were the bones of a sixty-year old man, an adult female, two children and several infants.

Pontius Pilate's name will forever be remembered as the Governor who tried to hand Jesus over to King Herod, ignored his wife's pleas 'to have nothing to do with Jesus,' approved Jesus' beating, then tried to have him freed. But what he was remembered for was the release of Bar Abbas. He will also be remembered for washing his hands publicly to reject responsibility for the results of the trial, approving the crucifixion of Jesus and

Conspiracy With Malicious Intent

the writing of the sign, 'Jesus the Nazarene, King of the Jews', in three languages. It was the sign that was placed above Jesus while he was on the cross.

In his discussion with Jesus about what is Truth, it is interesting that Pontius Pilate should write such a sign. Controversy surrounds this sign, for some scholars say that he wrote it to irritate the Jews, while others give the benefit of the doubt to Pontius, saying that he may have recognized who Jesus actually was and publicly proclaimed it. Some say it was an act to appease his wife, who had pleaded on his behalf to 'have nothing to do with Jesus.'

Pontius Pilate historically made poor decisions because of his arrogance, obstinate attitude and need to be in command which resulted in social, moral and ethical failures. He lacked empathy, used violence to maintain control, was quick to execute, and detested the Jews. He lost his commission as Governor in 36 AD when the Syrian Governor, Lucius Vitellius, sent him to Rome where he was exiled to Vienne. Some historians believe that he was exiled to Gaul. Some historians suggest that he to committed suicide while still in Rome but other suggest his suicide was in Gaul.

King Herod the Great murdered his wives and children, ordered the killing of the Hebrew boys just after Jesus was born and lived a most immoral, depraved and paranoid life. His son, King Herod known as Herod Antipas, was also a vile man, who was also known for total moral decay. He is remembered for his beheading of John the Baptist and his personal rendezvous with Jesus after Pontius Pilate referred Jesus to Herod because he was a Galilean. King Herod interviewed Jesus and was fearful that Jesus was actually John the Baptizer, so in turn he referred him back to Pontius Pilate. Historians tell us that he was exiled to Gaul while other historians say he was sent to Iberia (Spain).

Bar Abbas, an ardent member of a political activist group called Sicarii, a proactive militant group whose main goal was to overthrow the Roman influence by violence, disappeared from history the day he was released from the Praetorian. He is remembered for being the man, who was granted freedom in exchange for the life of Jesus. He is known as a murderer, thief and an extremely violent man. Little is known about his death. There existed a custom in Jerusalem that the Governor would commute a death sentence of a criminal during Passover, and when Pontius Pilate was unable to release Jesus, he tried to commute his death sentence but that was unsuccessful. The crowd demanded Jesus crucified, resulting in the release of Bar Abbas.

Herein lays an irony. Bar Abbas' formal name, according to scholars, was Iesous ton Bar Abbas or Jesus bar Abbas or Jesus Bar Abbas. Either way, it tickles one's mind to consider that Jesus of Nazareth replaced Jesus Bar Abbas prior to the crucifixion. It seems to have been God's plan for one innocent man to die for the guilty, regardless of how many there were.

Amon found his Messiah during Simon Peter's message and obeyed the message given by Jesus, to take the gospel to Samaria and Judaea and into the entire world. His life ended in Crete because of the Gospel of Jesus Christ. His search for the Messiah was in fact, a Messiah's search for him.

BIBLIOGRAPHY

Unless otherwise indicated, Bible quotations are taken from:

Jewish New Testament
Jerusalem, Israel, Clarksville, Md.
Copyright: Jewish New Testament Publication, Inc. 1989

The Interlinear Bible
Greek/English, Volume 4
Copyright: 1976, 1977, 1978, 1979, 1980, 1981, 1984 Second Edition
Copyright: 1985 by Jay P. Green, Sr.
The Greek Text Copyright: 1976
Trinitarian Bible Society London, England

The Interlinear Bible
Hebrew/English, 1-3 Volumes
Copyright: 1976, 1977, 1978, 1979, 1980, 1981, 1984
Second Edition Copyright: 1985 by Jay P. Green, Sr.

The English-Greek Reverse Interlinear New Testament (ESV)
Copyright: 2006 by Logos Research Systems, Inc.

The Holy Bible, English Standard Version
Copyright: 2001
Good News Publishers

English Standard Bible – Study Bible
Copyright: 2008 by Crossway Bibles
Good News Publishers

English Standard Bible
Copyright: 2001
Crossway Bibles Good News Publishers

The Holy Bible, New International Version
Copyright: 1973, 1978, 1984
International Bible Society

New American Standard Bible – Updated Edition
Copyright: 1960, 1962, 1963, 1968, 1971, 1972, 1973, 1975, 1977, 1995
The Lockman Foundation

The New Revised Standard Version Anglicized Edition
No Copyright found
The National Council of Churches of Christ in the USA

Holy Bible, New Living Translation
Copyright: 1996 by Tyndale Charitable Trust

TODAY'S PARALLEL BIBLE
Copyright: 2000 by Zondervan

J. B. Phillips
Copyright: 1960
Cox and Wyman Ltd.
Great Britain

New American Bible
Copyright: 1970
Confraternity of Christian Doctrine (CCD), Washington, DC

Revised New Testament of the New American Bible
Copyright: 1991 CCD

Catholic Edition of the Revised Standard Version of the Bible
Copyright: 1946, Second Edition: Copyright: 1971
The Catholic Edition of the NEW TESTAMENT, Copyright: 1965
Division of Christian Education of the Churches of Christ in the USA

Douay-Rheims Bible
No Copyright found.
Translated from the Latin Vulgate of St. Jerome in the 16th century with a revision to create the Douay-Rheims Catholic Bible - 1700s.

JERUSALEM BIBLE
Copyright: 1966, 1967, 1968
Darton, Longman & Todd Ltd. and Doubleday

New Jerusalem Bible
Copyright: 1985
Darton, Longman & Todd Ltd. and Doubleday

Good News Translation - Second Edition
Copyright: 1992 American Bible Society

The Word of Life Study Bible
Copyright: 1993, 1996
Thomas Nelson Inc.

The Way – The Living Bible
Copyright: 1971
Tyndale House Publishers, USA

Christian Community Bible
Copyright: 2004 Bernardo Hurault
Main Writer: Patricia Gorgan
Catholic Bishops' Conference of the Philippines
Quezon City, Philippines

Revised Standard Version
Translated from the original tongues being the Version set forth A.D. 1611, Revised A. D.1881-1885 and A.D. 1901
Revised A. D. 1952
Zondervan Publishing House, Grand Rapids, Michigan

Authorized King James Version
Copyright: 1947
The World Publishing Company, Cleveland & New York

New King James Version – New Testament
Copyright: 1979
Thomas Nelson Inc.

New King James Bible, New Testament & Psalms
Copyright: 1980
Thomas Nelson Inc.

The Holy Bible, New King James Version
Copyright: 1982
Thomas Nelson Inc.

The New King James Version
Copyright: 1979, 1980, 1982
Thomas Nelson Inc.

The John MacArthur Study Bible – KJV
Copyright: 1997
Word Publishing

Life Application Study Bible – NIV
Copyright: 1988, 1989, 1990, 1991
Tyndale House and Zondervan

NIV – Archaeological Study Bible
Copyright: 2005
Zondervan

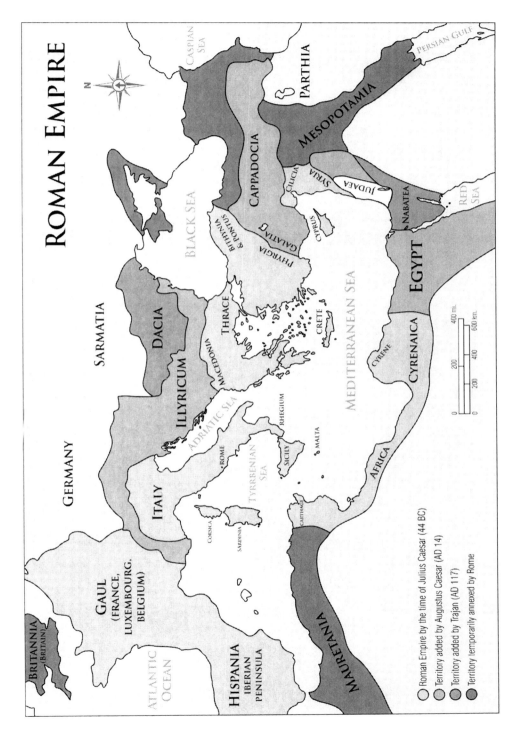

Conspiracy With Malicious Intent

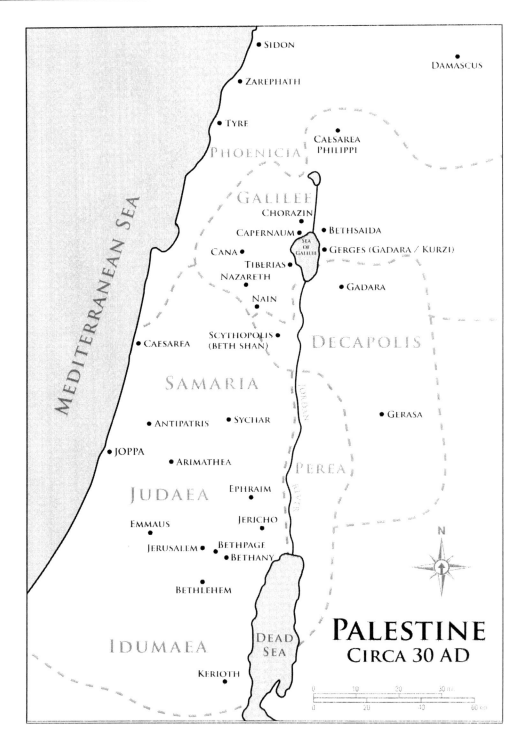

CPSIA information can be obtained at www.ICGtesting.com
Printed in the USA
LVOW111928010113

313900LV00006BA/485/P

9 781609 573355